WHY SOME DIRECT SELLING COMPANIES CRASH

WHY SOME DIRECT SELLING COMPANIES CRASH

Why some direct selling companies boom, why others collapse, and how to build one that survives.

Rob Sperry

First Edition

Printed in the United States of America

ISBN: 979-8-9963774-0-4

www.robsperry.com

For the builders who refused to confuse motion with momentum.

Contents

Introduction: Why Some Direct Selling Companies Crash.............................1

PART I: THE PROBLEM

Chapter 1: The Momentum Myth.............................20

Chapter 2: The Equation Nobody Solved.............................34

Chapter 3: The Momentum Spectrum.............................52

Chapter 4: Diagnosing Where You Actually Are.............................71

Chapter 5: The Product Alibi.............................92

PART II: THE FIVE DRIVERS

Chapter 6: Product-Culture Fit.............................118

Chapter 7: Platform Disruption.............................134

Chapter 8: Leader Migration.............................159

Chapter 9: Market Expansion.............................193

Chapter 10: Compensation Architecture.............................209

Chapter 11: The Perfect Storm.............................234

PART III: DECLINE PATTERNS

Chapter 12: The Four Phases of Decline.............................253

Chapter 13: The Regulatory Domino Sequence.............................267

Chapter 14: The Operational Ceiling.............................282

PART IV: THE PLAYBOOK

Chapter 15: Reading the Equation.............................296

Chapter 16: Timing, Sequencing, and the Boom-Bust Cycle.............................314

Chapter 17: Reigniting Stalled Growth.............................336

Chapter 18: The Quiet Compounders.............................361

Chapter 19: The Next Momentum Window.............................375

Conclusion: What Momentum Is Actually For.............................393

Appendix A: The 53-Company Dataset.............................403

Appendix B: The Momentum Diagnostic AI Prompt.............................406

Work With Rob.............................409

Introduction: Why Some Direct Selling Companies Crash

You didn't lose momentum. You never understood what created it.

The question this book exists to answer is this.

Why do some direct selling companies compound for thirty years while structurally similar companies collapse in five?

The 53-company dataset behind this book is the evidence. Real-time data from 82 verified top earners who are actively building right now runs through the arguments as proof points. Through all of it, one pattern has been consistent. The companies that achieve momentum almost never understand what created it. And the companies that lose momentum almost never understand what destroyed it.

Western Union is the clearest non-direct-selling example. In 1876, Alexander Graham Bell offered Western Union the patent for the telephone for $100,000. The company that owned the entire long-distance communication infrastructure of the United States declined the offer. As the story is usually told, the committee that weighed the offer turned it down. The telephone had too many shortcomings. The voice quality was inferior. The transmission distance was limited. Customers would have to buy expensive new equipment. Why would anyone use it when they could send a perfectly clear telegram for less money?

The committee was looking at the telephone through the lens of telegraph economics. They believed Western Union's momentum came from the telegraph network, the trained operators, the established cable infrastructure, the institutional relationships. The telephone, by their analysis, was a curiosity that didn't match any of those structural advantages.

They were wrong. Western Union's momentum had never been about the telegraph specifically. It had been about being the fastest way to send a message between two distant points. The telegraph was just the mechanism. When the telephone matured into a viable mass-market technology in the 1880s and 1890s, the underlying momentum migrated to the new mechanism. By 1909, AT&T had acquired a roughly 30%

controlling stake in Western Union under Theodore Vail's leadership. The arrangement lasted only four years. Under Wilson-era antitrust pressure, AT&T agreed in the 1913 Kingsbury Commitment to divest the Western Union shares. The displacement of telegraphy by telephony was a market-driven phenomenon over the next two decades, not a corporate consolidation. Bell's patent had become the most valuable patent in American business history.

The company was destroyed by attribution error. They had attributed their momentum to the wrong variable. And because they had attributed it to the wrong variable, they couldn't see the transition coming, even when the inventor of the future technology came to their offices and offered them the chance to own it.

Direct selling companies make the same mistake. Different industry. Same mechanism. They attribute growth to their product, their culture, their leadership, their vision. Those things mattered. But the primary cause was usually a combination of structural forces, market timing, platform dynamics, compensation architecture, and leader migration patterns that the company either stumbled into or deliberately engineered. When those forces aligned, momentum exploded. When they shifted, momentum evaporated. And the leadership team, which had taken credit for the growth, was left staring at a declining revenue chart wondering what they did wrong.

Usually, they did nothing wrong. The forces shifted. They had never understood the forces in the first place.

This book exists to fix that.

Before you read another page, run this one test. Take your revenue last quarter. Subtract every dollar that came from a distributor purchasing to qualify for a rank, a bonus, or a promotion. What is left is your real customer volume. If that number is less than 40% of your total revenue, put this book down and fix that first. Nothing else in these pages will help you until you do. Every framework, every driver, every diagnostic assumes you're building on a real customer base. If you're not, you're managing a recruiting machine dressed as a business, and the rest of this book will feel like criticism of your company because most of it is.

If your customer ratio is above 40%, keep reading. The book is written for you.

The companies in this book built something real. Many of them also made structural mistakes that cost them. We study both. The analysis isn't about assigning blame. It is about extracting the lessons that let the next generation of companies build on what these leaders learned the hard way. If any founder reads their company's story and feels I got something wrong, I welcome that conversation.

Every great company in history has faced challenges that looked fatal at the time. Apple was 90 days from bankruptcy in 1997 before Steve Jobs returned and Microsoft invested $150 million to keep them alive. Starbucks closed 600 stores in 2008 and brought Howard Schultz back as CEO. Ford nearly went bankrupt in 2006 and had to mortgage its entire portfolio of assets, including the blue oval logo, to secure a $23.6 billion line of credit. Netflix lost 800,000 subscribers in a single quarter in 2011. FedEx, in its early years, was so close to collapse that founder Fred Smith took the company's last $5,000 to a Las Vegas blackjack table and won $27,000, buying enough time to raise the funding that saved the company. Every one of those companies is now a textbook example of excellence.

This industry is no different. Amway faced an FTC investigation in the 1970s that could have ended the company. Herbalife survived a five-year public short attack led by a hedge fund manager specifically trying to destroy it. Nu Skin watched 33% of its stock value evaporate in a single day after Chinese government scrutiny. Mary Kay lost its founder in 2001 and still adapted across generations of cultural change. Every long-term winner in this profession has a chapter in its story that looked, at the time, like the end. Challenges aren't evidence of failure. They are evidence of doing something large enough to be tested.

Every CEO reading this book will face a moment that looks like an ending. The equation exists to help you read the moment correctly and respond before the pattern runs to completion.

A note on what this book is also about, because the early pages will read as diagnostic and the diagnosis is honest about what isn't working. The constructive case is just as important, and it runs through every chapter that follows.

Direct selling is one of only two legitimate ways to build a consumer brand. The other is paid advertising at scale. In any category where human trust matters more than algorithmic targeting, the model has an enduring structural role that no amount of platform disruption or category competition will eliminate. The long-term compounders prove this. Melaleuca has been growing across more than four decades on a real customer foundation. Amway has continued to operate at scale across more than sixty years. PM International has crossed three billion dollars in revenue with thirty-plus years of operational discipline, even though its revenue mix leans more on internal consumption than on the customer foundation this book advocates. These aren't exceptions. They are the proof of concept that the model can compound. The model works best when it's built on a real customer foundation and operated with strategic discipline.

The next generation of operators has structural advantages no prior generation has had. AI for customer personalization and operational forecasting. Real-time data on what is working across the industry. Lighter inventory models that reduce risk. Hybrid distribution architectures that combine the relationship-driven sales the model is good at with the operational discipline that modern consumers expect. The accumulated mistakes of every prior attempt available to study. A regulatory environment that has clarified what works and what doesn't. A modern customer who is more sophisticated about evaluating both products and opportunities. The companies that combine these tools with the timeless fundamentals of relationship-driven selling are positioned to write the next chapter of this profession's story.

The companies that build customer foundations and operate with strategic discipline are positioned to own the next decade. The companies that understand the equation in this book will create more momentum more often, sustain it longer, and reignite it more reliably than the companies that don't. That isn't a promise of guaranteed outcomes. It is a structural prediction based on what the dataset shows about what works and what doesn't. The opportunity is real. The frameworks in this book are designed to help any company capture it.

Two enemies run through every chapter that follows. Short-term thinking and artificial volume. Short-term thinking is the decision to optimize for this quarter at the expense of the next five years. Artificial volume is revenue that exists because the comp plan demands it, not because a customer wants the product. These two enemies are responsible for more destroyed companies than every regulatory action, market shift, and competitive threat combined. They are sitting in your boardroom right now.

The harder truth underneath both of them is this. The recruiting-first model that built this industry is dying. It has been dying for a decade. Regulators see it. Platforms penalize it. Customers distrust it. The next generation of builders refuses to sell it. The companies that understand this and rebuild their model around real customer acquisition will own the next decade. The companies that don't will be the flash crashes this book studies five years from now. Every framework, every ratio, every diagnostic in this book is built on that conviction. If you disagree, close the book now. Everything that follows assumes you're ready to face it.

And underneath both enemies is a single truth most leadership teams avoid: every momentum decision is a tradeoff. The move that creates speed usually costs something else. Control. Trust. Margin. Simplicity. Fairness. Long-term durability. Many companies don't collapse because they made one catastrophic decision. They collapse because they made a series of reasonable decisions without being honest about the price each one carried. This book will force you to see the price tags.

Everything in this book feeds a single tool: the Momentum Equation Scorecard. You will find it in Chapter 15. It takes every framework, every ratio, every driver, and every diagnostic in these pages and compresses them into one executive instrument you can run in 30 minutes. As you read, start scoring. The audits, diagnostics, scorecards, ratios, and assessments throughout the book are all the same thing: diagnostic tools designed to surface specific truths about your company that the standard dashboard obscures. By the time you reach the scorecard, you'll already know your numbers. If you're not using it, you're guessing.

One more thing before we begin. Most readers will engage with this book alone first, and that's the right way to start. Read it. Highlight what surprises you. Score the frameworks against your own company in your own head. Then bring it to your leadership team. The frameworks in this book reveal more when scored by multiple people on the same leadership team than when scored by one. The Momentum Attribution Audit reveals more when five people in a room give different answers and the disagreement surfaces a blind spot. The Flash Crash Scorecard reveals more when the CEO and the VP of Sales score the same five characteristics and discover they see the company differently. The Reignition Diagnostic reveals more when the people who set strategy and the people who execute it are looking at the same data and having the same conversation. Read alone first. Then put the book in front of the team that helps you build the company.

Get this book into the hands of every member of your leadership team. Your top corporates. Your VP of Sales. Your head of operations. Your comp plan architect. Your top field advisory council members. Have them read it independently before discussing it together. The conversations that follow will be more valuable than the book itself. The book gives you the lens. The conversations reveal what the lens shows you about your specific company.

How to use this book. If you read cover to cover, it builds sequentially from diagnosis to framework to playbook. If you're diagnosing a specific problem, go directly to the chapter that matches. If you only have 30 minutes, go to Chapter 15 and run the Momentum Equation Scorecard.

Underneath the scorecard, underneath every framework in this book, there's one decision that matters more than all the others. It is built on what I call the Two-Graph Model.

Graph One is the Momentum Illusion. It is volatile. It spikes when you launch a promotion. It spikes when a big leader goes on a building tear. It spikes when you open a new market or run a convention incentive. Then it drops. Then it spikes again. This graph tracks new sign-ups, new builders, recruiting velocity, promotional activity. It is exciting to watch. It is what many companies obsess over. And it's the most misleading number in your business.

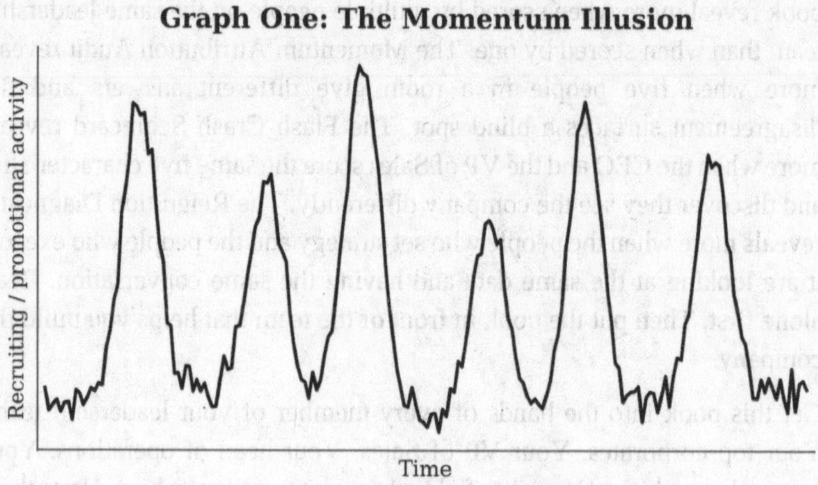

Graph One: The Momentum Illusion

Graph Two is Customer Reality. It is steady. It moves slowly. It doesn't spike after a promotion. It doesn't drop when a leader takes a month off. This graph tracks your true customer volume. How many real customers do you have? How much are they spending per month on average? How long are you retaining them? This is the true volume of your business. Everything else is noise on top of it.

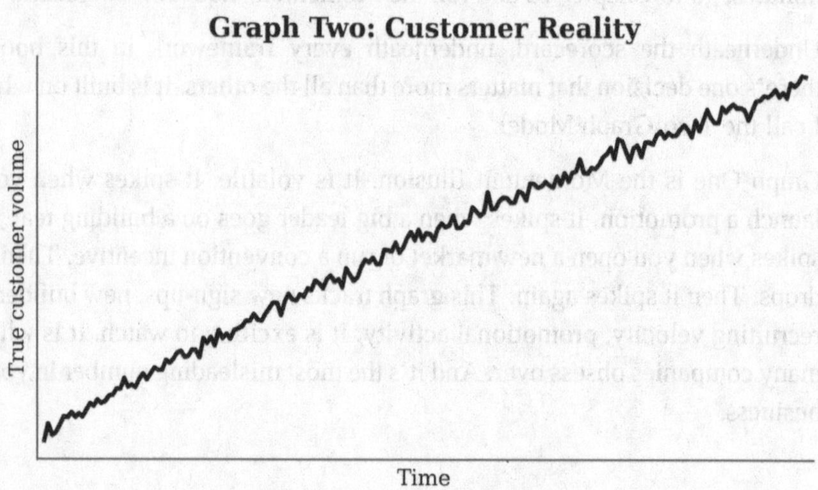

Graph Two: Customer Reality

Ask yourself one question. Which graph does your executive team review weekly? If the honest answer is Graph One, the rest of this book is going to be uncomfortable. That is the point.

When you're in momentum, the first graph dominates your attention. Revenue is climbing. Sign-ups are accelerating. The volatile line is going up and to the right and everyone is celebrating. The second graph barely gets discussed because who cares about steady customer retention when recruiting is on fire?

Then momentum stops. The first graph drops. Sometimes it drops hard. Promotions stop working. Leaders slow down. Recruiting cools. And when that volatile line falls away, what is left? The second graph. Your true customer base. It is the floor you fall to, and the number that determines whether your company survives the correction or collapses through it.

How to create momentum. How to stay in it longer. How to diagnose when it's fading. How to reignite it when it stalls. But the North Star through every chapter is that second graph. The true customer volume. Because in the end, every company falls to its customer floor. How high you build it while you have the chance is the part that lasts.

The simplest way to think about this is two worlds.

World One is the distributor world. Recruiting. Team building. Rank advancement. Incentive trips. Convention stages. Income recognition. This is the world of momentum, energy, and growth. It is exciting. It is visible. It is what fills a convention hall with cheering. Every company obsesses over World One because World One is where the scoreboard lives.

World Two is the customer world. People who buy your product because they want it. They reorder every month because the product works for them. Many of them have no idea there's a compensation plan attached. They don't know what a rank is. They have never been to a convention. They don't care about your business opportunity. They care about the product.

World Two doesn't know World One exists. And that's exactly the point.

The best companies in this industry build both worlds simultaneously. World One creates the growth. World Two creates the insurance. World One fills the pipeline. World Two builds the floor. When something goes wrong in World One, and something always eventually goes wrong, a leader leaves, a promotion fails, recruiting slows, the field loses energy, World Two is still there. Those customers are still ordering. That revenue is still coming in. That floor is still holding.

The companies that only build World One have no insurance. When the distributor world contracts, there's nothing underneath it. The companies that build both worlds have a foundation that survives whatever happens in the recruiting room. That is the entire thesis of this book in one metaphor. Build both worlds. Never stop investing in World Two, especially when World One is on fire.

In 2025, I published Built to Last in Direct Selling. That book diagnosed what is broken inside direct selling companies. It covered the infrastructure, trust, culture, and systems that companies need to survive. It was the defensive playbook. How to build a company that can withstand the forces that destroy most companies in this industry.

This book is the companion, not a sequel. It is a different question for the same audience.

Built to Last asked: why do companies collapse?

Why Some Direct Selling Companies Crash asks: why do some companies compound for decades while others collapse in five years, and what separates the survivors from the rest?

Built to Last was the defense. This book is the offense. Every company needs both. The best infrastructure in the world means nothing if you can't create growth. The most explosive growth in the world means nothing if the infrastructure underneath it can't sustain it. These two books sit together on the same shelf because they address the same problem from opposite directions.

If you've read Built to Last, this book will show you how to create the momentum that your infrastructure was designed to sustain. If you've not read it, this book stands on its own. But you'll find, by the time you finish the final chapter, that the two lenses together reveal more than either one alone.

This book matters right now, in this specific moment, for a specific reason.

The direct selling industry is facing simultaneous disruptions that have no historical precedent.

GLP-1 receptor agonist drugs are dismantling the weight management category. Medifast, one of the most successful coaching-model companies in the industry, has seen its stock decline 76% from peak. Herbalife, a nearly $5 billion company that survived the most public short-selling attack in financial history and a $200 million FTC settlement, saw its stock crater before beginning a partial recovery as the company adapted. This isn't a company-specific problem. It is the first systemic category disruption in the history of direct selling, where a pharmaceutical innovation is simultaneously threatening multiple billion-dollar companies.

The model exit wave is accelerating. In 2024 and 2025, BODi (formerly Beachbody), Rodan+Fields, Beautycounter, Modere, and Seint all exited the direct selling distribution model. BODi's executive chairman called the multi-level marketing model "outdated and unsustainable." Whether that statement reflects the industry's future or one company's miscalculation is a debate worth having. But five companies exiting in roughly the same twelve-month window is a pattern, not a coincidence.

Platform disruption is accelerating. TikTok Shop has created a distribution channel that reaches consumers at a fraction of the cost of direct selling distribution. The creator economy and the direct selling field are now competing for the same consumer attention using the same platforms. The algorithmic advantages that powered a decade of social-selling momentum are shifting.

The trust recession continues. Public perception of direct selling remains negative. Anti-direct selling content creators reach larger audiences than most direct selling companies' marketing efforts. Every new FTC enforcement action, every documentary, every viral complaint thread reinforces a narrative that the industry hasn't effectively countered.

AI is about to change the skills that matter. Automated content creation, AI-powered customer service, personalized marketing at scale. These capabilities will reshape what distributors do, how they reach customers, and which companies can compete effectively.

All of this is happening simultaneously. And many leadership teams are reacting to each disruption individually without seeing the pattern that connects them.

Every disruption in this list does one thing. It reduces the market's tolerance for artificial volume. Consumers have more options. Regulators have more scrutiny. Platforms favor real engagement. Young builders demand substance. The companies whose revenue depended on qualification purchasing, recruiting hype, and the comp plan doing the work the product couldn't do are the companies most exposed to every disruption listed above. The companies whose revenue depends on real customers buying real products for real reasons are the ones most insulated from all of them.

That is the through-line. Every force pressing on this industry right now is tightening the same screw.

This book gives you the pattern.

The analytical foundation of this book rests on 53 companies, their year-by-year revenue trajectories, SEC filings, court records, FTC enforcement documents, and documented leader concentration and internal consumption ratios. The dataset overrepresents big wins and big failures, which is exactly where momentum lessons live. The vast quiet middle of the industry, companies doing $20M to $80M profitably for two decades, operates under partially different rules. The patterns in this book apply most directly to companies pursuing significant scale.

When I claim every flash crash I systematically coded showed at least three of five structural characteristics, that's an observational finding from a deliberate coding pass through the dataset, not a theory. Every framework in this book was derived from that dataset and tested against it.

Additionally, the customer revenue ratios cited throughout the book are audited and court-documented for some companies (BurnLounge, Vemma, AdvoCare, Neora, Herbalife) and estimated from business model structure and available data for others. Where the ratio is precisely documented, the source is cited. Where it's inferred, it's labeled as an estimate. The 50% threshold is directionally supported across the dataset as the most consistent predictor of survival. It isn't claimed as a universally audited finding across all 53 companies. The principle matters more than the precise line. What matters is the direction of the ratio and the honesty with which leadership teams measure it.

The same sourcing discipline applies to the revenue figures throughout this book. Publicly traded companies, including Nu Skin, Herbalife, Medifast, Tupperware, Avon, Beachbody, USANA, and Zinzino, file audited financials, and their numbers are drawn from those filings. Most direct selling companies are privately held and don't publish audited revenue. For private companies such as Amway, doTERRA, Young Living, Mary Kay, Melaleuca, MonaVie, LuLaRoe, Rodan and Fields, and PM International, the revenue figures cited here are company-reported or estimated from the best available industry sources, and they should be read as reported figures rather than audited fact. Where a number is an estimate or a reported figure, the book labels it as such on first reference. The trajectories and the orders of magnitude are reliable. Individual figures for private companies may vary from whatever internal numbers those companies hold.

The data shows what happens next, not just what happened. The Three Hard Ratios. The Flash Crash Formula. The Four Phases of Decline. The Regulatory Domino Sequence. The 5-Act Boom-Bust Cycle. The Momentum Equation Scorecard. Each one emerged from the data. Each one has been tested against the dataset. Each one survived.

These frameworks aren't academic exercises. They are diagnostic tools designed to be used in a leadership meeting this quarter. They are scorecards that can be put on a whiteboard. They are checklists that can guide strategic decisions. This book was written to be used, not just read.

What this book will do and what it won't do.

It will show you the five structural forces that create momentum in direct selling. Product-Culture Fit. Platform Disruption. Leader Migration. Market Expansion. Compensation Architecture. Every major momentum period in the industry's history was driven by one or more of these forces.

You will learn to identify which ones are active in your company right now and which ones are dormant, absent, or reversing.

It will show you how to diagnose whether your growth is real or fragile. The Three Hard Ratios separate companies with genuine customer demand from companies with product alibis. The Flash Crash Formula identifies the structural characteristics that predict collapse. The Decline Phase Diagnostic catches erosion before it becomes visible in the revenue report. You will learn to read your own company's health with more precision than any dashboard currently provides.

It will show you the historical patterns that predict what happens next. The 5-Act Boom-Bust Cycle has repeated six times in seventy years. The Regulatory Domino Sequence follows a consistent four-stage timeline. The product category survival rates tell you the odds for your specific product type. History doesn't repeat exactly. But the patterns are consistent enough to be strategically useful.

It won't promise permanent momentum. It is impossible to always be in momentum. Markets shift. Products age. Platforms change. How to create momentum more often, stay in it longer, and see the decline coming before it arrives. That is a realistic promise. Permanent momentum isn't.

It won't sugarcoat the data. Some of the findings in this book will be uncomfortable. If your company's internal consumption ratio is above 70%, the data says you're at elevated risk. If your product category has a 0% historical survival rate, the data says the odds are against you. This book doesn't soften the data. You are sophisticated executives and leaders who read Harvard Business Review and Good to Great and Blue Ocean Strategy. You don't need to be protected from uncomfortable findings. You need the findings so you can act on them.

It will show you what to see and force the decisions that follow. The frameworks in this book are diagnostic and decisional. They show you where you are, what the data confirms about where you're heading, and what moves the situation demands. The strategic decisions belong to you. This book gives you better information to make them with and the pressure to make them now.

One thing this book isn't: an argument against direct selling. It is an argument against weak operating assumptions inside direct selling. The model works. It has created more entrepreneurial income for more ordinary people than any other distribution system in history. This book isn't here to question whether the model works. It is here to make the operators inside it more honest about what creates momentum, what sustains it, and what destroys it.

The structure of the book follows the logic of diagnosis.

Part I (Chapters 1 through 5) dismantles the myths about momentum and gives you the diagnostic lens you need before the driver chapters begin. The Momentum Myth. The Momentum Spectrum. The Three Hard Ratios. The Product Alibi.

Part II (Chapters 6 through 11) introduces the five drivers of momentum and shows what happens when they combine. Product-Culture Fit. Platform Disruption. Leader Migration. Market Expansion. Compensation Architecture. The Perfect Storm.

Part III (Chapters 12 through 14) documents the patterns of decline. The Four Phases. The Regulatory Domino Sequence. The Operational Ceiling.

Part IV (Chapters 15 through 17) is the playbook. Reading the Equation. Timing and the Boom-Bust Cycle. Reigniting Stalled Growth.

Each chapter contains a framework, scorecard, or diagnostic tool that can be used independently. Together, they form the Momentum Equation Scorecard, a unified system for reading your company's momentum in real time.

A word about the companies in this book.

You will read about companies that achieved extraordinary things and companies that failed spectacularly. Some companies appear as both. Nu Skin reached $3.18 billion in peak revenue, faced a Barbara Walters expose that nearly destroyed it, was saved by Japan, and then lost a third of its market value in a single day from a Chinese government investigation. That same company is still operating forty years later, still innovating, still adapting. That isn't a failure story. It is a resilience story with failures inside it.

MonaVie reached a reported $854 million in annual revenue within three years of launch, faster than almost any company in industry history. Its events were legendary. Its vision-casting was among the best the profession has ever seen. Dallin Larsen understood how to build belief in a room. The company's failure was structural, not a failure of talent or vision.

Every company in this book was built by people who worked hard, took risks, and tried to build something real. Some succeeded structurally and some didn't. The analysis in this book respects the effort while being honest about the outcomes. The point isn't to judge. The point is to learn. And the companies that failed teach as much as the companies that survived, sometimes more.

One last thing before we begin.

This is the best thinking I have, drawn from two decades of observation, the largest decline dataset ever compiled for this industry, and the real-time pattern recognition that comes from working with 1,800 top earners who see momentum from the inside every day.

A caveat that applies to every business book ever written, including this one. Jim Collins published Good to Great in 2001 and featured eleven companies he identified as having made the leap from good to great. Within a decade, several of those companies had stumbled hard. Circuit City filed for bankruptcy in 2008. Fannie Mae was taken into federal conservatorship in the 2008 financial crisis. Wells Fargo's reputation was destroyed by the fake accounts scandal. Collins' analysis wasn't wrong at the time he wrote it. The companies were great at the time he wrote it. The world changed. The companies that looked like permanent winners turned out to be winners for a season.

The same reality applies here. Some of the companies this book praises will struggle. Some will decline. Some may not exist in the form they exist today by the time you're reading this. That isn't a failure of the analysis. That is a feature of business. Change is the only constant. No company is permanent. No strategy works forever. No momentum lasts indefinitely. The best a book like this can do is give you the lens to see what is working now, identify what shifts are coming, and respond faster than your competitors when the conditions change. If a company I praise here collapses next year, the lens is still the lens. The equation didn't fail. The company did. And someone using the equation could have seen the decline coming if they had been looking at the right variables.

Hold every company in this book, including the ones I speak of positively, with the same skepticism you would apply to any business. They are all subject to the same forces. They all face the same pressures. They all could be wrong about what is coming. The point is never to trust the company. The point is to learn from the mechanism.

If this book does its job, you'll finish it seeing your company differently. Not with more optimism or more pessimism. With more clarity. You will know which drivers are active. You will know whether your foundation is sound. You will know which act of the cycle you're in. And you'll make better decisions because of it.

That is the equation. The book doesn't promise a formula for guaranteed momentum. It offers a lens for seeing momentum clearly enough to create it more often and sustain it longer.

THE ARCHITECTURE UNDERNEATH THE EQUATION

Before we go any further, you need to understand how the variables in this book relate to each other, because the structure isn't flat. It is layered.

At the foundation sits the Customer Ratio. The percentage of your revenue that comes from real customers buying real products for real reasons, independent of any compensation plan qualification requirement. This variable is the load-bearing concept of the entire book. It determines whether everything above it compounds or collapses. Without a real customer foundation, no driver can produce durable momentum. With a real customer foundation, every driver becomes more powerful.

This is the point where a careful reader starts to see an apparent contradiction, so it's worth resolving now rather than later. This book argues two things that sound opposed. The first is that real customers, people who buy because they want the product and would keep buying with no compensation plan in the picture, are the foundation of a durable company. The second, which comes later, is that without the field and the compensation plan, most great products would never reach a single customer, because the field is the discovery engine of this entire profession. Both are true. They aren't in tension once you see how they fit. The product has to deliver real value that a customer would pay for on its own merits. The field and the compensation plan are what put that product in front of the customer in the first place. The comp plan is the engine that drives discovery. The customer foundation is what determines whether that discovery turns into something durable or something temporary. A product nobody would buy without the comp plan is a problem no field can fix. A great product nobody ever discovers because there's no field is a tree falling in an empty forest. The whole game is building a product real enough to keep customers and a field strong enough to find them. Hold both ideas at once. The rest of the book depends on it.

Above the foundation sit the Five Drivers. Product-Culture Fit. Platform Disruption. Leader Migration. Market Expansion. Compensation Architecture. These are the variables that produce momentum when activated, individually and especially in combination. The drivers are real. Their effects are documented. But none of them produces durable momentum on their own when the customer foundation is absent. They produce spikes. The spikes recede.

Above the drivers sit the Constraints. Regulatory Gates. Operational Ceilings. The Boom-Bust Cycle. These are the structural forces that determine how long any momentum can be sustained, regardless of how skillfully the drivers are activated. The constraints don't create momentum. They limit how long momentum can hold once created.

Underneath the constraints, woven through every layer, is what I'll call the Underneath. The structural depth that sits below every surface variable. The foundation underneath the leader concentration. The customer base underneath the revenue chart. The infrastructure underneath the operational capacity. The data discipline underneath the dashboard. Every variable in this book has something underneath it, and the depth or absence of that underneath is what determines whether the variable is a strength or a vulnerability.

That is the architecture. Customer Ratio at the foundation. Five Drivers above it. Constraints around them. The Underneath threading through every layer.

If you remember nothing else from this book, remember this. The Customer Ratio is the variable that determines whether anything else you do compounds or collapses. The Five Drivers are accelerants. They can't replace the foundation. The Constraints are limits. They can't be overcome by skill at the driver level. The Underneath is what separates real strength from cosmetic strength at every level of the equation.

Every chapter that follows is in service of this architecture. When you get confused about why a chapter exists, ask which layer it's teaching about and how that layer connects to the foundation underneath.

The one line this book forces every leadership team to confront is this. You are either building customer volume, or you're borrowing momentum. There is no third category.

Part I: The Problem

Chapter 1: The Momentum Myth

Many companies that lost momentum never had it. They had a wave.

On the night of September 26, 2019, Peloton employees ate seafood and drank champagne in the glittering halls of Hudson Yards. The company had just gone public. Paper fortunes were being calculated on phone screens. People talked about second homes. Student loans they'd finally pay off. New cars. One former engineer later told CNBC it felt like nothing could get in the way.

Fourteen months later, nothing had.

By January 2021, Peloton's stock hit $171 a share. The company's market cap touched $50 billion. That made it worth more than Marriott International. More than Kraft Heinz. More than Capital One. CEO John Foley was telling employees in virtual all-hands meetings that the stock would hit $1,000. In May 2020, he told Time Magazine he could see "a couple hundred million people on the Peloton platform in 15 years."

The math seemed to justify the optimism. COVID-19 had shut down gyms worldwide. Thirty-eight thousand fitness facilities in the U.S. alone went dark. Peloton's connected bike, priced at $1,895 plus $39 per month for classes, became the fitness solution for millions of locked-down consumers with money to burn. Orders exploded. Subscriptions doubled. Wait times stretched past three months. Customers were paying in full and sitting around for weeks hoping their bike would show up. Revenue surged from $915 million in fiscal 2019 to $4 billion in fiscal 2021.

That is five to seven years of projected growth compressed into eighteen months.

So Peloton's leadership did what any confident executive team does when they believe they understand why they're winning. They doubled down. Hard.

In the span of six months, they committed $820 million to expanding capacity. They broke ground on a $400 million factory in Ohio called Peloton Output Park, designed to give them direct control over manufacturing. They acquired Precor, an established fitness equipment maker, for $420 million. They hired aggressively across every department.

Field operators were offered thousands in hazard pay just to keep delivering bikes through the pandemic's darkest days. In some regions, last-mile delivery was running $500 per bike before the customer touched the handlebars.

Every single one of these decisions made sense inside the narrative the leadership team had built. The narrative went like this: consumers have discovered that Peloton is a superior fitness experience. The pandemic accelerated a permanent behavioral shift. People don't want to go back to gyms. They want connected fitness at home. We are the market leader in a category that just became mainstream. Our job is to scale fast enough to capture this demand before competitors catch up.

That narrative felt logical. It was internally consistent. Every data point in front of them seemed to confirm it. Revenue was climbing. Subscribers were growing. Customer satisfaction was high. The churn rate sat around 1%. Wall Street was throwing money at them.

There was just one problem. The narrative was wrong.

Not completely wrong. Peloton did have a great product. The community was real. The instructor-driven model was truly innovative. But the explosive growth, the $4 billion spike, the 460% stock surge, that wasn't happening because of any of those things. Those things had existed before the pandemic. They'd produced steady, respectable growth. A $915 million company. A loyal niche.

The explosion was caused by a convergence of external forces that Peloton didn't create and couldn't sustain. Gyms closed. Forty million Americans filed for unemployment but stimulus checks padded consumer accounts. People were stuck at home and desperate for something that felt productive. A $2,000 bike with live classes and a social community scratched an itch that had nothing to do with Peloton's long-term value proposition. It had everything to do with a global crisis that temporarily eliminated every alternative.

The demand wasn't about Peloton. It was about circumstance. And circumstances change.

By mid-2022, gyms reopened across the country. Consumer spending tightened as inflation spiked. The used Peloton market flooded with barely-ridden bikes selling for half price. People who'd bought bikes in the heat of lockdown stopped using them. Peloton was sitting on more than $1.4 billion in gross inventory by mid-2022. The company itself, in its Q4 fiscal 2022 shareholder letter, described the stockpile as an existential threat to the business. Industry observers calculated the overhang at well over a year of sales at the company's collapsed run-rate.

Revenue fell from $4 billion to $2.5 billion. Then kept falling. Fiscal 2025 closed at $2.49 billion, down from $2.70 billion the prior year and roughly 38% below the $4.02 billion fiscal 2021 peak. The stock cratered 98% from its peak. Foley was pushed out in early 2022. Thousands were laid off. The Ohio factory was sold before it ever shipped a single bike. The Precor acquisition became a write-off. The company's market cap, which once exceeded $50 billion, shrank below $5 billion.

The postmortem is usually told as bad luck. "The pandemic boom ended." That is too generous. Peloton's collapse wasn't a function of timing. It was a function of misdiagnosis.

John Foley and his leadership team looked at explosive growth and asked themselves: what is driving this? They answered: our product, our brand, our platform. Then they invested $820 million based on that answer.

The actual answer was: a global pandemic closed every gym in the world and consumers had nowhere else to spend their fitness dollars.

They had momentum. Real, measurable, revenue-producing momentum. But they never understood what was creating it. So they poured resources into scaling the wrong thing. And when the actual driver disappeared, the momentum vanished with it.

Peloton is instructive because it's outside this industry. The same mechanism plays out inside it, and it's possible to see it coming if you know what to look for.

On July 8, 2024, I posted the following to my private community of 1,800 verified six- and seven-figure earners. It was public. It was dated. And it was specific.

> Leaders,
>

> Keep your teams close and no matter how good your culture is keep improving it!

>

> I know of at least 3 different companies that are about to IMPLODE with a mass exodus that hasn't even started yet. The companies aren't even aware yet.

>

> The rest of this year will be a WILD RIDE for this profession.

The reaction was exactly split. Half the community thanked me for the warning. The other half were furious. Some said I was fear-mongering. Some accused me of being anti-industry. Some private messages weren't printable.

I followed up that same day with a clarification. The goal wasn't to create fear. The goal was to create awareness and urgency. I had to be careful about that balance. I believe in this profession. I'm an advocate for what it can do when it's built right. But I also don't live in fairyland. A leader who is always optimistic can't see the hard stuff in time to address it. Realism matters. Awareness matters. And the only way to deliver either one responsibly is to create space for leaders to evaluate their own situations with honest eyes.

The post required a live follow-up inside the group. I wanted to pull people back from panic and into clarity. My job wasn't to tell anyone their company was good or bad. My job was to hand them a better set of questions to ask about their own company than the ones they were currently asking.

What happened in the months after the post is what proved the framework works. Leaders from dozens of different companies reached out. Not to ask me whether their company was on my list. They reached out to ask a better question. "What should I be watching? What patterns should I be looking for inside my own company right now? Am I missing something?" That is exactly the right question. It is the one the framework answers.

Some of those leaders looked at the variables, saw warning signs, and brought them to their executive teams. Some of those companies made adjustments. Some didn't. The companies that adjusted are still here. The ones that didn't are either in crisis now or will be soon.

This book is the framework those leaders were asking about.

What many company leaders believe about momentum is this.

They believe that when momentum arrives, they recognize it. They believe that when it leaves, they feel it go. And they believe that when they want to get it back, they can recreate the conditions that produced it.

Every part of that is wrong.

Start with recognition. Many leaders can't accurately identify which variables are driving their growth while they're in it. When revenue is climbing, everything looks like a genius move. The new product launch seems to be working. The comp plan redesign feels brilliant. The leader you just recruited from a competitor looks like a game changer. The conference you threw last quarter was "the best one ever." Every decision gets credit because every decision happened before the growth appeared on the scoreboard.

But correlation isn't causation. And the revenue climbing on your dashboard might have nothing to do with the decisions you're congratulating yourself for.

This is attribution error. And it's the most expensive mistake a leadership team can make.

In psychology, attribution error is the tendency to assign causes to outcomes based on incomplete or incorrect reasoning. You see a result. You identify the most available explanation. You lock it in. Then you build strategy around it. The explanation feels right. It feels rational. It might even be partially correct. But it's almost certainly incomplete. And incomplete diagnosis produces broken strategy.

What attribution error looks like at the company level.

"We're growing because our product is incredible." Maybe. Or maybe your product landed at the exact moment a cultural mega-trend was accelerating, and millions of consumers were already searching for something like it. Your product didn't create the trend. It caught the trend. The wellness boom that lifted doTERRA didn't start inside doTERRA.

The athleisure explosion that powered LuLaRoe didn't originate in a warehouse in Corona, California. Those companies inserted themselves into cultural currents that were already massive and accelerating. When the current shifts, the companies that confused riding the wave with building the wave find out the difference fast.

"We're growing because we signed a major leader." Maybe. Or maybe that leader brought 20,000 people from her last company, and the growth you see is the mathematical result of her pre-built network plugging into your comp plan. If her enthusiasm fades in eighteen months, if she gets a better offer from a competitor, if she decides she's tired and wants to coast, the growth leaves with her. You didn't build that network. You rented it. And rental agreements expire.

"We're growing because we opened three new countries." Maybe. Or maybe distributors were already shipping product into those countries through informal channels before you officially launched. Your expansion didn't create demand. It captured demand that was already flowing on its own. Whether that demand deepens after the novelty wears off, or whether your "new market" was really just a one-time formalization of existing behavior, is the test of real expansion.

In each case, the leadership team sees growth. They look at their most recent major decision. They draw a line from one to the other. Product launch to revenue. Leader signing to revenue. Market opening to revenue. Clean narrative. Clean cause and effect.

But momentum is almost never one variable. It is compound. Multiple forces operating at the same time, overlapping, reinforcing, masking each other. The growth you see on the top line is the combined output of all of them. When you attribute it to just one, you misread the equation. And when you try to recreate that growth by pulling that single lever, nothing happens. Because the lever you're pulling was never the engine. It was one part of a machine with five moving pieces, and you only noticed the one piece you installed.

That is why many companies can't recreate their own growth. They are trying to replicate something they never actually understood.

The enemy in this chapter isn't incompetence. The people running direct selling companies are frequently sharp, experienced, and dedicated. The enemy is something more subtle and more dangerous.

It is confidence built on a false diagnosis.

Momentum is the great exaggerator. It magnifies strengths. It hides weaknesses. Until it doesn't. While revenue climbs, every flaw in the foundation, low customer ratios, leader concentration, qualification purchasing, stays invisible. The same forces that create the spike also mask the structural cracks underneath. And the moment the spike plateaus, every hidden weakness announces itself at the same time.

Bill Belichick's New England Patriots teams in the 2000s and 2010s understood this. When the Patriots led by three touchdowns at halftime, Belichick didn't celebrate in the locker room. He ran the same film session he ran when they were down 21 points. He obsessed over every missed assignment, every tendency the opponent might exploit in the second half. The team never relaxed because the coach refused to let the scoreboard create complacency. Six Super Bowl titles. The most sustained dynasty in modern football. Built not on talent alone but on the discipline of diagnosing during the good times instead of waiting for the bad ones.

Direct selling leadership teams need the same discipline. Treat every quarter of growth as a film session, not a victory parade. The time to diagnose is when you're winning, because that's when you still have the resources and the credibility to fix what you find.

Ancient Rome understood this better than any modern business school. When a Roman general won a great victory, the Senate awarded him a triumph: a procession through the streets of Rome with his army, his prisoners, and the spoils of war. The crowds cheered. The general rode in a golden chariot wearing a purple toga. It was the highest honor the Republic could bestow.

But standing directly behind the general in that chariot was a slave. And the slave had one job. He held a laurel crown above the general's head and whispered, continuously, "Memento mori." Remember, you're mortal. Remember, this will end. You are a man, not a god.

The Romans didn't do this to dampen the celebration. They did it because they understood that the moment of greatest triumph is the moment of greatest danger. Victory distorts judgment. When growth is running, every decision feels validated. The next call feels easier than it should.

Every company in momentum needs a version of that slave.

In practice, that looks like this. Once per quarter, when things are going well, gather your top ten executive leaders in a room. The field stays out of this meeting. The corporate team. The people who see the financials, the operations, the compliance pipeline, the field analytics. Ask them one question:

If we're out of momentum two years from now, what was the reason?

Write down every answer. Do not debate them. Do not defend against them. Just collect them. Then look at the list. Those answers are your vulnerability map. They are the things your team already sees but nobody is saying out loud because nobody wants to be the person who questions the momentum while it's running.

The companies that do this exercise with honest data will find that their team already knows where the cracks are. The customer ratio somebody has been meaning to bring up. The leader concentration that makes everyone nervous. The operational bottleneck that hasn't broken yet but will if volume grows another 20%. The comp plan adjustment that keeps getting deferred because the numbers are still good enough.

Those are the things that destroy momentum. Everybody saw them. Nobody said them while there was still time to fix them.

There is a deeper pattern here that research on entrepreneurship has documented extensively. The skills that create a company are almost never the skills that scale it. The charismatic founder who recruited the first thousand distributors through personal force of will may not be the right person to build the operational infrastructure for a hundred thousand. The visionary who saw the product-culture fit before anyone else may not be the right person to manage the compensation architecture that sustains a billion-dollar organization.

To be clear: founder control is a strength in the early stages. It is often the reason the company exists. The founder's willingness to make every call, stay up until midnight solving problems, personally recruit the first wave of leaders, and impose her vision on every detail of the business is what gets the company from zero to something. That intensity and control is an asset during the startup phase and often well into the growth phase. The issue isn't that control is wrong. The issue is that what works at $10 million becomes a ceiling at $100 million and a crisis at $500 million. The transition isn't one-size-fits-all. Some founders come into this business having already scaled a previous company and arrive better equipped for the corporate-scale challenge. Others are first-time builders who have never managed an organization above 50 people. The right transition point depends on the founder's prior scaling experience, the company's current stage, the depth of the existing leadership bench, and the rate at which the company is growing. There is no universal milestone. There is only the discipline of recognizing when the company has outgrown the capacity of any one person to run it, and acting on that recognition before the bottleneck does visible damage.

The founder who insists on making every decision personally at scale becomes the bottleneck, not because she lost her talent but because the company outgrew the capacity of any single person to run it. The founder who recognizes that transition point and builds a leadership team that challenges her assumptions creates something that can outgrow her. Many founders in direct selling choose control longer than they should. The ones who choose growth at the right moment, and accept the discomfort of being challenged by people they hired, are the ones whose companies sustain momentum past the founder's personal capacity.

The most dangerous version of founder dependency isn't the founder who works too many hours. It is the founder who surrounds herself with people who agree with her on everything. A leadership team made entirely of yes-people produces validated decisions, not better decisions. The founder gets faster execution and worse strategy, and the company gets a slow erosion of the diagnostic muscle the leadership team is supposed to provide. By the time the strategic blind spot becomes visible in the revenue chart, the team that should have flagged it has spent years learning that disagreement gets punished.

The discipline that separates founders who scale from founders who hit their personal ceiling is the deliberate recruitment of trusted opposites.

Most founders know their strengths well. The work is in identifying the weaknesses without flinching and then finding people who are strong where the founder isn't, who can be trusted to push back, and who have the institutional standing to do it without flinching. The visionary founder needs an operator who insists on rigorous execution detail. The aggressive founder needs a steady CFO who pushes back on capital decisions. The product-obsessed founder needs a head of compliance who challenges the marketing claims. The operationally precise founder needs a culture and field leader who keeps the human dynamics in view. Trusted opposites aren't random opposites. They are people the founder respects enough to listen to when they disagree, and who care enough about the company to keep disagreeing even when it costs them something. That is what a real leadership team looks like. It is also what most founders avoid building, because being challenged by a team you hired is uncomfortable in ways that being challenged by a competitor or a market isn't.

When a company is in momentum, nobody wants to slow down and ask why. Growth feels like validation. It feels like proof that you're making the right calls. Revenue going up means the field is happy, the board is happy, the investors are happy. Recognition stages are full. Events are sold out. Social media is buzzing with transformation stories.

In that environment, asking "but do we actually know why this is working" feels like questioning a gift. It feels ungrateful. It feels like the analytical person at the party who wants to talk about the fire exits when everyone else is dancing.

So the question goes unasked, by the CEO and the top corporates and the VP of Sales and the board. The narrative solidifies unchallenged.

Then growth slows.

And the first instinct is always the same. Do more of what we think created it. Launch another product. Sign another big leader. Open another market. Bump the fast-start bonus. Run a bigger promotion. Throw a flashier convention.

When that doesn't work, the blame starts. The field isn't working hard enough. The market is shifting. The economy is soft. Competitors are poaching our leaders. The comp plan needs adjusting. The VP of Sales needs replacing.

And the most common shortcut of all: find more leaders. Revenue slowing? Recruit a bigger name. Field energy dropping? Sign a proven builder from another company. Customer depth weak? Ignore it and pour more volume in from the top.

It doesn't work. It has never worked long-term. And every executive reading this book knows it doesn't work because they've tried it. New leaders create a burst of activity. Revenue spikes for a quarter. The boardroom exhales. Then the new leader's initial surge normalizes, the structural problems that existed before she arrived are still there, and the company is back where it started except now it's also paying a signing bonus it can't recover. The bucket is still leaking. You just poured more water in from the top.

Too many executives think they know the playbook. They have the vocabulary. They have been to the conferences. They own all the books. But when the revenue chart dips, they skip every step in the diagnostic and go straight to the one move they're most comfortable with: find another leader. Strategy requires diagnosis. That is just a reflex. And reflexes don't fix structural problems. Diagnosis does.

The one thing that almost never happens is the leadership team questioning its original narrative. Because the original narrative was never tested. It was built during the good times from assumptions that felt obvious, and nobody had any incentive to challenge assumptions when the revenue line was going up and to the right.

By the time momentum is gone, the team has been operating on a bad diagnosis for months. Sometimes years. And now they're trying to fix a problem they can't even accurately describe.

This is how companies drift from momentum to decline while still fully believing they know what they're doing. The confidence never leaves. Only the growth does.

Through my private community of 1,800 verified six- and seven-figure earners, I watch this pattern play out in real time. The top earners talk openly behind closed doors about the gap between what corporate thinks drove growth and what actually drove it.

A version of a conversation that happens constantly goes like this. Corporate launches a new product line. Revenue spikes the following quarter. Leadership takes a victory lap. "The product is a hit." Meanwhile, the field knows that one specific leader who had been coasting for two years suddenly got hungry again. Something clicked. Maybe she saw a teammate pass her in rank. Maybe she set a new financial goal. Maybe she just woke up one morning and decided she wasn't done. Whatever the reason, she went on a 90-day building tear that had nothing to do with the product launch. Her effort alone accounted for a significant chunk of that quarter's growth. When she went back to coasting, the revenue flattened. But by then, corporate had already committed millions to expanding the product line they believed was the driver.

Or this one: a company opens a new international market. First-year revenue looks incredible. Corporate celebrates the expansion strategy. The field knows the truth. A massive leader in that country was already building informally before the official launch. She had been importing product, enrolling people, creating buzz for months. The "new market" just formalized activity that already existed. Year two, after the pent-up demand is absorbed, growth slows to a crawl. Corporate is confused. The field isn't.

This gap between the corporate narrative and the field reality is where momentum goes to die. The people making strategic decisions are operating on an incomplete picture, and the people who could complete the picture are never in the room when strategy gets set.

In the survey from the introduction, 65% of respondents identified "hype fatigue" as the fastest engagement killer. Their exact framing: "every launch is the next big thing but doesn't deliver." When two-thirds of your most experienced leaders are telling you they no longer believe the story, the story is the problem.

That isn't a complaint. It is a diagnostic signal. And it connects directly to what Peloton got wrong. The narrative feels true because nobody with the authority to challenge it has any incentive to challenge it during the good times. By the time the good times end, the narrative has calcified into organizational identity. And organizational identity is the hardest thing to change.

THE MODEL EXAGGERATES EVERYTHING

There is something specific about how direct selling works that makes momentum misdiagnosis especially dangerous. The model is built on word of mouth at scale. A volunteer field of thousands or hundreds of thousands of people sharing the same story at the same time. When the story is good, that distribution force amplifies it faster and farther than any traditional marketing channel could. When the story is bad, the same force amplifies the doubt and the frustration with the same speed.

This is the strength and the weakness of the model. It is the reason a company can go from zero to a billion in revenue in five years, which would be nearly impossible in most other industries. It is also the reason a company can lose half of its volume in eighteen months when the field narrative turns. The model exaggerates everything in both directions.

The pendulum swings hard either way. That has consequences for how the field perceives momentum, and the perception itself becomes part of the reality.

This profession is a perception-driven business in a way most industries aren't. A company doing $300 million in revenue that drops to $280 million looks like a company in decline to anyone watching it from the inside. A different company that goes from $20 million to $30 million, much smaller in absolute terms, looks like a rocket. From the outside, the comparison is silly. $280 million is many times larger than $30 million. From the inside of this industry, the smaller company is the one with momentum, and the bigger company is the one losing the story. The field follows direction, not absolute size. Top earners look at trajectory. Recruits look at trajectory. The story the company tells about itself moves the field's belief, and belief moves activity, and activity moves revenue.

This is why momentum management in direct selling is harder than momentum management in most other industries. You aren't just managing the underlying business. You are managing the perception of the underlying business inside a field that has the power to amplify whichever direction the perception is pointing. A small dip in absolute terms can become a story of decline that compounds. A small uptick in absolute terms can become a story of momentum that compounds in the other direction.

This is precisely why the customer foundation matters as much as it does in this book. When the perception swings against you, when the field narrative turns negative, when the storyline is that your company is in decline, the customer base that exists outside that narrative is the rock that holds. Real customers don't check the field's mood before placing their reorder. They buy because they like the product. The companies that built deep customer foundations during the good times have a structural shock absorber when the storm hits. The companies that didn't have nothing underneath the perception when it shifts.

The model exaggerates everything. The customer foundation is what keeps the exaggeration from breaking the company.

One company proved every one of these patterns at billion-dollar scale. Its story is next. A company that had three momentum drivers firing simultaneously, identified zero of them correctly, and built its entire strategic identity around a narrative that was never tested. When the narrative collapsed, there was nothing underneath it.

THE BOTTOM LINE: Many companies can't recreate their own growth because they misattributed what caused it. Run the Momentum Attribution Audit with your leadership team. If everyone gives the same answer, you've not dug deep enough.

Misdiagnosis is the most expensive mistake in this industry.

Chapter 2: The Equation Nobody Solved

From zero to $854 million in three years. Three drivers created it. The company identified zero of them. The failure was diagnosis.

MonaVie's story is famous in this industry. The common version of the story centers on hype and acai juice. That version misses the mechanism entirely. And it fails to acknowledge what MonaVie did remarkably well.

MonaVie launched in 2005 with one product: a premium acai berry juice blend in a wine-shaped bottle. By 2008, four years in, the company reached $854 million in annual revenue. Internal financial records confirm the company held near peak through 2009 at approximately $850 million in revenue on 6.5 million cases of juice, with 95% of revenue coming from the US market alone. International expansion was still negligible at peak. Those numbers represent one of the fastest growth trajectories in the history of direct selling. Dallin Larsen built a brand that was unmistakably premium. The events were world-class. The vision-casting from stage was among the best the industry has ever seen. The energy inside MonaVie at peak was something people who experienced it still talk about. None of that was fake. The execution was brilliant.

The question isn't what happened but which variables produced it.

If you had asked MonaVie's leadership at the time, they would have pointed to the product. And the comp plan. And the leaders they had recruited. They knew it was a combination. They weren't blind to the fact that Brig Hart's organization was driving massive volume or that the comp plan economics were attracting top talent from across the industry. They saw the pieces. What they didn't do was ask which pieces were permanent and which were borrowed. And the product story was real. Acai was the hottest ingredient in the wellness world. Oprah featured it. Dr. Oz promoted it. The antioxidant craze was in full swing. Health food stores couldn't keep acai products on the shelves. MonaVie positioned a premium juice blend right at the center of that cultural conversation.

But product-culture fit isn't what created the velocity. Product-culture fit lowered the friction. It made the conversation easier. It gave distributors something the culture was already validating. That foundation is meaningful. But on its own, product-culture fit produces steady growth, not the revenue trajectory MonaVie actually produced.

The velocity came from a different driver entirely: leader migration.

MonaVie's founding team recruited aggressively and strategically from established companies. The biggest move was Brig Hart. Hart had been among Amway's most prolific producers for two decades, with a massive organization and a level of earnings that placed him among the top earners in the industry's history.

Think about what it means when a leader of that magnitude moves. Hart didn't show up alone with a briefcase and a dream. He brought infrastructure. Relationships built over more than a decade. Tens of thousands of people in his network who trusted his judgment. When Hart moved, his network noticed. His top leaders evaluated the opportunity. Many followed. Their teams followed them. And then those teams' teams followed.

This is the cascade effect, and it operates like a chain reaction. One credible leader moves, which signals to the market that something real is happening, which attracts more leaders, which creates more volume, which attracts more attention, which accelerates the cycle. Hart's organization within MonaVie grew into what industry observers at the time described as the fastest-scaling downline the company had. Amway sued Hart and other former distributors in 2008, which tells you everything about the magnitude of the talent drain.

Now layer on a third driver: compensation architecture. MonaVie's comp plan guaranteed a 50% weekly payout of commissionable volume, which is a subset of total revenue but still aggressive by industry standards. It offered fast-start bonuses up to $240 per qualified signup. The plan was aggressive by design. For an experienced networker sitting inside another company making strong income, the math was simple. Move your organization to MonaVie, get a ground-floor position, earn a higher percentage from day one, collect fast-start bonuses on every person your team enrolls. It wasn't emotional. It was arithmetic.

Three drivers running simultaneously. Product-culture fit making the conversation easy. Leader migration injecting pre-built sales forces overnight. Aggressive compensation making the economics irresistible for experienced builders.

That is the actual equation that produced MonaVie's trajectory.

But the company told itself a more complete story than just the product. MonaVie's leadership believed they had the best of everything. The best product, at the center of the biggest health trend in a decade. The best compensation plan, paying out 50% of commissionable volume with fast-start bonuses that made the economics undeniable. The best leadership, with proven top earners who had built at the highest levels of the profession. The best events, with production value that rivaled companies ten times their size. The best opportunity, period. And they promoted it that way. The pitch wasn't "try our juice." The pitch was "this is the greatest economic opportunity in direct selling history."

When you believe you have the best of everything, you stop diagnosing which specific variables are actually driving the growth. You stop asking which pieces are structural and which are temporary. Everything blurs into one narrative: we're the best, and the results prove it.

Then came the international expansion, which is where the timing tells the real story. At peak in 2009, the company was 95% US. International was negligible. The aggressive international push came after domestic momentum began softening, as the company chased breadth across dozens of markets to replace the US revenue that was declining. MonaVie went from 10 countries in 2008 to 24 markets, then launched 15 European countries in a single announcement in 2014, reaching 40 markets. The expansion was fast, broad, and unfocused. Opening that many markets simultaneously stretched leadership attention, operational capacity, and field energy across too many fronts. Instead of building depth in a few strong markets, the company chased breadth across dozens. Each new launch created a burst of activity and then required sustained support that the company couldn't deliver at scale. By 2015, the geographic mix had inverted to 35% US and 65% international, but on a revenue base of just $160 million on 1.2 million cases of juice, an 81% decline from the 2009 peak. The international markets didn't save the company. They consumed resources while the original engine was failing.

When the acai trend faded, the damage was compounded by the overextension. The problem wasn't that one driver collapsed. It was that the company had never isolated which drivers were carrying the growth, which meant they had done nothing to protect them or build alternatives. The leaders who arrived fast left faster. The comp plan economics that attracted them worked equally well at the next ground-floor opportunity. The product-culture fit evaporated because acai stopped being culturally relevant. And the international markets that were supposed to replace domestic momentum never developed the depth to sustain themselves. In an internal memo later revealed through court documents, MonaVie's own chief science officer Ralph Carson, who had helped develop the original juice, described it as "expensive flavored water" and called the product claims "purely hypothetical, unsubstantiated and, quite frankly, bogus."

The distributor count tells the final story. At peak, MonaVie had recruited over a million distributors, with some estimates placing the total network including customers well above that. In 2015, the company defaulted on a $182 million loan and went into foreclosure. Jeunesse Global purchased MonaVie's assets for pennies on the dollar. The product that everyone said they loved, the product that built a billion-dollar company, could not sustain customer purchasing once the qualification pressure that drove monthly volume disappeared. That is the Smoke Detector Test administered by the market itself.

All three drivers collapsed within a narrow window. And because the leadership team believed only one driver was active, they had no playbook for what came next.

MonaVie didn't lose momentum because acai stopped trending. They lost momentum because they believed they had the best of everything, which meant they never diagnosed which specific variables were actually creating the growth and which were temporary. They expanded too fast internationally instead of building depth. They promoted the opportunity instead of the product's standalone value. And they couldn't see the collapse coming because their own narrative told them it was impossible.

They attributed a multi-driver equation to a single story: we're the best. And when the equation fell apart, they had no framework for understanding why.

The same pattern plays out in every industry. Netflix almost destroyed itself in 2011 with the same mistake.

In July 2011, Netflix announced it would split its DVD-by-mail service from its streaming service and charge for them separately. For customers who wanted both, the effective price increase was 60%. In September, Reed Hastings took it further and announced that the DVD business would be spun off into a separate company called Qwikster. Two brands. Two websites. Two billing systems. Two logins. The same customer would interact with Netflix for streaming and Qwikster for DVDs, and the two operations would never talk to each other.

Netflix subscribers at the time numbered about 23 million. The blog post announcing the changes drew thousands of angry comments within hours. By the next earnings report, Netflix had lost more than 800,000 subscribers. Within three months, the stock had dropped 70-75%. The company's market cap fell from $16 billion to under $4 billion.

In October 2011, three weeks after announcing Qwikster, Hastings reversed the decision. The spin-off was canceled. The brands would stay unified. The price increase stayed in place.

Hastings had made a real strategic error. He believed Netflix's momentum lived in the distribution technology. DVDs versus streaming. He reorganized the company around that belief. He was wrong. Netflix's momentum had never been about the delivery mechanism. It had been about the customer relationship, the queue, the recommendation engine, the single-login convenience of having your entire viewing life in one place. By splitting the brand, Hastings broke the very thing that was creating the momentum, which he had misdiagnosed as something else.

Hastings got the diagnosis wrong. But he got the recovery right. Within three weeks, he reversed the Qwikster decision publicly, admitted the error in writing, and kept the parts of the strategy that were defensible (the price increase, the long-term pivot to streaming). He corrected the attribution error fast enough to survive it. Netflix was worth under $4 billion in late 2011. By 2021, it was worth $300 billion. The recovery worked because Hastings could admit the equation had been misread.

MonaVie never got that chance. The acai trend didn't give the company three months to correct course. When the cultural wave collapsed, the three drivers collapsed together, and the company had no alternative narrative to fall back on.

The difference between the two outcomes wasn't talent. Hastings isn't a better CEO than Dallin Larsen. The difference was diagnosis speed. Netflix identified its own attribution error within three weeks. MonaVie hadn't identified its multi-driver equation years after the crash.

Attribution error, the psychological pattern Lee Ross formalized in 1977, explains why. Humans overweight internal factors and underweight situational ones. Kahneman showed we construct narratives from incomplete data. Rosenzweig's "halo effect" demonstrated the corporate version: when growth is running, everything looks brilliant. When it stops, the same elements look flawed. Nothing changed structurally. The halo shifted.

Three dynamics amplify this error in direct selling. First, growth tracks individual leader behavior more than corporate decisions. One top earner sprints for ninety days and the whole organization accelerates. Corporate credits whatever initiative they just launched. The initiative might have had zero effect.

Second, direct selling operates on lagging indicators. A comp plan change in January shows up in revenue in April. By the time results appear, the team has made ten more decisions and naturally credits the most recent one. The actual cause is buried three or four decisions back.

Third, the industry runs on narrative. "We're in momentum" becomes self-fulfilling. The story attracts leaders, leaders create growth, growth validates the story. When that cycle is running, the question of what is actually producing the growth rarely gets asked. When it stops, there's no diagnostic framework because nobody built one during the good times.

I learned this lesson twice. Once in my own business. Once sitting across from one of the founders of a company that was about to learn it the hardest way possible.

The personal version first. When I started building in direct selling in 2008, I went all in. I contacted 250 people in three weeks. Worked 80 hours a week. No TV. Read every personal development book I could find. Didn't miss a single training.

My first month was actually a massive success. I generated almost $40,000 in sales in three weeks doing the business part time. My check was big. My wife was having success too. Everything felt like it was working.

Then it went down. Month two, smaller. Month three, smaller again. Month four, smaller still. By my fifth month, working 80 hours a week, giving everything I had, my check was less than $400. Roughly a dollar an hour.

I had just quit a six-figure job coaching tennis. That position was filled the day I left. No going back. My family needed income. I was working harder than I'd ever worked in my life, earning less than minimum wage, and doing the math on how fast we'd foreclose on the house.

What happened between month one and month five was simple. I had transitioned from doing the work to managing the work. I went from personally inviting, personally sponsoring, personally recruiting to sitting back and trying to coach everyone else to do it. I became a manager instead of a builder. And my business died the way every business dies when the leader stops leading from the front.

Ralph Waldo Emerson said it: what you do speaks so loudly I can't hear what you say. Too many so-called leaders in this profession make that transition too fast. They go from the trenches to the conference call. From personally prospecting to just managing everybody. And they wonder why the growth stops.

My mentor, Lon Wardrop, a 20-plus million dollar earner, pulled me aside. He acknowledged my effort. Then he said something I didn't understand for four more years: "If you want to be good, recruit. If you want to be great, taproot."

Taprooting is building deep. Taking one person and working down through their network, then their network's network, building one deep line that produces massive volume instead of hundreds of shallow conversations that produce almost nothing. Width is for show. Depth is for dough. But the part that gets missed when you're starting is this: you can't just taproot. You have to keep driving new invites, new conversations, new people into the business while simultaneously building depth. Because the people you already have aren't always going to put you in front of new prospects. You have to drum it up yourself. Constantly. This is what separates builders from managers.

I had to wake up. Go back to new invites. Personal sponsoring. Recruiting. And then also teach others to do the same while taprooting deep into the organization. When those skills finally came together, the work compounded. I built to the top rank in my company, and I've since helped multiple field organizations apply the same depth-driven approach across different companies. The principle holds. Width is for show. Depth is for dough. But neither works without the discipline of personally driving new conversations into the business at the same time.

I was attributing my potential to the most visible input, raw volume of activity, when the real driver was the least visible one: depth, sustained personal production, and leading from the front while teaching others to do the same. Same attribution mistake. Personal scale.

But the moment that burned this lesson into me permanently happened a few years later, and it didn't involve my own business at all.

ViSalus had one of the most explosive growth runs the industry had ever seen. In just two years, revenue went from roughly $34 million in 2010 to $623 million in 2012, audited at 450% growth. The company grew its independent promoter force from about 8,000 to over 100,000. They were riding a fitness and weight-loss trend, and the energy around the Body by Vi Challenge was electric. Blyth Inc., the parent company, planned an IPO valued at up to $175 million.

Credit where it's due. The founding team understood branding, social proof, and event production at a level most companies in this industry never reach. They created the Body by Vi 90-Day Challenge, a concept that made the product feel like a movement rather than a purchase. The BMW car bonus program gave the field a visual proof of success that was more powerful than any income disclosure. The conventions were theatrical, aspirational, and engineered to create belief. These weren't lucky amateurs who stumbled into growth. They were exceptionally talented marketers who built a machine that generated extraordinary momentum. This chapter isn't asking whether they were talented. They were. It is asking whether they understood which variables were producing the momentum they created.

I attended one of their major conventions on the East Coast, somewhere around their peak. I was building in the field at the time, always evaluating, always paying attention to which companies had something real underneath the noise. And I have to tell you, I was impressed. The event was massive. The energy in the room was unlike anything I'd experienced at that point. The production was world-class. The field was on fire.

What stayed with me wasn't the size of the event. It was a moment that happened in a one-on-one conversation with one of the company's founders.

I had the chance to sit down with him directly. I asked him a simple question.

"What's the plan when growth slows or reverses? How do you handle the storm?"

He wasn't annoyed by the question. He was confused by it. Almost offended. Like I'd asked him what the plan was for if gravity stopped working.

His answer, in three words.

"That won't happen."

That was the end of my interest.

I also talked to a couple of top field leaders that weekend. The same conviction had flowed through to them. They couldn't conceptualize a scenario where the wind stopped blowing either. I did not have a chance to test the conviction with the rest of the corporate team, but the founder's certainty had clearly traveled at least into the top of the field organization.

The failure wasn't talent, product, or character. It was that the founder, whose conviction shaped the company's strategy and the field's belief, could not imagine external conditions changing. He had so fully attributed the company's momentum to their product, their brand, their vision, their leadership, that the possibility of a reversal was literally unthinkable. The conviction had spread far enough into the field that the people closest to the founder shared the same blind spot.

What happened next is public knowledge.

ViSalus's revenue collapsed from $623 million to roughly $350 million the following year. Almost half the revenue, gone. Promoters dropped from a peak of over 100,000 to about 30,000 within two years. The planned IPO was pulled due to lack of investor interest. A class-action lawsuit from shareholders followed. The company bled out over the next several years. It was eventually sold for a fraction of its peak value and ultimately ended up in bankruptcy, filing with what the court documents described as "no operating business."

From $623 million and 100,000 promoters to "no operating business."

According to Blyth Inc.'s SEC filings (as reported by Crain's Detroit Business), one co-founder's distributor organization accounted for 74% of company revenue. The number itself is striking, but the lesson for a CEO is not that the 74% should have been prevented. No CEO recruits. No CEO controls which leader builds the biggest organization or how fast that organization scales. Concentration like this happens organically in this industry. It is often a sign of an extraordinary builder, not a mistake by the company.

The lesson is what the company didn't have underneath the concentration. ViSalus didn't have a deep customer base independent of that organization. It didn't have a roster of mid-level leaders being cultivated three and four levels down who could carry volume if any single concentration shifted. It didn't have a customer retention infrastructure strong enough to hold revenue when a leader's attention or pace changed. The 74% itself wasn't the problem. The absence of structural depth underneath the 74% was the problem.

The same data point in a different company would have looked different. If 74% of revenue had been flowing through one organization but that organization itself was anchored by 200,000 real customers reordering monthly because they liked the product, the concentration would have been a strength rather than a vulnerability. The leader could slow down and the customer revenue would still flow. Another leader could rise underneath without disrupting the volume. The structural foundation would have absorbed any shift.

That is what a CEO actually controls. Not the concentration itself. The depth underneath it. Customer acquisition systems that build real demand independent of any leader's organization. Leadership development infrastructure that produces new top earners every year so the company is never one departure away from a revenue collapse. Operational and product investments that make the company itself the asset rather than any single field organization. The CEO of a flash crash company often feels powerless because she is watching variables she doesn't directly control. The CEO of a durable company is investing relentlessly in the variables underneath those concentrations, knowing that the concentrations themselves aren't the test. What is underneath them is.

The company had built its growth on aggressive leader acquisition, which meant a significant percentage of its volume came from experienced networkers chasing the hottest opportunity rather than loyal customers using the product. When you acquire that many leaders from that many different companies in a short period, you're also mixing dozens of different cultures, systems, and expectations into one organization. That creates energy on the way up but fragmentation on the way down. Leaders who joined for the economics evaluate their options the moment the economics slow.

Every company falls to its true customer floor when growth subsides. In this case, that floor wasn't high enough. The ratio of genuine repeat customers to opportunity-driven purchasers couldn't sustain the business once the recruiting engine slowed.

The company also had a well-known car bonus program that became one of its most visible recruiting tools. Distributors who hit a certain volume threshold qualified for a monthly bonus to cover their luxury car payment. During growth, that program was electric. It was aspirational. People posted photos of their new cars on social media. It filled convention stages with gleaming vehicles and created a powerful visual proof of the opportunity.

When volume dropped, the car program inverted. Distributors who had leased or purchased cars based on the bonus were now stuck with payments they couldn't afford. The program that had been one of the company's greatest recruiting assets became a symbol of the downside. Former distributors sharing stories about cars they could no longer pay for became some of the most damaging content on the internet. What built belief on the way up destroyed belief on the way down.

People will always debate the reasons for a company's decline. Some will say it was the leadership. Some will say it was the market. Some will say it was the comp plan. Some will say it was timing. Those arguments are subjective. Smart people who were equally close to the situation will disagree about which factor mattered most.

But one thing isn't debatable. If the customer base had been strong enough, the floor would have been dramatically higher. That isn't an opinion. That is math. A company with 60% real customers that loses half its distributors still has 60% of its revenue intact. A company with 20% real customers that loses half its distributors is in freefall. The customer floor is the one variable that determines how far you fall when everything else goes wrong. And everything else always eventually goes wrong.

I think about that meeting constantly. He was talented. Maybe one of the most naturally gifted salespeople I've ever been in a room with. Maybe one of the most naturally gifted salespeople I've ever been in a room with. I think about it because of how clearly it illustrated what this chapter is about. When things are going well, people always think they're better than they really are. When you're standing at the peak, it becomes almost neurologically impossible to visualize what happens when you leave it. The peak feels permanent. It feels earned. It feels like it belongs to you.

It doesn't. The peak is a combination of variables. Some you control. Some you don't. And if you can't even bring yourself to ask which is which, the decline will blindside you completely.

And at the center of every one of these stories is the same thing I saw in that meeting. A leader who couldn't bring themselves to question what was working while it was working. Who mistook the peak for the new floor. Who heard the question "what happens when things go backwards" and answered, with total conviction, "that won't happen."

It always happens. The only real variable is whether you saw it coming.

There is a shadow side to everything in this book. Including this chapter. If attribution error leads to bad strategy, overcorrection leads to paralysis.

Some leaders will hear the argument I just made and decide they can't trust any diagnosis. They will second-guess every growth signal. Delay every initiative for another round of analysis. Demand certainty before committing resources. They will become so afraid of misattributing their growth that they stop acting on it.

That is equally dangerous. Maybe more dangerous.

Momentum rewards speed. It rewards decisiveness. It rewards leaders who act on directionally correct information before the picture is perfectly clear. Platform windows don't wait for your diagnostic process. Leader migration opportunities don't pause while your team debates which driver to prioritize. Markets that are ready to open don't stay open forever.

The goal isn't perfect diagnosis. Perfect diagnosis doesn't exist in a complex, relationship-driven, multi-variable business. If you wait for complete certainty about what is driving your growth, you'll lose the window to capitalize on it.

The goal is better diagnosis. Asking the right questions while you're growing. Building a habit of inquiry into your leadership rhythm so that you're not blindsided when the growth shifts. The difference between companies that sustain momentum and companies that crash isn't that one group diagnosed perfectly. It is that one group asked the question at all.

The companies that got destroyed by attribution error, every single one I've studied, had one thing in common, and it wasn't a lack of intelligence or a lack of effort. A lack of curiosity during the good times. They were so busy celebrating growth that they never paused to understand it.

So how do you avoid attribution error? You build diagnosis into your rhythm. Not after momentum fades. During momentum. The faster you're moving, the more important it is.

A framework your leadership team can use in its next meeting is below.

THE MOMENTUM ATTRIBUTION AUDIT

Run this quarterly when you're growing steadily. Run it monthly when growth is accelerating. The hotter things get, the more critical this becomes.

Step 1: List every variable that could be contributing to your current growth.

Do not filter. Do not rank. Just list. Product launches, comp plan changes, leader activity spikes, individual field leader behavior, market openings, platform shifts, cultural trends, competitor stumbles, economic conditions, seasonal patterns, regulatory tailwinds, social media algorithm changes.

Most teams will generate ten to fifteen variables. Good. Growth is almost never one thing. If your team lists fewer than five, they're not looking hard enough.

Step 2: Sort each variable into one of two categories.

Category A: Created. We made a decision that produced this growth. We designed a comp plan feature. We developed a product. We trained a field behavior. We built a system.

Category B: Captured. This growth is happening because of an external condition we didn't create. A cultural trend. A platform window. A competitor collapse. A leader who walked in from another company with 10,000 people already enrolled.

Be brutal with the data. Many companies overcount what they created and undercount what they captured. The product riding a wellness mega-trend is captured momentum. You didn't create the wellness movement. The international market exploding because a major leader already built a shadow organization there's captured momentum. You didn't generate that demand. You formalized it.

Created momentum is what you own. Captured momentum is what you're borrowing. Both are real. Both produce revenue. But only one belongs to you when conditions change.

Step 3: For each variable, apply the removal test.

Ask: if this variable disappeared overnight, would our growth rate survive? If a specific leader stopped building tomorrow, would the numbers hold? If the cultural trend shifted, would our product still sell at this pace? If the platform changed its algorithm, would our field still be able to reach new customers?

Any variable that, when removed, would materially damage your growth rate is a critical driver. If you have a critical driver that sits in the "captured" column, you have a vulnerability.

The removal test isn't theoretical. In July 2007, a federal court ordered BurnLounge to stop paying recruiting rewards. The company was generating $476,516 in monthly revenue that June. By August, revenue had collapsed to $10,880. That is a 97.7% drop in sixty days. Court-documented. The most precise measurement of real demand versus artificial demand ever recorded in this industry. Every leadership team should be asking: if we removed qualification purchasing tomorrow, what percentage of our volume would still be there? The answer to that question tells you what the model is amplifying versus what it's manufacturing.

Step 4: Stress-test your twelve-month strategy.

Take your plan for the next year. Now remove every captured driver from the equation. What survives? If your strategy assumes that external conditions will continue, you're building on borrowed ground. If your strategy can absorb the loss of external tailwinds and still produce growth, you have a foundation worth investing in.

Step 5: Run the alignment test.

Ask every member of your leadership team to independently write down the single biggest reason your company is growing right now. No discussion first. No collaboration. Just write.

Then compare answers.

If the answers vary wildly, your team doesn't have alignment. You have multiple competing narratives about what is driving the business, which means your strategy is being built on an assumption that your own team can't agree on. That is a red flag.

If every answer is identical, that's worth examining too. Perfect agreement in a leadership team often signals groupthink. Everyone has adopted the same comfortable narrative, and nobody is stress-testing it. The most dangerous thing in a boardroom is a story that everyone believes and nobody has checked.

The healthiest result is rough alignment with productive disagreement. The team agrees on the primary drivers but debates the secondary ones. That debate isn't dysfunction. It is diagnosis. And diagnosis is the one thing many companies never do while they're winning.

Step 6: Calculate your Attribution Health Ratio.

Count the variables in Category A (Created). Count the variables in Category B (Captured). Now weight them. Not every variable matters equally. A comp plan feature that drives 30% of growth isn't equal to a minor seasonal tailwind that drives 2%. Rate each variable on its contribution to current growth: high, medium, or low. Assign three points to high, two to medium, one to low. Add up the total points for Category A. Add up the total points for Category B. Divide Category A by the combined total.

That percentage is your Attribution Health Ratio.

Above 70% Created: GREEN. You understand your growth. You can reproduce it. Most of what is working is something you built. When conditions shift, you still own the engine.

40 to 70% Created: YELLOW. You have directional understanding. A meaningful portion of your growth is borrowed. Build redundancy into what you control and create hedges against what you don't.

Below 40% Created: RED. You are riding momentum you didn't create. Assume the external conditions end and plan accordingly. The time to build your own foundation is while the borrowed tailwind is still blowing, not after it stops.

This ratio isn't static. Run it every quarter. A company shifting from 35% Created to 55% Created over two years is building durability, even if revenue growth looks unchanged externally. A company shifting from 60% Created to 45% Created is accumulating hidden risk, even if revenue is up and to the right. The revenue number tells you the weather today. The Attribution Health Ratio tells you what is holding up the roof.

Imagine a company where the leadership team actually knows why they're growing.

Not guessing. Not telling each other a story that sounds smart. Knowing. With specificity.

They know which drivers are active and which are dormant. They know which growth is owned and which is borrowed. They know which external conditions they're riding and they have a plan for when those conditions shift. They know which single leader accounts for 30% of this quarter's growth, and they're already building organic leadership underneath that concentration risk.

When a quarterly board meeting happens, the CEO does not just present revenue. She presents the driver map. Here is where the growth is coming from. Here is what we control. Here is what we don't. Here is what we're building to replace the drivers that won't last.

That company doesn't panic when a platform changes its algorithm. They had already identified platform dependency as a borrowed driver and were diversifying. That company doesn't collapse when a top leader leaves. They knew leader concentration was a risk and were investing in organic leadership development to reduce it. That company doesn't pour $50 million into scaling a product line that was riding a cultural trend. They can see the difference between a wave and a foundation.

That company creates momentum more often, stays in it longer, and recovers from dips faster. They see clearly what they're working with.

MonaVie didn't fail because acai stopped trending. Peloton didn't fail because the pandemic ended. They failed because their leadership teams built strategy on stories instead of diagnosis. Every driver in this book has a mechanism. Product-culture fit. Platform disruption. Leader migration. Market expansion. Compensation architecture. They are variables in an equation. And variables can be identified, measured, and managed.

The next chapter breaks apart the most dangerous assumption in the direct selling industry: that momentum means explosive growth. It doesn't. The most durable momentum you'll ever see might be the quietest thing in the room.

THE BOTTOM LINE: MonaVie had three drivers firing simultaneously and identified zero of them. The equation is always multi-variable. Map every driver that contributed to your current growth and ask which ones you control and which ones you're borrowing.

Momentum isn't a story you tell. It is an equation you solve.

Chapter 3: The Momentum Spectrum

Figure 2. Momentum has five shapes. The explosive spike gets the headlines. Steady compounding wins the decade.

The fastest-growing company in the room is usually the closest to collapse.

The enemy in this chapter: celebrating the spike instead of building the floor.

In 2017, LuLaRoe reported approximately $2.3 billion in annual revenue. Four years earlier, the company barely existed. Revenue in 2014 was $9.8 million. That means LuLaRoe grew roughly 23,000% in three years. From a standing start to one of the largest direct selling companies in North America. The growth rate was so extreme that industry analysts ran the numbers twice.

The story was everywhere. Eighty thousand consultants. Facebook Live selling parties that felt like entertainment. Limited-edition legging patterns that created collector psychology. A buy-in model that committed sellers financially from day one. The energy was unmistakable. People weren't joining a company. They were joining a movement.

That same year, doTERRA quietly crossed a reported $1.5 billion mark. The company had been founded nine years earlier, in 2008. Its growth had never made headlines for being explosive. There was no single year where revenue multiplied by ten. No viral moment. No cultural phenomenon that put the brand on the cover of anything. Just steady, consistent, compounding growth, year after year, for nearly a decade. By 2024, doTERRA surpassed $2 billion in annual sales with over 10 million customers across 155 countries. The company operates net debt-free.

LuLaRoe peaked in 2017. By 2019, the company was in freefall. Consultants dropped from a peak of roughly 80,000 in April 2017 to fewer than 20,000 active sellers by 2020, per industry reporting. Lawsuits piled up. Quality complaints destroyed the brand. Revenue collapsed. The company that grew 23,000% in three years lost most of it in two.

doTERRA is still growing. Sixteen years in. No documentary about its downfall.

Two companies. Both in direct selling. Both launched within a few years of each other. Both reached billion-dollar scale. One was a rocket that exploded on reentry. The other was a freight train that never stopped.

If you asked most people in the industry which company "had momentum" in 2016, they would have pointed at LuLaRoe without hesitation. The speed. The energy. The noise. That is what momentum looks like to most people.

They would have been wrong.

The assumption this chapter dismantles.

Most people in direct selling, and in business generally, believe that momentum means explosive growth. It means hockey-stick curves. It means doubling revenue year over year. It means packed conventions, sold-out events, social media buzz, and the feeling that something unstoppable is happening.

It is a wave, not momentum. And waves always crash.

Across a dataset of 53 direct selling companies, spanning seven decades and including every major growth story and collapse in the modern industry, one finding stands out above all others.

The faster a company reaches its peak, the faster it falls.

That statement will bother people. It should. Fast growth isn't the problem. Fragile fast growth is. Some companies earn speed because genuine product demand is pulling them forward and the infrastructure is keeping pace. Others manufacture speed through incentives, migration, and timing they don't control. The issue isn't the velocity. The issue is what the velocity is sitting on. The data doesn't punish speed. It punishes speed without foundation.

The trap is subtle: success can validate the outcome while hiding flaws in the structure. A company growing at 200% per year looks brilliant. Every decision the leadership team made appears vindicated. The product must be right. The comp plan must be right. The culture must be right. The timing must be right. Revenue going up feels like proof that the system is working. It isn't proof. It may only mean the system hasn't been tested yet. The test comes when the external conditions shift, when the cultural wave matures, when the platform algorithm changes, when the big leader evaluates her options. That is when you discover whether the speed was earned or borrowed. And many leadership teams don't make that discovery until the revenue chart tells them, which is always too late.

A note for the reader before going further. Every framework, scorecard, and diagnostic in this book requires one thing from the reader to actually work. Zero ego. Zero expectations. The leader who picks up this book assuming her company is one of the strong ones, and reads each chapter looking for confirmation, will miss every teaching the book has for her. The frameworks are designed to surface gaps, not to validate strengths. If you can't read each section with the discipline of asking what the framework reveals about what is missing in your own company, the frameworks will produce the same superficial reassurance every other strategic exercise produces. The leaders who get the most out of this material are the ones who arrive willing to be wrong about something they've been telling themselves for years.

The discipline is uncomfortable in a specific way. It requires holding the possibility that the company's success was less about the leadership team's brilliance and more about the underlying drivers doing their work. It requires accepting that the data may not match the story the company tells itself in board meetings and at conventions. It requires being willing to name the gap between the version of the company that exists in the leadership team's narrative and the version of the company that exists in the customer base, the comp plan, the regulatory exposure, and the operational infrastructure. That gap is where the real diagnosis lives. The leader who can stand inside it without flinching is the leader who can actually use this book.

The same posture extends outside the company. Two industry standards every corporate team should be holding themselves to.

First, attend Direct Selling News and Direct Selling University events. Why would any owner or executive insulate themselves in a bubble when there's a forum where the industry's most thoughtful operators gather, share what is working, share what failed, and stay current on the regulatory and strategic shifts that matter? The companies that show up to DSN and DSU consistently are the companies where the leadership team is building the muscle of cross-company learning. The companies that skip these gatherings because the team is too busy or too confident are the companies most likely to be surprised by something a peer figured out two years ago.

Second, attend the ANMP event, and encourage your top leaders to attend. The Association of Network Marketing Professionals is the only forum where corporate executives and top field leaders from across the industry sit in the same rooms as peers. Top earners share what is producing results in their organizations right now. Field-side practices that work in one company often translate directly to others. Owners and executives who attend ANMP hear the field's actual voice from across the entire industry, not just the polished version their own field gives them on stage. The leaders who have been on stage at one company and now operate quietly at another bring observations that no internal advisory council can replicate.

There is no need for arrogance or overconfidence. The ability to learn how to learn is the greatest ability anyone in business can have. The leadership teams that compound across decades treat continuous external learning as a fundamental discipline, not a nice-to-have when the calendar permits. The teams that stay insulated learn the hard way, after their company has already been hit by the pattern someone else figured out at last year's DSU panel.

Collaboration is the new competition. The phrase has become cliché. It is also true. Every long-term operator I know in this industry has built relationships with peers at other companies that produce mutual learning, mutual referral, and mutual protection. The companies that try to operate in isolation, treating every other operator as a threat to be defeated rather than a peer to learn from, are the companies that miss the patterns this book identifies until those patterns are already inside their own walls. The abundance mentality isn't just a field-side principle. It is a corporate-side discipline that determines which companies still exist in twenty years.

The pattern is documented across the 53-company dataset spanning seven decades.

Companies that peaked in zero to five years from founding had a median time from peak to major break of approximately one year. One year from the top to crisis. LuLaRoe. MonaVie. Organo Gold. BurnLounge. Color Street. The fastest risers were consistently the fastest fallers.

Companies that peaked in six to eight years broke in one to two years. ViSalus. Vemma. WorldVentures.

Companies that peaked in nine to twelve years had a longer runway, typically two to five years before the break. But the break still came. Tahitian Noni. AdvoCare. Thirty-One Gifts. Plexus. It Works.

The companies that took thirteen to twenty years to peak showed a completely different pattern. Some declined. Some plateaued. But the crashes were less severe and the timelines were longer. Isagenix. Young Living. Rodan + Fields. Younique. These companies had time to build infrastructure, develop leadership depth, and create real customer bases before external conditions shifted.

And the companies that took twenty-plus years to peak, the legacy companies like Herbalife, USANA, Nu Skin, Mary Kay, and Tupperware, experienced the slowest declines of all. They weren't immune. Several of them are declining right now. But the foundation was deep enough that the decline took years, not months.

The median across the full dataset: roughly ten years from founding to peak. Roughly four years from peak to break.

But those medians hide the real story. The distribution shows two distinct clusters. Flash crashes on one side. Slow erosions on the other. Almost nothing in between.

Figure 3-1: Each point is one company in the dataset. The horizontal axis is years from founding to peak revenue. The vertical axis is peak annual revenue on a log scale. Color indicates current status. The two-cluster pattern is visible at a glance. Companies clustered in the under-ten-years zone are dominantly red and amber. Companies in the over-twenty-five-years zone are dominantly green. The middle is sparse, which is the distribution this chapter is naming.

Flash crashes look like this.

A company reaches peak revenue in roughly six years. Growth is explosive. Recruiting velocity exceeds 100% year over year for two or more consecutive years. The conventions are massive. The income claims are loud. The field is on fire.

Then something breaks. A regulatory action. A leader exodus. A quality failure. The recruiting story loses its power. Sometimes all of them at once. Revenue drops 40% or more within twelve months. The company either collapses entirely or enters a death spiral that takes another two to three years to complete.

Median time from peak to major break in flash crash cases: approximately one year.

Every flash crash I systematically coded against this framework showed at least three of five characteristics, and the pattern has held in every additional case I've examined since. These five traits function as a diagnostic. If your company has three or more of them, you're structurally set up for a flash crash whether you realize it or not.

One: a single hero product driving more than 50% of revenue. When one product IS the business, the business has the risk profile of that product.

Two: revenue predominantly from distributor self-purchasing. More than 70% internal consumption. When the buyers are the sellers, the volume is artificial.

Three: recruiting growth exceeding 100% year over year for two or more consecutive years. The company enrolls faster than it can train, develop, and retain. Each person who quits becomes a negative story in the market.

Four: the top 5% of leaders generating more than 50% of total volume without sufficient leadership development underneath. Concentration like this happens organically in this industry. It is a feature of how distribution works, not a strategic mistake. The flash crash variable isn't the concentration itself. It is whether the company is investing in developing emerging leaders deep within those highly leveraged organizations who can carry volume if any single concentration shifts. ViSalus had 74% flowing through a single organization with limited secondary leadership development underneath.

Five: no meaningful customer verification system. If the company can't demonstrate real customers with data, both regulatory and structural risks are elevated.

The full analysis of each characteristic, with case studies and the complete Flash Crash Scorecard, is in Chapter 11.

Check those five boxes against your company. If three or more apply, the flash crash pattern is your structural profile. It doesn't mean you'll crash tomorrow. It means the architecture of your business matches the architecture of every company that crashed fast in the last twenty years.

That is worth knowing.

Slow erosions look completely different.

A company takes twenty or more years to reach its peak. Growth is gradual. The brand becomes institutional. The field force is mature. The product line is diversified. The company operates in multiple countries. It has survived recessions, leadership transitions, competitive pressure, and regulatory scrutiny.

Then the erosion begins. The shape is a slope, not a cliff. Revenue dips 3% one year. Flat the next. Down 5% the year after. The decline is so gradual that it doesn't trigger alarm. Each quarterly report looks like a rounding error. Each annual decline can be explained away. "Market conditions." "Temporary softness." "We're investing for the future."

But the compound effect is devastating. A 5% annual decline for ten years cuts your revenue nearly in half. A 3% annual decline for fifteen years does the same thing. The company is slowly evaporating while leadership tells itself the fundamentals are sound.

Tupperware is the purest example. Founded in 1948. A direct selling icon for seven decades. At peak, operating in over 100 countries with millions of consultants. But the slow erosion was relentless. Revenue peaked at roughly $2.67 billion in 2013 and declined to $1.31 billion by 2022, a 51% decline spread across nine years. It never felt like a crisis in any single quarter. It always felt manageable. Until it wasn't. Tupperware filed for Chapter 11 bankruptcy in September 2024.

The restructuring officer summarized the problem in one sentence: "Nearly everyone now knows what Tupperware is, but fewer people know where to find it."

That is what a slow erosion looks like from the inside. The brand still has recognition. The product still has nostalgia. But the distribution model has been outpaced by the market. Customers moved to e-commerce. Younger consumers never engaged with the party plan. The field aged without being replaced. And the decline was so gradual that nobody treated it as the emergency it was until the cash ran out.

Mary Kay tells a version of the same story. Founded in 1963. Revenue peaked in various estimates around $3 to $4 billion globally. The company remains private, so exact figures are harder to verify. But reported consultant counts have declined from a peak of 3.5 million globally to lower levels in recent years. The brand is iconic. The product is solid. The culture is legendary. But the slow erosion of the direct selling model itself, driven by e-commerce competition, changing consumer behavior, and an aging field force, has been grinding away for years.

Slow erosions are harder to diagnose than flash crashes because nothing dramatic happens. There is no regulatory action. No scandal. No leader exodus. Just a quiet, steady shrinking that compounds over time until the company looks up and realizes it's half the size it was a decade ago.

Outside direct selling, the purest flash crash in recent business history is WeWork.

In January 2019, WeWork was privately valued at $47 billion. The company had about 500,000 paying customers across 500 locations. SoftBank had poured billions into the company at the $47 billion valuation. The company had signed long-term leases on commercial real estate in major cities around the world. The growth rate had been extraordinary. By every industry metric, WeWork was the defining success story of the commercial real estate disruption story.

On August 14, 2019, WeWork filed its S-1 prospectus with the SEC in preparation for an IPO at that $47 billion valuation. The document was 300 pages long. For the first time, institutional investors outside SoftBank could see the financials. What they saw ended the company.

The S-1 revealed $47 billion in future lease obligations and only about $4 billion in committed income. Adam Neumann's governance arrangements included family members on payroll, the company paying him millions to license the trademark "We," and a dual-class share structure that gave him disproportionate control. Losses had reached $1.6 billion on $1.8 billion of revenue. The business model, which the marketing framed as technology-enabled community, was functionally commercial real estate arbitrage with none of the margin protection that established real estate companies had built into their contracts.

The market reaction played out in six weeks. Week one, analysts suggested the IPO should price at $25 billion. Week two, $20 billion. Week three, $15 billion. Week four, $12 billion. Week five, $10 billion. Week six, the IPO was postponed indefinitely. By late September, Neumann had been forced to resign. By the end of 2019, WeWork's valuation had fallen below $8 billion. SoftBank eventually wrote down its investment by more than $14 billion. In 2023, WeWork filed for Chapter 11 bankruptcy.

The pattern matches every flash crash in direct selling. Single hero narrative: "we're reinventing work." Massive concentration in one driver: commercial real estate arbitrage. No real customer validation: the business looked like demand but was structurally dependent on the continued availability of cheap capital. When the capital availability ended (which was triggered by the public filing exposing the financials), the demand vanished faster than the lease obligations did.

What makes WeWork instructive for this book is what it shares with every direct selling flash crash. It had the appearance of demand without the foundation. The growth was real in a technical sense. The customers existed. The revenue existed. But the structure was a time bomb. When it was forced into daylight by the S-1 filing, the valuation collapsed in weeks. Nothing about the business had changed. The business was the same on August 13 as it was on August 15. What changed was that the market could finally see what had been there all along.

Every flash crash in direct selling follows the same logic. The growth that feels miraculous while it's running is usually not miraculous at all. It is a specific set of structural conditions that worked for a narrow window. When the conditions end, or when outsiders can finally see the structure, the collapse is instantaneous.

Between the flash crash and the slow erosion, there's a third pattern. It is the rarest and the most valuable.

Sustained compounding.

This is the pattern that most people in the industry talk about wanting but almost never study. Because it doesn't make headlines. It doesn't create viral moments. It doesn't fill stadiums with 10,000 screaming distributors.

It looks like a company that grows 8% to 15% per year for a decade or more. Consistently. Without dramatic spikes. Without dramatic crashes. Just a steady upward trajectory that compounds into something enormous over time.

doTERRA is the clearest modern example. Founded in 2008 by a team of essential oils industry veterans. Revenue grew from startup to over $2 billion across sixteen years. No single year of explosive growth. No year where revenue multiplied by five. Just consistent performance compounding over a long runway.

What makes sustained compounding so powerful is the math. A company growing at 12% annually doubles in six years and quadruples in twelve. That doesn't feel dramatic in any single year. But after a decade, the company that grew steadily at 12% is often larger than the company that spiked at 300% and then crashed.

LuLaRoe's cumulative revenue: roughly $4 to $5 billion. doTERRA's cumulative revenue across its existence is well north of $15 billion. PM International, a company that most readers outside Europe have never heard of, has grown consecutively for over thirty years, reaching $3.25 billion in 2024 from a German startup in 1993. That is operational compounding at scale, even though, as noted in this chapter, the customer architecture underneath PM International leans more on internal consumption than the model this book advocates.

PM International is an instructive case in operational discipline and longevity. The company has had thirty-plus consecutive years of growth, built on obsessive standard operating procedures for every function (market launches, product releases, conventions), a world-class personal development program, and a deliberate refusal to chase trends. Its lead product, a nutritional supplement line called FitLine, has been reformulated over a dozen times rather than replaced. That is the iPhone strategy applied to a product line: do not abandon what works. Improve it. Each reformulation gave the field an enhanced version of the same story rather than asking them to learn a completely new one. That kind of product focus, where the company invests in upgrading the existing narrative rather than constantly switching directions, is one of the rarest disciplines in direct selling. The qualifier worth noting is that PM International, like a number of long-term operators, has a higher proportion of internal consumption volume than the customer-foundation model this book advocates. The operational discipline is real and worth studying. The customer architecture is a separate question, and readers shouldn't infer that thirty years of compounding alone equals the kind of customer foundation Melaleuca has built.

The companies that achieve sustained compounding share three characteristics that flash crash companies almost always lack.

First, they've diversified revenue. Not dependent on one hero product. Not dependent on one leader's organization. Not dependent on one country. When any single variable shifts, the impact is absorbed rather than catastrophic.

Second, they have real customers. The product alibi chapter applies directly here. Companies with high real customer ratios can absorb recruiting slowdowns because the revenue base doesn't depend entirely on field activity. Customers keep buying even when the field takes a breath.

Third, they invest in infrastructure proportional to growth. They don't overexpand during hot streaks. They don't build factories for demand that might be temporary. They scale their operations, their compliance, their training, and their leadership development at a pace that matches their growth rate. When the growth rate fluctuates, the infrastructure holds.

There is a fourth characteristic that PM International exemplifies and that deserves its own mention: they don't switch directions.

Think of it this way. You build a team to play basketball. You train them for basketball. You develop systems for basketball. Everyone understands the playbook. The culture is built around basketball. Then one day the CEO announces: "Weight loss is trending. We are launching a weight loss product line. Now we play football."

Your basketball team doesn't know how to play football. The messaging changes. The training changes. The belief system that took years to build has to be rebuilt from scratch. And you're asking tens of thousands of distributors, who finally got comfortable telling one story, to learn an entirely new one. Many companies underestimate how difficult it's to get a large field rowing in the same direction. Switching directions resets that alignment to zero.

The companies that chase every new trend, launching new product categories because a competitor is having success there, sacrifice long-term sustainability for short-term excitement. The field feels the whiplash. The messaging gets confused. The culture fractures. Nu Skin demonstrated the right approach with its Galvanic Spa: rather than abandoning the device when it matured, they integrated their ageLOC technology into the existing product line, enhancing the story rather than replacing it. That produced a meaningful revenue increase in the markets that adopted it.

The irony of the momentum spectrum is this: the most dramatic growth stories are almost always the least durable. And the most durable growth stories are almost always the least dramatic. The industry celebrates the spike. The data celebrates the compound.

What the data says about where you sit right now.

I want to show you five revenue trajectories. All of them come from SEC filings. They are verified. They can't be argued with. They tell the story of momentum more clearly than any framework or theory.

Medifast. Revenue was $302 million in 2017. The OPTAVIA coaching model caught fire. Revenue climbed to $501 million in 2018, then $714 million in 2019, then $935 million in 2020, then $1.53 billion in 2021. At peak in 2022, the company hit $1.6 billion with over 60,800 active earning coaches. The stock reached $337. It was the most impressive growth story in the publicly traded direct selling space.

Then GLP-1 weight loss drugs gained mainstream adoption. Revenue dropped to $1.07 billion in 2023. Down 33% in one year. Then $602 million in 2024. Down another 44%. Full year 2025 revenue closed at $385.8 million per the company's reported financial results, down another 36%. Active earning coaches dropped from 60,800 to 16,100. A 74% coach decline in two and a half years.

The company is right now almost exactly where it was before the OPTAVIA spike happened. Eight years of growth and decline that ended where it started. $302 million to $1.6 billion and back to $385.8 million. The spike created the illusion of permanent transformation. It was a temporary event driven by a coaching model that intersected with a cultural health moment, and it was undone by a pharmaceutical innovation the company had no ability to compete with.

Nu Skin. Peak revenue of $3.18 billion in 2013, driven largely by an ageLOC TR90 system launch in Greater China that produced the highest revenue quarter in company history. By 2024, revenue had declined to $1.73 billion as the company worked through a multi-year restructuring. Then the People's Daily published an article questioning the company's business practices. A government investigation followed. The stock dropped 33% in a single day. Revenue fell to $2.57 billion in 2014. It never fully recovered. A partial rebound to $2.68 billion in 2018 was reversed by China's "100-day crackdown" on health product companies in 2019. Revenue has declined every year since. By 2025, it stood at $1.49 billion. Sales leaders down 23%. Customers down 14%. Twelve years of post-peak decline and counting. A company that built 37% geographic concentration into a single market discovered what happens when that market turns hostile.

Herbalife. Peak of $5.8 billion in 2021. Revenue has settled around $5 billion. The weight management category is under structural pressure from GLP-1 drugs. Herbalife's diversified geography and Nutrition Club model provide a buffer that single-market companies don't have. The company that Bill Ackman bet $1 billion would go to zero is still operating globally four decades after its founding. That is a survival story still being written.

Beachbody/BODi. $874 million peak in 2021. The company went public through a SPAC at a $2.9 billion valuation. The stock opened at $25. Then reality hit. Revenue dropped to $692 million in 2022. Then $527 million in 2023, with cumulative losses exceeding $575 million since going public. In November 2024, the company exited the direct selling model entirely, cutting 33% of its workforce. By 2025, revenue had fallen to $252 million. A 71% decline from peak. The company's cash-flow breakeven point fell from approximately $900 million in 2022 to roughly $180 million by 2025 after eliminating the 40 to 50% direct selling commission structure and executing a multi-stage cost reduction. The executive chairman called direct selling "outdated and unsustainable."

Whether the post-exit company is healthier long-term is a question that hasn't yet been answered. The cost structure improved on paper. The breakeven threshold dropped because the field commission structure was eliminated. But the company also lost the entire distribution and word-of-mouth engine that had built the brand to nearly a billion in revenue in the first place. The early read is that BODi traded a high-cost distribution model with growth potential for a lower-cost distribution model with a smaller revenue ceiling. The math improved. The runway shortened. I've been watching this profession for more than two decades, and I've not yet seen a single company successfully switch from direct selling to a corporate distribution model and come out stronger on the other side. Not one. BODi may be the first. Or it may be the next case that confirms the pattern. The data so far doesn't settle the question.

Now contrast all four of those with this trajectory.

PM International. Founded in Germany in 1993. Grew steadily for over thirty years to $3.25 billion in 2024. No viral moment. No cultural phenomenon. No period of explosive headline-making growth. Just consecutive year-over-year compounding for three decades. The company is unfamiliar to most readers outside Europe. It operates quietly in over 40 countries with a product portfolio spanning nutrition, skincare, and performance. No regulatory action. No mass exodus. No crash. No documentary.

Five trajectories. Same industry. Same time period. Four spikes. One compound. The compound won.

Same industry. Same model. Same time period. Completely different trajectory. Because the type of momentum was different.

I've seen the full range of this spectrum firsthand. Not from the outside. From inside the rooms where the people building these companies talk candidly about what they're experiencing.

Inside the private community I run with over 1,800 verified six and seven-figure earners, I get real-time data on how momentum feels from the field side, not the polished version or the stage version. The real version. The version you hear at midnight in a hotel suite after the convention is over and the cameras are off and someone finally says what everyone has been thinking.

The top earners in a flash-growth company can feel the difference between real momentum and a sugar rush. They describe it in remarkably similar language across completely different companies and different product categories.

"It feels like we're running downhill and the ground is getting steeper."

"I'm making more money than I've ever made but something doesn't feel earned."

"My retention is awful. Everyone joins excited and quits in four months. I'm refilling the same holes over and over."

"Nobody on my team is actually using the product. They're buying it to stay active. There's a difference."

"I know this can't last but I don't want to be the one who says it."

That last one. I hear it more than any of the others. A top earner who can see the structural problem, who can feel the spike cresting, but who doesn't want to name it because naming it feels like disloyalty. Because naming it means questioning the company's narrative. And in a profession where belief drives behavior, questioning the narrative is the one thing nobody wants to do.

The top earners in a sustained-compounding company describe their experience in fundamentally different terms.

"It feels like we're building something. Not riding something."

"My leaders are getting better, not just getting bigger."

"When someone joins my team now, they stay. Five years ago they came and went. Now they stick."

"Our customers reorder without being reminded. They actually like the product."

There is another dynamic that every owner and leader needs to understand about momentum and perception. In direct selling, direction matters more than magnitude. A company that grows from $10 million to $20 million is celebrated. Everyone feels the momentum. But a company that goes from $300 million to $280 million, a modest 7% decline that any Fortune 500 CEO would manage without drama, creates panic in the field.

The survey of 82 top earners confirms this. When asked the biggest reason they slowed down, the number one answer at 40% was not compensation, not recognition, not burnout. It was: "The opportunity didn't feel the same as before." It wasn't the product. It wasn't the pay. The feeling. The perception of direction had shifted and that shift in feeling preceded any shift in their behavior. They stopped building before the numbers confirmed the problem.

The decline is small. The perception is enormous. Because in a profession where everyone is promoting the dream and the direction, any negative direction becomes a crisis of belief. Human nature kicks in. The field amplifies the narrative. Social media spreads the doubt. And a manageable revenue adjustment becomes a momentum-killing story.

This is why the smartest companies manage perception as carefully as they manage performance. They are transparent about the numbers but they frame the direction. They acknowledge the dip and they show the plan. They never pretend everything is fine when the field can see the numbers. But they also never let a modest correction become a narrative of collapse. The companies that lose the perception game lose the field. And losing the field accelerates the decline, creating a self-fulfilling prophecy that turns a small dip into a real crisis.

"It's not as exciting as the companies doing three hundred percent growth. But I sleep at night."

That last line matters. The leaders who have been in this profession long enough to have experienced both a spike and a compound will tell you, unanimously, that they would trade the spike for the compound every time. The compound doesn't pay better in year one. It usually doesn't. But they've watched friends, teammates, and entire organizations evaporate when the spike reversed. They have seen what happens when the external conditions that created the momentum disappear and there's nothing underneath. They have seen the aftermath. The leader who was making $80,000 a month who drops to $6,000 and can't cover the mortgage on the house the $80,000 paid for. The team that was 10,000 strong that's down to

400 in eighteen months. The company that was "the next billion-dollar story" that's now a case study in what happens when the spike reverses.

The compound feels boring. The spike feels magical. But boring is the only thing that lasts.

There is a shadow side to this argument. And it matters.

If you take this chapter's message to its extreme, you'd conclude that fast growth is always bad and slow growth is always good. That is wrong.

Fast growth isn't inherently dangerous. Fast growth driven by genuine product demand, real customers, and structural advantages can be magnificent. If a company hits product-culture fit with a genuine consumer need, and the field is growing because customers are pulling product through the channel rather than distributors pushing it through the comp plan, that speed is healthy. It is organic. And it can be sustained if the company invests in infrastructure proportional to the growth.

What makes fast growth dangerous is when it's driven by recruiting economics rather than product demand. When the speed comes from comp plan incentives, ground-floor positioning, leader migration, and income claims rather than from customers who love the product. That kind of speed has a structural expiration date. And the faster it goes, the sooner it expires.

The diagnostic isn't "are we growing fast?" It is "why are we growing fast?" If the answer is "because customers can't get enough of our product," lean in. Scale. Invest. Build. If the answer is "because our recruiting is on fire and the field is excited about the opportunity," proceed with extreme caution. That growth has a ceiling, and when it hits the ceiling, the reversal will be proportional to the speed.

The framework for this chapter is below. Use it to determine which kind of momentum you actually have.

THE MOMENTUM TYPE DIAGNOSTIC

Answer each question without self-deception. Use data, not hope.

Question 1: How long did it take your company to reach its current revenue level?

If you reached it in under five years from launch, you're in the flash-growth window. Historically, companies in this window have the highest crash rates and the shortest peak-to-break timelines. Your margin for error is very small. Every decision matters more because the foundation underneath you is thinner.

If you reached it in five to twelve years, you're in the normal growth window. You have some foundation. You have had time to develop leadership, build infrastructure, and create customer depth. But you're not immune. The break can still come, and typically arrives within two to five years of peak.

If you've been growing steadily for more than twelve years, you're in the sustained compounding zone. Your risk profile is lower. Your foundation is deeper. But slow erosion is your threat, not flash crash. Monitor for the gradual declines that compound over time.

Question 2: What is your growth rate, and where is it coming from?

If growth exceeds 50% year over year, identify the source. Is it driven by customer acquisition? New market openings? Or recruiting velocity? Recruiting-driven growth above 100% annually is a structural warning sign. It means you're consuming your prospect pool faster than it replenishes. That isn't sustainable regardless of how good it feels.

Question 3: What happens to your revenue when recruiting slows for one quarter?

If a single quarter of reduced recruiting produces a visible revenue dip, your growth is recruiting-dependent. That places you on the spike end of the spectrum. If revenue holds steady during recruiting slowdowns because customer reorders sustain the base, you're on the compounding end.

Question 4: How diversified is your revenue?

One product driving more than 50% of revenue: concentrated risk. One leader organization accounting for more than 30% of volume: concentrated risk. One country generating more than 40% of sales: concentrated risk. Each concentration point amplifies the speed and severity of a potential decline.

Question 5: Which revenue trajectory matches yours?

Look at your revenue chart for the last five years. Does it look like a hockey stick going up? A plateau? A gradual upward slope? A spike that's starting to flatten? Match your shape to the patterns in this chapter and be honest about what that match implies.

Picture a CEO who knows exactly where her company sits on the spectrum.

They aren't telling themselves a momentum story. They are reading a momentum chart. They see the growth rate, the growth source, the concentration risk, and the trajectory shape. They can distinguish between a spike they're riding and a compound they're building. When the board asks "are we in momentum?" the CEO doesn't answer with enthusiasm. She answers with data. "Our revenue growth is 14% year over year. It is driven 62% by customer reorders, 23% by new customer acquisition, and 15% by new distributor enrollments. Our top five organizations account for 31% of volume, which is within acceptable concentration limits. We are in sustained compounding and our current trajectory projects to $1.2 billion in three years at this rate."

That isn't the answer many boards get. Many boards get "we're on fire right now." And they don't push further to ask what kind of fire.

The next chapter introduces the diagnostic that separates the companies in momentum from the companies in trouble. Three ratios. Three numbers. The clearest picture of company health this industry has ever had.

THE BOTTOM LINE: Fast growth isn't the problem. Fragile fast growth is. Check your company against the five flash crash characteristics. If three or more apply, your growth is structurally fragile regardless of how good the revenue looks.

The most dangerous momentum is the kind everyone celebrates. The most valuable momentum is the kind nobody notices.

Chapter 4: Diagnosing Where You Actually Are

Figure 3. Three numbers predict company survival more reliably than revenue, distributor count, or convention attendance combined.

Three numbers will tell you more about your company's future than your last ten board meetings combined.

The enemy in this chapter: vanity metrics masquerading as health.

In 2017, AdvoCare disclosed that 67% of its distributors earned zero income. Not low income. Zero. Two out of every three people in the business made nothing.

Before we go further with that number, context matters. Because if you're a company executive reading that and your first reaction is panic, you need to understand what that number actually contains.

Direct selling has the lowest barrier to entry of any entrepreneurial model on the planet. Starting costs somewhere between zero and a few hundred dollars. Compare that to getting a real estate license (thousands of dollars, months of study), buying a franchise (tens or hundreds of thousands), or launching a traditional business (often six figures of capital). The accessibility is a genuine strength of this model. More people get to try. More people get to test whether entrepreneurship fits them. And the cost of failure is orders of magnitude lower than in any other model.

But easy in also means easy out. A significant percentage of people who sign up as distributors never do a single thing. No calls made. No product shared. No training attended. They signed up, life happened, and they moved on. That is the nature of a low-barrier model, not a company failure. You can't give someone a $200 entry point and then be surprised when some of them treat it like a $200 experiment that they never followed through on.

There is another group inside that 67% that matters even more. Many of those "zero earners" are actually glorified customers. They signed up intending to try the business. They loved the product, stopped building but kept buying, and never recruited a single person. On the income disclosure, they show up as "zero earners." In reality, they're happy customers who happen to have a distributor account. When a company has strong products with real demand, a meaningful percentage of its "failures" are actually loyal product users who found what they were looking for. That outcome is good for the company and good for the person. The FTC has historically struggled with this distinction because on paper, these people look like failed distributors. In practice, they're customers who entered through the distributor door.

So the 67% is not as simple as "two out of three people failed." Some never tried. Some became customers. Some gave it a genuine shot and discovered it wasn't for them, which is a normal outcome in any entrepreneurial model.

But the context stops being comfortable here.

AdvoCare wasn't a small company. At peak, it had over 500,000 distributors. It had endorsement deals with Drew Brees and other professional athletes. Its events filled arenas. The brand was synonymous with performance nutrition across the American South. ESPN ran a feature story. The company was visible, respected, and growing.

The structural question isn't whether 67% earned zero. It is how much of those people's purchasing was driven by genuine product demand versus comp plan qualification requirements. AdvoCare had a meaningful real customer base. The company reported nearly 400,000 preferred customers at the time of the FTC settlement, and legal analysts have estimated that approximately 18% of total revenue came from those preferred customers alone. By industry standards that's a real foundation, and it deserves acknowledgment. AdvoCare wasn't a pure alibi case in the way some flash crash companies were.

The deeper issue was structural. The FTC did not credit the preferred customer revenue as protective because the company's growth engine still depended heavily on distributor qualification volume tied to enrollment, and the income claims being made about the opportunity itself were the focus of the agency's case. From a regulatory standpoint, even strong customer programs can be insufficient when the surrounding business model leans too far toward recruitment-driven volume. The lesson isn't that AdvoCare had no real customers. The lesson is that even a meaningful real customer base may not protect a company when other parts of the architecture create regulatory exposure.

That was the fire alarm hiding in plain sight.

Two years after that disclosure, the FTC hit AdvoCare with a reported $150 million fine and banned the company from the direct selling model permanently. Over 224,000 distributors received refunds. The FTC's case focused on income claims about the business opportunity and the structure of distributor compensation. The company had a meaningful preferred customer base of nearly 400,000 people, but the surrounding regulatory exposure on income claims and recruitment incentives was what produced the enforcement action.

The data was there the entire time. Not hidden. Not leaked. Published. On the company's own website. If a leadership team had taken that single number seriously, taken it as a diagnostic finding rather than an industry norm to be explained away, the outcome might have been different. They might have restructured. They might have pushed customer acquisition. They might have survived.

Nobody took it seriously. Because nobody was looking at the right numbers.

This is the problem with how most direct selling companies assess their own health. They look at the wrong metrics. They track total revenue. Distributor count. Convention attendance. New enrollments per month. Social media engagement. These are activity metrics. They tell you how much motion exists. They don't tell you whether the motion is sustainable.

The companies that collapse are almost never surprised by a lack of activity. They are surprised by the sudden discovery that the activity wasn't building anything durable. The revenue was there. The distributors were there. The events were packed. And underneath all of it, the foundation was hollow.

Three metrics actually predict whether your company survives. Not whether it grows. Not whether it has momentum. Whether it survives.

What many leadership teams monitor.

They monitor total revenue. Revenue going up means things are working. Revenue going down means things aren't. Simple. Comforting. And dangerously incomplete.

Revenue tells you the size of the engine. It doesn't tell you what the engine is running on. A company generating $500 million in revenue from 80% real customers is a fundamentally different business than a company generating $500 million from 80% distributor self-purchasing. The revenue line looks identical. The structural health is opposite.

They monitor distributor count. More distributors means growth. Fewer means decline. But distributor count is a gross number, not a net number. If you recruited 50,000 people this year and 48,000 quit, your net growth is 2,000. That looks like growth. It is actually a treadmill running at near maximum speed just to stay in place. The gross number is exciting. The net number is terrifying. And many companies only report the gross.

They monitor new enrollments. This is recruiting velocity. It is one of the most celebrated metrics in the industry. "We enrolled 10,000 new people this month." Standing ovation. But new enrollments without retention data is like measuring rainfall without measuring evaporation. You can have impressive inflows and still be drying up.

They monitor convention attendance. This is a belief metric. It tells you how many people are engaged enough to show up. It is useful. But it's a lagging indicator of enthusiasm, not a leading indicator of sustainability. Conventions are often best attended in the year before decline begins, because the company is spending heavily on incentives to fill the room precisely when it can least afford to.

None of these metrics are useless. But none of them predict survival. The companies that collapsed across the 53-company dataset were often performing well on all of these metrics in the year before their break event. Revenue was up. Enrollments were strong. Conventions were packed. And twelve months later, the company was in crisis.

What they weren't monitoring are the three numbers that would have told them the truth.

The clearest non-direct-selling illustration of this failure is Blockbuster.

In 2000, Blockbuster had nearly 9,000 stores, 60 million customers, and $6 billion in annual revenue. The company dominated home video rental. It was profitable. Its metrics all looked healthy. Store counts grew. Membership grew. Revenue grew. One line on the income statement in particular looked spectacular: late fees generated roughly $800 million per year. That was pure margin. No inventory cost. No marketing cost. Just customers paying for their own failure to return a movie on time.

The same year, a struggling startup called Netflix flew to Dallas to meet with Blockbuster CEO John Antioco. Reed Hastings and Marc Randolph offered to sell their DVD-by-mail business for $50 million. They would run Blockbuster's online presence. Blockbuster would promote Netflix in its stores. The merger would have been cheap insurance. Antioco, per his co-founders' later accounts, laughed them out of the room and called the dot-com hysteria "completely overblown."

What Antioco was tracking, and what Netflix was tracking, were fundamentally different metrics. Blockbuster measured store revenue, membership growth, and late fees. All up. All good. Netflix measured something different: subscriber retention, time-to-first-click on the site, average recommendation conversion, and most importantly, customer feelings about late fees. That last metric wasn't on any Blockbuster dashboard. It didn't need to be. Late fees were a profit center, not a problem.

Except customers hated late fees. And when a business model arrived that eliminated them, customers left Blockbuster as fast as they could sign up for Netflix. The metric Blockbuster had been ignoring (customer resentment about the $800 million profit stream) turned out to be the metric that predicted the future. In 2005, Blockbuster launched a "No More Late Fees" campaign that came with hidden restocking fees. 47 state attorneys general sued over the bait-and-switch. In 2010, Blockbuster filed for bankruptcy. The $800 million profit stream was never a profit stream. It was a time bomb.

Blockbuster didn't lack data. It tracked everything. It just tracked the wrong things. The metrics that confirmed the existing strategy got celebrated. The metrics that would have challenged it weren't measured at all.

Every direct selling company has its own version of this. Every dashboard includes the metrics that make the current strategy look good. Every dashboard excludes the metrics that would force a hard conversation. The AdvoCare leadership team was looking at revenue, distributor count, and endorsement deals with professional athletes. They weren't focused enough on the structure of how revenue was being generated, what the regulator would see as protective, and what the regulator would see as exposing. The data was there. The scoreboard was wrong.

The Three Hard Ratios emerged from coding every company in the dataset against a consistent set of variables and then asking one question: which metrics reliably separated the survivors from the casualties?

Three ratios separated survivors from casualties. Three numbers that, when tracked together, predict a direct selling company's trajectory with more accuracy than any other combination of metrics available.

They are called the Hard Ratios because they require honest data, they produce uncomfortable answers, and they can't be gamed without actually changing the business.

RATIO 1: RETAIL VS. INTERNAL CONSUMPTION

What percentage of your total volume comes from people who aren't enrolled in the compensation plan?

This is the master ratio. The single most predictive number in the industry. Chapter 5 makes the case for why this ratio separates the living from the dead. This chapter shows you how to measure it and what the thresholds mean.

Above 50%: Survival Zone. More than half your revenue comes from real customers. You have a product business. The FTC has never successfully prosecuted a company with this ratio. Neora's 80% customer revenue was the specific fact the judge cited when she denied every claim the FTC brought.

30% to 50%: Caution Zone. You have real customer demand, but it's not dominant. Your business can survive a recruiting slowdown, but it will feel it. At this level, the company is structurally viable but needs to actively push the ratio upward. Every percentage point of real customer revenue you add is a percentage point of structural resilience.

15% to 30%: Danger Zone. The majority of your revenue depends on people inside the comp plan continuing to purchase. If recruiting slows, if autoship attrition rises, if the field loses enthusiasm, your revenue base is directly exposed. You are one bad quarter from a visible decline.

Below 15%: Death Zone. Historically, every company in the dataset with documented internal consumption above 85% is dead, dissolved, or banned from direct selling. This isn't a correlation. It is a pattern without exception. Vemma at 86% internal. WorldVentures at 95% internal. BurnLounge with 97.7% collapse when rewards were removed. AdvoCare at high internal consumption levels even with a meaningful preferred customer program. If your ratio is in this range, a crisis isn't a possibility. It is a timing question.

How to measure it. Pull the data from your back office. Count every order placed by someone who doesn't hold a distributor ID, affiliate position, or any enrollment in the compensation plan. That is your real customer revenue. Divide by total revenue. That is your ratio.

That instruction sounds easy. In practice, getting an honest answer is the hardest data discipline most companies in this industry have ever attempted, and it's the reason CEOs end up reporting customer ratios in board meetings that aren't actually defensible.

Three problems show up immediately. First, the back-office system was probably built to track distributors, not customers. The default tagging treats every account as a participant in the comp plan unless someone manually flags it otherwise. That means the customer count in the dashboard is whatever the data team estimated, not whatever the data actually contains.

Second, the preferred customer category is often muddied beyond use. Many companies count preferred customers who enrolled through a distributor link, receive wholesale pricing, and may or may not be actual customers in the regulatory sense. If those preferred customers are buying because the product is useful to them and they would continue buying without any relationship to a distributor, count them. If they're friends and family doing a favor, or distributors who enrolled under a spouse's name to hit a team volume requirement, do not count them. The ratio only works if the underlying classification is rigorous, and the rigor takes work.

Third, the FTC reality from earlier in this chapter applies. Distributors who behave like customers don't become customers in the regulator's eyes no matter how product-loving their behavior is. That means even if your back office has clean data, it has to track the original enrollment classification, not the subsequent behavior. A person who enrolled as a distributor five years ago and has been buying $80 a month with zero income from the business isn't in your customer count. She is in your distributor count, regardless of how customer-like she behaves.

The discipline this requires is to build a customer-only enrollment path. New customers enroll as customers. New distributors enroll as distributors. The classification is locked at signup and the back office reports each population separately. Companies that have done this work, including Zinzino and Herbalife post-2016, can produce a customer ratio that holds up under scrutiny. Companies that haven't done this work are reporting a number that may or may not match what an FTC investigator would conclude using their own methodology.

For a CEO walking into a leadership meeting and saying "we have X percent real customers," the underlying question isn't just what the dashboard says. It is whether the data discipline behind the dashboard is rigorous enough that the number would survive being examined by someone outside the company. If you're not sure of the answer, the first project is the data infrastructure, not the ratio itself.

RATIO 2: ACTIVE SELLER CHURN RATE

What percentage of your distributors quit or go inactive annually?

Churn is the silent killer. It is the number that many companies track but few take seriously because "that's just how this industry works." And it's true that direct selling has structurally higher churn than traditional employment. People join with low commitment. The barriers to exit are nearly zero. Churn rates of 50% to 70% are considered normal in this industry.

Normal doesn't mean healthy. It means normalized. There is a difference.

But before we diagnose the problem, we have to be honest about why the number is high. Two out of three people who sign up in direct selling won't build a business. That sounds alarming until you remember three things.

First, the entry cost is nearly zero, which means people try who would never try any other entrepreneurial venture. Many of them are testing, not committing. Second, a large percentage of those who stop building continue buying the product. They are customers with distributor accounts. They didn't fail. They found what they actually wanted, which was the product, not the business. Third, the comparison matters. Real estate agents wash out at over 90% in the first two years. Insurance agents at over 80%. Small businesses fail at roughly 50% within five years, and those require tens or hundreds of thousands in capital. Direct selling's churn rate is high. It isn't uniquely high for entrepreneurial models. The difference is that direct selling's churn is more visible because income disclosures publish it.

Now, some of you reading this are already composing the counterargument. "Every commission-based industry has high washout rates. Real estate agents? Over 90% of people who get their license never sell a single house. Insurance agents? More than 80% wash out in the first two years. Franchise owners? Significant failure rates even with six-figure investments. This isn't a direct selling problem. This is an entrepreneurial reality."

You are right. The washout rates across commission-based and entrepreneurial models are brutal everywhere. And direct selling deserves credit for something the other models don't offer: an absurdly low barrier to entry. Getting a real estate license costs thousands of dollars and months of study. Buying a franchise costs tens or hundreds of thousands. Starting in direct selling costs somewhere between $0 and a few hundred dollars in most companies. The accessibility is a genuine strength of this model. More people can try. More people can test whether entrepreneurship fits them. The cost of failure is orders of magnitude lower than in real estate or franchising.

That comparison is fair and it matters. I'm not here to pretend this profession has a monopoly on churn.

There is also a positive dynamic that the raw churn numbers obscure. When low-barrier entry meets strong customer acquisition, many participants become lifelong product users who never build a business. They signed up intending to try. They loved the product. They kept buying.

They never recruited a single person. On the income disclosure, they show up as "zero earners." In reality, they're happy customers who happen to have a distributor account. That outcome is good for the company and good for the customer. When a company has strong products with real demand, a significant percentage of its "washouts" are actually glorified customers. And that's fine.

Trouble starts when the company counts their qualification volume as core revenue and builds its entire economic model on it. The 67% who earned zero at AdvoCare weren't all unhappy. Some were product users. The structural question is two-layered. Commercially, you want to know how much of their purchasing was driven by real product demand versus comp plan qualification, because product-driven purchasing is sticky and qualification-driven purchasing evaporates the moment the comp plan changes. Regulatorily, the distinction doesn't protect you. The FTC counts enrolled distributors as distributors regardless of motivation, which means even a heavy population of loved-product enthusiasts inside your distributor base will appear in the regulatory math as internal consumption rather than as external customer demand.

But the comparison, while valid, can't become a hiding place. Here is why.

In real estate, when 90% of licensed agents never sell a house, those agents cost the brokerage almost nothing. They paid for their own license. They pay their own desk fees. They generate zero revenue for the brokerage. Their failure is a personal disappointment, not a structural threat to the company.

In direct selling, the washouts are often the revenue. They are buying product to qualify. They are on autoship to maintain rank. They are purchasing starter kits and monthly minimums. Their volume shows up in the company's topline revenue even though they're not building, not selling to real customers, and are about to quit. When they leave, their purchases leave with them.

The structural difference comes down to this. In traditional commission models, the people who fail cost the company nothing. In direct selling, the people who fail may be generating a significant portion of the company's volume. Their churn isn't just a field-level failure rate. It is a revenue event. And if a large enough percentage of your volume is coming from people who are about to quit, your revenue is sitting on a trapdoor.

Every entrepreneurial model has churn. What actually predicts survival is how much of your revenue depends on people who are churning. This is the measurement many companies never run. Your growth didn't slow. Your system stopped producing real customers.

Below 50% annual churn: Healthy. Your field is retaining more than half its members year over year. This is rare in direct selling and indicates genuine product stickiness, strong culture, or a comp plan that rewards staying over starting. Companies at this level have significantly longer peak-to-break timelines.

50% to 70%: Normal direct selling. This is where most companies operate. It means you need to recruit roughly one new person for every person who leaves just to stay flat. Growth requires recruiting at a rate that exceeds this churn. It is sustainable if recruiting capacity remains strong, but it creates a treadmill effect where the company must run constantly to avoid going backward.

70% to 85%: Structural Problem. At this level, you're losing more than two-thirds of your field every year. Recruiting can't sustainably outpace this rate indefinitely. The math becomes increasingly difficult. Some will argue that you never run out of contacts if you teach people how to prospect correctly, and there's truth in that. But at 70%+ churn, even excellent prospecting skills struggle to keep pace with the volume of departures. The field isn't running out of people to talk to. It is running out of people who stay long enough to produce durable volume. The distinction matters: the problem isn't a finite prospect pool. The problem is that the system is consuming people faster than it retains them.

Above 85%: Collapse Imminent. Across the dataset, churn rates above 85% preceded every flash crash. At this rate, the company is effectively replacing its entire field every fourteen months. No recruiting engine can sustain this. It is the business equivalent of a car burning oil faster than you can refill it. The engine will seize.

The critical insight about churn is that it's invisible during growth. If you're recruiting 10,000 people per month and losing 7,000, your net growth is 3,000. That looks like progress. It feels like momentum. The conventions are growing. The revenue is climbing. But the gross churn, the 7,000 leaving, is the leading indicator. When recruiting slows from 10,000 to 8,000, your net growth drops from 3,000 to 1,000. When it drops to 7,000, you're flat. When it drops below 7,000, you're declining. And at no point did the churn rate change. The churn was always 70%. You just stopped being able to outrun it.

This is Phase 1 of every decline in the dataset: invisible churn acceleration. The rot is hidden inside the gross numbers. It only becomes visible when recruiting can no longer mask it. By then, the structural damage is already done.

Herbalife's FTC investigation produced data that illustrates this perfectly. The FTC found that the majority of distributors quit within their first year. Nearly half of all participants quit in any given year. But because Herbalife was simultaneously recruiting new people at a massive rate, the headline distributor count remained relatively stable. The net number looked healthy. The gross number, the sheer volume of people cycling through the system, told a completely different story. The company wasn't retaining a sales force. It was processing a throughput.

Medifast's OPTAVIA model shows the same dynamic in real time. At peak in late 2022, the company had over 60,800 active earning coaches. By mid-2025, that number had fallen to roughly 22,800. A 63% decline. But there's a detail that reveals the underlying churn: average revenue per coach also dropped, from $4,972 to $4,630 per quarter. Both the number of coaches AND the productivity per coach were declining simultaneously. That isn't a recruiting slowdown. That is a structural unraveling where the remaining coaches are producing less because the addressable market for their product is shrinking. When the "who" and the "how much" are both falling, the decline accelerates on two axes at once.

AdvoCare's 67% zero-earner rate was a churn signal of the same kind. The 67% were cycling through the distributor side of the business, and the company needed constant fresh enrollment to replace them. The preferred customer side of the business was real, but the recruitment-driven distributor side was where the structural fragility lived. To AdvoCare's own leadership team, monitoring gross enrollment and total revenue, the signal was buried.

RATIO 3: PAYOUT INFLATION VS. REVENUE TREND

Are your commission payouts growing faster than your revenue?

This ratio is the financial early warning system. It tells you whether the company is buying its momentum with unsustainable economics.

In a healthy direct selling company, commission payouts grow proportionally with revenue. Revenue goes up 10%, payouts go up roughly 10%. The margin stays consistent. The business can afford its growth.

In a company buying momentum, payouts grow faster than revenue. The company is increasing fast-start bonuses, adding promotional incentives, offering performance agreements to recruited leaders, funding rank advancement bonuses, and subsidizing trips and prizes at rates that exceed what the revenue can support.

This happens for a specific reason. When organic growth slows, leadership teams try to stimulate it artificially. They increase the incentive. They add bonuses. They create promotions designed to spike activity. Each of these costs money. If they work and revenue accelerates proportionally, the ratio stays healthy. If they don't work, or if they produce temporary spikes that fade, the company has increased its cost structure without increasing its revenue base.

The pattern across the dataset is consistent. Companies that showed payout inflation exceeding revenue growth for two or more consecutive quarters were in the early stages of a margin compression that, left unaddressed, led to financial distress within eighteen to thirty-six months.

MonaVie's 50% commissionable-volume payout was aggressive from the start. Combined with signing bonuses, fast-start bonuses, and performance agreements, the total cost of distribution exceeded what the product margins could support long-term. When volume growth slowed, the payout structure consumed the company's cash reserves. The math was unsustainable from inception. It just didn't become visible until the recruiting engine decelerated.

How to monitor it: track total commission and bonus payouts as a percentage of revenue, quarter over quarter. If the percentage is rising while revenue is flat or declining, you're in payout inflation. The trend matters more than the absolute number. A company paying out 42% of revenue consistently is fine. A company that was paying 38% last year and is paying 44% this year has a problem, even if the 44% looks "normal" in isolation.

These three ratios work because they measure fundamentally different dimensions of company health.

Ratio 1 measures demand reality. Is your revenue real? Is it coming from people who actually want the product, or from qualification purchasing?

Ratio 2 measures field sustainability. Is your distribution force stable enough to sustain the business, or are you running a treadmill?

Ratio 3 measures financial sustainability. Are you paying for your growth out of healthy margins, or are you borrowing from your future?

A company can be weak on one ratio and survive if the other two are strong. A product company with high customer revenue and healthy margins can tolerate moderate churn because the customer base provides stability independent of field turnover. A company with low churn can tolerate a weaker customer ratio because the field itself is sticky enough to sustain volume.

But weakness on two or more ratios simultaneously is the danger signal. High internal consumption plus high churn means your volume depends on a field that's constantly leaving. High churn plus payout inflation means you're spending more to replace people who are quitting. High internal consumption plus payout inflation means you're paying escalating commissions on volume that's not driven by real demand. Each combination is a specific type of structural fragility.

All three ratios weak simultaneously? That is the profile of every company in the dataset that experienced a flash crash.

Decision triggers:

If Ratio 1 is red (below 30% real customers): stop all recruiting incentives until customer acquisition programs are producing results. Every dollar spent on recruiting with a red Ratio 1 is building on sand.

If Ratio 2 is red (above 70% annual churn): your first-90-day experience is failing. Fix onboarding, training, and early wins before any other initiative.

If Ratio 3 is trending red (payout inflation for 3+ quarters): restructure the comp plan this quarter. Not next quarter. This one. Payout inflation left unchecked becomes a financial crisis within 18 months.

If all three are green: you've earned the right to invest aggressively in drivers. This is rare. Protect it.

What I see across the community that makes this data personal.

The top earners I work with, the ones who have been in this industry for ten-plus years and have survived company transitions, market shifts, and the full emotional spectrum of building a direct selling business, every one of them has developed an intuitive version of these three ratios. They may not call them by these names. But they measure them.

Before they join a company, they ask questions that map directly to these ratios. "What percentage of your customers aren't distributors?" That is Ratio 1. "What does your twelve-month retention look like?" That is Ratio 2. "Has the comp plan been adjusted in the last two years, and in which direction?" That is Ratio 3.

The ones who don't ask these questions are the ones who chase the spike. They join the hottest company. They ride the recruiting wave. They make big money for eighteen months. And then they start looking for the next hot company. The industry calls them "jumpers." The data calls them the predictable casualties of flash crash economics.

The seven-figure earners who have sustained their income for a decade or more aren't jumpers. They are diagnosticians. They pick companies the way a venture capitalist picks investments. They look at the fundamentals underneath the excitement. They want to see the ratios before they commit. Because they've been burned before. They have joined the exciting company with the packed convention and the charismatic founder and the "we're in momentum" narrative, and they've watched that company lose 60% of its revenue in two years.

Experience teaches you to look at the ratios. This chapter saves you the cost of learning that lesson the hard way.

There is a necessary caution here.

These ratios are diagnostic tools, not destiny. A company with a poor customer ratio can fix it. A company with high churn can improve retention. A company with payout inflation can adjust its compensation structure.

The ratios tell you where you are. They don't tell you where you have to stay.

The danger isn't having unfavorable ratios. The danger isn't knowing your ratios. The danger is a leadership team that monitors convention attendance and new enrollments while the three numbers that actually predict survival sit unexamined in the back office.

The second danger is denial. Some leadership teams know their ratios and choose not to confront them. They know the customer percentage is low. They know the churn is high. They know payout inflation is creeping. But confronting those numbers means confronting uncomfortable strategic decisions. It means potentially slowing growth to build a healthier foundation. It means telling the field that some of the metrics they celebrate, like enrollment velocity, are less important than metrics they've never heard of, like customer retention rate. It means being the leader who says "we need to slow down" when everyone around you is saying "let's go faster."

That is hard. It is also the job. The companies that survived across this dataset weren't the ones with the best ratios from day one. They were the ones whose leadership teams were willing to look at hard numbers and make hard decisions before the market forced those decisions on them.

The framework is below. It is the diagnostic your leadership team should run quarterly.

THE MOMENTUM HEALTH SCORECARD

For each ratio, enter your actual number. Not an estimate. Actual data from your back office, your financial statements, and your field analytics.

Ratio 1: Customer Revenue Ratio

Total revenue from non-participant customers / Total revenue = ____%

Score: - Above 50%: GREEN. Real product business. - 30-50%: YELLOW. Viable but needs improvement. - 15-30%: AMBER. Structurally fragile. - Below 15%: RED. Historical death zone.

A clarification owners frequently ask about. The non-participant customer category doesn't include distributors who behave like customers. Many companies have what insiders call "glorified customers." These are people who enrolled as distributors, never built a business, and continued ordering products month after month because they actually love what they bought. The product enthusiasm is real. The reordering is real. From the inside, these people look indistinguishable from real customers, and on a dashboard they often get lumped in.

The FTC does not lump them in. Once a person has enrolled as a distributor, the FTC counts them as a distributor for life. No amount of subsequent customer-like behavior reclassifies them. This isn't a debatable interpretation. It is the regulatory reality every direct selling company operates under. A company can have 40,000 enrolled distributors who never recruited a single person and only ever bought product for personal use, and the FTC will still count those 40,000 as distributors when calculating the company's customer ratio.

This is exactly what tripped Vemma. They had real product enthusiasts who bought energy drinks every month with no income from the business. Many of those people would have been customers in any economic sense of the word. The chargeback rate was minimal, which is itself evidence that the people buying the product actually wanted it. The kids drinking Verve actually liked the drink. But because they had enrolled as affiliates, the FTC counted them as affiliates, and the company's internal consumption ratio looked structurally suspect even though much of that consumption was driven by genuine product preference. The lesson isn't that Vemma didn't have real demand. The lesson is that real demand inside an affiliate classification doesn't protect a company from regulatory action when the income claims and recruitment incentives create exposure on their own.

The implication for any company reading this: customer counts and customer ratios only protect you when those customers are actually classified as customers in your enrollment system. A program that enrolls everyone as a distributor by default and figures out later who is really building is structurally exposed regardless of how strong the product is. The companies with the cleanest regulatory posture have separate enrollment paths. Customers enroll as customers. Distributors enroll as distributors. The system distinguishes between them at the moment of signup, not retroactively after the FTC starts asking questions.

This is one reason Zinzino, Herbalife post-2016, and other structurally clean operators have invested heavily in customer-only enrollment programs. The customer ratio is a regulatory shield only when the underlying classification is rigorous. Everything else is a story you tell yourself about your customer base that the FTC is not obligated to believe.

Ratio 2: Annual Field Churn Rate

Total distributors who quit or went inactive in the last 12 months / Total distributors at the start of the period = ____%

Score: - Below 50%: GREEN. Exceptional retention. - 50-70%: YELLOW. Industry normal, manageable. - 70-85%: AMBER. Structural problem. - Above 85%: RED. Collapse-level churn.

Think of your business as a bucket. Recruiting is the water you pour in. Churn is the holes in the bottom. If you have a high churn rate, it doesn't matter how fast you pour water in. It is all coming out. You can be exceptional at acquisition and still lose because you never fixed retention. Many companies invest 90% of their energy in pouring faster and 10% in plugging the holes. The math says that's backwards.

And retention isn't passive. Customers don't stay because they signed up. They stay because they're continuously sold on the value of what they bought. When someone commits to a product, they want to know it's working. They want to feel smart about the purchase. They want to be reminded why they chose it. The companies with the highest retention rates are the ones whose field leaders and corporate systems are constantly reselling the customer on the product. Not with hype. With results, education, and reinforcement. A customer who understands what the product does, sees it working, and feels supported in using it doesn't cancel when money gets tight. She cuts the thirty things that matter less.

Ratio 3: Payout Inflation Index

Commission + bonus payout as a % of revenue this quarter vs. same quarter last year.

Rising while revenue is flat or declining: RED. Rising proportionally with revenue growth: GREEN. Declining or stable: GREEN.

Combined Assessment:

Three greens: You have a structurally sound business. Invest in momentum drivers with confidence.

Two greens, one yellow: You have a foundation with one area that needs attention. Address the yellow before it becomes orange.

One or more oranges: You have structural fragility. Before investing in growth, fix the ratios. Growth on a fragile foundation accelerates toward collapse rather than success.

Any red: This is a crisis whether the revenue line shows it yet or not. Every month you delay addressing a red ratio is a month closer to a break event. The data across 53 companies is unambiguous. Reds don't fix themselves. They compound.

Imagine a CEO who walks into a board meeting with this scorecard.

She doesn't lead with revenue. She doesn't lead with enrollment numbers. She doesn't lead with convention attendance.

She leads with three ratios. "Our customer revenue ratio is 54%. Green. Our annual churn is 62%. Yellow. Our payout inflation index is flat. Green. Two greens and a yellow. The yellow is churn. Here is our 90-day plan to push churn below 55% by improving our first-120-day onboarding experience and increasing product subscription retention by 8%."

The board doesn't need to guess whether the company is healthy. The board doesn't need to interpret revenue trends or listen to narratives about momentum. The three ratios tell the story in numbers that can't be argued with.

Every company in this industry has access to this data. Most choose not to look at it because the numbers might not match the story they're telling themselves. The leadership teams that look anyway, that insist on truth over comfort, are the ones who show up in the "survivor" column of the dataset instead of the "casualty" column.

A pattern observation about how leadership teams behave around their own numbers. The teams that show up in the survivor column of any dataset usually share a habit. They run their metrics monthly. They bring them into leadership meetings. The ratios aren't a surprise to anyone in the room. The dashboard is part of the rhythm of the business.

The leadership teams that end up in the casualty column usually share a different habit. They have a lot of data, often too much, and they can't identify which of it actually predicts survival. The metrics that matter are buried under the metrics that are easy to track. That confusion itself is a signal. A leadership team that doesn't know which of its own numbers matter has been running on the wrong dashboard for some time, and the gap between what they're tracking and what they should be tracking widens until something breaks. The companies that get this right strip the dashboard down to a small number of ratios that actually predict structural health, and they look at those ratios on a recurring cadence regardless of what the topline revenue is doing in any given quarter.

The next chapter reveals the dividing line between a real business and a product alibi. You already know your three ratios. Now you're about to learn what they mean for whether your company is building something real or decorating something temporary.

PRODUCT VALUE AND DEFENSIBILITY: THE INPUTS UNDERNEATH THE RATIO

The customer ratio is the outcome variable. The inputs that produce it are product value and product defensibility. A company can run every customer acquisition campaign in the playbook, redesign its comp plan around customer rewards, and still fail to build a real customer base if the underlying product doesn't deliver enough value relative to alternatives, or if the value it delivers is easily replicated by competitors at lower prices.

Product value drives customer acquisition. A consumer who tries your product and concludes that it's meaningfully better than alternatives, or solves a problem that alternatives don't solve as well, will continue to buy. A consumer who tries your product and finds it marginally different from cheaper alternatives won't. The customer acquisition rate any company achieves at scale is a direct function of how much real value the product delivers, full stop.

Product defensibility drives lifetime value and retention. If your product is easily replicated by a competitor at a similar price, customer churn will be high regardless of what your comp plan or culture does. Defensibility comes from many sources. Proprietary formulation. Trademarked process. Manufacturing relationships that are hard to copy. Regulatory approvals that take years to obtain. Brand equity that competitors can't replicate quickly. Service ecosystems and community that travel with the product. The companies in the dataset with the strongest customer retention curves are almost always the companies whose products are hardest to substitute.

If a company's product has weak value or weak defensibility, the customer ratio can't be fixed by comp plan engineering or field development. The ratio is downstream of the product. A leadership team running the customer ratio diagnostic and finding the number is too low has to ask, before redesigning anything else, whether the product itself is producing real customer demand at sustainable volume. If it's not, the structural problem is the product, not the comp plan.

Customer Ratio is the clearest example of The Underneath. The revenue line is the surface variable. The percentage of that revenue coming from real customers is what sits underneath it. Two companies can show identical revenue and have opposite structural health, because what is underneath their revenue is opposite. Whenever you see a number in this book that looks healthy on the surface, the question to ask is what is underneath it.

THE BOTTOM LINE: Track three ratios: real customer revenue percentage, active seller churn rate, and payout ratio trend. These three numbers predict survival more reliably than revenue, distributor count, or convention attendance combined.

The scoreboard everyone watches measures activity. The scoreboard that matters measures health. Know your three numbers.

Chapter 5: The Product Alibi

Figure 4. Every direct selling company operates in two worlds. The ratio between them predicts whether the business is real or an alibi.

Remove the comp plan. Watch what happens. That is your real business.

In June 2007, a company called BurnLounge was generating $476,516 in monthly revenue. It sold digital music packages through a direct selling model. It had recruited over 56,000 paid members. By every metric the industry uses to measure momentum, BurnLounge was on fire.

In July 2007, a federal court halted BurnLounge's ability to pay recruiting rewards.

By August 2007, revenue had collapsed to $10,880.

That is a 97.7% collapse in sixty days. Not sixty months. Not sixty weeks. Sixty days.

By that point, the number was effectively zero. The company was dead. Not dying. Dead. The entire revenue engine had been the compensation plan. The music? The packages? The "product"? Nobody wanted them without the business opportunity attached.

This is the single most important data point in the research behind this book. Court-documented. Not estimated. It answers a question many company owners have never asked themselves.

If you removed qualification purchasing tomorrow, what percentage of your volume would still be there?

BurnLounge's answer was 2.3%.

That means 97.7% of the revenue wasn't product demand. It was opportunity demand dressed up as product demand. People were buying packages to participate in the business opportunity, not because they wanted digital music. The product wasn't the business. The product was the alibi.

The flipped assumption in this chapter, and it's the most uncomfortable one in the book.

Having a product doesn't mean you have a product business.

Many direct selling companies believe they're product companies with consumer-distributed brands. Some of them are. But a significant number are actually recruiting economics engines with a product attached to make the economics legal. The product exists. It is real. People consume it. The question is what is driving the consumption.

Comp plans aren't the enemy. They are the engine. Every successful business uses systems to drive customer acquisition. Procter and Gamble spends billions on advertising. Costco builds a membership model. Apple builds an ecosystem. Direct selling companies build compensation plans. Each of these systems exists to amplify real demand for a real product. None of them is illegitimate just because it exists. Telling a direct selling company to "shut off the comp plan and see who is left" is like telling a consumer brand to "shut off advertising and see who is left." The point isn't whether the system is producing volume. Of course it is. That is what systems do. The point is whether the system is amplifying real demand or manufacturing the appearance of demand.

This is the durability test. And the diagnostic is more sophisticated than a single switch. It asks several questions in sequence.

What percentage of your buyers continue purchasing after they've stopped pursuing rank advancement? If a meaningful percentage of them keep buying, the product has independent demand. If almost none of them keep buying, the comp plan was the entire reason for the purchase.

What is the average tenure of the consumers who order monthly without earning a commission check? If you have thousands of people who have been ordering for three, five, or seven years with no income from the business, you have evidence of independent product love. If your purchasing population turns over every fifteen months as people qualify, miss qualification, and disappear, the product isn't the engine.

When the comp plan adjusts in ways that change qualification thresholds, what happens to volume? A product business absorbs comp plan adjustments because the underlying demand is real. A recruiting economics engine collapses because the qualification structure was the engine.

When external conditions change, demand for genuine products holds. Demand for qualification volume evaporates. The companies that survive long enough to compound have built businesses where the comp plan is amplifying something the customer actually wants. The companies that flash crash have built businesses where the comp plan is the entire reason the volume exists.

The difference comes down to this. Not whether the comp plan is doing work. The comp plan is always doing work. The difference is what it's working on.

A necessary clarification before we go further. This isn't a legal argument. It is a durability argument. A company can be fully compliant and still be structurally fragile. Distributor consumption may be genuine. Many distributors love their products and would buy them regardless. Whether insiders use the product isn't the test. The real measure is how much of your volume survives when recruiting slows, when a major leader leaves, or when the opportunity loses its heat. That is a stability question, not a morality question. And it's the question this chapter forces every leadership team to answer with data instead of assumptions.

This isn't a moral argument. I'm not here to call anyone a fraud. Most of the companies caught in this pattern are run by people who deeply believe in their products. The founders use the products. The field leaders love the products. The testimonials are real. None of that is the test.

The test is mathematical. What percentage of your revenue comes from people who would buy your product even if no compensation existed? That single ratio, more than any other metric in this industry, predicts whether your company survives.

The clearest non-direct-selling case of product alibi is Beanie Babies.

In the late 1990s, Ty Warner's Ty Inc. reached $1.3 billion in sales in 1998. Warner personally reported $662 million in income in 1999, more than Hasbro and Mattel combined. Beanie Babies accounted for roughly 10% of all eBay sales in the platform's early days. The average resale price on eBay was $30, six times the $5 retail price. Self-published price guides predicted what each Beanie Baby would be worth in 2008. One guide sold more than three million copies. People built spreadsheets. Stored their collections in plastic protectors. Treated $5 stuffed animals as investments.

Ty Warner ran a brilliant scarcity strategy. He sold only to small specialty stores, not big box chains. He retired characters to create artificial scarcity. He released new designs constantly to keep the speculation market churning. The strategy worked. The demand was massive. The revenue was real. The profits were extraordinary.

But the demand wasn't for the product. The demand was for the speculation.

People weren't buying Beanie Babies because they wanted stuffed animals. They were buying them because they believed the stuffed animals would appreciate in value and could be resold at a profit. The purchase was a speculative investment dressed up as a toy purchase. The "product" was a placeholder for the real transaction, which was financial.

On one night in 1999, Ty announced a character retirement. Historically, announcements like this had triggered a spike in secondary market prices for the retired characters. This time, nothing happened. The eBay prices didn't move. Collectors realized, all at once, that the scarcity game had limits. Then the selling began. Within months, Beanie Baby prices collapsed. Today a "rare" Beanie Baby that sold for hundreds of dollars in 1998 is worth approximately fifty cents.

Ty Warner hadn't done anything wrong. His company made real products that he shipped to real customers. The crash didn't happen because of a regulatory action or a scandal or a leader exodus. It happened because the demand was structurally speculative, and speculative demand evaporates the moment the speculative premise stops being believable.

Every product-alibi company in direct selling has the same structural problem. The product exists. The company is usually compliant. The distributors are often passionate. But the underlying demand isn't driven by the stated product. It is driven by some other incentive, usually the compensation plan, that makes the product the cover for a different economic transaction. When the incentive weakens, the demand evaporates, and everyone discovers simultaneously that nobody actually wanted what they had been buying.

The Beanie Baby bubble's one visible difference from the direct selling version is speed. Speculative bubbles collapse in weeks or months. Product-alibi direct selling companies collapse in years, because the compensation structure masks the fragility for longer than a speculation market can. The mechanism is identical. The timeline is different.

The data is brutal in its clarity.

Across the 53-company dataset behind this book, every company where we can document greater than 80% internal consumption (revenue from participants rather than retail customers) is dead, dissolved, or banned from operating as a direct selling company.

Every single one.

Holiday Magic. 95% internal. Dissolved. SEC fraud.

WorldVentures. 95% of members were reps, not customers. Bankruptcy. Dissolved.

Vemma. 86% internal consumption in 2013. Only 14% retail. FTC shutdown.

YTB International. 85% of revenue from membership purchases by participants. Flash crash.

AdvoCare. Strong distributor enrollment alongside a meaningful preferred customer program of nearly 400,000 people. The FTC's case focused on income claims and the structure of recruitment incentives. Fined $150 million. Banned from network marketing permanently. Over 224,000 distributors received refunds.

TelexFree. 98% internal. DOJ fraud conviction.

Equinox International. Over 90% of participants earned nothing. Minimal retail. Dissolved. $40 million in penalties.

BurnLounge. Package-driven revenue with negligible retail. 97.7% collapse when recruiting rewards were removed. FTC shutdown.

Now look at the other end of the spectrum.

Neora. Approximately 80% of revenue from real customers. 20% internal. The FTC sued them in 2019, alleging they were a pyramid scheme. The case went to trial in 2022. In September 2023, Judge Barbara Lynn of the

Northern District of Texas denied every single claim the FTC brought. All five of them. Pyramid scheme allegation. False earnings claims. False product claims. Agency claims. Means and instrumentalities.

The judge's ruling was 56 pages long. One sentence tells you everything: "The fact that 80 percent of revenues come from ultimate user sales weighs heavily against a finding that Neora focuses exclusively or almost exclusively on recruiting as opposed to sales."

Eighty percent real customers. That was the number that saved Neora. That was the fact the judge pointed to when she rejected the government's case. It wasn't the culture, the events, or the compensation plan design. The customer ratio.

Neora became the first direct selling company to defeat the FTC's pyramid scheme allegations in a federal court trial. The previous benchmark, Amway's 1979 victory, had come before an FTC administrative law judge rather than in federal court. Nearly fifty years between meaningful regulatory victories. The variable that gave Neora its strongest defensible position was one ratio. An honest caveat about the headline ratio. Neora's high customer volume figure at the time of the trial was partly a function of the recruiting and overall business having contracted significantly during the years of FTC litigation. When the distributor base shrinks and the customer base remains, the customer ratio rises mechanically. The legal architecture was real and the defense was earned. The high customer ratio was both an architectural choice and a bittersweet outcome of the years of regulatory pressure that preceded the verdict. Both things are true. A company defending itself in court for years sees its recruiting collapse, which mechanically lifts the customer percentage even before any architectural changes are credited.

CEO Jeff Olson put it plainly: "Because Neora has always been built on a solid foundation with science-based products that bring true value to the market, a massive non-distributor customer base that represents nearly 80 percent of the company's total revenue, and a modern e-commerce sales system that removes the need for brand partners to carry inventory or incur unnecessary extra costs, we were able to take on and win this important fight."

There is a dividing line in this industry. It is visible in one number. And it separates the companies that survive from the companies that end up in court filings and bankruptcy dockets.

The dividing line works like this.

If more than 50% of your revenue comes from real customers, people who aren't in the comp plan, people who buy because they want the product and would continue buying if the business opportunity disappeared, you have a real business with a direct selling company distribution channel. The direct selling model is how you sell. But the product is why people buy.

The closer you move toward a majority of revenue from real customers, the more stable your business becomes. Companies well above 50% have the strongest foundations. Companies well below it are structurally fragile.

The exact threshold will vary by category, phase, and model. The principle is more important than the line. Some companies with 40% real customers are healthier than companies with 55% because the trajectory is moving in the right direction and the leadership team is actively investing in customer acquisition. The number is a diagnostic signal, not a verdict. The direction of dependency matters more than the number, and so does the honesty with which you measure it.

If you're a company owner reading that and your first instinct is to argue with the definition, you're proving the point. Defensiveness about the customer ratio is itself diagnostic. A leadership team confident in its customer foundation engages with the number directly. A leadership team afraid of what the number will reveal looks for reasons the metric doesn't apply to them. Companies that get defensive about the customer ratio are almost always the companies with the worst ratios. Companies that get curious about it are the ones that fix it.

A critical caveat for companies not pursuing massive scale: this framework is designed for companies building toward $100 million, $500 million, or a billion dollars. There are hundreds of direct selling companies operating at $20 million to $80 million annually, profitably, for decades, with internal consumption ratios that would flag as risky under this framework. Many of those companies have loyal distributor bases who use the products every day because they work. The distributors are the customers. The business is stable because it's small, focused, and not trying to scale past its natural ceiling. Those companies aren't broken. They are operating a different model at a different scale. The customer ratio pressure increases with scale because scale attracts regulatory attention, scale requires recruiting velocity that increases churn, and scale makes the gap between real demand and artificial volume larger and more visible. If your ambition is steady profitability at a manageable size, your risk profile is different from the companies in this dataset.

A second caveat for new and fast-growing companies: if you're in Act 1 or Act 2 of your growth cycle, you'll almost certainly not hit the 50% real-customer mark in the first 24 to 36 months. That is normal. Growth-phase companies are recruiting-heavy by nature. The obsession should be directional: is the ratio moving upward every quarter? Are you investing in customer acquisition programs from day one? What is acceptable in phase one becomes fatal in phase three. The companies that build their customer floor during the growth years are the ones that survive when the growth slows. The companies that wait until the growth slows to start building customers discover they're too late.

That language is blunt. It should be. Because the consequences of being on the wrong side of that line aren't abstract. They are specific, documented, and devastating.

Companies above the line survive regulatory scrutiny. They retain customers during downturns. They can weather leader departures because customers are loyal to the product, not the upline. They can price competitively because real demand supports the price.

Companies below the line are structurally fragile in ways that no amount of field culture, leadership development, or event production can fix. When recruiting slows, revenue drops, because recruiting IS the revenue engine. When a leader leaves, her entire volume walks with her, because nobody underneath was buying for the product. When the FTC comes calling, there's no defense, because the ratio tells the whole story.

Whether your product is good is beside the point. Whether your product sells without the compensation plan attached is everything. Those are two completely different questions. And many companies in this industry have only ever answered the first one.

This pattern is amplified by product category. Some categories are structurally more likely to produce product alibis than others. The following survival rates are based on the 53 companies in the dataset. They aren't universal statistics for the entire industry. There are hundreds of direct selling companies that aren't in this dataset, and a broader sample might shift the percentages. But these are the most documented cases available, and the patterns within them are directionally reliable. Use them as risk indicators, not as destiny.

Exotic juice and superfruit companies have a 0% survival rate within the 53-company dataset (1990-2025). Tahitian Noni. MonaVie. XanGo. Zija. Every single superfruit juice direct selling company in the dataset is dead. Combined peak revenues exceeded $2 billion. Combined current value is approximately zero. The pattern is consistent across these cases. An exotic ingredient captures cultural attention. A premium juice product enters the market at a meaningful price premium relative to comparable retail options. The direct selling distribution model supports that premium through business opportunity economics, not consumer value perception alone. Then the ingredient shows up at retail at a fraction of the original price as the supply chain matures. The premium becomes harder to defend. What had been a story about exclusivity and discovery becomes a story about why the same fruit costs more through the distributor channel than at the grocery store.

Travel and membership companies have faced significant structural challenges. WorldVentures and YTB both failed at scale. When the "product" is a membership, the line between customer and opportunity-seeker blurs. However, the category isn't dead. Niche players focused on cruises, group travel, and high-touch experiences have carved out sustainable segments. The structural risk remains high because memberships can blur the line between product and opportunity, but writing off the entire category would ignore the companies that are finding ways to make it work.

Clothing and accessories at scale have proven extremely volatile in direct selling. LuLaRoe, Thirty-One Gifts, and Stella & Dot all experienced sharp declines after explosive early growth. Fashion cycles move faster than direct selling inventory models can handle. Quality consistency across mass production is brutal. That said, niche players in athleisure and accessories have found sustainable segments at smaller scale. The lesson isn't that fashion can't work in direct selling. It is that fashion at massive scale, built on a single hero product and an inventory-heavy model, has not sustained peak momentum in the dataset. Companies entering the category with better inventory management, wider product lines, and stronger customer programs may write a different story. The history simply says it will be harder.

Weight management shakes: 33% still operating, all in decline. ViSalus. Medifast. Isagenix. Herbalife. It Works. And here, the category itself is now under siege from something no direct selling company has ever faced before.

What is happening right now in weight management is unprecedented. It is the first time in the history of this industry that an external technology is simultaneously threatening multiple billion-dollar companies, and the threat isn't a competitor or a regulatory action. A pharmaceutical breakthrough.

GLP-1 receptor agonist drugs, sold under brand names like Ozempic and Wegovy, are rewriting the weight loss category from the outside. These drugs work. Clinical evidence supports them. Insurance is beginning to cover them. And they're making the conversation around weight management shakes, meal replacements, and challenge-based programs feel dated almost overnight.

Medifast is the clearest case study. The OPTAVIA coaching model drove revenue from $302 million in 2017 to $1.6 billion in 2022. That is a $1.3 billion acceleration in five years. Explosive momentum by any standard.

Then GLP-1 drugs gained mainstream adoption.

2023 revenue: $1.07 billion. Down 33%.

2024 revenue: $602 million. Down another 44%.

Full year 2025 revenue: $385.8 million per reported financials. Still falling.

Active earning coaches dropped from over 60,800 at peak to approximately 16,100. That is a 74% decline in the people who ARE the business. In two and a half years.

Medifast's decline isn't a company-specific failure. The product works. The coaching model is well-designed. The leadership is competent. The decline is a category event. GLP-1 drugs made the weight management shake category structurally less relevant for a large segment of consumers. It is the equivalent of what happened to film cameras when smartphones arrived. The product didn't get worse. The world changed around it.

Herbalife has weathered more existential threats than any company in this industry: the Ackman short-selling assault, a $200 million FTC settlement, and now GLP-1 category disruption. Each time, the company adapted rather than collapsed. Whether the Nutrition Club value proposition offsets the pharmaceutical headwind is a question the next several years will answer.

This is what happens when your product category faces existential disruption and your customer base was never deep enough to absorb the shock. If 80% of your volume was coming from real customers who loved the product and used it daily regardless of the comp plan, a category disruption hurts but doesn't kill you. You still have customers. They might slow down. Some might leave. But the core holds.

If 50% or more of your volume was driven by distributors buying to qualify, autoship to maintain rank, and product purchases to earn commissions, a category disruption doesn't just hurt. It eliminates the justification for the purchasing behavior. The distributor was buying shakes to stay active in the comp plan. Now the comp plan is less attractive because recruiting is harder because the category is losing relevance. Remove the comp plan incentive and the product volume evaporates. The shakes didn't stop working. The shakes were never the real reason people were buying.

The product alibi collapses when the category collapses. And the company discovers, too late, what percentage of its revenue was real.

I want to be direct about something. This chapter will make some people reading this book uncomfortable. Maybe you. If your internal consumption ratio is above 50%, I understand why you don't want to look at this data. If your autoship numbers are high and your retail customer verification is soft, I understand why this framework feels threatening.

What I know from sitting with top earners across this entire industry for nearly two decades.

The leaders who build long-term, the ones who are still earning seven figures a decade after they started, every single one of them will tell you the same thing. They build on product. Real product demand. Customers who love what they use and reorder because of results, not because of rank requirements.

The leaders who burn out, who hit big numbers fast and then watch everything collapse, are almost always the ones who built on recruiting economics. They recruited hard. They hit fast-start bonuses. They filled rooms with people who were excited about the opportunity. But nobody underneath them was actually using the product for its own sake. The volume was a function of the comp plan structure. When enthusiasm cooled, volume evaporated.

I've watched this pattern play out hundreds of times inside the community. The difference between a sustainable business and a house of cards is always the same thing. It is always the customers themselves, not the testimonials or the "I love our products" posts on social media. The actual, measurable, verifiable percentage of volume that comes from people who have no financial incentive to buy.

That percentage is the number. It is what this chapter is about. And every company owner reading this book needs to know theirs.

There is a shadow side here, and it's important.

Some companies hear this argument and overcorrect toward pure retail. They strip out business opportunity incentives. They make it harder to earn. They implement customer verification requirements so burdensome that the field stops recruiting entirely.

That kills momentum just as effectively as a product alibi kills sustainability.

This book is about momentum. And momentum requires an engine. The compensation plan IS the engine. It creates the economic incentive that drives field activity, which produces the conversations, which creates the customers. Without the engine, you have a great product sitting on a shelf that nobody talks about.

The goal isn't to eliminate the comp plan. The goal is to build a business where the comp plan amplifies genuine product demand rather than manufacturing artificial demand. The comp plan should make the field more effective at reaching customers who actually want the product. It shouldn't be the reason customers exist.

Neora understood this. Eighty percent of their revenue came from real customers. But they also had a compensation plan that rewarded brand partners for selling to those customers. The engine was running. But it was fueled by actual demand, not qualification purchasing.

The companies that get this balance right create momentum that lasts. The companies that let the engine become the product create momentum that looks real but has an expiration date printed on it in invisible ink.

From the field side, this looks different than the corporate dashboard suggests.

Through my private community of 1,800 verified six- and seven-figure earners, I see this constantly. These are people who have been in the profession for years. Many of them have built across multiple companies. They have seen inside the numbers in ways that most corporate teams never hear about.

One pattern surfaces constantly. A top earner joins a new company. She is excited about the product. She starts building. Within the first six months, she notices something. Her team is growing, but the customers are thin. Most of the volume on her team is coming from distributors buying their monthly autoship to stay qualified. The rank requirements are structured so that maintaining a position requires $150 to $200 in personal monthly purchases. Her team is buying product to keep their spots, not because they woke up craving it.

She raises the concern to corporate. She says, "We need more real customers. The volume is almost entirely internal." Corporate thanks her for the feedback. Nothing changes. The revenue line is going up. The company is "in momentum." Nobody wants to hear that the momentum is hollow.

Eighteen months later, recruiting slows. It always slows eventually. When it does, the autoship volume drops immediately because new people stop joining, which means fewer people buying to qualify. But the existing distributors also start dropping their autoship because their paychecks are shrinking and the $200 monthly purchase no longer feels justified by the commission it generates. The volume decline accelerates. Corporate panics. Launches a new product. Throws a promotion. Bumps the fast-start bonus.

None of it works. Because the problem was never the product or the promotion. The problem was that the volume was never real demand. It was comp plan participation masquerading as product consumption.

I've watched this play out so many times that I can predict the timeline within a few months just by asking one question. What is the ratio? If a top earner tells me that fewer than 30% of their team's customers are people outside the comp plan, I already know how the next two years end. The only variable is how long it takes for recruiting to slow down.

That is pattern recognition across thousands of data points. The leaders who build the longest careers in this industry figured out early that the customer ratio is everything. They would rather grow slower with real customers than faster on qualification purchasing. Because they've seen what happens when the qualification volume disappears.

The best builders in this profession aren't the best recruiters. They are the best at creating customers. Recruiting without customers is a Ponzi scheme with a product label on it. Recruiting with customers is a distribution business. The difference is one ratio. And it determines whether you're building something that lasts or something that collapses the moment the field stops running.

This is the diagnostic. Use it in your next leadership meeting. Use it without self-deception.

THE PRODUCT REALITY TEST

This is a five-question diagnostic. Answer each question with verified data, not estimates, not feelings, not what you hope is true. If you can't answer a question with data, that gap is itself a finding.

Question 1: What percentage of your total volume comes from customers who are NOT in the compensation plan?

This is the master ratio. The single most predictive number in the entire industry. Pull the actual data from your back office. Not "customers" who are also enrolled as distributors buying at wholesale. Real external customers with no distributor ID.

- Above 50%: You are in the survival zone. You have a real product business.
- 30-50%: You are in the caution zone. Your business has real demand but it's not dominant.
- 15-30%: You are in the danger zone. The majority of your revenue depends on comp plan participation.
- Below 15%: You are in the death zone. Historically, every company in this range has either been shut down by regulators, dissolved, or gone bankrupt.

Question 2: What percentage of your distributors' product purchases are required for rank qualification or commission eligibility?

This is the qualification purchasing ratio, and the math is more nuanced than it first appears. Take a company where distributors must spend $150 per month on autoship to remain active and earn commissions. If the average distributor personal purchase is $160 per month, the surface-level math suggests qualification is driving nearly all the volume. The reality is usually more layered. Some distributors would naturally consume $130 in product and add $20 to hit the qualification threshold. The $20 is qualification-driven. The $130 is real demand. Some would naturally consume $80 and stretch to $150 only because the comp plan requires it. Most of that volume is qualification-driven. Some would naturally consume $200 in product and the $150 minimum is well below their actual usage, which means none of the qualification requirement is doing structural work for that distributor.

The diagnostic is to understand the distribution. Run an analysis. What percentage of your distributors are at or just above the qualification threshold every month, suggesting their order is calibrated to the minimum rather than to their actual usage? What percentage consistently order well above the threshold, suggesting genuine usage that exceeds qualification requirements? What percentage drop below the threshold during stretches when they're not actively building, then return when they're pushing for rank? The shape of that distribution tells you how much of your autoship volume is real demand and how much is comp plan compliance. A healthy company has a meaningful population well above the threshold and a meaningful population that orders below the threshold during inactive periods because they like the product. A structurally dependent company has most of its distributors clustered exactly at the qualification minimum, which is the signature pattern of qualification-driven volume that disappears when distributors stop building.

Question 3: If you removed all autoship requirements and rank qualifications tomorrow, what do you estimate would happen to your total volume in 90 days?

This is the smoke detector test, and it has to be answered with nuance. Autoships aren't a problem on their own. They are an effective mechanism for building consumption habits, which is exactly why every successful subscription business in any industry uses them. Netflix uses autoship. Costco's renewal model is a form of autoship. Amazon Subscribe and Save is autoship. The mechanism is legitimate. It serves the customer who wants the product to arrive without having to reorder. The question isn't whether autoship volume would drop. Of course it would, just as Netflix subscriptions would drop if Netflix removed automatic renewals tomorrow. The question is what shape the drop would take, and what would remain.

The diagnostic is about the size and sustainability of the floor underneath the autoship volume. If your leadership team believes volume would drop by more than 60% within 90 days and stay down, the autoship was carrying most of the demand rather than amplifying it. If volume drops 30 to 40% and stabilizes, the autoship was doing healthy work amplifying real demand and the company has a meaningful customer floor underneath. If volume drops sharply and then recovers as customers and distributors voluntarily place orders to maintain their consumption, you've built a real product business that uses autoship as a convenience layer rather than as a structural crutch. The shape of the recovery matters more than the depth of the initial drop.

Question 4: Is your product priced in a way that the customer would defend on its own merits?

This is more nuanced than a Target comparison. Premium pricing is legitimate when it's supported by something the customer actually values. Louis Vuitton bags sell at multiples of comparable quality bags because customers value the brand, the heritage, and the social signal. Apple products sell at premiums to comparable specs because customers value the ecosystem, the design, and the experience. Whole Foods sells groceries at premiums to Walmart because customers value the curation, the trust, and the in-store experience. None of these premiums are illegitimate. They are paid willingly because the customer believes the additional spend is worth it for reasons beyond the spec sheet.

The diagnostic question for a direct selling product is whether the premium is supported by something real that the customer values, or whether the premium exists only because the comp plan margin requires it. The signals are usually clear once you look. Do customers continue purchasing at the premium price after the business opportunity has stopped being relevant to them? Do customers refer the product to friends and family who have no interest in becoming distributors? Do customers describe specific reasons they prefer your product, beyond saying "my friend sells it"? Are there independent reviews, testimonials, or third-party validation that supports the premium positioning?

A product that has a high price and also has community, brand, science, results, experience, education, or service that the customer values is a premium product, the same way Louis Vuitton or Apple or Whole Foods is. A product that has a high price supported by nothing but the comp plan margin is exposed when the comp plan changes or the opportunity weakens. The premium itself isn't the test. What sits underneath the premium is.

Question 5: What is your product category's survival rate?

Check it against the data. Exotic superfruit juice? No long-term survivors at original scale in the dataset. Weight management shakes? 33%, and declining under GLP-1 pressure. Travel memberships? High-risk, with a few niche survivors. Clothing and accessories at scale? Extremely volatile, with sharp declines after peak. If your category has a difficult history, your margin for error on the customer ratio is smaller. You need stronger customer depth, better differentiation, and deeper community than a company in a category with a more favorable track record.

These numbers aren't death sentences. They are difficulty ratings. Every category has companies that beat the odds because they executed at a higher standard than their competitors. The history tells you the standard required. It doesn't tell you whether you can meet it. That is up to you.

Scoring:

If you have real data for all five questions and the answers are favorable, you have a foundation. Build on it. Protect it. Make customer acquisition as central to your strategy as distributor recruiting.

If you can't answer these questions with data, start there. The inability to answer is the most common finding in this exercise. Many companies don't track the ratio because they don't want to know the answer.

If the answers are unfavorable, you have a choice. You can fix the ratio while you still have momentum. Or you can wait until the market, the regulators, or a category disruption fixes it for you.

THE PRODUCT DEMAND TEST

Before we go further, a critical clarification about what this test is actually measuring.

The direct selling model exists because relationship-driven distribution works. Great products get lost in crowded retail shelves. Great products fail launches because they have no budget for traditional advertising. Great products sit in warehouses because no retailer will take a chance on an unknown brand. The direct selling model solves real problems that the traditional distribution system can't solve. It gives products a human voice in the market. It creates communities around those products that retail can't replicate. It generates word-of-mouth at scale in ways that no advertising can match. Good companies with good products benefit enormously from the model.

None of that is in question. The model isn't the problem. The model is often the reason the product reaches anyone at all.

The comp plan matters enormously. Compensation drives human behavior. A well-designed comp plan is essential infrastructure. It is what gets distributors out of bed in the morning, what rewards the relationship-building work that generates sales, what funds the lifestyle changes that get families out of financial stress, what creates the leadership development pipeline that any serious direct selling company requires. Every company in this book has a comp plan, and every owner reading this has spent hundreds of hours thinking about theirs. Comp plans aren't the enemy. They are the engine.

Whether you have a comp plan isn't the test. Of course you do. What actually matters is what your comp plan is incentivizing your distributors to do.

The best comp plans incentivize distributors to push the value of a product that already has value. This is the healthy posture. The field is motivated to find real customers, explain why the product matters, create the social proof and community and education that retail can't replicate, and build repeat-ordering relationships. The comp plan is paying distributors to do work that expands a genuine market. The product has to be strong enough that those customer relationships hold once they exist.

The company has work to do here too. A strong product doesn't market itself. The company has to build product-culture fit, invest in credible marketing, commission the studies and certifications that support its claims, cultivate the values and story that connect the product to something larger than the transaction, and maintain quality control so that the product keeps performing for the customer who buys it. A great product with a weak company story still fails in the market. A great product with a strong story and an incentivized field is the combination that builds durable companies.

The wrong posture is the reverse. "We have an incredible comp plan, and the product is whatever we happen to sell through it." That is when the comp plan stops being an engine and starts being the reason the company exists. The product becomes a placeholder for the real transaction, which is the compensation flow. Distributors buy not because they want the product but because buying is how they earn. Customers are a rounding error. The company may have a great comp plan. It doesn't have a business.

A data point worth sitting with. When MonaVie collapsed in 2015, the public record shows the company defaulted on a $182 million note and Jeunesse Global purchased the underlying asset for $15 million. Think about what that number means. A company that had done over $800 million in annual revenue at peak was worth $15 million at the end. Every person in the industry who watched MonaVie operate in its final years saw the same pattern: the distributor count stayed in the hundreds of thousands on paper long after the count of people who were actually ordering juice for themselves had dropped dramatically. The field was held together by the comp plan, the leader events, and the belief that the company could be restarted. The customers were mostly gone. When the comp plan structure broke, the product alibi became visible in the valuation. $15 million for assets that had been valued in the billions was the market's answer to the question this chapter keeps asking.

The test is something narrower and more specific.

Is the compensation plan amplifying real customer demand, or is the compensation plan manufacturing the appearance of demand?

There is a massive difference between those two states, and the test that separates them is this:

If we removed qualification purchasing requirements tomorrow and let every distributor choose what they bought based solely on whether they wanted the product, would a meaningful percentage of current volume still be there? Would customers who have already been introduced to the product continue buying and referring friends? Would the product have pull in the market on its own merits, with the comp plan acting as the amplifier rather than the origin of the demand?

A fair objection is worth addressing directly. A CEO reading this might say, of course nobody would buy if I removed the entire field. The field is the marketing channel. They are the storytellers. Without distributors introducing the product, there are no customers. That objection is correct and important. The Smoke Detector Test isn't asking whether you should remove the field. The field is your distribution and storytelling engine, the same way Apple has retail stores and Nike has athletes and a beverage brand has shelf space at Costco. The test is asking a different question. It is asking whether the qualification pressure that the comp plan creates, the financial requirement to buy a certain volume each month to remain eligible for compensation, is doing the heavy lifting that the customer base should be doing. The field can keep introducing the product. The promoters can keep telling the story. The question is whether, once a customer has been introduced and tried the product, the customer keeps buying because they want it, or only because the comp plan structure makes the purchase mandatory for the distributor to remain qualified. Two different mechanisms. The first is amplification. The second is manufacturing. This is the resolution to the apparent contradiction raised at the start of the book. Real customers and an essential field aren't opposing ideas. The field introduces the product and tells the story. The customer foundation determines whether the story holds once the introduction is over. A company needs both, and the comp plan should be paying to amplify real demand rather than to manufacture the appearance of it.

If yes, you have a real product business. The comp plan is doing what it's supposed to do. It is accelerating adoption, rewarding the distributors who create the relationships that generate sales, and amplifying a product that has real merit. This is the ideal state. Everything in this chapter is about protecting and expanding it.

If no, you have a compensation business with a product alibi. The comp plan isn't amplifying demand. It is creating the illusion of demand. Revenue exists because the qualification structure requires purchases, not because customers independently want the product. This is the dangerous state. Everything in this chapter is about fixing it before the market, the regulators, or a competitor fixes it for you.

A strong product without a strong model goes nowhere. Every owner in this industry knows that. A strong model without a strong product eventually collapses. Every owner in this industry has seen that happen too. The companies that last are the ones where both are strong, and where the leadership team can tell with clarity which is carrying which at any given moment.

THREE CORRECTION LEVERS (act on these this quarter)

Lever 1: Build a preferred customer program that makes it easy for the field to acquire and retain customers. Give your distributors a simple, low-friction path to enroll customers who want the product but have no interest in the business opportunity. Track customer acquisition and retention as separate metrics from distributor enrollment. Set a target: 25% of new volume from customers who aren't in the comp plan within 12 months. The goal isn't to replace the field. The goal is to validate that the product has demand beyond the compensation plan and to give your distributors a tool that makes customer acquisition as rewarding as recruiting.

Lever 2: Decouple qualification from purchasing. Reduce or eliminate the personal volume required to earn commissions. Replace it with customer acquisition metrics. Pay distributors for acquiring and retaining customers, not for buying product themselves. Every dollar of qualification purchasing you remove from the system is a dollar of artificial volume you're replacing with real demand or exposing as hollow. Both outcomes are better than the status quo.

Lever 3: Measure your product's intrinsic demand. Ask your field leaders this question: if a customer's sponsor quit tomorrow, would the customer keep ordering? If the answer is yes for the majority of customers, your product has real demand. If the answer is no, your product is being carried by the relationship, not by its own merit. Both dynamics exist in every company. What matters is the ratio. Track customer reorder rates independent of distributor activity. That number tells you more about your product's real value than any focus group or market research study.

The first option is painful but survivable. The second one isn't.

Imagine a company that knows its ratio. Really knows it.

The CEO walks into a board meeting and says: 62% of our volume comes from real customers. 38% comes from distributors purchasing to qualify. Our retention rate on real customers is 74% annually. Our product has demand the comp plan is amplifying, not manufacturing. Two-thirds of our revenue is independent of the qualification structure.

That CEO is not guessing. She isn't telling a story. She is presenting a fact that her entire strategy can be built on.

When a leader leaves, she knows exactly how much volume walks out the door. It's the 38%, not the 62%. When a competitor launches a copycat product, she knows her customers are buying for reasons that go beyond opportunity economics. When the FTC calls, she has the data that Neora had. The data, not the hope that things will work out.

That company can take intelligent risks. It can invest in momentum drivers knowing that the foundation holds. It can recruit aggressively because every new distributor is adding to a machine that produces real customers, not just recycling the same volume through comp plan qualification.

That company is playing a different game than the one most of this industry is playing. And it's the only game that lasts.

Neora survived because 80% of its revenue was real. BurnLounge died because 97.7% of its revenue was artificial. Both were in direct selling. Both had products. Both had compensation plans. Both recruited distributors.

One was a product business with direct selling distribution.

The other was a direct selling company with a product alibi.

The data doesn't care which one you think you are. It only cares which one you actually are.

A PAIRWISE COMPARISON: MONAVIE AND FOREVER LIVING

Both companies built businesses around health-positioned consumable products. Both reached substantial scale. Both had strong international operations. The outcomes diverged on a structural variable that matters in this book: how aggressively the comp plan rewarded enrollment volume versus measured customer-base building.

MonaVie launched in 2005 around a premium acai-blend juice. Revenue grew explosively, peaking at $854 million by 2008. The company added market expansion, leader migration from Amway, and aggressive comp plan acceleration. Three drivers stacked. Revenue scaled fast. By 2015, the company defaulted on a $182 million note. Jeunesse purchased the underlying asset for $15 million. A company that had peaked near a billion dollars in revenue was worth $15 million at the end. The market answered the durability question with brutal precision.

Forever Living was founded in 1978 around aloe vera as the anchor product. The company never produced the kind of explosive single-year revenue growth that MonaVie did. It compounded across decades, eventually operating in over 160 countries with peak revenue exceeding $1.7 billion. The comp plan was less aggressive on the enrollment side than MonaVie's, which produced slower growth and longer operational durability. The company built across nearly fifty years rather than collapsing inside ten. That is the comparison this section is making.

But the durability comparison shouldn't be confused with a verdict on the customer foundation. Forever Living concluded its US recruiting operations in April 2026, citing in the company's own words unmanageable regulatory exposure under the evolving US regulatory environment. A company with a deeply protective real customer foundation doesn't typically need to wind down a recruiting model under regulatory pressure. The structural lesson is that Forever Living's measured comp plan produced longer operational durability than MonaVie's aggressive one. It doesn't prove that Forever Living's customer architecture was as deep as the durability comparison might imply.

The lesson is the comp plan structure, not the product. A measured comp plan that doesn't lean heavily on enrollment-driven volume produces a longer runway and slower compounding, even when the underlying customer foundation isn't as protective as the surviving years suggest. An aggressive comp plan that pays handsomely on enrollment volume produces a faster spike and a harder crash. Both companies had real products with real consumers who liked them. The variable that produced different durability outcomes was how each company's comp plan and field activity converted product into revenue. The companies in this dataset that have built the deepest customer foundations, Melaleuca being the clearest example, have measured comp plans plus customer-acquisition systems that the comp plan supports rather than substitutes for. Forever Living had the comp plan half of that equation. The customer-acquisition half is harder to assess from the outside.

The next chapter introduces the first and most universal driver of momentum in this industry: Product-Culture Fit. What you're about to learn is how the companies that achieved the most explosive growth in history did it by inserting their product into a cultural conversation that was already happening. But now you have the lens from this chapter. Product-culture fit without real customer demand is just a louder version of the alibi. The wave carries you up faster, and the crash brings you down harder.

THE BOTTOM LINE: Run the Smoke Detector Test. If you removed qualification purchasing tomorrow, what percentage of your volume would come from customers who actually wanted the product? That percentage is what your model is amplifying. Everything above it's what your model is manufacturing.

A real business uses the direct selling model to amplify real demand. A product alibi uses the direct selling model to manufacture the appearance of demand. Same model. Different underlying reality. Know which one you're running.

Part II: The Five Drivers

Chapter 6: Product-Culture Fit

Nobody had to convince women to wear yoga pants to the grocery store. That was the market telling you something.

The enemy in this chapter: riding a wave you mistook for a foundation.

In 1998, Chip Wilson attended a yoga class in Vancouver and hated what he was wearing. The available athletic clothing was designed for men or adapted poorly for women. Cotton fabrics absorbed sweat. Nothing stretched right. Nothing looked good. Wilson had spent years in the technical surf and snowboard apparel business, and he recognized a gap that was less about fabric and more about timing.

Yoga was crossing over. What had been a niche practice for a specific subculture was becoming a mainstream wellness activity, particularly among affluent, health-conscious women in urban areas. The cultural shift was already in motion. Women weren't just exercising differently. They were rethinking what wellness meant, how they wanted to feel in their bodies, and what they wanted their clothing to communicate about their identity.

Wilson founded Lululemon in a yoga studio that doubled as a design space. The first product was a pair of black stretchy pants made from a technical fabric that felt like cotton but performed like athletic wear. The pants were flattering. They were functional. And they arrived at the exact moment a massive cultural wave was forming.

Lululemon didn't create the yoga trend. It didn't create the wellness movement. It didn't create athleisure. It inserted itself into a cultural conversation that was already accelerating and gave it a physical product to wear.

Revenue was $5.9 million in 2002. By 2007, it was large enough to go public, raising $327 million in its IPO. By 2021, revenue exceeded $5.9 billion. Lululemon stock has grown roughly 13-fold since its IPO. The company effectively created a new category of clothing that didn't exist before and then rode the cultural wave of athleisure from niche to ubiquity. Sports-inspired apparel nearly doubled in market size between 2011 and

2021. Merriam-Webster added "athleisure" to the dictionary in 2016. That is how deeply the cultural shift penetrated.

The lesson isn't that Chip Wilson was a genius. He was talented. He saw the gap. But the genius was in the timing, not the vision. If Lululemon had launched in 1988 instead of 1998, the yoga movement wasn't big enough. If it had launched in 2008, the wave was already crowded. The product hit the cultural moment with near-perfect precision.

That is product-culture fit. And it's the most universal driver of momentum in direct selling.

The mechanism works like this.

When millions of people are already talking about a topic, already searching for solutions, already building an identity around a lifestyle, a product that embodies that conversation spreads through networks with almost no friction. The distributor isn't pushing against consumer skepticism. She is riding a wave of pre-existing desire. She is sharing something the culture has already validated. The product doesn't need to be explained. It needs to be offered.

This is fundamentally different from selling a product that requires education. If your product needs a 20-minute explanation of why someone should care, you're pushing uphill. If your product is the answer to a question the culture is already asking, you're running downhill. The speed difference isn't incremental. It is exponential.

Product-culture fit lowers the friction of every single conversation in the field. It makes the distributor more credible because the culture is backing her up. It makes the product more shareable because consumers are already primed for it. It makes recruiting easier because the story writes itself. "I found this thing that everyone is looking for" is a more powerful message than "I found this thing and let me tell you why you should care."

Nearly every hyper-growth story in direct selling history starts here. Not all of them. But the vast majority. The product caught a cultural wave.

doTERRA, whose growth trajectory we documented in Chapter 3, launched in 2008 as essential oils crossed from niche wellness circles into mainstream consumer consciousness. The clean living movement was accelerating. Consumers were questioning synthetic chemicals in their homes, their personal care products, their medicine cabinets. Essential oils became cultural shorthand for a natural, intentional lifestyle. The company inserted itself into the center of that conversation and rode it from startup to over $2 billion across sixteen years. By 2024, the essential oils direct selling channel had captured nearly 47% of total essential oil revenue. The category leaders didn't create the wellness trend. They positioned themselves inside it at the right time.

What made the fit particularly durable was the breadth of the product category. Essential oils aren't a single-use product. They serve aromatherapy, cleaning, personal care, emotional wellness, and dozens of other applications. A customer who starts with lavender oil for sleep might expand into peppermint for headaches, lemon for cleaning, and frankincense for skincare. The product line grows with the customer's interest. That breadth created a retention dynamic that single-product companies never achieve. The customer doesn't buy once and leave. She goes deeper into the category over time.

MonaVie launched in 2005 as the superfood craze was at full roar. Oprah featured acai. Dr. Oz promoted antioxidants. Health food stores couldn't keep acai products in stock. MonaVie's premium acai juice blend rode the wave to $854 million in annual revenue by 2008. The product-culture fit was so strong that distributors barely had to sell. They were sharing something the culture already wanted.

But MonaVie's product-culture fit had a fatal flaw. It was anchored to a single ingredient in a single product format. Acai juice. One bottle. One story. When the cultural conversation moved on, when acai became available at every grocery store for a fraction of MonaVie's price, when MonaVie's own chief science officer Ralph Carson, who had helped develop the juice, described it in an internal memo as "expensive flavored water," the story evaporated. There was no depth to the product category. No adjacent use cases. No reason for a customer to stay once the novelty faded. The cultural wave gave MonaVie its start. The lack of product depth ensured it couldn't survive the wave's peak.

LuLaRoe is the most complex product-culture fit story in the dataset. The company launched in 2013 as athleisure was going fully mainstream. Lululemon had spent a decade training women across North America to wear stretchy pants as everyday clothing, and the trend had spread to most developed markets. The cultural permission structure was already in place. What LuLaRoe added was accessibility. Lululemon sold $100 yoga pants in upscale retail locations. LuLaRoe sold $25 leggings through Facebook parties. The product was affordable. The patterns were unique. The limited-edition model created scarcity and collector psychology. Women weren't buying leggings. They were hunting "unicorns," the rare patterns that became status symbols within the community.

Revenue went from $9.8 million in 2014 to approximately $2.3 billion in 2017. That is product-culture fit operating at maximum velocity, amplified by a platform driver (Facebook Live, which we'll cover in the next chapter) and a compensation architecture that required $5,000 to $9,000 in upfront inventory purchases.

But LuLaRoe's product-culture fit contained its own destruction mechanism. Fashion is cyclical. Trends move fast. And LuLaRoe's model required consultants to purchase inventory blind, receiving randomly assorted patterns they couldn't choose. When the legging trend peaked, when quality issues emerged (the infamous "buttery soft" fabric started tearing), when 80,000 consultants were all selling the same product in overlapping social networks and the field's credibility eroded, the product-culture fit didn't just fade. It inverted. The same social media that had amplified the brand now amplified the complaints. Facebook groups dedicated to LuLaRoe selling transformed into groups dedicated to GOOB (Going Out Of Business) sales. The cultural conversation shifted from "where can I find those leggings" to "those leggings are falling apart."

Product-culture fit gave LuLaRoe four years of explosive growth. The lack of product depth, combined with quality failures and fashion-cycle risk, ensured that the crash was as dramatic as the rise.

Plexus caught the gut health wave with its "Pink Drink" and grew 2,833% from 2012 to 2015. Rodan+Fields caught the selfie-era skincare obsession and reached a reported $1.5 billion by 2017. Monat caught the anti-aging hair care trend and grew 860% from 2016 to 2019.

In every case, the company didn't create the cultural trend. The trend was already building. The company created a product that fit the trend. And then the direct selling distribution model amplified the fit through thousands of personal conversations happening simultaneously.

That amplification is what makes product-culture fit so powerful specifically in direct selling. A traditional retail brand can catch a cultural wave too. Lululemon did. But a direct selling company catches the wave and then puts ten thousand surfers on it at the same time. Each distributor is a node in a network, and when every node is sharing a product that the culture already wants, the compounding effect is massive.

The equal and opposite is brutal. And it's brutal.

Product-culture fit without real customer depth is the most dangerous kind of momentum in the industry.

Because the growth feels so natural, so organic, so obviously right, the leadership team concludes that the product is the engine. "People love our product." "The product sells itself." "We have the best product in the category." And in the moment, they're partially correct. People do love the product. It does sell more easily. It might even be the best in the category.

But the product is riding a wave. And waves break.

The superfruit graveyard documented in Chapter 5 is the purest proof. Every superfruit juice company in the 53-company dataset is dead. Combined peak revenues exceeded $2 billion. Combined current value: approximately zero. They had product-culture fit. It was real. But it was fit with a cultural moment, not fit with a durable need. When the moment passed and acai showed up at Costco, the fit evaporated.

MonaVie is the most instructive case. At peak, the company was generating $854 million annually. The acai story was compelling. The branding was premium. The field believed in the product passionately. But the actual momentum equation involved three drivers: product-culture fit, leader migration, and aggressive compensation architecture. The product-culture fit created the story. The other two drivers created the velocity. When the cultural moment faded and the product's scientific credibility was publicly questioned, the story collapsed. And because the other two drivers were borrowed rather than owned, there was nothing underneath.

The company that rode the same wellness mega-trend but survived, doTERRA, did something fundamentally different. Essential oils weren't a single-ingredient fad. The product category was broad. It served multiple use cases: aromatherapy, cleaning, personal care, wellness support. The cultural conversation around essential oils was deeper and more durable than the superfood craze because it connected to an entire lifestyle identity, not just a single health claim. And crucially, the company built real customer depth. Over 10 million customers by 2024. Not all of those customers are active at any given time. But the breadth of the customer base meant that even as the essential oils trend matured and Amazon availability eroded the premium, the foundation held.

Product-culture fit gave both companies their start. The difference in outcome was determined by what they built underneath it.

Right now, in real time, the most dramatic product-culture fit collapse in industry history is unfolding.

GLP-1 receptor agonist drugs are rewriting the weight management category. We covered the revenue impact in Chapter 4. Medifast dropped 76% from peak. Herbalife's stock cratered before beginning a partial recovery as the company adapted. This is the first systemic category disruption in the history of direct selling, where an external technology simultaneously threatens multiple billion-dollar companies.

But for this chapter, the mechanism matters more than the revenue numbers.

GLP-1 drugs didn't just create a competing product. They changed the cultural conversation. Weight management through meal replacement shakes, challenge programs, and coaching models was a product-culture fit that lasted for decades. The cultural assumption was: losing weight requires discipline, accountability, special foods, and sustained behavioral change. That assumption made the direct selling model a natural fit. The distributor was the accountability partner. The shake was the tool. The 90-day challenge was the framework.

Pruvit caught the keto wave with its ketone supplement line and grew rapidly as the ketogenic diet became one of the most searched health topics on the internet. The product-culture fit was real: millions of consumers were already experimenting with keto, and a supplement that promised to put your body into ketosis without the strict dietary requirements was an easy conversation for the field. The question for Pruvit, as for every company that catches a cultural wave, is whether the product creates a durable need that outlasts the trend or whether it remains tied to the wave's lifecycle.

GLP-1 drugs replaced the cultural assumption. The new assumption is: losing weight is a medical issue with a pharmaceutical solution. You don't need a coach. You don't need a shake. You need a prescription.

When the culture shifts, the product-culture fit dissolves. The product didn't stop working. Shakes still work for weight management. But the cultural conversation moved. The consumer who would have searched for "best meal replacement shakes" in 2020 is now searching for "Ozempic eligibility" in 2025. The distributor who would have said "let me tell you about our 90-day challenge" now faces a prospect who says "my doctor put me on Wegovy."

The product didn't fail. The culture left.

This is what makes product-culture fit both the most powerful momentum driver and the most dangerous dependency. When you have it, everything accelerates. When you lose it, nothing the company does internally can substitute for the external tailwind that disappeared.

Inside the mastermind community, I get to see how product-culture fit operates at the ground level, in the daily conversations of the people actually building.

The difference between a company that has product-culture fit and one that doesn't is visible in one metric that nobody tracks formally but every field leader feels: the ratio of inbound to outbound conversations.

When a company has product-culture fit, the field reports that people are coming to them. "My friend asked ME about it." "She saw my post and messaged ME." "He heard about it from someone else and found me." The conversations are inbound. The culture is doing the prospecting. The distributor is simply present and available.

When a company doesn't have product-culture fit, the field is doing all the work. Cold outreach. Follow-ups. Explanations. Overcoming objections. Convincing people to try something they didn't know they wanted. It is effortful. It is slow. And it produces a completely different growth trajectory.

I've seen leaders build successfully in both environments. The best networkers in the world can build without product-culture fit. They create their own conversations. They generate their own demand through sheer skill and work ethic. But the leaders who built the biggest organizations in the fastest time almost always did it inside companies that had product-culture fit. The cultural tailwind multiplied their effort. Instead of pushing against indifference, they were channeling existing desire.

The warning I always give is this: do not confuse the tailwind with your skill. If you're building inside a company that has product-culture fit, a meaningful portion of your success is attributable to the wave, not your surfing. That isn't an insult. It is a strategic reality. The moment you believe you're the wave rather than riding the wave, you'll make decisions that assume the tailwind is permanent. It isn't. Every cultural wave has a lifecycle. Whether the wave will peak isn't the open question. Whether you've built something real underneath it before it does is.

I watched this play out with weight management companies in the community starting in 2023. Leaders who had built massive organizations on shake-based challenge programs started seeing their customer acquisition slow. Not their recruiting. Their customer acquisition. The people who used to say "yes, I want to do your 90-day challenge" were now saying "actually, my doctor is talking to me about Ozempic." The cultural conversation was shifting underneath them in real time.

The leaders who had built deep customer relationships, who had customers buying product for reasons beyond weight loss, who had diversified their personal brands beyond a single product category, those leaders adapted. Their income dipped but didn't collapse. The leaders who had built entirely on the weight loss challenge narrative, whose entire customer base was motivated by a single use case that was now being disrupted by a pharmaceutical, those leaders watched their businesses dissolve in months. Same company. Same product. Same comp plan. Completely different outcomes based on how deep the customer foundation went.

Product-culture fit is a gift. But gifts can make you lazy if you're not careful. The field leaders who treat the tailwind as temporary and build real customer depth during the good years are the ones who survive when the wind shifts.

There is a flip side to this shadow that deserves attention.

Some companies look at the product-culture fit data and conclude that they need to chase trends. Every new cultural wave becomes an opportunity to launch a product. Gut health is trending? Launch a probiotic. Keto is trending? Launch a ketone supplement. CBD is trending? Launch a tincture.

Trend-chasing is the opposite of product-culture fit. Product-culture fit means your product authentically embodies a cultural conversation because it was designed for that purpose from the beginning. Trend-chasing means you're grafting a trending ingredient onto an existing platform to capture short-term attention. The field can tell the difference. Consumers can tell the difference. And the lifecycle of a trend-chased product is dramatically shorter than a product that was built from genuine conviction.

The companies that achieve durable product-culture fit share a common trait. The founders deeply believe in the product category. They aren't chasing a trend. They are building inside a space they care about. doTERRA's founding team were essential oils industry veterans before they launched the company. Their conviction about the product category was authentic. That authenticity transmitted through the field and made the product story credible.

Companies that chase trends without authentic conviction produce products that sell during the trend and die when it passes. Companies that build from authentic conviction inside a growing cultural space produce products that can outlast the trend's peak because the product serves a real need even after the cultural wave matures.

There is a meaningful difference between trend-chasing and strategic repositioning, and the difference deserves to be named directly. A company can legitimately decide to switch product categories, reposition its core offering, or commit to a new strategic direction. Pivots aren't always trend-chasing. The variable that separates a real pivot from a trend-chase is the level of commitment the leadership team brings to the decision.

If a leadership team is going to switch the product line, reposition the company, or commit to a new strategic direction, the keyword is commitment. Make sure the decision was made after a full review of the company, the culture, the customer base, the field, the operations, and the financial reality. Make sure every relevant input was on the table before the decision was finalized. Then, once the decision is made, commit to it for longer than one or two years. The level of commitment will determine the level of success more than almost any other input. It is hard enough to make anything work when the leadership team is fully committed. When the leadership team is half-committed, success becomes nearly impossible unless luck intervenes, and luck-based success is short-lived. The companies that have successfully repositioned in this industry made the decision once, committed to it for a multi-year window, and absorbed the short-term cost of the transition as part of the strategy. The companies that try a pivot for twelve months and quietly retreat when the numbers don't respond fast enough end up worse off than if they had never pivoted at all, because they've signaled both directions and committed to neither.

Vida Divina offers a modern, post-2016 case of multi-driver momentum built on authentic product-culture fit. Launched in September 2016 by Armand Puyolt, a former Total Life Changes master distributor, the company focused on wellness teas, mushroom coffees, and supplements with strong cultural resonance in Latin American and Hispanic markets. The company has reported significant year-over-year growth and made strategic acquisitions of MIALÉ in Peru and Radien skincare to diversify the product line. The migration of experienced leaders like Ada Caballero created the classic cascade effect documented in the Leader Migration chapter. Specific annual revenue figures for Vida Divina haven't been independently verified through CPA or CFO attestation and aren't cited here on that basis. The structural lesson doesn't require precise revenue numbers. The pattern of leader migration plus authentic cultural positioning is the teaching point.

The momentum was driven by three drivers in alignment: product-culture fit in wellness within a culturally tight community, founder credibility built across decades in the profession, and leader migration from established organizations.

What makes Vida Divina's product-culture fit instructive is the specificity. "Vida Divina" means "Divine Life" in Spanish. The annual convention, called Imparables ("Unstoppable"), is conducted entirely in Spanish. The founder's cancer survival narrative, his Mexican immigrant background, and his conviction about the traditional herbal ingredients he credits with his recovery created a brand that felt indigenous to the Hispanic community rather than marketed to it. As Puyolt told Direct Selling News: "I think it's drawn more people because they feel at home. They feel like they're important instead of feeling second rate anywhere else."

Vida Divina made the Hispanic community the center of the brand, not the periphery. The product-culture fit was cultural identity, not ingredient lists. And during COVID, when restaurants closed and Hispanic service workers lost livelihoods overnight, Vida Divina reportedly quadrupled in size within the Hispanic market. The growth didn't come from a digital strategy. It came because economic desperation within a community that already knew the brand created organic distribution at a scale no algorithm could match.

The company has faced the regulatory scrutiny that every company in momentum eventually faces, including TINA.org and DSSRC decisions on health and income claims and an FTC Notice of Penalty Offenses in 2023. No enforcement action or shutdown has occurred. Vida Divina remains active. The question for every company at this stage is the same: is the customer floor deep enough to sustain the business when the initial driver alignment matures?

What the field says about product-culture fit from the inside is this. In the survey of 82 top earners, when asked what would make them more likely to personally sponsor again, the number one answer was a clear, compelling vision for the next five years at 46%. Only 24% said "a product I'm excited to share." That doesn't mean they dislike their current product. It means that for the majority of experienced builders, the product alone isn't the barrier to re-engagement. They need to believe in where the company is going. But for the quarter who did cite product excitement, the message is clear: product-culture fit isn't a one-time achievement. It erodes. And when it erodes in the field, no amount of vision-casting compensates for a product the field no longer feels compelled to share.

Apply this now.

A PAIRWISE COMPARISON: DOTERRA AND YOUNG LIVING

Both companies sold essential oils. Both rode the same cultural wave. Both built large multi-million-customer fields. Both peaked in roughly the same era. The outcomes diverged dramatically.

Young Living was co-founded by D. Gary Young and Mary Young in 1993, with the company incorporated in 1994. Young Living built the modern direct-to-consumer essential oils category over the following decade and a half. In 2008, several former Young Living executives, including David Stirling and David Hill, co-founded doTERRA, which entered the same category with a different sourcing model and compensation architecture. Both companies grew through the 2010s, with Young Living reporting over a billion dollars in annual revenue from 2015 onward and doTERRA also crossing the billion-dollar threshold during the same window. By the early 2020s, doTERRA had grown to a larger annual revenue figure than Young Living, with doTERRA reaching a reported two billion dollars in annual sales by 2024 and Young Living's growth compressing relative to its peak years.

Same category. Same cultural tailwind. Same fundamental product. Different outcomes. The category alone didn't produce the divergence. Two companies riding the same cultural wave produced two different long-term trajectories, which means the variable separating them was something other than the wave itself. That something is the architecture underneath each company's growth, which is what this chapter and the chapters that follow examine in depth across the dataset. The pattern repeats across other categories. Two companies in the same wave can produce sharply different outcomes, and the difference is almost always in the foundation each company built underneath the cultural moment.

This isn't a story of one perfect company and one troubled one. Every great company faces challenges. Challenges are inevitable at scale, and the strongest companies in any industry move through rounds of them. doTERRA is no exception. It expanded internationally earlier than Young Living, and that broader base helped its revenue hold up better as the category matured, but it has worked through its own difficult chapters along the way, including workforce reductions and a leadership transition that brought co-founder David Stirling back as CEO. None of that diminishes what doTERRA built. It simply confirms that durability isn't the absence of challenge. It is the ability to keep building through it. The point of the comparison isn't that one company succeeded and the other failed. Both built large, real businesses, and both earned their place in this analysis. The point is that two companies in the same category with the same cultural tailwind produced different long-term trajectories, and the variable that separated them was the structure each built underneath the growth, not the wave they both rode.

THE PRODUCT-CULTURE FIT ASSESSMENT

This diagnostic has two parts: a fit evaluation and a vulnerability scan. Both matter.

Part 1: Fit Evaluation

Question 1: Is your product category growing in the broader culture, independent of your company?

Search Google Trends. Read market research. Look at retail shelf space. Is the category itself expanding? Are mainstream retailers adding products in your space? Are mainstream media outlets publishing content about your product category? If the answer is yes, you have cultural tailwind. If the answer is no, you're creating demand rather than capturing it.

Question 2: When your distributors share the product, do prospects already know what it is?

If the prospect says "oh, I've been hearing about that" or "my friend uses something like this," you have cultural pre-awareness. The culture has done the education for you. If the prospect says "what is that?" or "why would I need that?" you're starting from zero. Both can work. But the growth trajectories are fundamentally different.

Question 3: Is inbound interest increasing over time?

The vast majority of customers in direct selling are generated by the field. That is how the model works. The test isn't whether prospects magically appear without effort. The test is whether the product itself creates enough pull that a meaningful and growing percentage of conversations begin with the prospect already interested. "My friend told me about this." "I saw someone using it and asked what it was." "I've been hearing about this." If your field leaders are reporting that these conversations are increasing over time, your product-culture fit is strengthening. If every conversation still requires a cold approach with zero prior awareness, the field is carrying the entire load and the product isn't pulling its weight in the culture.

Question 4: Does your product serve a single trend or a durable need?

Acai was a trend. Weight management is a durable need. Essential oils serve multiple durable needs. Leggings serve a durable need but specific patterns are a trend. The more your product anchors to a durable need rather than a passing trend, the longer your product-culture fit window stays open.

Part 2: Vulnerability Scan

Question 5: Is your product category facing competitive pressure from retail or digital channels?

Almost every product category faces some version of this. Products can be copied. Whether retail alternatives exist isn't the test. What you offer that the retail alternative can't replicate is. Community. Coaching. Accountability. Education. Personal relationships. A system that helps people get results rather than just selling them a product. If your company has built a strong community and a differentiated experience around the product, the retail alternative isn't a direct substitute even when the ingredients are similar. If your company hasn't built those things, the retail price advantage will win over time.

Question 6: Are external forces changing your consumer's relationship with your product category?

GLP-1 drugs shifted consumer behavior in weight management. That isn't a judgment on the drugs. It is an observation that external forces can rapidly shift demand regardless of what anyone inside the company believes about their product. The question for every company: is there an external force, whether pharmaceutical, technological, or regulatory, that could fundamentally change how consumers think about your product category? If yes, how are you adapting? The companies that see these shifts early and evolve their product line or value proposition accordingly survive them. The companies that deny the shift or wait for it to pass don't.

Question 7: What does your product category's history tell you?

Check the data in Chapter 5. Some categories have proven extremely difficult to sustain at scale. Others have shown remarkable durability. Your category's history doesn't determine your company's future, but it tells you where the risks are and how much margin for error you have. If you're in a category with a difficult history, you need stronger customer ratios, better differentiation, and deeper community than a company in a category with a more favorable track record. Harder doesn't mean impossible. It means the execution standard is higher.

Scoring:

Strong fit + low vulnerability = you have one of the most powerful momentum drivers working for you. Invest in it. Build customer depth underneath it before the wave matures.

Strong fit + high vulnerability = you have a window. The growth is real right now, but the structural risks are material. Build fast, but build real customer depth while you have the tailwind.

Weak fit + low vulnerability = you have a stable but slow business. Growth will come from other drivers (platform, leaders, compensation, international), not from cultural tailwind.

Weak fit + high vulnerability = this is the worst position. The culture isn't helping you, and external forces are threatening you. This company needs a fundamental strategic review.

Picture an executive team that understands exactly where their product sits in the cultural cycle.

They know their product category is growing. They know their fit is strong. They also know that their category has a historical survival rate of 50% and that retail alternatives are multiplying. So they're not complacent. They are building customer depth while the tailwind lasts. They are diversifying their product line to anchor in durable needs rather than trending ingredients. They are tracking the vulnerability scan quarterly and watching for early signals that the wave is maturing.

When the wave does mature, and every wave does, they're not surprised. They aren't scrambling. They have customers who buy because they love the product, not because the culture told them to. They have a product line that serves needs beyond the original trend. They have a field that knows how to sell without cultural tailwind because they were trained for it before they needed to be.

That company turns a temporary advantage into a permanent foundation. That is what product-culture fit is supposed to build. Not dependency on the wave. Infrastructure underneath it.

The next chapter covers the second momentum driver: Platform Disruption. What you're about to learn is that the way your field reaches customers matters as much as what they're selling. And the platforms that built the biggest direct selling companies of the last decade are the same platforms that are now threatening to make the model obsolete.

THE BOTTOM LINE: Product-culture fit is the most universal momentum driver but it has an expiration date. Evaluate whether your product is riding a trend or anchored in a durable need. Build customer depth while the cultural tailwind lasts.

You don't create the wave. You catch it. What you build while you're riding it's what determines whether you survive it.

Chapter 7: Platform Disruption

Every major era of direct selling growth started when someone figured out a new way to reach people. Every major era ended when the platform changed the rules.

The enemy in this chapter: platform dependence disguised as strategy. This isn't an argument against social selling. It is an argument against dependency. Platforms can accelerate momentum. But borrowed distribution isn't the same as owned demand.

In the mid-1940s, a woman named Brownie Wise had an insight that would define an entire industry for the next seventy years.

Tupperware's products were sold in retail stores. They weren't selling well. The plastic containers were innovative but consumers didn't understand how the seals worked. They sat on shelves and gathered dust. Earl Tupper had a product without a distribution method.

Wise, a single mother in Florida who had been selling Stanley Home Products through in-home demonstrations, recognized that Tupperware needed to be experienced, not displayed. The seal needed to be demonstrated. The "burp" of the lid needed to be heard. You had to put the container in someone's hands.

She invented the Tupperware party.

The concept was radically simple. A hostess invites friends to her home. A Tupperware dealer demonstrates the products in the kitchen. People try the seal. They feel the quality. They buy. The hostess earns free products for hosting. The dealer earns commission. Tupperware gets a sale that could never have happened on a retail shelf.

Within two years of Wise taking over distribution, Tupperware pulled its products from all retail stores. The party plan became the exclusive channel. Revenue exploded. By the 1950s, a Tupperware party was reportedly starting somewhere in the world every 2.5 seconds. Wise appeared on the cover of Business Week, the first woman ever to do so.

The Tupperware party wasn't a sales technique. It was a platform. It combined postwar suburbia (women at home, new neighborhoods, social networks built around kitchen tables), the automobile (dealers could drive to houses), and the cultural role of the hostess (entertaining was a social expectation) into a distribution channel that was perfectly engineered for its era.

That platform lasted for decades. It built a multi-billion-dollar global company. And its mechanics were eventually replicated by hundreds of direct selling companies, from Mary Kay to Pampered Chef to Thirty-One Gifts.

But the lesson that matters for this chapter is this. The Tupperware party worked because it exploited a specific set of conditions. Suburban housewives. Limited mobility. Face-to-face social networks. A culture of home entertaining. When those conditions changed, when women entered the workforce, when social networks moved online, when home entertaining declined, the platform stopped working. Tupperware's decline didn't start with a product failure. It started with the erosion of the conditions that made the party plan possible.

The platform gave Tupperware its momentum. The platform's expiration took it away.

The mechanism that makes platform disruption the most powerful amplifier in direct selling.

New platforms temporarily eliminate competition by rewarding early adopters with outsized, disproportionate reach. The first companies to build systems around a new platform gain an asymmetric advantage. They reach more people, faster, at lower cost, than anyone using the previous platform. This advantage lasts until the platform matures, algorithms shift, competitors catch up, or a newer platform emerges.

The window is typically three to five years. Sometimes less.

Inside that window, the growth is extraordinary. Outside it, the advantage disappears. And companies that built their entire operation around a single platform's mechanics discover, painfully, that the platform owes them nothing.

Facebook's evolution is the single cleanest case study for this pattern. Three distinct waves of direct selling momentum mapped directly to

Facebook's platform changes, and each wave created billion-dollar companies before the window closed.

Wave one: the Facebook virtual party. Younique, founded in 2012, was the first major direct selling company to market and sell almost exclusively through social media. The company replaced the in-home Tupperware party with a Facebook party. The mechanics were adapted but the social dynamic was preserved: a hostess invites friends, a presenter demonstrates products, orders are placed in real time. Except now the "living room" was a Facebook group, and the friends didn't need to live in the same zip code.

The results were staggering. Younique went from 100 units per day at its July 2013 launch to over 10,000 units per day by July 2014. Revenue reached approximately $400 million. In 2017, cosmetics giant Coty acquired a 60% stake, valuing the company at $1 billion. Younique didn't just use Facebook. It reinvented what a "party" meant in direct selling by removing geographic constraints entirely.

Then Facebook's algorithm changed. Organic reach declined. Group engagement shifted. The mechanics that had made the virtual party explosive became less effective. Coty eventually sold its stake back, with reporting citing "decreased hype" around the brand. The platform gave. The platform took.

Wave two: Facebook Live. LuLaRoe existed before Facebook Live launched in 2015, but its trajectory changed overnight once consultants could broadcast their inventory in real time. Viewers watched live and commented "SOLD" on screen. The limited-edition pattern model turned each broadcast into an event. Scarcity created urgency. The 5,000-per-pattern production limit meant every livestream was a hunt for "unicorns," rare patterns that became collector items.

Revenue leapt roughly 20 times in a single year. From approximately $70 million in late 2015 to an estimated $1.3 to $1.8 billion in 2016. It is a detonation, not growth. Facebook Live didn't just help LuLaRoe sell leggings. It created an entirely new selling behavior that had never existed before: live-broadcast commerce where the transaction happened inside the social interaction.

SeneGence's LipSense products surged on the same platform, with the company reportedly reaching nearly $1 billion by 2018. Multiple beauty and accessories companies rode the Facebook Live wave to rapid growth.

But the Facebook Live window closed too. The algorithm deprioritized live commerce. Consumer behavior shifted. The novelty wore off. And the companies that had built their entire field system around going live three times a week suddenly had to figure out how to sell without the platform's organic amplification.

Wave three: Instagram and the visual economy. Rodan+Fields made the most deliberate platform bet of any company in this chapter. The founders, both dermatologists who had previously created Proactiv, explicitly designed their social selling model around smartphone culture. They printed camera icons on product packaging to encourage before-and-after photos. They built their entire customer acquisition strategy around the idea that skincare results are visual and that visual social platforms would turn every customer into a walking advertisement.

CEO Diane Dietz noted that "everything in Rodan+Fields is run on your smartphone." That wasn't marketing language. It was the operating model. The company was designed from the ground up to exploit Instagram's visual discovery mechanics.

Revenue grew from approximately $10 million to $1.5 billion over eight years. A 150-times increase powered by one platform insight about how consumers discover and share skincare experiences. At peak, Rodan+Fields was reported as the number one premium skincare brand in North America by revenue, surpassing premium brands with decades more history and far larger advertising budgets.

Then the conditions that had built the business started working against it, and platform shift was only one of them. Instagram's algorithm evolved and organic reach for network marketers declined. TikTok emerged as the dominant short-form video platform, with discovery mechanics that favored individual content creators over product-sharing consultants. But the platform change was only the accelerant on a fire that had several other sources of ignition burning at the same time. The skincare category itself was shifting underneath the business. Direct-to-consumer brands like The Ordinary and Glossier reached younger consumers with transparent ingredient stories at substantially lower price points, repositioning premium direct selling skincare as overpriced to a generation that researched formulations before they bought. Sephora and other retailers used TikTok and influencer partnerships to reach the same consumers at a fraction of the distribution cost. Consultant markets had saturated across North America, making it harder for new recruits to build sustainable businesses and eroding morale across the field. Private equity had taken a minority stake at a $4 billion valuation in 2018, adding a returns clock that the revenue trajectory eventually couldn't satisfy. In April 2020, the FTC issued a warning letter about COVID-related earnings claims. A class action related to one of the flagship products surfaced in 2022. The compound was brutal. Each factor on its own would have been survivable. The combination wasn't.

Rodan+Fields' decline from the $1.5 billion peak was steady and relentless. The company eventually joined the model exit wave in 2024, transitioning from multi-level direct selling to an affiliate program. The platform window that had helped build the business had closed. But the platform was never the whole story. The category had shifted. The competition had repositioned. The regulatory environment had tightened. The field had saturated. And the financial structure behind the company needed growth that the combined headwinds would no longer allow. Any company that tries to explain the Rodan+Fields decline with a single cause is oversimplifying, and any company trying to prevent the same pattern needs to understand all of the variables, not just the platform one.

Three waves. Three sets of billion-dollar companies. Three platform windows that opened, created extraordinary momentum, and closed.

The equal and opposite of platform disruption is platform dependency. And it's one of the most dangerous structural vulnerabilities a direct selling company can have.

When a company builds its field systems, its training, its selling behaviors, and its customer acquisition strategy around a single platform, it becomes hostage to that platform's decisions. Algorithm changes. Policy updates. Feature deprecations. Advertising cost increases. Any of these can erode the foundation overnight without the company making a single mistake.

Younique's billion-dollar valuation was partially built on Facebook's organic reach. When that reach declined, the economics of the business changed. Younique hadn't done anything wrong. Facebook had decided to show fewer organic posts to non-paying pages.

LuLaRoe's explosive trajectory was inseparable from Facebook Live's initial rollout. When Live's prominence in the algorithm faded, the selling behavior that powered the company's growth became less effective. The company hadn't done anything wrong. The platform's priorities had shifted.

This dynamic creates a specific strategic tension. To capture a platform window, you must go all in. You must build systems around the platform. You must train your field to use it. You must optimize everything for the specific mechanics that make the platform work right now. Half-hearted platform adoption doesn't produce momentum. Commitment does.

But full commitment to a single platform creates the dependency that makes you fragile when the platform changes. The very thing that created the momentum becomes the thing that threatens it.

The companies that handle this well are the ones that exploit platform windows aggressively while simultaneously building platform-independent capabilities. They ride Facebook Live while also teaching their field how to sell in person. They dominate Instagram while also developing an email list and a customer database that they own. They go deep on one platform while maintaining the ability to pivot to the next one.

The companies that get destroyed are the ones that mistake the platform for the strategy. They assume TikTok will always work. They assume Instagram's algorithm will always favor their content. They build their entire business on rented land and are surprised when the landlord changes the lease.

And now the platforms are threatening something even more fundamental than individual companies. They are threatening the model itself.

In 2024 and 2025, a wave of companies exited the direct selling model entirely. These weren't failures. The platform landscape had simply made a different model more viable for them.

BODi, formerly Beachbody, announced in September 2024 that it would transition from direct selling to a single-level affiliate program effective November 1, 2024. Executive Chairman Mark Goldston's statement was remarkably blunt: "We recognize that in light of today's current market dynamics, as well as consumer preferences, the multi-level marketing distribution model is outdated and unsustainable."

That is a company with 26 years of history, over 30 million customers served, and iconic programs like P90X and Insanity, publicly declaring that the distribution model it had used for nearly two decades no longer works.

BODi wasn't alone. Rodan+Fields, which had peaked at $1.5 billion in revenue using the social selling model, announced its own transition away from direct selling. Beautycounter, which had built a brand around clean beauty and direct selling under a $1 billion Carlyle Group valuation, went into foreclosure in 2024. Founder Gregg Renfrew bought back the assets and relaunched in 2025 as Counter, a new entity built on an affiliate-style model rather than the original multi-level structure. Modere followed. Seint Makeup followed.

Five companies exiting direct selling in roughly the same twelve-month window. That isn't a coincidence. It is a pattern. And the pattern has a cause.

The cause is platform disruption at the structural level. When direct selling was the primary way to reach consumers through personal relationships, the direct selling model made sense. The distributor was the marketing channel. The comp plan funded the distribution. The multi-level structure incentivized network building that expanded reach geometrically.

But social media, DTC e-commerce, Amazon, TikTok Shop, and influencer marketing have created alternative distribution channels that reach the same consumers at lower cost. A company that once needed 50,000 distributors to generate $500 million in revenue can now potentially reach that revenue through digital marketing, affiliate programs, and retail partnerships at a fraction of the distribution cost.

The September 2024 restructuring step alone, transitioning from direct selling to affiliate and cutting 33% of staff, was projected to lower the company's revenue breakeven point from less than $430 million to less than $225 million in annual revenue. That single change transformed the company's financial model. The products could be priced competitively for the first time because the distribution cost had been removed.

That math is what every company owner reading this book should be paying attention to. Clayton Christensen's disruption theory predicted exactly this pattern: when a lower-cost alternative reaches "good enough" quality, the premium distribution model loses its economic rationale. Whether the direct selling model is "outdated" is the wrong question. For many companies, it remains the best distribution strategy because the product category requires education, demonstration, and personal trust that digital channels can't replicate. Essential oils. Skincare with complex routines. Wellness products that benefit from coaching and accountability.

But for product categories where the consumer can make a purchase decision without distributor involvement, where the product sells on its own merits through content, reviews, and digital marketing, the direct selling distribution cost becomes a competitive disadvantage. The 40 to 50% paid to the field can be redirected to lower pricing, digital advertising, and direct consumer acquisition.

The model exit wave isn't the death of direct selling. It is the market telling certain companies that their distribution model no longer matches their product's path to the consumer. The platform landscape has shifted. And companies that don't recognize the shift will watch their competitors reach the same customers at lower cost.

The top earners I work with in the community are watching this shift carefully. And they're adapting faster than many companies.

The smartest field leaders I know are no longer platform-dependent. They build audiences on social media, but they know the audience is rented. The platform owns the reach. The algorithm decides who sees what. The only thing a leader actually owns is her skill set and her relationships. If Instagram disappears tomorrow, can she have a conversation that leads to a sale through any channel available to her? Can she use AI tools and 24-hour chat to maintain customer relationships at scale? Can she walk into a room of strangers and start a relationship that leads to a customer? Can she reach out to someone she hasn't talked to in a year and restart a conversation without it feeling forced, whether that's through text, voice message, video, or a face-to-face meeting?

Those skills are platform-proof. They work on any platform. They work without a platform. And they're the skills that many companies stopped training during the social media boom because content creation was easier to teach and more fun to practice.

I watched a six-figure leader realize this the hard way. She had built her entire business on Instagram. Twelve thousand followers. Consistent content. Strong engagement. Then Instagram changed its algorithm in a single update and her reach dropped 70% overnight. She went from 30 inbound messages a week to 4. Her income dropped by half in 60 days. She hadn't lost her skills. She hadn't lost her product belief. She had lost her platform. And she had no backup because she had never learned to sell without it. She rebuilt. It took eight months. She now teaches her entire team: if you can't make a sale without your phone, you don't have a business. You have an algorithm rental.

The lesson isn't to avoid social media. The lesson is to never let social media become the only thing you know how to do.

Every few years, a new platform window opens in this industry and the conversation inside the field shifts to it. Facebook parties were the window for a stretch. Then it was Instagram posts. Then Facebook Live. Then Instagram Stories and Facebook Stories. Then Reels on both platforms. Then TikTok. Then TikTok Shop. By the time you're reading this, there's likely another platform or platform feature that the community is talking about with the same intensity that each of the previous ones commanded at their peak. The names change. The pattern doesn't. A new mechanic opens, a small number of leaders figure out how to exploit it before it becomes saturated, the field rushes in, the platform adjusts its algorithm or its monetization rules, and the window narrows. Then the next window opens somewhere else, and the cycle repeats.

I'll use TikTok Shop as the current example because it happens to be the platform creating the most conversation and the most anxiety in the community as this book goes to print. But the strategic teaching applies to whatever platform is dominating the conversation when you read this, because the mechanics repeat.

TikTok Shop, or its successor, represents both a platform opportunity and a model threat simultaneously. On the opportunity side, the algorithm is a powerful discovery engine. It surfaces content to people who have never followed you, never heard of your brand, never been in your network. For direct selling, that's enormous. The traditional model relies on warm-market networks. A strong discovery platform expands the market to cold audiences at scale.

But platforms that enable direct transactions also enable something that fundamentally threatens the distribution model: anyone can sell any product through a simple affiliate link. No distributor enrollment. No comp plan. No team building. Just content, a link, and a commission. The creator economy and the direct selling field are now competing for the same consumer attention using the same platforms, and the creator doesn't need to buy a starter kit or hit a monthly autoship to participate.

The leaders who are thriving on whatever the current platform is are the ones who understood this immediately. They use the platform for audience building and authority, but they convert that audience into customers through their company's systems, not through the platform's built-in checkout. They treat the platform as a top-of-funnel awareness tool, not a transaction platform. The ones who are struggling are the ones trying to compete with affiliate creators on price and convenience. That is a fight the direct selling model can't win because the distribution cost built into the price is higher than the affiliate commission creators earn.

This is platform disruption happening in real time, and it will keep happening. The companies that recognize each new platform as both an opportunity to reach new customers and a threat to their distribution model will adapt. The companies that only see the opportunity will be blindsided by the threat. The companies that assume they can skip the new platform entirely will be blindsided by both.

The leaders who are struggling are the ones who built everything on one platform and never diversified. They went all in on one mechanic and never adapted when the dominant discovery channel moved. They built their entire business inside one algorithm's organic reach and watched engagement crater when the algorithm shifted. They are working harder than ever and reaching fewer people, and they don't understand why.

The answer is that the platform window they entered through has closed. And they didn't build the capability to open the next one.

I tell every leader in the community the same thing. Build on the platform. Do not build FOR the platform. The difference is strategic. Building on the platform means using it as a tool while maintaining capabilities that are platform-independent. Building for the platform means making the platform the foundation of your business. The first approach survives platform changes. The second doesn't.

There is a shadow side that cuts the other direction.

Some companies see the model exit wave and panic. They conclude that social media is killing direct selling and that the only answer is to run from the direct selling model entirely. They start stripping out compensation. They reduce the field's earning potential. They shift investment toward DTC at the expense of field support.

That overcorrection is as dangerous as platform dependency. The direct selling model's core advantage has never been the platform. It has been the human relationship. The distributor who looks a prospect in the eye and says "this changed my life, let me show you." The coach who follows up on day 14 when the customer is about to quit. The leader who builds a team culture that makes people want to belong.

No algorithm can replicate that. No Amazon listing can replicate that. No TikTok video can replicate that.

The companies that will thrive in the next decade are the ones that use platforms to amplify human relationships rather than replace them. They will adopt new platforms aggressively. They will build field systems that are platform-flexible. But they'll never lose sight of the fact that the relationship is the asset. The platform is just the amplifier.

When you lose the amplifier, you lose speed. When you lose the relationship, you lose the business.

What the model exit companies got wrong is this. And I say this as someone who respects the difficulty of the decisions they faced.

They looked at the 40 to 50% distribution cost and saw a line item to cut. They didn't see what that 40 to 50% was actually buying them.

Direct selling, when it's done right, does not just distribute products. It builds a sales force that no amount of digital advertising can replicate. A sales force that recruits itself. That trains itself. That motivates itself. That creates culture and community around the product that turns customers into advocates and advocates into builders. That sales force doesn't exist on a balance sheet. It doesn't show up in a cost-per-acquisition spreadsheet. But it's the most powerful commercial asset in the direct selling model.

An affiliate clicks a link and moves on. A direct selling distributor builds a team, invests her identity in the brand, shows up at convention with her family, cries on stage when she hits a rank, trains three people underneath her to do the same thing. That level of commitment, that depth of human investment, is what produces the community and culture that makes direct selling companies impossible to kill when the foundation is right.

Look at the companies that survived decades in this industry. Amway. Herbalife. Mary Kay. Melaleuca. Nature's Sunshine. PM International, which has grown consecutively for over thirty years to a reported $3.25 billion without a single viral headline. Every one of them has a field culture so deep that distributors describe it as a family. They celebrate together. They grieve together. They show up for each other's weddings and funerals. Try building that with an affiliate program and a coupon code.

The companies that exited the model looked at that culture and decided it wasn't worth 40% of revenue. I've been watching this profession for more than two decades, and I've not yet seen a single company successfully switch from direct selling to a corporate distribution model and come out stronger on the other side. Not one. The math on paper often looked defensible. The human reality has consistently refused to cooperate with the math.

The companies that made the switch didn't realize what they were walking away from until the walk was already complete. The field that had been their growth engine went somewhere else, often to competitors. The culture that had been their moat evaporated within months. The customers who looked like they were going to follow the brand into its new model turned out to have been loyal to the person who introduced them to the brand, not to the brand itself. The savings from cutting the field structure rarely showed up as improved competitive position, because the field structure had been doing far more work than the executives who cut it understood.

I'm not saying the direct selling model is the right fit for every product. It isn't. BODi's math was defensible on paper for a fitness content company competing against free YouTube workouts and $10 per month streaming apps. A product that doesn't require human education, coaching, or community may not benefit from the distribution cost that direct selling builds in.

But if you're considering the switch because the short-term numbers look better, understand the pattern. The companies that made this move believed they were cutting an expensive distribution model. What they discovered was that they were dismantling the emotional infrastructure that had been quietly carrying the business. Every one of them has either struggled, been acquired at a distressed valuation, restructured again, or quietly exited the consumer side of their business within a few years of the switch. The full pattern may still be incomplete. But the track record so far is remarkably consistent, and the consistency is a warning worth taking seriously.

The companies that exited because they were chasing lower costs without understanding what they were losing made a different kind of mistake. They abandoned a distribution model that was creating something their competitors could never buy: a self-replicating sales force with emotional investment in the brand's success. You can't purchase that loyalty with an affiliate commission. You can't manufacture that culture with a marketing budget. You can't replace ten thousand people who believe in your product and wake up every morning trying to share it with someone new.

EVERY PRODUCT NEEDS A STORYTELLER

There is a deeper truth underneath the model exit conversation that this industry doesn't talk about enough.

Every product needs a storyteller. Without one, even great products go nowhere.

Stanley made essentially the same vacuum-insulated tumbler for over a hundred years. Solid product. Reliable engineering. Almost nobody outside outdoor enthusiasts had heard of it for most of that century. By 2019, the company was preparing to discontinue its Quencher tumbler entirely because nobody was buying it. The product didn't change. What changed was the storyteller. A small online shopping blog called The Buy Guide started recommending the Quencher to its female audience. Influencers picked it up. TikTok creators turned it into a cultural moment. The cup became shorthand for a lifestyle. Sales jumped from $73 million in 2019 to roughly $750 million by 2023. Same cup. Same factory. Different storytellers.

Saunas were considered a Scandinavian curiosity for decades. Then a small group of health influencers started telling stories about cold plunges, heat exposure, and longevity protocols. The category exploded. Same saunas. Different storytellers. Weighted vests existed for thirty years as a niche fitness item. Then a wave of fitness creators started wearing them on walks and posting the science behind rucking and load training. Now you can't scroll a fitness feed without seeing one. Same vest. Different storytellers.

The lesson isn't that TikTok creators replaced direct selling. The lesson is that products don't sell themselves. Every product, no matter how good, requires somebody who knows how to tell its story to the right people in a way they'll actually believe.

There are exactly two ways to do that at scale. The first is traditional business: build a brand through advertising, content, retail partnerships, and DTC marketing. Spend tens of millions of dollars buying attention until enough customers know your product exists and trust the brand enough to buy it. This works. It is what built Apple, Nike, Lululemon, and most of the consumer brands you know.

The second way is direct selling. Recruit and train a sales force of real people who believe in the product, give them a compensation structure that rewards them for telling the story, and let the human relationships do the storytelling at scale. This also works. It is what built Amway, Mary Kay, Melaleuca, Shaklee, Herbalife, PM International, and every other durable direct selling company in this book.

Both models are legitimate. Both produce real businesses. Both can build billion-dollar brands. The choice between them depends on the product category, the founder's capital position, the customer education required, and the kind of business the founders actually want to build. There is no moral hierarchy. There is only fit.

What doesn't work is using one model to build the brand and then switching to the other to extract the margin.

THE WHIPLASH OF BETRAYAL

This is the part the executives making the cut-and-run decision don't understand.

The math looks simple from the executive suite. A company has built a $500 million brand using direct selling. The compensation plan consumes 45% of revenue. That is $225 million per year going to the field. Cut the field, the executive thinks, and you keep most of that $225 million. The customers will keep ordering. The brand recognition is established. The product works. Why would the customer care which channel they buy through? Move them to a DTC website and become wildly profitable overnight.

That math has been run in boardrooms across this industry for the past three years. The companies that have actually pulled the trigger have learned something the spreadsheet didn't show.

The field isn't just a distribution channel. The field is the brand.

When you built that $500 million company through direct selling, those customers didn't buy because of an ad they saw on Instagram. They bought because someone they knew, often someone they loved, told them this product changed her life. The trust transferred from the storyteller to the product. The customer's relationship with the brand exists inside the relationship with the distributor.

When you cut the distributor, you don't just lose a salesperson. You lose the storyteller who created the trust the customer is operating inside. And the customer notices.

But that's not the worst of it.

The executives running the math don't see this clearly. The distributors you're about to fire aren't employees. They aren't contractors waiting for their next gig. They are people who built businesses inside your brand. They quit other jobs to do it. They poured their identity into it. They sold the dream to their friends, their family, their neighbors, their sisters, their college roommates. They built teams. They mentored people. They cried on stages at your conventions when they hit ranks. Their kids have grown up watching them build this thing. Their family vacations were paid for by your comp plan. Their mortgages got refinanced because of your residual income.

When you cut their checks, you don't just end their income. You end their identity. And you do it after they spent the last five or ten years telling everyone they know that your company was different. That your company wouldn't do this. That your founders cared about the field. That the comp plan was protected. That this was the place to build a long-term business. You betrayed them. That is what they feel. And they're not wrong.

What happens next is the part the math doesn't predict.

Those former distributors don't quietly disappear. They were the loudest voices for your brand for years. They taught their entire network to love your product. Now they redirect that same energy in the opposite direction. They tell their friends to cancel autoship. They post videos explaining what the company did to them. They write reviews on every platform that will host them. They warn their customers about the change. They tell their families never to order from you again. They share their stories in support groups, on Reddit, on TikTok, in the same Facebook groups they used to use to recruit. The same network that you built your brand on becomes the network that destroys it.

The customer who was buying because she loved her sponsor now hears from that same sponsor that the company she trusted has changed. The customer's loyalty was always to the relationship, not to the brand. When the relationship turns hostile, the loyalty follows. The DTC site gets the order cancellation, not the new subscription.

This is the field-betrayal whiplash. It is documented in the data of every company that has tried it.

The executives ran the cost math. They didn't run the trust math. They forgot that the brand they were trying to keep was built out of human trust, and that trust evaporates the moment you do something that proves the brand was never what people thought it was.

There is a version of significant compensation plan change that the field can absorb without destroying trust. It still requires long lead times, generous transition compensation for affected leaders, real economic alternatives for distributors whose income structure is being adjusted, and complete transparency about why the change is happening. Companies that have made meaningful comp plan adjustments while keeping the field intact have done it through this kind of careful sequencing. The change still hurts in the short term. But the trust is preserved because the change was communicated, compensated, and executed in a way that respected the people who built the company.

This is fundamentally different from a model exit. A comp plan adjustment, even a significant one, keeps the company in the direct selling channel. The relationship between the company and the field continues. The economic structure changes, but the partnership remains. That is a manageable transition with the right discipline.

The version that doesn't work, that has been proven not to work in the data so far, is the version where executives exit the direct selling model entirely with a press release, slash field compensation overnight, and assume the customers will follow the brand to the new channel. That version has produced outcomes that destroyed billions of dollars in enterprise value. I've been watching this profession for more than two decades, and I've not yet seen a single company successfully switch from direct selling to a corporate distribution model and come out stronger on the other side. The companies that adjusted compensation while staying inside the model have a different track record. The ones that exited the model entirely have produced consistent, predictable damage every time.

WHAT THIS MEANS FOR OWNERS

The decision about what distribution model to use should be made when you start the company, not when you're trying to fix it.

If you build a product that doesn't need education, demonstration, coaching, or community, build it through traditional business channels. DTC, retail, advertising, content, affiliate. There are great companies in every product category that did exactly that. They aren't worse than direct selling companies. They are different.

If you build a product that benefits from the human trust that only relationship-driven storytelling can create, build it through direct selling. Recruit a field. Train them. Pay them well. Build the culture. Honor the people who built your brand by protecting the model they built it inside.

But don't build a brand using one model and then try to switch to the other to extract the margin. The customers were never yours. They were borrowed from the storytellers. The moment you cut the storytellers, the storytellers take the customers back.

Direct selling isn't outdated. It is one of two legitimate ways to build a consumer brand. It will continue to be a legitimate way to build a consumer brand for the next decade and beyond, in any category where human trust matters more than algorithmic targeting. The companies that succeed in this model will be the ones that respect what the model actually is. They will protect the field. They will pay it well. They will build cultures worth belonging to. They will earn the trust they're asking the field to extend on their behalf.

The companies that try to have it both ways will keep generating case studies for books like this one.

Some of those companies will discover this the hard way. Their affiliate revenue will look cleaner on a spreadsheet. Their margins will improve. Their investor decks will be prettier. And their growth will flatten. Because affiliates don't build teams. Affiliates don't create culture. Affiliates don't show up at a convention and recruit thirty people in the hallway because they believe this company changed their life.

The direct selling model isn't for every product or every company. This book has made that clear. But for the companies where the model fits, where the product benefits from education, demonstration, coaching, and community, the distribution cost isn't an expense. It is an investment in the most powerful sales force structure ever created. And the companies that understand that will outlast the ones that traded it for a cleaner P&L.

Never be held hostage by an algorithm. But never abandon your army because an accountant told you they cost too much.

YOUR MOVE THIS QUARTER:

If your product requires human involvement (education, coaching, demonstration, accountability): invest in making your field's human skills stronger, not in chasing the latest platform. Allocate training budget to one-on-one conversation skills, live presentation skills, and customer follow-up systems that work with or without any specific platform. Build platform-flexible systems so the field can shift to the next window in 30 days instead of 12 months.

If your product sells without human involvement: run the BODi math with real numbers. Calculate your customer acquisition cost through direct selling versus DTC, affiliate, and retail channels. If DTC is cheaper per customer acquired, you have a structural problem. Either add a human-value layer that justifies the distribution cost (coaching, community, accountability) or start building a hybrid model that reduces your dependence on the field for customer acquisition while preserving the field for relationship-intensive functions.

Run this audit.

THE COUNTER-CYCLICAL OPPORTUNITY IN HUMAN CONNECTION

There is a secondary observation that needs to be made here, because it has strategic implications for companies deciding where to place their bets over the next three to five years.

When an entire industry rushes in one direction, the counter-cyclical bet often becomes the more valuable one.

The industry rushed online during COVID. The platforms scaled. The virtual conventions proliferated. Training went digital. Recruiting went digital. The field got comfortable operating entirely through a phone screen. And the industry largely stayed there after the pandemic ended because the cost structure was more attractive and the habits had formed.

But the structural advantage of direct selling was never the platform. It was the human connection. The face-to-face conversation. The shoulder-to-shoulder training. The physical proximity of a leader standing in a room with twenty builders and changing what they believed was possible. Every platform the industry has ever used has been a delivery mechanism for something that's fundamentally human. When the delivery mechanism becomes the product, the product loses its distinguishing value.

Partner.Co, which consolidated several legacy direct selling brands that had previously come together under New Age, made a deliberate bet on the in-person format exactly when the rest of the industry was economizing on travel and physical gatherings. The founders of the predecessor companies went on the road together. The field from each legacy company was brought into the same rooms. The unified culture was built through physical presence, not through webinars and brand guidelines.

The result was reportedly one of the strongest US growth stories of the 2023 to 2025 window, in an industry climate that was mostly unkind to new company formations. That outcome isn't a coincidence. It is a demonstration of the counter-cyclical principle.

The companies that over-index on platforms during a platform-heavy cultural moment are the ones that will be most exposed when the next platform shift arrives. The companies that continue to invest in the human-connection infrastructure that platforms amplify but can't replace are the ones that will have a defensible advantage when the next algorithm change makes every competitor's organic reach collapse at the same time.

This isn't an argument against platforms. They are essential. It is an argument against letting platforms become the entire strategy. The leaders who can hold a room, train a team in person, and build relationships that don't depend on any specific platform are the leaders who will produce the most durable volume across any platform cycle. The companies that invest in developing that kind of leader are the companies least exposed to platform disruption even as they ride each new platform window.

THE PLATFORM DEPENDENCY AUDIT

Question 1: What percentage of your new customer acquisition comes through a single platform?

If more than 60% of new customers are acquired through one platform (Facebook, Instagram, TikTok, etc.), you have platform concentration risk. Any algorithm change on that platform directly impacts your growth rate. Diversify before the algorithm decides for you.

Question 2: Does your field have selling skills that work without the platform?

Survey 20 random active distributors with one question: "If your primary social media platform shut down tomorrow, could you still hit your monthly volume target using other channels, whether that's text, voice messages, video calls, AI-assisted outreach, 24-hour chat tools, in-person meetings, or any combination?" If fewer than 25% say yes with confidence, your field is platform-dependent. That means one algorithm change can disable your entire sales force overnight. You don't need to test it in practice. The answers will tell you everything. Target: at least 50% of your field should be confident they can produce volume through non-platform channels.

Question 3: Can your field communicate with customers and teams without relying on a social platform?

Every modern direct selling company owns its customer data the moment a purchase is made through the company website. That isn't the live risk. The live risk is how your field actually talks to customers and teams on a daily basis. If your distributors run their businesses primarily through Facebook groups, Instagram DMs, or private messaging inside any single platform, your entire field communication layer depends on decisions made by that platform. A policy change, a feature retirement, a group functionality update, or an algorithm shift can break team cultures and customer conversations overnight. The companies that hold up through platform shifts are the ones where the field has direct channels with customers and teams, through texting, the company app, email lists the leaders control, or voice and video tools that don't depend on one platform's feed. If you can't answer yes to this question with confidence, your field is more fragile than you think.

Question 4: How old is the platform window you're operating in?

Platform windows don't always mean entirely new platforms. Sometimes the window is a major new feature rollout on an existing platform, like

Facebook Live in 2015 or Instagram Reels in 2020. Sometimes it's an algorithm resurrection that heavily promotes a previously underused format, giving early adopters of that format outsized reach. The field should be scanning not just for new platforms but for any shift in how existing platforms distribute attention.

If you're in year one or two of a platform window, lean in hard. You have asymmetric reach. Build systems around it. Train the field. Move fast. If you're in year four or five, the window is maturing. Organic reach is declining. Start developing capabilities for the next window while you still have momentum on the current one. If you're in year six or beyond on the same platform window, the asymmetric advantage is gone. You are competing on a level field. Your field needs skills that work independent of any single platform's algorithm.

Question 5: Is your product category at risk of model disruption?

If your product can be effectively sold through Amazon, DTC websites, TikTok Shop, or retail without a distributor's involvement, your distribution model may be more expensive than alternatives. Monitor the BODi-style math: would your business be more competitive without the 40-50% distribution cost? If the answer is yes and your customer ratio (from Chapter 4) is weak, you have a structural vulnerability that platform shifts will expose.

Scoring:

High concentration + old platform window + model-vulnerable product: you're in the danger zone. Diversify immediately.

Moderate concentration + multiple platforms + relationship-driven product: you're positioned well but should be actively developing the next platform capability.

Low concentration + platform-independent field skills + owned customer data: you have platform resilience. Use it as an advantage when competitors' platforms shift.

Imagine a company that treats every platform as a three-to-five-year window.

When TikTok emerges, they don't debate whether it's "right for our brand." They deploy a small team to test and learn. They develop field training for the new platform within 90 days. They move fast while the organic reach is highest. They capture the early-adopter advantage.

Simultaneously, they ensure every customer acquired through TikTok is also captured in a company-owned database. Email. Phone. App account. The platform is the acquisition channel. The owned database is the retention channel. If TikTok disappears tomorrow, the customers remain.

When the platform window matures and organic reach declines, this company doesn't panic. It has already identified the next platform opportunity. Its field has been cross-trained. Its customer relationships are platform-independent. The transition is strategic, not desperate.

That company doesn't need any single platform. It needs the skill of recognizing and exploiting platform windows faster than its competitors. That skill, more than any individual platform, is the sustainable advantage.

One pattern I see constantly in consulting conversations. A company rides a platform wave to extraordinary growth. Then the platform shifts. The algorithm changes. The feature that built the business gets deprioritized. And the leadership team's first instinct is to ask how to replicate the old playbook on a new platform.

That is usually the wrong question. The platform didn't just give the company reach. It gave the company a specific selling behavior, a specific way of building trust, a specific content rhythm that matched the platform's native format. Moving that exact behavior to a new platform usually fails, because the new platform rewards different behaviors and punishes the old ones. The companies that successfully bridge platform transitions are the ones that treat the new platform as a new medium entirely, not a new distribution channel for the old message.

I've watched this pattern play out across Facebook parties, Instagram Live, TikTok Shop, and now AI-native platforms. The companies that keep adapting successfully have one thing in common. They don't try to force their platform-specific playbook onto the new environment. They build a new playbook from scratch, informed by how the platform actually works, and let the old one retire gracefully. That is much harder than it sounds, because the field will resist abandoning the behaviors that made them successful. But the field that resists most is often the field that crashes hardest when the old platform dies and they have nothing to replace it with.

WHAT TO DO WHEN THE WINDOW HAS PASSED

Most companies reading this chapter aren't in the early days of a platform window. They are downstream of one. The platform that built them has matured, the algorithm has shifted, the field's organic reach has compressed, and the recruiting numbers tied to that platform have flattened. The window is closed and the company is left figuring out what to do next.

The instinct most leaders have is to chase the next platform. TikTok was hot last year, so the company pours resources into TikTok content. TikTok Shop is the new opportunity, so the field gets pushed into TikTok Shop. The next platform after that becomes the next chase. This isn't a strategy. It is a series of reactions, each of which requires the field to learn a new platform from scratch and abandon the muscle memory it built on the previous one. By the time the field is competent on the new platform, the window on that one is closing too.

The companies that handle a closed window well do four things in sequence.

First, they diversify the platform exposure of the field. If 80% of recruiting and customer acquisition was happening through one platform during the window, the post-window strategy is to deliberately rebalance toward three or four platforms with no single dependency exceeding 40%. The diversification isn't just defensive. It is offensive in the sense that it positions the field to be ready when the next window opens on any of the platforms in the rotation, rather than being stuck on the wrong one.

Second, they invest aggressively in in-person fundamentals. Platform windows come and go. The structural advantage of direct selling, the in-person relationship, the live event, the shoulder-to-shoulder training, does not. When a platform window closes, the companies that have maintained strong in-person infrastructure recover faster because the field still has channels for building belief and momentum that don't depend on any algorithm. Partner.Co's growth in 2023 to 2025, mentioned earlier in this chapter, is a working example of this principle in action.

Third, they rebuild the customer foundation directly. Platform-dependent recruiting often produces customer-light revenue because the speed of the platform incentivizes signing up new distributors over building deep customer relationships. When the window closes and the recruiting velocity drops, what remains is the customer base. If the customer base is shallow because everyone was busy chasing recruiting volume, the post-window company is exposed. The reset is to use the slower period to rebuild customer acquisition and retention systems that the previous platform window obscured rather than developed.

Fourth, they position for the next window without becoming hostage to it. The next platform window will open. It always does. The companies that ride it best are the ones that stay aware of platform shifts without committing the entire field to any single one. They develop a small group of leaders who are early on each new platform, gather data, and make a measured commitment based on whether the platform is producing real customer demand or just temporary recruiting velocity. They never again let any single platform represent more than 40% of total volume.

This isn't a glamorous playbook. There is no big announcement, no convention reveal, no flashy new initiative the field can rally around. It is patient infrastructure work. Diversification, in-person investment, customer foundation rebuilding, measured platform rotation. The companies that do this work in the post-window period set themselves up for the next decade. The companies that just chase the next platform set themselves up for the next collapse.

The next chapter covers the fastest-acting momentum driver: Leader Migration. What happens when a top earner with 20,000 people in their organization decides to leave one company and join another. The economics are dramatic. The risks are enormous. And the companies that depend on it the most are the ones most likely to collapse when it reverses.

THE BOTTOM LINE: Platform windows last three to five years. Exploit them aggressively while building platform-independent skills. Survey your field: if the primary platform disappeared tomorrow, could they still produce volume?

The platform is never yours. The relationship always is. Build accordingly.

Chapter 8: Leader Migration

The same door that lets talent in lets talent out. And the door swings both ways at the same speed.

The enemy in this chapter: rented growth mistaken for owned growth. Not every external leader is rented. Some join because they believe in the product and the vision. The distinction is whether the growth they create is portable or permanent. This chapter teaches you to answer that question.

In professional sports, a single free-agent signing can transform a franchise. When LeBron James announced "I'm taking my talents to South Beach" in 2010, the Miami Heat went from a good team to a championship contender overnight. Two titles in four years. The city changed. The culture changed. The revenue changed. One person's decision to move created instant, measurable, transformative momentum.

Then he left. Went back to Cleveland. And the Heat, which had built its identity, its ticket sales, its brand equity, and its championship window around one player's presence, had to start over.

This is the sports analogy that direct selling executives love to use when they talk about leader migration. Signing a top earner from another company is like signing LeBron. Instant credibility. Instant volume. A signal to the market that something real is happening.

The analogy is accurate. It is also incomplete. Because in the NBA, when LeBron leaves, the ticket sales decline but the franchise survives. The arena is still there. The other players are still under contract. The fans are still fans of the team.

In direct selling, when a mega-leader leaves, the arena might empty entirely. Because the fans were never fans of the team. They were fans of the player. And when the player moves, they follow.

The structural reality of leader migration is that simple. It is the fastest-acting momentum driver in the industry. It produces the most dramatic short-term growth. And it creates the most dangerous dependency of any driver in this book.

Here is how leader migration works mechanically.

A company wants to accelerate growth. Organic growth through new distributor enrollment and customer acquisition is steady but slow. The leadership team decides to recruit established top earners from other companies. These are people with existing organizations, existing credibility, existing recruiting infrastructure, and existing monthly volume.

The economics evolved over time, and that evolution tells its own story. Between roughly 2008 and 2013, several companies offered significant upfront cash to attract top earners. Signing bonuses. Guaranteed monthly income. Contracts that paid leaders before they produced a dollar of volume for the new company. The logic was simple: pay for talent, get instant volume. And it worked in the short term. The leaders came. The volume spiked. Conventions filled up. The numbers looked incredible.

Then the pendulum swung. The upfront deals created a massive problem. Leaders who were paid to show up had no economic urgency to build. Some collected the guarantee and coasted. Others built briefly, cashed the bonus, and moved to the next deal. The companies that paid the most for talent often got the least durable growth in return. The volume spike was real but temporary, and when the deals expired, the volume often left with them.

The industry learned. Mostly. By the mid-2010s, the standard shifted to Business Development Agreements, or BDAs. Performance-based structures with no upfront cash. The leader earns through the comp plan based on actual results. Milestones. Volume thresholds. Rank qualifications tied to real production. The BDA aligns the leader's incentive with the company's growth rather than paying for the hope of growth.

Some companies still offer rank placement that allows recruited leaders to skip qualification periods. Others provide enhanced commission structures for the first 90 or 180 days. But the era of writing six-figure checks on day one has largely passed. The companies that tried it learned the hard way that purchased loyalty has an expiration date printed on the check.

Even with performance-based agreements, the migration mechanics are powerful. Pre-launch phases serve as leader magnets. The allure of ground-floor positioning is real because early leaders often receive enhanced economics and fresh energy. Everything is new, exciting, and full of possibility. There is nothing negative to compare to yet. The story writes itself.

However, the economics of being first aren't automatic. Many of the most successful leaders in this industry's largest companies joined well after launch and still created massive organizations. The advantage of being early is real. The assumption that being early guarantees success isn't. What matters more than timing is the depth of the leader's commitment and whether the company underneath them is built to sustain what they create.

When a leader of significant scale decides to move, the cascade effect begins.

Her personally-sponsored frontline leaders evaluate the opportunity. Many follow. They haven't done independent due diligence on the new company. They trust her judgment and they're loyal to her. They've been building together for years. She made them money. She trained them. She's their mentor, not the company.

Then those leaders' organizations notice. When your upline's upline moves, it sends a signal. Something is happening. The new company must be real. More people follow.

The broader field observes the migration. Other top earners from other companies see who has joined and interpret the moves as market validation. If four or five recognized names are moving to the same company, the bandwagon effect accelerates. Nobody wants to be late to a party that the biggest names are attending.

There is a dynamic here that companies often underestimate. Even when a departing leader is no longer actively building, even if the company privately feels the leader wasn't contributing, the move still sends a signal. Stage recognition creates perceived ownership in the minds of the rank-and-file. That person was celebrated at convention. Their name was on the screen. Their story was told from the stage. Any existing doubts in the field, about culture, compensation, or direction, become magnified when a recognized name leaves. The departure creates a crack in the foundation that's visible to the broader field, even if the leader wasn't driving daily volume. And for people in the field who had been quietly considering their own options, the departure gives them courage to act.

Standard industry non-compete clauses, typically six months, and non-solicitation provisions, typically two years, attempt to slow this process. They rarely stop it. The leader waits out the non-compete. Her network migrates informally during the waiting period. And when the restriction lifts, the formal enrollment begins.

Lawsuits sometimes follow. And lawsuits create a mess for both sides. They are expensive. They generate negative PR in both directions. The departing leader tells the story as "the company thinks they own me." The company tells the story as "this leader is stealing our people." The distributor argues she isn't soliciting, that people are coming to her, that everyone is an independent contractor. The company argues she is being passive-aggressive and indirectly recruiting. The public narrative becomes "company versus leader" instead of "opportunity versus opportunity," and it damages trust across the entire profession. Neither side wins the PR war. Both sides spend money that could have been invested in building.

MonaVie is the defining case study of leader migration as a momentum driver.

CEO Dallin Larsen was a former USANA marketing director. He understood the mechanics of the industry from the corporate side. When he launched MonaVie in 2005 with an acai juice product, he didn't just build a product company. He built a leader acquisition machine.

The biggest move was Brig Hart. Hart had been one of Amway's most prolific producers for two decades. His organization was massive and his personal earnings placed him among the highest-earning distributors in industry history.

Think about what that move represented. Hart didn't just bring himself. He brought credibility that took decades to build. He brought relationships with thousands of leaders who trusted his judgment. He brought a track record that made the pitch to other potential leaders almost effortless: "Brig Hart is here. Brig Hart, the Amway legend. If Brig is in, this must be real."

Other major leaders followed. Hart's MonaVie organization grew into one of the largest downlines in the company. When you study MonaVie's growth trajectory, what you're actually seeing isn't organic product demand. You're seeing the mathematical output of pre-built networks plugging into a new compensation structure.

MonaVie hit $854 million in annual revenue by 2008, three years after launch. The company reported extraordinary growth rates. Those numbers are staggering. They are also almost entirely attributable to leader migration rather than to the acai product itself.

The proof came when the leaders left. The same economics that made MonaVie attractive to incoming leaders made the next opportunity attractive to those same leaders. When MonaVie's growth plateaued and the acai trend faded, the big producers evaluated their options. They found new ground-floor opportunities. New comp plans. New products riding new cultural waves. And they moved. Again. Taking their organizations with them. Again.

MonaVie's revenue collapsed. The billion-dollar company was eventually absorbed. The leaders who built it had moved on to the next thing. Because they were never building MonaVie. They were building their organizations, and MonaVie was the temporary vehicle.

doTERRA presents a fundamentally different version of leader migration.

Its founding CEO came from the senior ranks of an established essential oils company. He launched the company in 2008 with several other industry veterans who brought deep essential oils expertise and relationships.

The initial leader migration was significant. Experienced distributors with established essential oils credibility crossed over, giving the company a network of knowledgeable leaders from day one. This is leader migration. The mechanism is the same as MonaVie's.

But what happened next is what separates this story from every other leader migration case in the dataset.

The company invested in building something that didn't depend on the migrated leaders. It built a product line with genuine depth. Multiple oils. Supplements. Personal care. Dozens of use cases that kept customers engaged and purchasing over long periods. It invested in sourcing that created a genuine competitive moat, partnering with local growers across 45 countries through its Co-Impact Sourcing program. It built a customer base that reached 10 million by 2024, with more than 3 million Wellness Advocates.

The leaders who migrated in gave the company its launch velocity. But it didn't let leader migration remain the primary driver. It layered product-culture fit (essential oils during the wellness mega-trend) and platform disruption (Facebook groups and the virtual party model) on top of the initial leader foundation. Over time, the customer base became deep enough that no single leader's departure could threaten the business structurally.

doTERRA used leader migration as a launch accelerant, then transitioned to a model where the brand and the customer base carried the growth. MonaVie used leader migration as the permanent engine and never built anything underneath it.

Same driver. Same mechanism. Opposite outcomes. The difference was The Underneath. ViSalus had concentration with no foundation underneath it. Modere had concentration with a real customer base underneath it. The concentration itself wasn't the test. What was underneath it was. The difference is what you build after the leaders arrive.

The data from the decline research makes the risk quantifiable.

The Leader Concentration Trap isn't a theory. It is a documented pattern with specific numbers attached.

ViSalus: one leader's organization accounted for 74% of total company revenue. When external circumstances changed and the foundation was tested, the concentration was exposed. The leader was still building. But the structural holes underneath the concentration, low customer depth, rapid growth that outpaced the infrastructure, became visible once momentum slowed. Revenue dropped 80% within two years.

Concentration of that magnitude isn't a strategic mistake. It often emerges from genuine field excellence. The 74% reflects how hard one organization built. What the company can control is what sits underneath the concentration. ViSalus didn't have the customer depth, the secondary leadership development, or the retention infrastructure that would have caught the revenue when external pressure tested it. That is the variable a leadership team actually owns.

Organo Gold: the company was built around a three-person leadership core. Founder and CEO Bernie Chua, global master distributor Shane Morand, and EVP of Sales Holton Buggs. Industry estimates of peak revenue vary widely, ranging from company-reported figures in the hundreds of millions to industry observer estimates approaching $800 million. What isn't in dispute is the magnitude of the collapse. When the leadership trio departed, the company cratered. Current estimated revenue is a fraction of peak, a decline in the range of 85 to 95%. The structural lesson doesn't depend on the exact peak. The culture, the field energy, the recruiting momentum, all of it was tied to three people.

THE PRIVATE EQUITY DIMENSION

The private equity dimension deserves explicit treatment here, because it changes how leader migration gets used at certain companies. Private equity sponsors operate on a timeline. Most fund structures require a liquidity event within five to seven years of acquisition. That clock creates pressure to accelerate revenue growth in a window that's shorter than the natural cycle of building a direct selling company organically. When the sponsor needs growth on the sponsor's calendar rather than the field's, leader migration becomes the fastest lever available. The company signs big checks to acquire established top earners, pulls volume forward, hits revenue targets, and positions for a sale or recapitalization. Sometimes the growth is real and durable. Sometimes it contracts as soon as the signing bonuses stop flowing.

Arbonne is a useful case study because it shows both sides of the pattern. In 2004, the company reported approximately $200 million in annual sales. Over the next three years, following aggressive recruitment of established top earners, the consultant base reportedly expanded from 434,000 in 2005 to 612,000 in 2006 to 1.3 million by 2007. Revenue scaled into the hundreds of millions.

Then the math reversed. Between 2007 and 2009, the consultant base contracted to under 800,000, a decline of roughly 40% in two years. In January 2010, the parent holding company filed for bankruptcy protection to restructure the debt that had funded the aggressive growth years. The private equity sponsors exited.

What is notable about Arbonne is what happened next. The company didn't disappear. The culture that had been built in the pre-acquisition years had genuine depth. Enough of it survived the restructuring that the brand continued operating. In 2018, Groupe Rocher acquired Arbonne for approximately $145 million and has operated the company since. Current revenue estimates vary widely depending on methodology, but the company is still an active participant in the profession.

The pattern is instructive. Aggressive leader migration combined with debt-financed expansion can produce real revenue on the sponsor's timeline. But the debt structure and the leader cohort both have expiration dates. When the debt comes due or when the signing-bonus period ends, the volume can contract faster than the operating cost structure can adjust. The resulting financial distress is often the trigger for a restructuring event.

None of this makes private equity ownership wrong. Sponsors can provide capital, discipline, and operational support that family-owned companies sometimes lack. The point is narrower. When private equity capital is combined with leader migration as the primary growth lever, the compound of financial leverage and volume concentration creates a specific form of fragility that has played out repeatedly in the industry.

ACQUISITION-LED GROWTH AS LEADER MIGRATION AT SCALE

There is a newer variation of this pattern playing out in real time, because one company in the industry is currently running it at a scale and pace that the profession hasn't seen before. When a direct selling company acquires another direct selling company, the asset it's primarily buying is the distributor field. Product formulations can be reformulated. Supply chains can be rebuilt. IT systems can be replaced. The distributor network is what justifies the acquisition price. Which means acquisition-led growth is essentially leader migration executed through corporate M&A rather than through individual recruiting. Same structural mechanism. Different delivery system.

Zinzino, a Swedish-founded public company listed on the Nasdaq First North Premier Growth Market, offers one of the few current examples of an acquisition-led growth strategy that has remained profitable and disciplined over a sustained period.

The company built its initial momentum organically. Its BalanceOil product line, combined with dry blood spot nutritional testing, created a product-culture fit that drove consistent growth for over a decade. By 2023, reported revenue reached approximately $168 million with 17% annual growth. The organic foundation was strong, the product story was differentiated, and the company had built real customer depth.

Starting around 2020, Zinzino began layering acquisitions on top of that organic base. VMA Life in 2020. Enhanzz in 2022. Xelliss and ACN in 2024. Then the pace accelerated dramatically. In 2025 alone, the company announced or completed acquisitions of Zurvita, Valentus, Ecosystem, Truvy, Bode Pro, Sanki, a minority stake in Xion International, and the assets of It Works. Revenue grew from $168 million in 2023 to approximately $367 million in 2025, a 51% annual growth rate in the most recent reported year. EBITDA margins expanded alongside the revenue growth, suggesting integration discipline and synergy capture rather than revenue-at-any-cost.

The financing structure of the acquisitions is strategically interesting. Rather than paying cash or taking on debt, the company finances acquisitions by issuing new shares. The balance sheet stays clean. No debt burden. No cash outflow. The trade-off is dilution: every acquisition issues new shares, which spreads ownership across more holders. This is a deliberate corporate strategy bet that total company value will grow faster than share count. It is the same approach Berkshire Hathaway and many other public acquirers have used successfully for decades. Whether the bet pays off depends on execution. If the acquired businesses integrate well and drive real growth, the dilution is offset by the larger pie. If they don't, the math runs the other direction.

What makes this case important to track is that it's currently succeeding at something the industry has repeatedly failed at. Direct selling consolidation plays have a long history of disappointing outcomes. The acquired distributor networks often fragment during integration. Cultural mismatches between the acquiring and acquired companies create field attrition. The economics that looked good on paper deteriorate as the complexity of running multiple brands overwhelms the operational infrastructure. Many companies that have tried to build through acquisition eventually either slow the pace or reverse course.

Zinzino has instead accelerated. The open strategic question is whether the compound of larger acquisitions executed faster can maintain the integration quality that has characterized the earlier, smaller deals. Integrating one direct selling company into another is a multi-year effort involving comp plan harmonization, field politics, IT systems, regulatory filings in multiple jurisdictions, and cultural assimilation. When acquisitions come quarterly, the integration work for each new deal begins before the work on the previous deal is complete.

I have no prediction to offer about how the strategy will ultimately resolve. The execution track record is clearly impressive, and the financial discipline at scale is the strongest the industry has seen from an acquisition-led strategy in years. What I'll say is that every owner and executive watching the direct selling industry right now should be studying this case carefully. If the strategy keeps working at the accelerated pace, it will rewrite the assumptions about how a modern direct selling company can grow. If it begins to show strain, it will confirm the limits of acquisition-led growth that the industry has seen before. Either outcome is a lesson playing out in real time.

Partner.Co is the other acquisition-strategy case to track closely, and the strategy is the opposite of Zinzino's. Instead of acquiring companies and running them as separate brands, Partner.Co consolidated several legacy direct selling companies into a single unified platform. The brands had come together earlier as part of New Age, and after acquiring the combined entity, Partner.Co accelerated the integration of brands that hadn't yet been merged. One brand. One product line. One culture. The field from every predecessor company rolled into the same organization.

What makes the Partner.Co story instructive is that multi-company consolidations in this industry almost never work. The usual failure mode is predictable: each legacy company had its own founders, its own culture, its own product heritage, and its own field identity. Ask a field leader from one of those companies to suddenly share a stage, a compensation plan, and a brand with leaders from three or four other companies, and the friction breaks the integration. Cultures clash. Top earners from each predecessor expect their particular history to be honored above the others. The "unified" company ends up as four smaller companies operating under one logo, with field politics that make every decision harder than it needs to be.

Partner.Co took the problem seriously from the start. The leadership team went on the road, physically, to bring the predecessor cultures together in person. They understood that cultural integration couldn't be announced through a press release and wouldn't happen through Zoom calls. The founders from the merging companies traveled together, appeared on stage together, and demonstrated the new unified identity in the one setting that matters most in this industry, which is the one where builders can see leaders in the same room breathing the same air.

They also made a counter-cyclical bet on the format itself. The industry at large went online during COVID and largely stayed there. Partner.Co understood that the structural advantage of direct selling is specifically the in-person human connection, and they doubled down on it exactly when everyone else was economizing on travel, events, and physical gatherings. The result was a company that reportedly generated some of the strongest growth in the US market between 2023 and 2025 despite operating in an industry climate that was mostly unkind to new company formations.

The Partner.Co model isn't for every company. It requires acquisition targets that are willing to subordinate their individual identities to a unified brand, founders who are willing to share authority rather than protect their legacy positions, and a leadership team willing to do the physical travel work that cultural integration actually requires. Zinzino's "keep brands separate" approach is less work and lower risk but also produces less integration upside. Partner.Co's "consolidate into one" approach is higher risk and more work but produces a single unified company with a cleaner long-term structure if the integration holds.

Two different acquisition strategies. Two companies currently making them work at scale. The industry hasn't had two simultaneous live case studies on acquisition strategy at this level of ambition in a long time, and both deserve continued attention in the years ahead.

MonaVie: heavy hitters were recruited with their entire organizations. When the next opportunity emerged, they jumped with those same organizations. Downlines followed their uplines. Revenue collapsed not because the product stopped working but because the people who were generating the volume left.

LuLaRoe: top consultants drove the majority of volume. When the comp plan changed and quality issues emerged, consultants dropped from a peak of roughly 80,000 in April 2017 to fewer than 20,000 by 2020 per industry reporting. The concentration wasn't in one leader but in a small percentage of high-volume sellers whose departure devastated the total.

Jeunesse Global may be the most dramatic modern example of what happens when leader migration is the primary growth strategy without organic culture underneath it. The full case study follows later in this chapter.

The pattern is consistent. The more concentrated your volume is in a small number of leaders or organizations, the more fragile your business is. And the leaders who generated that volume through migration are, by definition, the leaders most likely to migrate again.

The survey data reveals what accelerates that migration window. When 82 top earners were asked what kills their engagement fastest, 42% said "corporate only listening to the newest, flashiest leaders" and 35% said "lack of appreciation for long-term contributions." The companies that lose their legacy leaders aren't losing them to better comp plans. They are losing them to neglect. A leader who built your company for a decade watches the newest signing get the keynote slot, the CEO dinner, and the product development input. She doesn't complain publicly. She goes quiet. She takes calls. And six months later she is on someone else's stage.

Now look at the opposite pattern. Because it exists, and it proves the thesis from the other direction.

Modere, formerly Neways, had built its business around a customer-centric model with a strong product line anchored by its Liquid BioCell collagen products. In 2017, Modere terminated Jessie Lee Ward, who would go on to become one of the most recognized and highest-earning leaders in the entire direct selling profession. Ward wasn't a small departure. She was a force. She later built an organization at Pruvit that spanned 41 countries with over 1.6 million cumulative customers and 21,000 promoters. Forbes recognized her as one of the most influential women in America in 2022.

When Modere terminated Ward, the expected outcome, based on every other leader departure in this chapter, was a revenue hit. A significant leader leaves, volume follows, the company takes a visible blow.

That isn't what happened. Modere's revenue held. The company continued to grow in subsequent years, reportedly reaching approximately $368 million by 2020 to 2021, its peak revenue period. The customer base that Modere had built was loyal to the products, not to any individual leader. The Liquid BioCell collagen line had genuine consumer demand that existed independent of the field's recruiting activity. When the big name left, the customers stayed.

Modere did eventually decline, falling from that $368 million peak to roughly $150 million by 2024, before eventually ceasing independent operations. But that decline came years later and was driven by entirely different factors: competitive pressure, the broader model exit trend affecting the industry, and private equity dynamics. It had nothing to do with the 2017 leader departure.

A PAIRWISE COMPARISON: VISALUS AND MODERE

The Modere example is the mirror image of ViSalus. Both companies had extreme concentration in a single organization. Both companies faced external pressure. ViSalus saw revenue drop 80% even though its top leader kept building, because the structural weaknesses underneath that concentration surfaced the moment growth slowed. Modere lost its top leader outright and kept growing, because the business was built on a loyal customer base that existed independent of any individual builder. Same mechanism of extreme concentration. Opposite outcomes.

The variable that made the difference was the customer ratio from Chapter 4. When real customers are the foundation, concentrated leaders can leave or slow down and the company still functions. When the comp plan is the foundation, any shift in the structural engine exposes the company, regardless of whether the top leader is still building.

Vida Divina is the most recent textbook example of leader migration as a launch mechanism. When Armand Puyolt, a former top earner and president at Total Life Changes, launched Vida Divina in September 2016, 43,000 people signed up on the opening weekend. He had prepared product for 10,000. Those 43,000 did not discover a new company. They followed a leader they already knew. By year-end 2016, over 100,000 had enrolled.

Puyolt had spent 24 years building organizations across multiple companies. When he launched Vida Divina, his existing network migrated en masse. The company then pioneered an unusual extension of leader migration: acquiring entire companies to absorb their leader networks and distributor bases. OvaNutric Worldwide in Mexico was acquired in 2017, bringing established teams across seven Latin American countries. MIALÉ in Peru was acquired in 2023, adding 120,000+ members. Each acquisition was essentially a mass leader migration event executed through corporate M&A rather than individual recruiting.

The company's revenue reportedly reached near $1 billion by 2023, though independent estimates vary significantly and the figures are self-reported. The early indicators of customer depth are promising, particularly the cultural resonance documented in the Product-Culture Fit chapter. Whether the customer floor is deep enough to sustain the business through inevitable leader transitions will be determined by the same variables this chapter documents.

Here is the strategic tension at the heart of this chapter. And it's a real tension with no easy resolution.

You need big leaders to grow fast. Leader migration is the fastest-acting driver in the industry. A single leader signing can inject more volume in 90 days than a year of organic recruiting produces. For a company that needs to reach critical mass, that needs to create the perception of momentum, that needs to fill a convention hall with energy, leader migration is the most efficient tool available.

But leader migration carries a structural risk that compounds with scale. Some leaders who migrate find their home. They join because they believe in the product and the vision. They build for a decade. They become the culture. doTERRA's founding team migrated from an established essential oils company and built the most durable momentum story of the modern era. Those leaders weren't renting. They were relocating permanently.

Other leaders migrate because the economics are better. They follow the opportunity. They build fast and move fast. Their organization followed them to your company. It will follow them out.

The challenge for every company is that you can't always tell the difference on day one. Both types show up with energy, with volume, with conviction, and with a story about why this time is different. That difference takes time to show. Which is why the vetting matters more than the signing. And why the ratio of migrated leaders to organic leaders in your top earner ranks should be shifting over time toward organic.

The faster you grow through migration without building organic leadership underneath, the more fragile your foundation becomes. When several migrated leaders leave simultaneously, the revenue impact is severe. Migration itself isn't the problem. Concentration in any single source of leadership is structurally dangerous, regardless of how those leaders arrived.

The companies that survive the longest in this dataset, Herbalife, Mary Kay, Amway, resolved this tension in a specific way. They built brands strong enough that distributor identity tied to the company rather than to the upline. When a Mary Kay consultant introduces herself, she says "I'm with Mary Kay." Not "I'm on Sarah's team." The brand IS the identity. That brand loyalty creates a buffer against leader departure because the field's connection is to the company, not to any individual leader.

Companies that never build brand identity, that allow the field's loyalty to remain entirely with their upline, have no buffer. When the leader moves, the brand means nothing to the people left behind. They don't stay because they love the company. They stay only if they have nowhere else to go.

In the mastermind work, I see both sides of leader migration constantly. I see the company side and the leader side. And the gap between how companies think about leader acquisition and how leaders think about it is one of the biggest disconnects in the industry.

On the company side, the temptation is always the same. "If we could just sign one more big leader, we'd break through." I hear this from owners and top corporates constantly. They are chasing the one signing that will change everything. The one leader whose organization will put them over the top. The one deal that will fill the convention and create the bandwagon effect.

The conversations I've observed over years of working with top earners reveal something many company owners don't realize. When a company signs a big leader, the initial reaction is almost always positive. The field feels a surge of confidence. If this proven winner chose us, we must be doing something right. That early validation can be powerful. It fills convention halls. It creates belief. It signals that the company is attracting talent, not just growing organically.

The dynamic shifts when preferential deals become visible or widespread. Homegrown leaders who have ground it out for years start to feel the quiet frustration of "why them and not us?" Owners sometimes feel the opposite frustration, and they have a point: legacy leaders who built the company a decade ago may no longer be active, yet still receive full recognition and compensation. Both perspectives are valid. The issue isn't that leaders are right or owners are right. The issue is that perception drives behavior. And when the perception shifts from "this company rewards effort" to "this company rewards deals," the culture shifts with it.

The healthiest companies manage both sides. They give fair, transparent bridge arrangements to proven builders who are actually transitioning. They create clear activity requirements that reward current builders. And they don't pretend that every legacy leader who stopped building a decade ago deserves the same treatment as the leader who is actively creating growth today. The balance isn't easy. But the companies that find it retain both their legacy leaders and their rising stars.

Companies regularly lose their best organic leaders because those leaders watch a migrated leader receive in a contract what they spent three years earning through performance. The homegrown leader doesn't leave loudly. She just stops building as hard. She starts taking calls from other companies. And when she leaves, corporate is confused. "She was one of our best. What happened?" What happened is that you told her, through your actions, that the fastest path to value in your company is to leave and come back with leverage.

On the leader side, the calculation is thorough. The top earners I work with, the ones who have been in the industry long enough to know what matters, evaluate a new company the way a CEO evaluates an acquisition. They aren't asking about positioning. The vast majority of experienced leaders know what they can do. They know they can build. They have done it before. They aren't worried about where they sit on a depth chart.

What they're evaluating is everything else. Who are the owners? What is their track record? What is the compensation plan structure, not just the payout percentages but the behavioral incentives? What is the product? Is it real? Would they use it themselves? What is the community and culture like? Is it healthy or is it hype? What is the trajectory of the company? Is it stable? Is it growing? Is it showing honest progress? How do they fit into this specific culture and community?

These are the questions that experienced builders ask. And the product is almost always the starting point, not the afterthought. The leaders who have been through a collapse, who have experienced building inside a company where the product couldn't stand on its own, will not make that mistake again. They lead with conviction about the product because they know everything else is temporary if the product fails the Smoke Detector Test.

There is a smaller percentage, maybe 20%, who do lead with the economics. What is the payout? What is the fast-start? How many people are ahead of me? What does the comp plan ceiling look like? These leaders aren't bad people. They are experienced operators making rational calculations. But the companies that attract primarily economic evaluators build fragile organizations. The companies that attract leaders who evaluated the full picture, owners, product, culture, trajectory, build durable ones.

That isn't cynicism. It is pattern recognition from leaders who have seen enough companies to know what lasts and what doesn't. The leaders who evaluate the full picture tend to stay longer because their decision was based on multiple factors, not just one number. When the comp plan has a slow quarter, they stay because they believe in the product and the people. When a competitor offers a bigger deal, they stay because they invested in a culture they don't want to leave. That multi-factor commitment is harder to break than a single economic calculation.

The leaders who stay long-term, the ones I've seen build seven-figure incomes that last a decade or more, are almost always the ones who reached a point where their customer base generates enough volume that migration economics can't compete. They have real customers. Real reorders. Real income that doesn't depend on recruiting velocity. At that point, starting over at a new company means walking away from a machine that produces income while they sleep. The economic incentive to stay becomes overwhelming.

The companies that retain leaders long-term are the ones that make staying more economically attractive than leaving. Not through handcuffs. Not through non-competes. Through economic reality. If a leader's income is growing at her current company, if her customer base is producing consistent reorders, if her organization is developing new leaders below her who are generating volume she doesn't have to personally drive, the economics of staying outweigh the economics of starting over somewhere new.

The economics of leaving only win when the current income is stagnant or declining. That is why leader departures cluster during slowdowns. When a company's momentum fades, the leaders' incomes flatten. At that point, the next ground-floor opportunity doesn't just look attractive. It looks mathematically superior. And the migration begins.

Retention of leaders, then, is not a relationship problem. It is an economics problem. Make the economics of staying better than the economics of leaving, and leaders stay. Let the economics of staying deteriorate, and no amount of culture, relationship, or recognition will hold them.

There is a shadow side that has to be acknowledged.

Some companies hear the leader migration argument and get nervous. They wonder whether they should be out there recruiting leaders from other companies. The answer is no. Not as a strategy. Not as a priority.

The emphasis and the focus should always be growing the right way. Organic growth. Developing your own leaders. Building your own culture. Creating your own success stories from people who started with zero experience and became six-figure earners inside your brand. Those are the leaders who build your foundation. That is where you invest your time, your resources, and your leadership energy.

And here is what happens when you do that well. When your culture is healthy. When your operations are strong. When your customer acquisition is working. When your field is developing new leaders who are actually succeeding. When your company is showing visible, honest progress. You become attractive. Naturally. Without chasing anyone.

Leaders who are looking for their next home start hearing about you. The field talks. Because your company's results are visible. Because the leaders you developed organically are posting real results on social media, attending industry events with genuine enthusiasm, and telling a story that experienced builders recognize as real. The process of becoming a compelling long-term home for great leaders is a natural byproduct of doing everything else right.

That is fundamentally different from making leader acquisition a strategy. There is something this industry avoids saying out loud.

Every single company owner would welcome a great leader with high integrity who has decided to leave their current company. Every one. Even the owners who preach abundance mentality and would never wish a departure on a competitor. If a leader is already leaving, if she has already made the decision, if she is walking out the door regardless of what you do, then of course you would rather she join your company than someone else's. You want to provide a great opportunity. A great culture. A great fit. You want her to have a good experience in the profession. And yes, you want the volume she brings to help your company grow.

That isn't predatory. That is common sense.

Where the bad karma starts, where the reputation damage begins, where the industry's trust erodes, is when companies target leaders who are happy where they are. When companies throw big money and short-term deals at someone who wasn't looking to leave. When the pitch isn't "we have a great home for you" but "here is what I'll pay you to leave your current company." That is the behavior that poisons the well. And everyone in this profession knows exactly which companies operate this way.

The goal isn't to hunt leaders. The goal is to build a home so compelling that leaders who are already considering a move naturally choose you.

There is a meaningful difference between actively recruiting leaders from other companies and being a viable option for leaders who are going to leave anyway. Every company wants strong leaders to join. Every single one. But the companies that earn that trust without manufacturing it, through product quality, culture, systems, and genuine opportunity, are the ones that sustain momentum longest. The companies that are known primarily for leader acquisition, for being the place that writes the biggest checks to the newest signings, develop a reputation that ultimately works against them. The field across the industry talks. Everyone knows who the hunters are.

The healthiest approach is to invest in creating a company worth joining. Build the culture. Build the product story. Build the systems that make duplication possible. Build the personal development infrastructure that makes leaders better. When those things are real, leaders who are looking for their next home will find you. That is a fundamentally different dynamic than calling someone on their phone with a number.

THE SHADOW SIDE OF PURE ORGANIC GROWTH

The pendulum swings in both directions, and the book has to tell the truth about both. Heavy leader migration creates the easy-in, easy-out dynamic, the rented growth, the culture dilution, all of it. That has been the core argument of this chapter. But there's a shadow side to the opposite extreme that has to be called out, because I've seen it do real damage too.

Companies that build entirely organic, that never bring in an outside leader, that take pride in the fact that every one of their top earners started at zero inside the brand, are doing something right. The culture is deep. The loyalty is real. The story is authentic. None of that is in dispute.

But when that approach hardens into a strict policy, it produces its own set of problems that owners rarely diagnose correctly, because the culture around them has convinced them the approach is superior on every dimension. It isn't.

The first problem is intellectual insulation. A company that refuses to bring in leaders from other parts of the industry also tends to refuse to bring in perspectives, frameworks, or learnings from other parts of the industry. The field is encouraged to see outside companies as distractions, as threats, as noise. Over time, the company stops benchmarking itself against the broader profession. Leaders stop attending outside events. Executives stop reading what other companies are doing. The comp plan stops evolving because the company stops seeing how its plan compares to current industry standards. I've worked with companies whose compensation structures were ten or fifteen years behind the rest of the profession, and the leadership team didn't know it, because there was no mechanism in the culture for honest comparison. The field had been taught that the company was the best, and the executives had been surrounded by that message so long that it had become their assumption rather than their question.

The second problem is what experienced operators call the scarcity mentality dressed up as abundance. A purely organic culture often develops an internal narrative that the company is special, that outsiders don't understand what happens inside these walls, that the company's methods are superior and its challenges are unique. In healthy doses, this is conviction. In unhealthy doses, it's isolation. The company stops asking whether its practices would hold up to outside scrutiny. Outside consultants aren't trusted. Outside data is filtered through an internal lens. Over time, decision quality deteriorates because the decision-making process has lost its corrective mechanisms.

The third problem is the hardest to say out loud. A culture with no outside audit can slowly slide into accountability gaps that it would never tolerate if it were comparing itself to the broader industry. A top leader who mistreats her team but drives volume stays on stage. A policy that would be flagged as regulatory risk by any outside counsel is defended as an in-house nuance. A comp plan tweak that would be rejected by a neutral reviewer as fragile is celebrated internally as innovative. Companies with strong organic cultures regularly develop internal behaviors that wouldn't survive five minutes of honest outside review, with the culture around them having been trained to dismiss anyone who raises concerns as not understanding the company's unique magic.

This doesn't mean organic companies are corrupt. Most aren't. It means that a culture without outside mirrors can't accurately see itself, and without accurate self-perception, even a well-intentioned leadership team can drift into patterns it would correct immediately if it could see them clearly.

The solution isn't to abandon organic culture. Organic depth is a genuine competitive advantage. The solution is to pair organic depth with deliberate outside exposure. Industry conferences. Third-party audits of the comp plan. Board members who have operated at other companies. Consultants who will tell you what your field won't. Peer relationships with other owners where honest conversations happen. None of that weakens the culture. All of it strengthens the culture's ability to see itself accurately and correct before small issues become structural ones.

The healthiest companies I've worked with are the ones that take organic growth seriously as a priority and take outside benchmarking equally seriously as a discipline. They refuse to become leader-hunting machines. They also refuse to become insulated echo chambers. Both extremes produce decline patterns the industry has seen repeatedly. The balance isn't exciting to talk about at conventions, but it's what separates companies that sustain for decades from companies that looked unstoppable for five years and then quietly eroded.

But even when a leader joins for the right reasons, there are risks that many companies underestimate.

The first is the culture clash. A leader who built a massive organization at another company didn't build it in a vacuum. She built it inside a specific culture, with specific language, specific training systems, specific expectations about how things are done. When she arrives at your company, she brings that subculture with her. Ten thousand people who were trained to do things a certain way, who have a certain set of expectations, who may not align with your existing culture at all.

Sometimes the subcultures blend well. Sometimes they collide. The new leader's team expects a certain level of recognition. Your existing leaders feel like the newcomer is getting preferential treatment. The new leader's training system conflicts with yours. Personality clashes emerge between the migrating leaders and the organic leaders who built your company from the ground up. The existing field watches a leader who showed up six months ago get celebrated on stage alongside people who invested five years building from scratch. That creates resentment that festers quietly until it becomes a retention problem of its own.

The second risk is the edification trap. When a big leader joins your company, you celebrate them. You put them on stage. You feature them in marketing. You build them up in front of the entire field for months, sometimes years. Their name becomes associated with your brand. Your field looks up to them as proof that the opportunity is real.

Then they leave.

Now you've spent two years building credibility for someone who just walked out the door. And your field, the people who watched you edify that leader from every stage, is asking themselves: if she left, what does she know that I don't? The departure of an edified leader doesn't just remove volume. It removes belief. And belief, once cracked, is the hardest thing to rebuild in this profession.

This is why vetting matters more than recruiting. The companies that treat leader migration as a numbers game, that sign anyone with volume without screening for fit, are the companies that end up cycling through talent every eighteen months while their organic culture erodes underneath.

I tell every owner the same thing about vetting. Look at the leader's history, not just their volume. The history shows the truth.

If someone was with one company for five, six, seven, eight, ten years and is now looking to move, there's usually a legitimate reason. Maybe the company's direction changed. Maybe the leadership shifted. Maybe the product category got disrupted. A long tenure at a single company signals commitment, loyalty, and the ability to build through hard seasons. That person is a fundamentally different risk profile than someone who has been at three companies in the last two years.

The serial mover tells you everything you need to know. She will tell you that your company is different. That this time it's real. That she has finally found her home. She will sound convincing because she has had this conversation before. Multiple times. And eighteen months from now, she will be having the same conversation with the next company. Because the pattern isn't about the company. It is about the person. And people who switch that often have demonstrated, with documented behavior, that they'll switch again.

You want to believe your opportunity is the one that changes the pattern. It almost never is.

Screen for tenure. Screen for the reason behind the move. Screen for culture alignment. Screen for whether this person builds customers or builds recruiting machines. And screen for whether their organization's loyalty is to the leader or to the product. If the organization will follow the leader anywhere regardless of the company, that's a risk you need to price in. But if the leader is joining because she found a genuine home, if she is committed to building something permanent, if her history shows she plants roots rather than passes through, that's a fundamentally different calculation. The best migrated leaders become your most loyal builders. The worst become your most expensive departures. Vetting is the only way to tell the difference before you find out the hard way.

There is a deeper point here that most corporate teams miss entirely. And it sounds so simple that people dismiss it.

The best way to attract great leaders is to have a great company.

Not a great signing bonus. Not a great BDA. Not a great pitch from the CEO in a private meeting. A great company. Great culture. Great community. Great operations. Great customer acquisition. Great customer retention. A company that's showing progress. Not even massive momentum. Just visible, honest, directional progress.

That is what attracts the leaders worth having. Because the leaders worth having aren't shopping for the biggest check. They are shopping for the best home. They have been in this profession long enough to know the difference between a great deal and a great company. They have seen what happens when you join for the deal. They want something real underneath them this time.

The companies that think the fix is a leader are solving the wrong problem. If your company has holes in it, if your operations are weak, if your customer retention is poor, if your culture is fractured, if your product story has lost its edge, then signing a great leader doesn't fix those things. It masks them. Temporarily.

Think of it as a leaky bucket. The water represents sponsoring and recruiting. A great leader pours water into the bucket faster than anyone else. But if the bucket has holes, if customers are leaving, if new distributors are churning out in 90 days, if the product experience is inconsistent, then the water pours out as fast as it pours in. The leader creates an illusion of momentum. Revenue spikes. Conventions fill up. The numbers look incredible for a quarter or two. Then the leader's initial surge normalizes. The holes in the bucket become visible again. And the company is back where it started, except now it also has to explain to the field why the leader they celebrated for six months isn't producing the results everyone expected.

Fix the bucket first. Patch the holes. Build the operations, the customer experience, the retention systems, the culture that makes people want to stay. Then when a great leader arrives, the water she pours in actually accumulates. It compounds. It builds something durable.

The companies that attract the best leaders consistently aren't the ones with the best offers. They are the ones with the best fundamentals. Because great leaders can see fundamentals. They have been in enough rooms and evaluated enough companies to know the difference between a company that's built to hold water and a company that's hoping the next leader will pour fast enough to hide the leaks.

Performance agreements and bridge arrangements exist on a spectrum. Transparent, time-limited bridge payments to help proven leaders transition, bridging income gaps while they rebuild in a new environment, have been used successfully by selective companies. The key is transparency, selectivity, and a clear sunset. The leader earns the bridge through documented production, not through showing up. The field knows it exists. It isn't a secret backroom deal.

The companies that turn bridge arrangements into entitlement programs for anyone who switches create a different dynamic entirely. When there are no secrets in this profession, and there aren't, the story of the special deal gets out. Then everyone wants their deal. The culture shifts from duplication to entitlement. Instead of "what can I build?" the conversation becomes "what can I negotiate?" That poisons the well for every organic builder who earned their rank through the comp plan while someone else negotiated theirs.

Simultaneously, companies must invest in developing leaders from within. Built to Last covers the personal development and leadership development infrastructure in depth. Many companies got away from that investment and wanted the shortcut of only finding experienced leaders from elsewhere. The shortcut works in the short term. In the long term, the companies with the deepest organic leadership pipelines are the ones with the most durable organizations.

Over time, the ratio of experienced leaders who joined from other companies to organic leaders who grew up inside your culture should shift. The maturation of a company is measured partly by this ratio. When your most successful leaders are the ones who started with zero experience and built their careers inside your brand, your organization's loyalty is with the company, not with any individual. That is the most resilient structure possible.

A powerful long-term indicator of healthy duplication is the percentage of your six- and seven-figure earners who are first-time successful direct sellers. People who never built at another company. People who learned the profession inside your culture. If your company is ten years old and the majority of your top earners are experienced leaders who migrated from other companies, you have a recruiting culture. If the majority are people who had their first meaningful success inside your brand, you have a duplication culture.

A critical caveat: this metric doesn't apply to newer companies. If you launched two or three years ago, your top earners are almost certainly experienced leaders from other companies. That is normal. That is how companies start. You need proven builders to create the initial momentum, the first success stories, the early culture that attracts the next wave. Nobody expects a three-year-old company to have a roster full of homegrown seven-figure earners. That takes time.

The metric matters as the years go on. It is a directional indicator, not a snapshot judgment. Track it over time. At year three, your top earner list will be dominated by experienced leaders who joined early. At year five, you should start seeing homegrown success stories emerging. At year ten, the ratio should be shifting meaningfully toward organic leaders. The goal isn't to hit a specific number at a specific date. The goal is that the percentage of homegrown leaders in your top ranks is increasing every year. If that ratio is moving in the right direction, your systems are working. If it's stagnant or moving backward, you're still dependent on importing talent rather than developing it. Track this ratio over time. It tells you whether your systems are creating new leaders or just importing them. The companies with the highest first-time success ratios also tend to have the highest loyalty ratios, because a leader whose identity was formed inside your culture has no comparison point. Your company isn't one option among many. It is home.

The companies that never make that transition, that stay permanently dependent on outside leader acquisition, are the ones that appear in the decline dataset. The leaders who built them were the leaders who eventually left them. And there was nothing underneath to hold the organization together.

There is a related metric that's just as important and even simpler to track: leader tenure. How long have your top leaders been with your company?

But before we get to the metrics, there's one case study that matters more than any other in this chapter. Because it proves, with devastating clarity, that a company can do almost everything right on paper and still collapse if it builds its foundation on leader acquisition instead of organic growth.

Jeunesse Global became, by company-reported figures, the youngest company in direct selling history to reach $1 billion in annual sales. It did it in six years. By 2018, annual revenue hit approximately $1.46 billion. The company operated in over 140 countries with 32 fully operational offices. It had nearly 675,000 distributors. It appeared on the DSN Global 100 for seven consecutive years, ranking as high as number 13. It won over 30 growth-related awards. Five consecutive years on the Inc. 5000. $8 billion in cumulative sales by January 2021. Five consecutive years above $1 billion in annual revenue from 2015 through 2019.

Read those numbers again. This wasn't a fragile company on paper. This was diversified across countries. It had multiple product lines spanning skincare, supplements, and nutritional products. It had global infrastructure. It had brand recognition. It had the awards, the rankings, and the cumulative sales that would make any company owner's résumé look bulletproof.

And by 2024, Jeunesse had ceased operations. Its assets were acquired by Velovita. The DSSRC referred the company to the FTC and the Florida Attorney General after repeated failures to respond to compliance inquiries. The co-founder filed a lawsuit alleging that executives had stolen tens of millions from the company. By the end of 2024, Tracxn listed the company's employee count at one.

From the youngest billion-dollar company in the industry's history to one employee. That isn't a slow decline. That is a structural collapse.

What happened?

Jeunesse built its growth primarily on leader acquisition. The company was known throughout the industry as one of the most aggressive recruiters of established top earners from other companies. The deals were significant. The positioning was attractive. The economics were designed to pull proven producers from wherever they were building and plug them into the Jeunesse system.

And it worked. Spectacularly. For about five years.

But here is what leader acquisition without organic culture produces. It produces a company where the top earners are loyal to their deals, not to the brand. Where the subcultures of a dozen different companies are mixed together under one roof, each with different expectations, different training systems, different languages for how business gets done. Where there's no shared identity because nobody grew up together. Where the community and culture that make direct selling companies resilient never had a chance to form because the people at the top were always transient.

Jeunesse had the diversification. Multiple product lines. Over 140 countries. Global infrastructure. On paper, it checked the boxes that this book says matter. Product diversification. Geographic diversification. Operational scale.

But the one thing it didn't build was loyalty. Because loyalty in direct selling comes from shared experience over time. It comes from leaders who struggled together in the early days. Who were there when the company was small and unproven. Who built their identity inside the brand. Who have five, eight, ten years of history with the company and can't imagine being anywhere else. That kind of loyalty isn't available for purchase at any price. It can only be grown. And it takes years.

When leaders join for the deal, they leave for the deal. That isn't a character flaw. It is rational behavior. The deal at Jeunesse attracted them. A better deal somewhere else attracted them more. The same economics that made leader acquisition the company's growth engine made leader departure the company's decline engine. The door swings both ways at the same speed.

The leaders who left took their organizations with them. Because the organizations had followed the leaders to Jeunesse in the first place. The loyalty chain ran from distributor to leader to leader to deal. The company was never in that chain. When the leaders moved, the chain moved with them.

And the edification trap compounded the damage. Jeunesse had celebrated these leaders on stages around the world. Put their names on screens. Told their stories to hundreds of thousands of distributors. Built belief around individual personalities rather than around the brand. When those personalities left, the belief left with them. The field was left wondering: if the people we were told to admire are leaving, why are we still here?

There is something else that happens when a company's culture is built on imported leaders rather than organic growth. Title inflation. When you recruit proven top earners and give them rank placement or accelerated advancement, you create a hierarchy that wasn't earned through the company's systems. The existing field watches someone show up on day one at a rank that took them three years to achieve. That creates resentment. It creates a two-tier culture: the leaders who earned it and the leaders who negotiated it. And over time, the negotiators set the tone because they're the ones on stage. The culture becomes transactional. "What is my deal?" replaces "What can I build?" And once that shift happens, it's almost impossible to reverse.

Jeunesse is the single most important case study in this chapter because it proves that diversification of products, diversification of markets, and operational scale aren't enough. Those things matter. They are necessary. But they're not sufficient. Without organic loyalty, without a culture that was grown rather than purchased, without leaders whose tenure and identity are anchored to the brand, the diversification becomes a decorative facade over a hollow foundation.

The leaky bucket metaphor from earlier in this chapter applies perfectly. Jeunesse's bucket had impressive dimensions. Global reach. Multiple product lines. Strong branding. But the holes in the bucket were the leaders who were always one deal away from leaving. No amount of water poured in from the top could compensate for the structural drain at the bottom.

The lesson isn't that leader migration is wrong. doTERRA's founding was leader migration. Many of the most successful companies in the industry were accelerated by proven leaders who joined and stayed for decades. The lesson is that leader migration must be paired with organic culture-building, honest vetting, long-term retention economics, and a deliberate strategy to grow homegrown leaders who will never leave because they have no reason to. Jeunesse did the first part brilliantly and neglected the second part entirely. That collapse is the most dramatic proof in the industry's history that you can't buy your way to durability.

The math is basic. If your top leaders are there because of the deal, they'll leave because of the deal. And when they leave, they take everything they brought with them. Including the illusion that you had a company underneath them.

The math is basic. If your company has been around for ten years and your top twenty earners have an average tenure of seven or eight years, you have stability. Those leaders have been through hard seasons. They have seen the company manage challenges. They stayed. That tenure isn't just a number on a spreadsheet. It is proof that the economics of staying have consistently outweighed the economics of leaving. It means your comp plan rewards long-term building. It means your culture retains people. It means your product keeps customers reordering. Tenure is the compound interest of loyalty.

If your company has been around for ten years and your top twenty earners have an average tenure of two years, you have a revolving door. You are constantly replacing leaders. Each new arrival gets edified, celebrated, and promoted for eighteen months. Then they leave. Then the next one arrives. The field watches this cycle and draws the obvious conclusion: this company can't hold its best people.

A brand new company can't have long tenure. That is obvious. At year two, your longest-tenured leader has been with you for two years. But you should know what you're building toward. The goal is that every year, the average tenure of your top earner group increases. That number moving up is one of the strongest signals of organizational health in direct selling. It means people are staying. It means they're building something they don't want to walk away from. It means the foundation is holding.

Track it alongside the homegrown ratio. Together, those two numbers tell you whether your company is building a culture of permanence or a culture of turnover. And every year that both numbers move in the right direction, your company becomes harder to disrupt, harder to raid, and harder to break.

Measure this.

THE LEADER CONCENTRATION RISK ASSESSMENT

Question 1: What percentage of your total company volume is generated by your top five organizations?

If the top five organizations account for more than 50% of total volume, you have significant concentration risk. Any single departure can create a visible revenue impact. If the top five account for more than 70%, you're in the danger zone where the departure of one or two leaders could trigger a cascading decline.

Question 2: What percentage of your field leaders arrived through migration versus organic development?

If more than 60% of your top earners came from other companies, your leadership bench is structurally mobile. These leaders have demonstrated their willingness to move. They may move again. Track this ratio over time. It should be declining as you develop organic leaders.

Question 3: How strong is your customer base independent of any single leader?

The company doesn't own the relationship. The leader built it. That is how direct selling works and it's unrealistic to expect otherwise. But the company owns the reason the relationship continues: the product, the systems, the fulfillment, the reorder experience. When a leader leaves, some people will always follow. If the leader is talented and has deep personal relationships, a significant portion of their organization will go with them regardless of how good the company is. That is simply how this model works. The real protection isn't preventing departure. It is building a customer base so strong that even when distributors leave, the customers stay. If customers love the product and reorder because of the product, the departure of a leader hurts recruiting but doesn't destroy revenue. This is the Modere lesson from earlier in this chapter: the company lost a major leader and kept growing because the customers were loyal to the product, not to the person who introduced them to it.

Question 4: What is the economic incentive for your top leaders to stay?

Is their income growing? Are their customer reorders increasing? Are they developing new leaders below them who reduce their personal workload? Or is their income flat, their customer base stagnant, and their daily reality a grind of maintaining what they've built? If the economics of staying are deteriorating, the migration window is opening.

Question 5: Do you have a leadership development pipeline that produces organic leaders?

Not mentorship programs. Not training modules. Actual organic leaders who have risen through your system from new distributor to top earner without having been recruited from another company. If you can't name at least five such leaders, your leadership bench is migration-dependent.

Scoring:

High concentration + high migration ratio + leader loyalty + deteriorating economics + no organic pipeline: you're one or two departures from a crisis. Address this immediately.

Moderate concentration + mixed migration/organic + growing economics: you're in a transitional position. Invest heavily in organic development while you have the revenue to fund it.

Low concentration + organic-dominant leadership + strong brand identity: you've built the resilience that most companies in this industry never achieve.

Consider a company that uses leader migration as a tool rather than a crutch.

They sign strong external leaders during growth phases to accelerate momentum. They give those leaders fair compensation and genuine support. But they also track concentration risk quarterly. They know exactly what percentage of their volume sits inside each organization. They invest disproportionately in developing organic leaders who have no history of migration.

When a migrated leader starts showing signs of restlessness, they don't panic. They already know how much volume is at risk because they've been tracking it. They've already been building organic depth underneath that leader's organization. The departure hurts. It always hurts. But it doesn't threaten the company's existence because the foundation was never entirely dependent on one person's commitment.

That company has used leader migration without becoming hostage to it. That is the only way to deploy this driver safely.

A recurring conversation in the masterminds I run with seven-figure field leaders. The question of when to move. Leaders are always evaluating their current company against the alternatives. Every significant earner in this industry is getting recruited constantly. Whether they're being pursued isn't the variable. What they're weighing is.

The pattern I see over and over is this. Leaders don't leave when the money gets bad. They leave when the belief gets bad. Long before the income drops, the leader starts noticing that corporate is making reactive decisions, that the product pipeline is thin, that the executive team doesn't have a clear answer for where the company is going, or that the promises made at the last convention haven't been kept. The money is still coming. But the confidence is already gone. And once confidence is gone, the leader is evaluating every other company they hear about with fresh eyes.

The signal that a company is about to lose a major leader isn't usually visible in the compensation data. It is visible in the communication data. Is the leader still attending corporate calls? Are they still posting about the company voluntarily? Are they bringing up the company's vision in their own team training? When those markers fade, the departure is usually 12 to 18 months out. Corporate teams that want to retain leaders should stop tracking only income and start tracking belief. Belief is the real leading indicator. Income is the lagging one.

The next chapter covers the most reliable momentum driver for established companies: Market Expansion. What happens when you open a new country where your product category has no direct-selling competition. The math is different. The risks are different. And the lessons from Amway's $11.8 billion peak and Nu Skin's China shock tell you everything you need to know about the reward and the danger.

THE BOTTOM LINE: Leader migration is the fastest-acting driver and the most dangerous if not paired with organic culture-building. Track your ratio of migrated leaders to homegrown leaders. If it's not shifting toward organic over time, your growth is rented.

Rented growth is still growth. Just know your lease terms.

Chapter 9: Market Expansion

Every new country is a reset button. Fresh networks. No brand fatigue. Ground-floor energy. Whether you're pressing reset on purpose or out of desperation determines whether the reset works.

The enemy in this chapter: expansion used to hide domestic stagnation.

In 1959, Amway was an American cleaning products company selling door-to-door in Michigan. Thirty years later, it was still largely an American company. Revenue had plateaued at roughly $1 billion. The U.S. market was mature. The domestic recruiting story had lost its energy. Growth had stalled.

Then Amway went international. And the math changed completely.

Between 1990 and 1996, Amway's reported global revenue grew from $1 billion to $7 billion. A 600% increase in six years. The growth came almost entirely from new markets: Japan, Korea, China, Latin America, Eastern Europe. By the mid-1990s, international sales accounted for more than 70% of total revenue. The domestic American business that had defined the company for three decades became the minority of its own revenue.

China was the transformation. Amway entered China in 1995 and built it into the company's largest single market. By 2008, China alone was generating $2.5 billion in revenue with 28% year-over-year growth. At Amway's all-time peak in 2013, reported global revenue reached $11.8 billion, with China contributing over $4.3 billion. More than a third of the largest direct selling company in history came from a single country that the company hadn't even entered two decades earlier.

That is market expansion as a momentum driver, not incremental growth or a 5% bump from adding a small European market. A complete transformation of a company's trajectory, driven by accessing tens of millions of consumers in a market where the product category had zero direct selling competition.

The mechanism is specific to direct selling and it's powerful. In traditional retail, international expansion is enormously expensive. You need stores, distribution infrastructure, marketing campaigns, local management teams, regulatory compliance, and years of investment before the market produces a return. In direct selling, the distributors absorb most of the sales and marketing cost. The company provides the product, the comp plan, and the back-office systems. The field does the rest. That makes international expansion cheaper than in traditional retail models.

But cheaper doesn't mean cheap. And this is where many companies underestimate what international expansion actually costs.

The hidden expenses add up fast. Product registration and regulatory approval in each market can take months and cost tens of thousands of dollars per product per country. You need a general manager for the market, someone who understands the local business culture, speaks the language, and has authority to make decisions without calling headquarters for every approval. You need localized shipping and inventory management, which means either a local fulfillment center or a reliable third-party logistics partner. Pricing has to be adapted for local economics, which requires market research, competitive analysis, and often a different margin structure than your domestic business. Some countries require the company to maintain a minimum bank balance in-country as a condition of operating. You need local legal counsel who understands the direct selling regulatory framework in that specific jurisdiction. And you need cultural intelligence, not a translated website, but a genuine understanding of how business relationships work in that market, what the local customs around selling are, and which practices that work in the United States will actively offend people in another culture.

Companies that do this right invest real money upfront. Companies that try to open on the cheap, skipping the GM, skipping the product registration, shipping from the U.S. at inflated prices, using Google Translate for their materials, create exactly the kind of "fake opening" that the field reads immediately and never forgives.

The field has heard the stories. Leaders talk across companies and across borders. A reputation for half-committed market launches spreads faster than the launch itself. The leader in Colombia who got burned by a company that opened without real infrastructure tells her friends in Mexico. The leader in Thailand who built for six months on promises that "corporate is coming" and then watched the company pull out tells everyone at the next industry event. These stories accumulate. And the leaders worth having, the ones who would actually build a real business in your new market, screen for them before they commit.

International expansion in direct selling is more affordable than traditional retail expansion. That is true. But treating it as cheap or easy is how companies end up with a dozen open markets, none of which are producing meaningful volume, all of which are draining management bandwidth and cash.

The timing balance is critical, and there's no formula for it. This is one of the hardest strategic decisions a company faces.

Diversify too soon and you kill what is working. A company that's growing well in its domestic market and diverts leadership attention, field energy, and capital into an international launch too early can disrupt the momentum that was funding the growth in the first place. The new market becomes the shiny toy. Everyone is excited about the launch. The domestic business, which was the engine, gets neglected. Leaders who were focused on building at home start spending time and money flying to the new market. The domestic growth slows. The international market, which was supposed to be additive, becomes a distraction that subtracts from the core.

Diversify too late and you miss the window. A company that waits until its domestic growth has stalled before exploring international expansion has already lost years of potential growth. The best international markets have windows. Leaders who are excited about your product today may not be available in three years. Cultural relevance has a shelf life. Competitors may enter the market first and establish the narrative. Waiting until you need international revenue to survive is the definition of expanding from weakness, which we covered above.

The companies that time it right are the ones that begin laying international groundwork while the domestic business is still healthy and growing. Not launching. Laying groundwork. Researching markets. Building relationships. Testing product-market fit informally. So that when the domestic growth naturally matures, the international pipeline is ready, not rushed.

A new country provides three acceleration points simultaneously. A fresh market means recruiting is easier because nobody is tired of hearing about the opportunity yet. Cultural novelty around the product generates organic buzz because the market has never seen it before. As we saw in the Chapter 1 example where a leader was already building informally before the official launch, pent-up demand often exists because products have been flowing informally across borders for months or years before the official launch. When Amway officially entered a new market, there were usually already people using the products, imported through informal channels, waiting for the company to show up and formalize what was already happening.

This is why market expansion is the most reliable momentum driver for established companies. Product-culture fit depends on timing a cultural wave. Platform disruption depends on technology shifts. Leader migration depends on individual relationships. Market expansion depends on a map. There is always another country.

But the map is also the trap. And the most instructive company for understanding both the salvation and the danger of market expansion is Nu Skin, because they lived through both. Twice.

Nu Skin was founded in 1984 and grew rapidly through the late 1980s. By 1991, annual sales had multiplied to approximately $500 million. The distributor force had grown to 100,000. Management was talking about reaching $10 billion in a decade. The trajectory looked unstoppable.

Then in July 1991, ABC's Nightline aired a devastating expose. Guest host Barbara Walters asked the question that would nearly destroy the company: "Is Nu Skin nothing but a scheme promising the American dream while for many delivering only the nightmare?"

The segment featured former distributors with thousands of dollars of unsold product in their basements. State attorneys general pounced. Michigan and Connecticut accused Nu Skin of operating an illegal pyramid scheme. In 1992, the company settled with five states over allegations of deceptive advertising and misleading recruiting practices. The U.S. business was in crisis. Revenue cratered domestically. The brand that had been growing explosively was suddenly toxic in its home market.

What saved Nu Skin was the map. The company had begun operations in Asia in 1991, starting with Hong Kong. Japan became the lifeline. While the American business reeled from the Barbara Walters fallout and regulatory scrutiny, the Japanese market provided revenue and momentum that kept the company alive. International expansion didn't just grow Nu Skin. It saved Nu Skin from a domestic crisis that could have been fatal.

That survival created a template. And the template became a trap.

Because Nu Skin's experience taught the entire industry a lesson that was half right and half dangerous. The half-right lesson: international expansion can rescue a company from domestic problems. The half-dangerous lesson: it will always work.

Companies watched Nu Skin survive and concluded that international markets were the answer to every growth stall. Revenue flattening in North America? Open Asia. That thinking led directly to the epidemic of premature market launches that plagued the industry for the next two decades. Companies opened markets before they were ready. Before they had local infrastructure. Before they had adapted products and pricing. Before they had committed the resources to succeed. They opened markets because they needed a headline, not because they had a strategy. And most of those launches failed, costing both money and credibility. The money was recoverable. The credibility with international field leaders who had been promised real support wasn't.

Nu Skin's own story illustrates the danger of the template it created. The company that was saved by Japan became dangerously concentrated in China twenty years later.

In 2012, Nu Skin's revenue was $2.17 billion, the product of nearly three decades of building, adapting, and reinventing. Then the company launched its ageLOC TR90 weight management system in Greater China in the third quarter of 2013. What happened next was one of the most dramatic single-quarter surges in direct selling history.

Revenue in the Greater China region surged 240% year-over-year. Sales leader count improved 255%. In a single quarter, the region generated $464.6 million. Nu Skin reported its first-ever billion-dollar quarter. Full-year revenue hit $3.18 billion. The stock reached $94. It was the highest revenue the company had ever achieved.

The problem was concentration in a volatile market. At peak, China accounted for 37% of Nu Skin's total global sales.

A necessary caveat. Every company that expands internationally is going to have heavy concentration in one market during its early international years. If you open Japan and it takes off, Japan might represent 50% or more of your international revenue for the first several years. That is normal. That is the math of having one strong market and several developing ones. Concentration isn't automatically a problem. It is a phase. The goal is to diversify over time, gradually reducing the percentage that any single country represents.

What matters more than the raw percentage is which country that concentration is in. Thirty-seven percent of revenue from the United States is a very different risk profile than 37% from China. The U.S. has a stable regulatory environment for direct selling. The FTC's rules are known. The legal framework is established. Concentration in a stable market is a strategic consideration you manage over time. Concentration in a volatile market is a structural vulnerability that can detonate without warning.

It isn't wrong to be in China. The growth potential is enormous. Companies have built billions there. But you have to understand that you're building in a market where the regulatory environment for direct selling is uniquely complicated, where government investigations can be triggered by a single media article, and where political dynamics can shift overnight. Building there's a legitimate strategy. Building there without pricing in the volatility is reckless.

That is what happened to Nu Skin.

In January 2014, the People's Daily, the official newspaper of the Chinese Communist Party, published a series of articles questioning Nu Skin's business practices. A government investigation followed. Nu Skin's stock dropped 33% in a single day. Not over a month. Not over a quarter. In one day. One-third of the company's market value, erased by a newspaper article in the market that represented more than a third of its revenue.

Revenue fell to $2.57 billion in 2014. A partial rebound to $2.68 billion in 2018 was reversed by China's "100-day crackdown" on health product companies in 2019. Revenue has continued to decline, reaching $1.73 billion in 2024 with guidance of $1.48 to $1.62 billion for 2025.

But here is what deserves recognition. Nu Skin is still here. Forty years after its founding, the company has continually found ways to overcome its trials. The Barbara Walters expose. State investigations. The China crackdown. Each time, the company adapted. It reinvented its product line, from personal care to ageLOC anti-aging to beauty devices to intelligent wellness platforms. It restructured its comp plan. It invested in new technology categories and new geographic markets. The company that was nearly destroyed by a Nightline segment in 1991 is still operating, still innovating, and still employing thousands of people four decades later. That resilience is rare in any industry. In direct selling, it's extraordinary.

Nu Skin's setback wasn't because the product was bad. It wasn't because the field wasn't talented. The setback came from building 37% geographic concentration into a single volatile market with no plan for what would happen when that market turned hostile. The company has spent the years since absorbing the cost of that concentration and rebuilding around new markets, new product categories, and new field strategies. The lesson sits in the concentration decision, not in any verdict on the company itself.

Amway's China story contains the same lesson, told over a longer timeline. China's $4.3 billion contribution to Amway's $11.8 billion peak was magnificent. It was also a concentration risk of the same kind. When China's direct selling regulatory environment tightened, when consumer sentiment shifted, when domestic Chinese competitors emerged, Amway's global revenue declined. From $11.8 billion in 2013 to reported estimates in the $8 billion range in recent years. The decline wasn't a collapse. It was a slow erosion of the single market that had driven the peak.

The equal and opposite of market expansion is geographic concentration. The same force that creates the most dramatic growth creates the most dangerous vulnerability. When one market accounts for more than 30% of your global revenue, your company's fate is tied to the political, regulatory, economic, and competitive dynamics of that one market. You aren't a global company. You are a single-market company with a global mailing address.

There is a non-DS parallel that makes this pattern visceral.

In the early 2000s, Nokia dominated the global mobile phone market. At peak, Nokia held roughly 40% of global market share. More than a billion people used Nokia phones. The company was Finland's largest corporation, contributed 4% of the country's GDP, and was one of the most valuable companies in Europe.

Nokia's dominance had been built through geographic expansion. While Motorola and Ericsson focused primarily on the U.S. and European markets, Nokia aggressively pursued emerging markets in Asia, Africa, and Latin America. The company was among the first to build distribution infrastructure in India, where it eventually captured 70% of the mobile phone market. It was among the first in China. Among the first across sub-Saharan Africa. By the mid-2000s, Nokia sold phones in more than 150 countries and had a presence in markets that most Western technology companies hadn't even considered.

The expansion strategy was deliberate and brilliant. Nokia designed phones specifically for emerging market consumers. Cheap. Durable. Long battery life. Simple interfaces. Phones that could survive dust, heat, and rural conditions. The company invested in understanding local cultures, local distribution networks, and local price points. It wasn't exporting a Western product. It was building products for the markets it wanted to win.

Revenue tripled in the decade between 1998 and 2008. Nokia became the textbook case study in how geographic expansion could transform a company's trajectory. Business schools taught it. Investors celebrated it. The company seemed unstoppable.

But Nokia's expansion created a specific organizational vulnerability. The emerging markets that drove its growth wanted cheap, reliable phones. Not smartphones. Not app ecosystems. Not touchscreens. Basic devices for voice and text. Nokia built its entire product development pipeline, its manufacturing infrastructure, its cost structure, and its organizational culture around serving those markets. The company became exceptionally good at building the phones that its biggest markets demanded.

When Apple launched the iPhone in 2007 and Google launched Android in 2008, Nokia was caught between two worlds. Its emerging market customers didn't want smartphones yet. Its developed market customers suddenly wanted nothing else. Nokia's organizational DNA, shaped by a decade of building for emerging markets, could not pivot fast enough. The skills, habits, and assumptions that made Nokia dominant in one era made it irrelevant in the next.

By 2013, Nokia's phone business was sold to Microsoft for $7.2 billion. A company that had been valued at over $250 billion at its peak. Sold for less than 3% of that value.

The direct selling lesson is this. Market expansion shapes your company's DNA. The markets that grow you teach you how to operate. Your comp plan adapts to work in those markets. Your field systems optimize for those markets. Your corporate culture orients around those markets. That adaptation is necessary. It is also a constraint. When the next phase of your business requires a different approach, the habits formed during expansion can become the very thing that prevents you from evolving.

What I see in the community that connects directly to this driver. And what I've experienced personally, having spoken in 25 countries and seen international expansion from every angle.

The field always knows before corporate does when an international market is real versus when it's a flag on a slide.

The top earners who have built internationally share a consistent observation. When a company opens a new market with genuine investment, with boots on the ground, with localized product and pricing, with a comp plan adapted for the local economy, the field responds. Leaders fly in. They hold events. They invest their own time and money because they believe the company is committed.

When a company opens a market as what I call a "hope and a prayer" launch, the field reads it immediately. No in-country management. No localized materials. No adapted pricing. Just a website, a shipping address, and a press release. The field knows this is a company trying to buy time with a headline. "We just opened six new countries!" sounds great on a conference call. It means nothing if those countries have no real infrastructure behind them.

I've been on the ground in markets where both scenarios played out. Standing in a room in Asia where a company had invested in a local office, a local general manager with authority to make decisions, translated materials, adapted pricing, and a field team that felt fully supported. The energy in that room was unmistakable. People believed they were part of something real. They were right.

I've also been in rooms in markets where the company had done none of those things. Where the local leaders had been building for months on promises that corporate was "coming soon." Where the products were overpriced because nobody had adjusted for local economics. Where the training materials were in English and the field was supposed to figure it out. Where the local leaders had already started losing belief because they could feel the half-heartedness radiating from headquarters.

The difference between a real market launch and a fake one isn't about the size of the investment. Some markets can be opened effectively with modest resources. The difference is commitment. Real commitment means the company has decided this market matters for the next five years, not the next quarter. It means the local field can see evidence of that decision in every touchpoint. Fake commitment is visible too, and the field's response is predictable: they stop building, they stop believing, and they tell their friends at other companies that the launch was a joke.

The companies that use market expansion as a legitimate momentum driver invest upfront. They spend money before they make money. They hire local. They adapt the product and the comp plan for local economics. They commit for years, not quarters. And they ensure that the market's growth doesn't create dangerous concentration by continuing to invest in their established markets simultaneously.

The companies that use market expansion as a desperation move, as a way to mask domestic decline with an international headline, almost always fail in the new market and accelerate their decline at home. Because the field isn't fooled. And when the new market doesn't materialize, the narrative damage is worse than if they had never launched at all.

Herbalife offers a third model of market expansion that deserves direct analysis because its broad early distribution softened the concentration trap that caught Nu Skin and Amway, even though the company developed its own concentration to manage over time.

Herbalife operates in more than 90 markets worldwide, and its growth from roughly $1.2 billion in 2003 to $4.96 billion in 2014 was driven substantially by international markets distributed across Latin America,

Asia-Pacific, Europe, and North America. The Nutrition Club concept was particularly effective in Latin American and Hispanic communities, creating physical gathering points where consumers could experience the products daily. That said, broad market distribution doesn't make a company immune to concentration. Herbalife has built a business in India that now exceeds a billion dollars in annual revenue, which is a genuine success and also a genuine concentration exposure in a market that has proven difficult and unpredictable for direct sellers. The lesson isn't that Herbalife avoided concentration entirely. It is that broad early distribution gave the company more places to absorb a shock in any single market, even as success in a market like India eventually created its own concentration to manage.

The Nutrition Club model is worth examining because it created something that most direct selling companies never achieve in international markets: a genuine daily consumption habit tied to a physical location. A Nutrition Club is essentially a smoothie bar run by a distributor. Customers come in every day. They drink a shake. They socialize. They develop a routine. The product becomes embedded in their daily life in a way that online ordering or monthly autoship never achieves.

In Latin America specifically, the Nutrition Club concept aligned with existing cultural patterns. Gathering at a local spot for a morning drink or an evening snack was already a social norm. Herbalife didn't impose an American distribution model on a foreign culture. It built a distribution model that matched the culture's existing behavior. That alignment produced retention rates in club-based markets that exceeded what the company achieved through traditional distributor-to-consumer selling.

This model produced durable international growth because the customers were real. They were showing up every day. They were paying for a product they consumed on the spot. The relationship was with the product and the community, not with the comp plan. When Herbalife faced the $200 million FTC settlement in 2016 and was required to restructure its U.S. business to document genuine retail customers, the Nutrition Club model in international markets was largely unaffected. The clubs already had real customers. The regulatory pressure that threatened the U.S. business barely registered in the markets where the customer model was strongest.

Herbalife still faces headwinds. But the diversified geographic model means that no single market's decline threatens the company's existence. When one market softens, others hold. That resilience is a direct function of diversification, and proof that the leadership team was willing to adapt through multiple crises across four decades.

The contrast with Nu Skin is instructive. Nu Skin's peak was higher on a relative basis (revenue tripled from $1.18 billion to $3.18 billion). Herbalife's peak was reached more gradually (quadrupled from $1.2 billion to $4.96 billion over eleven years). But Nu Skin's decline has been steeper and more sustained because the concentration risk was higher. Herbalife's decline has been shallower because no single domino triggers a cascade.

There is a shadow side that deserves attention.

Some companies hear the market expansion argument and conclude that the answer to every growth problem is a new country. Revenue flattening in North America? Open Asia. Revenue declining in Asia? Open Latin America. Revenue stalling in Latin America? Open Africa.

This is geographic escape, not geographic strategy. Each new market launch costs money. Each one stretches management bandwidth. Each one creates new compliance requirements, new cultural complexities, new logistical challenges. If the company's core business is unhealthy, opening new markets doesn't fix the underlying problem. It just spreads the symptoms across more geographies.

A note on what international expansion actually costs. The number varies enormously by market, regulatory environment, infrastructure requirements, and the company's existing operational maturity. There is no single cost figure that fits every launch. What I can say is that the cost categories are predictable even when the dollar amounts aren't. Regulatory and legal compliance to enter the market. Local fulfillment and warehousing infrastructure or partnerships. Local-language customer service capability. Local payment processing. Local product registration, often involving testing, label translation, and reformulation if ingredients are restricted. Local marketing materials and field training translated and culturally adapted. Local team hires or contractor relationships for the first eighteen to thirty-six months. Pre-launch and launch event costs for the first generation of leaders. Each category has a base cost that doesn't go away just because the launch happens to be small. A leader projecting an international launch should run the worst-case scenario on each category, add a contingency for the costs that always emerge during the first year, and ask whether the projected revenue justifies the projected investment over a three to five year window. Many international launches that look cheap on paper become expensive in execution because the second-order costs were never modeled. Many that look expensive on paper turn out to be the right investment because the underlying market has the demand to support it. The discipline is to model the full cost with discipline, not to start with the revenue assumption and back into a cost number that supports it.

I've sat in rooms where a company's top field leader in Asia said quietly: "They opened our country because they needed a press release, not because they were ready." That leader had spent six months trying to get customer service responses in her language. Her team was ordering product from the U.S. website because the local fulfillment center wasn't stocked. The "international launch" that made the corporate newsletter was, on the ground, a half-built operation that was eroding belief faster than it was building volume. The field always knows the difference between a real commitment and a headline.

The diagnostic question is this: is international expansion an extension of domestic strength or an escape from domestic weakness?

Amway expanded internationally from a position of domestic maturity. The U.S. business was stable and profitable. International expansion was additive. Nu Skin expanded from a position of domestic success and used China to reach an entirely new growth tier. The problem wasn't the expansion itself but the concentration that resulted.

The companies that fail at international expansion are almost always the ones expanding from weakness. They need the new market to work because the core business is in trouble. That desperation transmits to the field. Leaders sense it. They know the company is running from something, not building toward something. And desperate launches produce desperate results.

Score your readiness.

THE INTERNATIONAL MOMENTUM SCORECARD

Question 1: What is your geographic revenue concentration?

If any single country accounts for more than 40% of total revenue, assess the volatility of that market. Concentration in a stable regulatory environment like the United States or most of Western Europe is a strategic consideration to manage over time. Concentration in a volatile regulatory environment like China or markets with unstable direct selling laws is an urgent vulnerability. For newer companies, heavy concentration in one or two markets is normal and expected. The goal is directional: is the concentration decreasing over time as you add markets? My recommendation is always to open fewer markets, invest more into each one, and do them properly rather than spreading thin across a dozen countries with half-committed launches.

Question 2: Are you expanding from strength or from weakness?

Is your domestic business healthy and growing? Or is it flat or declining and you're looking for international revenue to offset the loss? The former produces durable expansion. The latter produces desperate launches.

Question 3: What is your investment commitment per new market?

Are you hiring local management with decision-making authority? Localizing products and pricing? Adapting the comp plan for local economics? Providing in-language, in-timezone customer service? If the answer to any of these is no, you're doing what this industry calls a "fake opening" and the market will punish you for it.

Question 4: Does real demand signal already exist in the market?

Before you officially launch, can you see organic interest from inside the target country? Are people there searching for your brand or category online? Are prospective customers and builders reaching out asking when the company will open? Are consumers in that country already aware of your category through adjacent brands or media coverage? Are distributors in neighboring countries you already operate in hearing from contacts in the target market who want to build once the company is legally available? These are the signals that tell you whether you're formalizing existing demand or manufacturing it from scratch. Important: this question is about reading demand signals, not about creating distribution before you're legally registered. Many countries prohibit product flow, business registration, or distributor activity before regulatory approval is complete, and premature activity can disqualify a company from ever operating legitimately in that market. Read the signals. Do not front-run the approval.

Question 5: What is the regulatory risk profile of the market?

Is direct selling legally recognized and regulated? Is the regulatory environment stable or volatile? Have other direct selling companies faced government action in this market? China, India, and several other high-growth markets carry regulatory risk that must be priced into the expansion decision. The growth potential is enormous. So is the downside.

Scoring:

Low concentration + expanding from strength + high commitment + organic demand + stable regulation: you have one of the most reliable momentum drivers available. Execute aggressively.

Moderate concentration + expanding from strength + moderate commitment: you're in a reasonable position but should monitor concentration risk and invest in diversification.

High concentration + expanding from weakness + low commitment + volatile regulation: you're in danger of compounding your problems rather than solving them. Fix the core business before adding markets.

Consider a company that approaches international expansion the way Herbalife did it. Not as a single-market bet. Not as a desperation play. But as a systematic diversification strategy where each new market adds to a portfolio without creating dependence on any one of them.

That company doesn't panic when one market's regulatory environment shifts. It doesn't face a 33% stock decline from a single newspaper article in one country. It doesn't watch a third of its revenue evaporate because one government investigation disrupted one geography.

That company uses market expansion as the reliable, repeatable momentum driver it's designed to be. Not a lottery ticket hoping one market saves the quarter. A strategic expansion of the company's geographic footprint, executed with commitment, resourced with capital, and managed for diversification.

The next chapter covers the least visible but most important accelerant underneath every other driver: Compensation Architecture. How comp plan design steers field behavior, for better and worse. Why the plans that drive the fastest growth also produce the lowest retention. And why the most important question about your comp plan isn't what it pays. It is what it incentivizes.

THE BOTTOM LINE: Expand from strength, not weakness. If domestic growth is stalling, international expansion won't fix the structural problem. Run the International Readiness Scorecard before committing resources.

A new country isn't a strategy. A diversified portfolio of markets is a strategy. Know the difference before you plant the flag.

Chapter 10: Compensation Architecture

Your comp plan isn't what you pay people. It is what you tell them to do. Every behavior your field exhibits, good and bad, was designed into the plan.

The enemy in this chapter: paying for maintenance instead of creation.

In 2003, Netflix had a problem. The company's DVD-by-mail business was growing, but its best engineers were leaving for companies that paid bigger bonuses. Reed Hastings could have done what many CEOs do: match the competing offers, add a retention bonus, layer on stock options. Instead, he redesigned the entire compensation architecture.

Netflix eliminated bonuses entirely. No performance bonuses. No retention bonuses. No annual bonus pool. Instead, the company paid top-of-market base salaries and let employees choose how much of their compensation they wanted in stock options versus cash. The logic was simple. Bonuses incentivize short-term performance gaming. An engineer optimizing for a quarterly bonus will ship code that looks impressive this quarter, even if it creates technical debt next quarter. Pay them a salary that reflects their market value and they'll do the work that matters, not the work that triggers the bonus.

The results were counterintuitive. Netflix's engineering productivity increased. Employee satisfaction improved. Turnover among top performers dropped. The company went on to become one of the most valuable media companies in the world.

The insight wasn't about generosity. It was about architecture. Netflix understood that compensation isn't a reward system. It is a behavior system. Whatever you incentivize, you get. Whatever you fail to incentivize, you lose. The structure of the payment determines the behavior of the workforce.

Direct selling companies understand this instinctively on the recruiting side. Every comp plan is designed to incentivize specific enrolling behaviors. But many companies have never applied the same architectural thinking to the behaviors that sustain momentum: customer retention, product education, team development, and long-term building.

Melaleuca understood something many companies avoid: legacy should be respected, but activity should be rewarded.

The company had been using compensation mechanics to reward active leaders and reduce payouts to less-active ones for years. Leadership Points requirements meant that directors who stopped producing saw their organization commissions reduced proportionally. The principle was embedded in the plan long before it had a branded name.

Then came the Critical Activity Bonus. The CAB required the company's highest-ranking leaders to maintain a personal customer retention rate of 90% or higher AND enroll an average of four new members per month to qualify for a significant monthly bonus. Leaders who had been earning passive residual income for years were suddenly told: build or lose your bonus.

The field reaction was predictable. Anger. Frustration. Accusations that the company was changing the rules. Some leaders left. The short-term disruption was real.

But Melaleuca had been here before. In the late 1990s, the company's growth had stalled at roughly $300 million because senior leaders were coasting on residual income without recruiting or serving customers. Founder Frank VanderSloot had responded by restructuring payments to penalize passivity. The result: revenue reignited from $300 million to $547 million by 2003, and ultimately to over $2 billion by 2017. Two decades of growth, triggered by compensation decisions that forced activity.

The CAB was the same principle, made more visible and more structured. And the result was the same. The leaders who stayed adapted. Activity increased. Customer retention became a measured, incentivized behavior rather than a hoped-for outcome. The company reported a 43% increase in enrollments among senior leaders and a 72% increase in growing businesses after the CAB launched.

This story matters because it illustrates the most important truth about compensation architecture: the plan doesn't just distribute money. It distributes instructions. Every structural feature tells the field to do something specific. And the field follows those instructions with remarkable precision, not because they read the comp plan document and consciously decide to comply, but because the economic incentives are baked into every daily decision.

Melaleuca's CAB told the field: serve your customers and keep building. The field served customers and kept building. That isn't a coincidence. That is architecture.

Zinzino is a modern example of comp plan design that pushes the field toward customer acquisition as a structural requirement.

The company was founded in 2005 in Sweden by Orjan and Hilde Saele. Orjan had been a distributor first. He had built. He had seen the math from the inside. And the math told him something many company founders avoid admitting: if your compensation plan doesn't require the field to acquire real customers, your revenue is built on qualification purchasing that will eventually collapse. Attrition would always outrun recruiting. It was arithmetic.

So when he built Zinzino's compensation plan, he designed it so that the path to meaningful earnings runs through personal customer acquisition. To access the full earning potential of the plan, a partner has to build a real customer base, not just recruit and rely on distributor autoship. Higher ranks require progressively more customer activity. The structure deliberately makes it harder to earn through recruiting alone.

The field pushed back. New people complained. It was harder than other companies where you could earn commissions by signing up a few friends and hitting an autoship. Orjan held the line, because he understood that the short-term friction of requiring customer acquisition would produce long-term stability that no recruiting-first model could match.

The results speak for the decision. Zinzino reported revenue of approximately $367 million for full-year 2025, a 51% increase over the prior year. Q1 2026 continued the trajectory with 26% growth. The company is publicly traded on Nasdaq First North, which means the numbers are audited. The company operates in more than 100 markets, a figure confirmed in its 2025 annual report. Full-year 2025 revenue reached approximately $363 million, up 51% year over year. Its flagship product, BalanceOil+, is paired with a blood test that gives customers measurable results, creating a retention loop built on evidence rather than hype.

Orjan and Hilde have been public about their vision of building toward 100 million customers. Not distributors. Customers. That distinction is the point. The compensation architecture told the field: build customers first. The field built customers. And the company's growth curve reflects a foundation that gets stronger over time instead of weaker.

There were complaints along the way. There still are. New partners who join from other companies where the customer expectation was lower sometimes struggle with the transition. Orjan has said publicly that even with the momentum the company has now, there are still complaints about the customer requirement. He keeps it anyway, because the behavior it produces is the behavior that builds a durable business.

That is compensation architecture as a momentum driver. The plan that drives momentum isn't the plan that pays the most or the plan that's easiest to explain. The plan that produces the right behavior. Zinzino's plan told the field to acquire and retain real customers. The field did exactly that. And the revenue curve shows what happens when the behavior matches the strategy.

Here is how compensation architecture works as a momentum driver.

Every comp plan has three levers. Front-end speed. Middle-layer stability. Back-end leverage. No plan can maximize all three simultaneously. Where you put the emphasis determines the shape of your growth curve and the durability of the business you build.

The front end is what a new person experiences in their first 30 to 90 days. Fast-start bonuses. First-order commissions. Quick wins that put money in someone's pocket before they have time to doubt their decision. The front end answers the question every new distributor asks on day one: "Can I make money at this?"

If the front end is strong, new people see results quickly. They stay. They tell friends. Duplication happens naturally because the story is real: "I just made $200 in my first week." That story is more powerful than any training module or motivational speech. It is proof.

If the front end is weak, new people work hard and see nothing for weeks or months. They quit. They tell friends it didn't work. The story becomes:

"I tried it and nothing happened." That story kills recruiting faster than any competitor.

The middle layer is what a builder experiences from month three to month eighteen. Team commissions. Volume bonuses. The income that comes from having a growing organization of customers and distributors producing monthly volume. The middle layer answers the question: "Can this become a real income?"

If the middle is strong, builders develop consistency. They see their income grow as their team grows. They invest more time because the return justifies it. This is where duplication becomes self-sustaining.

If the middle is weak, builders hit a ceiling. They have been working for six months and their income plateaus because the plan doesn't reward the volume their team is producing at their level. They start looking at other opportunities where the middle pays better. This is where you lose your most promising people: not the beginners who never start, and not the top earners who are making significant income, but the builders in the middle who are doing the work and not seeing the return.

The back end is what a top leader experiences after year two and beyond. Leadership bonuses. Matching commissions on deep generations of their organization. Pools that share in total company volume. The back end answers the question: "Can this become legacy income?"

If the back end is strong, top leaders stay. They have invested years building an organization and the income rewards that investment compoundingly. Their earning potential grows even when their personal recruiting slows because the organization produces volume independently. That makes the economics of staying better than the economics of starting over somewhere new.

If the back end is weak, top leaders plateau and start evaluating other companies. They have done the work but the plan caps their earning potential. The economics of leaving become attractive because a new company with better back-end leverage lets them rebuild at a higher ceiling.

There is one important nuance that owners often miss when thinking about back-end strength. Back-end strength isn't only a function of the back-end percentage. It is a function of how much volume is flowing through the back end. A company with a moderate back-end payout percentage but a strong front end (great duplication, fast new-builder starts, high customer acquisition) can produce stronger absolute back-end checks than a company with the highest back-end percentage in the industry but a weak front end. The percentage isn't the only variable. Total volume is the other variable, and total volume is created by front-end behavior.

This is why companies that may not look the strongest on paper at the back-end percentage can still retain top leaders. If your front end is producing real customers and real new-builder activity at scale, the absolute dollars flowing through the back end can be more attractive than what a competing company with a higher percentage on a smaller volume base would pay. The art is to design the front end to drive enough total volume that the back end produces meaningful absolute checks even at a moderate percentage. A company that does this well has the strategic option to invest the difference in product, customer experience, and corporate infrastructure rather than spending it all on back-end leverage. That investment pays off across the whole business, including back at the field through the experience the field has of working with a well-supported company.

Here is the tension. You can't pay maximum rates on all three levers without weakening the company. There is only so much you can pay on a dollar. If you pay too much in commissions, you take from product development, corporate employees, conventions, customer service, technology, and every other investment that sustains the business. Pay too little and the field can't earn enough to stay. The art of compensation design is balancing these three levers so that the right behaviors are rewarded at every stage of a builder's career. The right diagnostic question for any comp plan is the same: which lever is the company underinvesting in, and what behavior is that producing?

There is a nuance here that defenders of high payout ratios raise, and they're not entirely wrong. The 40 to 50% payout to the field isn't inherently wasteful. It is a customer acquisition cost. Whether that cost is efficient compared to the alternatives is the real question. A company selling a $150 per month wellness supplement through direct selling pays roughly $60 to $75 per month to the field for every customer that volume supports. The same company trying to acquire and retain that customer through Facebook ads, Google search, and DTC e-commerce might spend $80 to $120 per acquisition with no ongoing relationship and no repeat purchase guarantee. In categories where the product benefits from education, coaching, and personal accountability, the direct selling distribution cost can be the most efficient customer acquisition channel available.

The payout becomes a problem when it's not buying real customers. When the 40 to 50% is paying for qualification volume that churns out in 90 days, the company is spending its distribution budget on artificial revenue that produces no lasting value. The efficiency question isn't "is 40% too high?" It is "what is that 40% actually purchasing?" If it's purchasing real, retained, reordering customers, the payout is an investment. If it's purchasing distributor qualification volume that evaporates when recruiting slows, the payout is a subsidy for fragile revenue.

The industry has shifted meaningfully in how it approaches this balance.

Modern plans are moving toward stronger front-end economics. The reason is competitive. New builders today aren't only comparing your comp plan to other direct selling companies. They are comparing it to affiliate marketing, e-commerce, content creation, and gig platforms that pay instantly. A new builder can post a TikTok with an affiliate link and earn a commission the same day. If your comp plan requires eight weeks of effort before the first meaningful check arrives, you're losing to platforms that pay in real time.

This competitive pressure has pushed many companies to redesign their first 90 days. Faster bonuses. Lower qualification thresholds. Simpler pathways to the first check. Some companies now pay customer acquisition bonuses within days of a new customer's first order. The goal is to shrink the gap between effort and reward so that the new builder's experience competes with the immediacy of the digital economy.

Younique understood this early. Starting in 2012, the company paid retail commissions within three hours of an online sale, deposited directly into the distributor's account. That speed made the opportunity feel real in a way that waiting four to six weeks for a monthly commission check never could. A new presenter could make a sale at 2 pm and see the money in her account by 5 pm. That instant feedback loop was one of the key accelerants behind Younique's explosive early growth, alongside the Facebook party model that made social selling accessible. Speed reduces the psychological distance between effort and reward. In a digital economy where affiliate commissions, gig payouts, and creator earnings arrive within hours, any direct selling company still paying on a monthly cycle is competing with one hand tied behind its back.

The other significant shift is toward rewarding active builders over passive earners. For decades, the industry's implicit promise was: build it once, earn forever. That promise attracted builders. It also created organizations where high-ranking leaders coasted on income generated by teams they no longer supported. The residual income that was supposed to reward past effort became an entitlement that drained compensation dollars from the active builders producing current volume.

The survey data makes this concrete. Among 82 top-level leaders, 57% identified "paycheck flat, effort no longer feels worth it" as the number one cause of disengagement on their teams. Not product issues. Not regulatory pressure. Flat paychecks. The middle layer of the comp plan had stopped rewarding their effort. And when asked how corporate should decide who has a seat at the table, 78% said a mix of current production and mentorship. Not legacy rank alone. Not past achievement. Current activity combined with impact.

When asked what recognition would feel most meaningful, 54% chose "being asked to help shape company strategy" over every other option, including income milestones, public stage recognition, and private acknowledgment. They don't want another plaque. They want to matter. They want influence that's real, not performative. The companies that give legacy leaders genuine strategic input, and then visibly act on it, will retain those leaders. The companies that create token advisory councils with no follow-through will lose them.

The field is telling you exactly what it wants: a plan that rewards what you're doing now, combined with influence that proves corporate is listening.

Melaleuca's CAB is one response. Other companies have introduced their own variations: power rankings that require ongoing activity to maintain full earning potential. Qualification adjustments that reduce payouts to leaders who aren't actively building. Recognition systems that celebrate current activity alongside lifetime achievement. The principle is the same across all of them: the plan should reward what you're doing, not just what you did. If your highest-paid leaders are your least active builders, you didn't create a compensation plan. You created a retirement program funded by the people who are actually working.

None of this erases what legacy leaders built. They took the early risk. They recruited when the company had no reputation. They filled the first convention halls. They created the base others inherited. The issue isn't whether they matter. They do. The issue is whether today's compensation still rewards the behavior the company now needs most. Respect past contribution. Pay current behavior. Those two things can coexist in the same plan if the leadership team designs it with both in mind.

The deeper principle here applies to every compensation decision: trust, responsibility, and reward must stay aligned. Trust is the relationship between corporate and the field. Responsibility is what owners, executives, and leaders are actually accountable for. Reward is who gets paid, recognized, and protected. When those three match, the organization moves in one direction. When they drift apart, when the field trusts corporate less but corporate rewards itself more, when leaders carry responsibility for growth but owners capture the reward, momentum erodes internally long before the revenue report shows it. The comp plan is where misalignment becomes measurable. If your plan rewards behaviors that your culture punishes, or punishes behaviors your strategy needs, the misalignment will produce exactly the dysfunction you see in your field and wonder where it came from.

These changes aren't universally popular. Legacy leaders who built their income under the old rules feel that the company is changing the deal. And they're right. The deal is changing. Because the old deal, where leaders could earn top-tier income without current activity, created a structural drag on compensation that reduced what active builders could earn. The companies making this shift have concluded that rewarding current activity is more important than honoring historical entitlement. Some leaders leave when these changes happen. The ones who stay and adapt often discover that the new structure produces better results because the entire organization is more active.

The most dangerous compensation architecture problem in direct selling connects directly to the Three Hard Ratios from Chapter 4: the gap between what the plan requires people to buy and what they actually want to consume.

Many companies require a monthly personal volume to maintain active status and earn commissions. The amount varies. Some require $100. Some require $200. Some have reduced or eliminated these requirements in response to regulatory guidance.

When the required volume exceeds what a distributor would purchase for genuine personal use, the excess becomes what the industry calls qualification purchasing. The distributor buys product she doesn't need in order to maintain her rank and her commission check. That volume appears on the company's revenue report indistinguishable from a genuine customer purchase.

The math matters. If a company has 50,000 active distributors and the qualification gap averages $90 per person per month, that's $4.5 million per month in artificial volume. $54 million per year. Revenue that exists only because the plan demands it, not because anyone wants the product.

That $54 million is fragile. When a distributor decides the commission check no longer justifies the monthly purchase, she cancels. When recruiting slows and her income drops, the purchase becomes harder to justify. When she quits entirely, the volume vanishes. The cascading effect is why recruiting slowdowns produce revenue declines that are disproportionate to the change in distributor count.

The regulatory environment has noticed. The FTC's guidance since the Herbalife settlement in 2016 has pushed companies toward documenting real retail customers and reducing the incentive structures that encourage self-purchasing. Many modern companies have responded by reducing or eliminating forced monthly minimums, restructuring bonuses to reward verified customer purchases rather than personal volume, and building preferred customer programs that separate genuine consumption from qualification behavior.

The companies that are ahead of this curve will have cleaner economics and less regulatory exposure. The companies that are behind it are carrying artificial volume on their books that will evaporate the moment the plan changes or the regulatory environment tightens further.

Inside the private community, I see comp plan architecture from the field's perspective. And the field understands plans better than most corporate teams realize.

The top earners I work with evaluate comp plans the way financial analysts evaluate investment structures. They can look at a plan and tell you within an hour whether it's designed for growth or retention. Whether the fast-start economics will attract builders or jumpers. Whether the qualification requirements will produce real volume or closet-qualifying. Whether the depth of the plan is sufficient to incentivize leadership development or whether it caps out too early and kills the mentoring incentive.

What I hear most often behind closed doors, and it's a conversation that would make most corporate teams uncomfortable.

"The plan pays me to recruit. It doesn't pay me to keep customers." That sentence, or a version of it, comes up in almost every leadership session I facilitate. A leader looks at the comp plan and does the math. Enrolling one new distributor who buys a $500 starter kit pays more in bonuses than retaining twenty customers who each reorder $50 per month. The math is clear. The behavior follows the math.

The leaders who see this and deliberately choose to build on customers anyway are the ones with the longest careers. They understand that the plan may not reward customer retention in the short term, but that customer retention is what produces income that survives when recruiting slows. They are playing a different game than the plan was designed for. They are building durability inside a structure designed for speed. That takes discipline. And not everyone has it.

The other conversation I hear: "I know I'm spending more than I need to maintain my rank. But if I drop, I lose my monthly income." This isn't limited to new distributors. Top earners get trapped in the same cycle. The cost of maintaining rank exceeds genuine consumption. They know it's irrational. They do it anyway because the alternative costs more.

These conversations happen constantly at the field level. They almost never reach corporate leadership. Because the field knows that saying "your plan incentivizes the wrong behavior" sounds like complaining. And in a culture that celebrates positivity and forward motion, nobody wants to be the person who questions the compensation structure. So the feedback stays behind closed doors. And corporate continues designing plans based on assumptions about field behavior that don't match reality.

There is a critical insight here that connects compensation to the book's central thesis.

When momentum subsides, you fall to the level of demand from your real customers. Your raving fans. The people who would buy your product even if there were no comp plan attached. Everything above that level was driven by the incentive structure: qualification purchasing, recruiting-driven volume, promotional spikes. When those incentives weaken or the recruiting slows, all of that volume drops away and you're left with your true floor.

Picture a chart with dramatic spikes. Revenue surges during product launches, incentive trips, rank advancement promotions. Then it settles back. Surges again. Settles back. Each time it settles, it returns to roughly the same level. That level is your real customer base. Your true north star. Everything above it was temporary. The comp plan created the spikes. The customers created the floor.

The healthiest companies in this industry are the ones where the floor is rising. Where genuine customer acquisition, retention, and average monthly spend are growing steadily, independent of promotional activity. The floor may not be exciting. It doesn't produce the headline numbers that fill a convention hall with cheering. But it's the metric that determines whether the company survives the next cycle.

A FORWARD-THINKING EXPERIMENT TO TRACK

Here is the structural question behind every comp plan conversation in this industry. Traditional advertising has been largely off-limits to direct selling companies for six decades. The math doesn't work. When 40 to 50% of revenue goes to the field, the margin left for television spots, billboards, and celebrity campaigns is thin. The assumption has been that the distributor is the marketing channel. The comp plan is the advertising budget. Everything else is inefficiency.

A few companies are now attempting to break that constraint through compensation architecture. The most visible experiment is the Super Patch Company, a wearable wellness brand founded in 2023, which built an internal platform it calls CapX. The company describes it as crowd advertising. Super Patch funds large-scale traditional media itself, including reported Times Square billboards, television spots, and celebrity-featured content, while crediting the customers acquired through that media back to distributors in the field through the compensation plan. The corporate investment doesn't replace the field. It amplifies the field.

Think about what this is actually doing. The distributor isn't being asked to choose between her comp plan and mass advertising. The company is funding the advertising on top of the comp plan, and the field earns commissions on customers who arrive through channels the field couldn't have created on its own. Whether the economics are sustainable over a full cycle is a question time will answer. The attempt itself is the point.

After sixty years of comp plans optimizing around the assumption that the field is the entire marketing channel, a new generation of companies is testing whether corporate capital and field commissions can coexist inside the same customer acquisition funnel. If experiments like this work, the implication is significant. It would mean a direct selling company could build a brand at consumer scale through traditional media without stripping compensation from the people who built the business. It would mean the historical tradeoff between mass reach and field economics may not be permanent.

This is the kind of structural innovation to track closely. No specific company's version is guaranteed to succeed, but the problem they're attempting to solve is real. Every CEO in this industry has wrestled with the same question. How do I reach more customers at scale without taking money away from the people whose labor built this company? If anyone solves it cleanly, the entire industry benefits.

The broader pattern worth recognizing is that the companies doing interesting things right now are the ones combining old-school methods with new-school execution. Super Patch is using billboards, television, and celebrity endorsement, methods that have been driving consumer brands for a hundred years, and pairing them with modern digital attribution and direct selling distribution. That isn't a rejection of tradition. It isn't a rejection of innovation. It is a synthesis.

Partner.Co is doing a version of the same thing. In-person events and shoulder-to-shoulder training are as old as this industry. Doubling down on them in 2023 through 2025, when the rest of the industry had gone almost entirely digital, was a counter-cyclical choice to integrate an old method back into a modern company structure.

Zinzino is doing a version of the same thing. Public company discipline and audited financials are traditional corporate practices that predate most of this industry. Applying them inside an acquisition-led growth strategy at direct selling scale is a new synthesis.

The owners and executives building the next generation of successful companies aren't choosing between old and new. They are integrating both. Every strong company in the current cycle has figured out at least one thing that traditional industries have done well for decades and one thing that only recent technology or cultural shift makes possible, then combined them into a structure that wouldn't have been possible in either era alone.

That is the pattern to watch for. Not innovation for its own sake. Not tradition for its own sake. The synthesis is where the durable advantage is being built.

The top metric every company should track: the health of your customers. Customer acquisition rate. Customer retention rate. Average monthly spend per customer. The company needs to take 100% responsibility for these numbers. Everything you do in product development, comp plan design, field training, marketing, and operations should be evaluated against one question: does this improve customer acquisition, customer retention, or average monthly spend? If the answer is no, it may feel productive but it's not building the floor.

THE LEGACY LEADER PROBLEM

There is a second structural challenge that every mature direct selling company eventually faces, and few plan for. I want to address it here because I believe it's the next frontier of compensation architecture in this profession.

Legacy leaders built the company. The top earners of ten, fifteen, twenty years ago created the field infrastructure, the culture, and the downlines that made the company what it's today. They deserve to be rewarded for what they built. That isn't in question. The model works because builders can build something that pays them for a long time after they stop actively building every day. That promise is what gets people to invest years of their life in creating an organization.

But here is the problem that every mature company eventually hits. If legacy leaders are paid in perpetuity at peak levels regardless of current activity, the company eventually can't afford to reward the people who are building now. The comp plan becomes a pension fund for retired builders. The money that should be flowing to the leaders creating momentum today is locked up in residual payments to leaders who stopped working years ago. The engine stalls because the fuel is going to people who are no longer pulling.

This isn't a theoretical problem. Look at the companies in the decline dataset that went through slow erosion rather than collapse. In many cases, the structural issue underneath the erosion wasn't a product failure or a platform shift. It was a comp plan that had locked in decades of legacy earnings to a small cohort of leaders at the top, leaving insufficient economics for the next generation of builders. The legacy leaders had earned their positions through real work over real years. The company honored the compensation structure that had attracted them decades earlier. But the math stopped working. There wasn't enough commission available to reward the builders who needed to become the next generation of leaders, so those builders went elsewhere.

The tension is real and it has no easy answer. Companies that cut legacy leader compensation aggressively trigger the field-betrayal whiplash described earlier. Companies that leave legacy compensation untouched eventually starve the engine that creates new momentum.

The next generation of comp plan architecture, I believe, will solve this tension through a dual structure. Legacy earnings remain. What was earned stays earned. But active production earns more. Someone who goes completely inactive continues to receive residual income from what they built, but at a level that's meaningfully lower than what an active builder at the same rank earns. The gap between active and inactive at the top of the plan becomes a real economic signal, not a rounding error. The message is clear. You built something. We honor it. We are still paying you. But the company isn't the same as it was when you built it, and the people building now need the economics too.

A few companies are testing versions of this. Some use activity qualifiers that scale legacy residuals by current engagement. Some layer activity bonuses on top of legacy earnings so the top line is higher for active leaders without the residual structure being cut. Some restructure new enrollment volume to be less dependent on the legacy tree. None of these models are perfect. All of them are attempting to solve the same underlying problem.

Before any company designs its own version of activity-based compensation reform, the leadership team should look at the engine they already have without flinching. The first variable is the front-end to back-end ratio of the comp plan. A company paying eighty-five percent of its compensation pool on back-end residuals and fifteen percent on front-end new-business behaviors isn't rewarding the human activity that creates new growth. When momentum slows, that imbalance shows up structurally. The fix isn't always a new activity bonus on top of the existing plan. Sometimes the cleaner fix is rebalancing the front-end and back-end split so the company is paying for the behavior it actually wants more of in the first place.

The second variable is width requirements at rank. A leader can occasionally luck into one big leg, and a fortunate leader might occasionally luck into two. Three or more strong legs is almost always real work. Companies that require meaningful width to achieve and maintain rank are already filtering for active building, because the structure itself doesn't let a leader sit in management mode at the top while one legacy leg carries the rank. Companies that allow rank to be achieved with a single dominant leg have created a structural invitation for management-mode top earners, and the activity bonus they bolt on later is often trying to solve a problem the comp plan design created in the first place.

This is why the right approach depends heavily on the company's current state. A newer company that has already designed a generous front-end split and meaningful width requirements may need only modest activity requirements at the very top of the plan, because the underlying architecture is already pulling for active building. An older company with a back-end-heavy split and minimal width requirements typically needs more substantial reform, because the structural drag is bigger and the gap between what the comp plan pays for and what the company now needs is wider.

The distributor counterargument has to be addressed directly, because it's legitimate. Consider the top leader who has been with the company for twelve years, has watched her rank stabilize, and over the past year has doubled the volume of her existing organization through depth-building and taprooting. She did the work. She produced the growth. Under a poorly designed activity bonus, she can still be told her compensation is being reduced because she didn't create a new outside leg or hit a specific new-enrollment number on the front line. Her response is fair: I just grew this company more than most leaders ranking above me, and you're penalizing me because the growth came from inside my existing tree rather than from a new leg. That objection is right. A reform that punishes real internal growth isn't a reform. It is a different kind of misalignment dressed up as discipline.

The solution is to design activity requirements that recognize multiple kinds of growth. New enrollments matter. New first-line legs matter. But total organizational volume growth, depth expansion, and customer base growth inside an existing tree also matter, because all of them produce the same thing the company is trying to reward, which is real new business activity. The leader who doubles her existing tree through taprooting is producing growth. The activity structure should recognize her contribution alongside the leader who built a new leg, not instead of her.

Before any rollout, the leadership team needs to run the scenarios. What happens to the leader who grew her current organization by forty percent but didn't add a new front-line leg? What happens to the leader who added a new leg but did nothing in her existing tree? What happens to the leader who increased her customer count substantially but didn't add new builders? Each scenario should be modeled through both lenses. The corporate lens, which is whether this leader is producing the kind of growth the company needs to sustain momentum. The distributor lens, which is whether this leader is being recognized and compensated fairly for the work she actually did. The system has to make sense from both seats. If a scenario only makes sense from one seat, the design is incomplete.

The last piece, which most companies miss, is communication. Top leaders shouldn't first hear about activity bonus changes when their commission statement arrives. They should have been walked through the scenarios, the rationale, and the gotchas months ahead of any rollout. The companies that make these transitions well include their top leaders in the design conversation, surface the legitimate objections before rollout rather than after, and adjust the structure based on what those conversations reveal. The companies that announce activity reform unilaterally and then deal with the field reaction afterward are creating the field-betrayal whiplash they were trying to avoid. The goal isn't to win an argument with your top leaders. The goal is to design a system both sides can defend in public. That requires both sides being in the room while the system is being designed.

RECOGNITION IS THE OTHER HALF OF THE ANSWER

Money isn't the only tool. In fact, for leaders at the top of the plan who are already financially secure, money is often not the most effective tool. Recognition is.

Here is a pattern that works. Keep the legacy rank structure intact. The leader who earned Presidential Diamond fifteen years ago is still a Presidential Diamond. That title isn't taken away. But layer a second recognition system on top of it that's based entirely on current activity. Call it whatever you want. Power rankings. Active leader board. Momentum circle. The name doesn't matter. The structure does.

Partner.Co is one of the clearer current examples of this approach in practice. The company was formed in 2023 through the combination of several legacy direct selling companies, which meant it inherited a field of leaders who had reached top ranks under the previous brands. Those legacy ranks carried forward. A leader who had built a significant organization inside one of the predecessor companies didn't lose what she earned. The title stayed. The residual income from the organization she built stayed.

But Partner.Co also introduced a separate recognition system called Power Rankings that identifies top active producers based on current activity, not legacy position. A builder who is producing now can earn that title regardless of whether she was in the company five years ago or five months ago. The legacy leader who is still actively producing can also earn it. The legacy leader who has gone passive doesn't. The recognition follows the work, not the history.

What that produces is the two-message stage the recognition architecture requires. Legacy titles are still honored. Lifetime achievement is still celebrated. And the Power Rankings give the field a visible, ongoing signal of who is currently building. Nothing is being taken away. Something is being added. The builders at the front of the room change based on current activity. The builders at the side of the stage, the ones who earned their lifetime ranks years ago, are still in the room. Both messages coexist in a way that many companies haven't figured out how to structure.

The human behavior this produces is what matters. A legacy leader who is still actively building sees her name in both systems and feels honored twice, for what she built and for what she is still doing. A legacy leader who has gone passive still has her rank and her residual, but she sees the Power Rankings happening around her and has to decide whether she wants back in the game. A new builder with no legacy at all sees a clear path to recognition that doesn't require waiting a decade for lifetime rank. Every group in the field gets a version of the same message: the company sees what you're doing right now.

This is what the next generation of recognition architecture looks like in practice. The customer track isn't a replacement for legacy recognition. An addition to it. And it communicates to every builder watching that the company still cares who is pulling the wagon today, regardless of how long someone has been at the top.

Now your convention stage has two kinds of recognition happening. Legacy ranks are honored. Lifetime achievement is celebrated. The people who built the company are still acknowledged in the way they earned. And the people who are actively building the company right now, regardless of when they reached their legacy rank, are recognized in a separate and equally visible way.

This matters because you're what you recognize. If the only people on stage are the top lifetime earners, you're telling the field that activity doesn't matter once you've arrived. If the only people on stage are this quarter's top producers, you're telling the field that what they built is forgettable. Both messages are wrong. The company needs both messages to coexist, visibly, every time the field gathers.

The leaders who are currently building watch the recognition system carefully. They are evaluating whether the company is going to reward them the way it has historically rewarded the legacy tier. If the only people consistently recognized are the ones who have been at the top for a decade or more, the current builders lose faith that their work will eventually be seen. They either burn out or leave. Either way, the pipeline dies.

The two-system recognition structure solves this. Legacy leaders get the respect they earned. Current builders get the visibility they need to sustain the work. Nobody is being erased. Nobody is being ignored. The stage reflects the truth of the company, which is that it was built by people who deserve honor and it's being built by people who deserve attention.

The financial architecture and the recognition architecture work together. Compensation that rewards activity without cutting legacy earnings. Recognition that celebrates lifetime achievement without erasing current effort. That one-two punch is what the next generation of direct selling companies will need to get right, and the companies that solve it cleanly will have a structural advantage that competitors struggling with the legacy versus activity tension can't replicate.

This is the fine line. Honor what was built. Reward what is being built. Build the infrastructure to do both at the same time, visibly and consistently. The companies that figure out how to keep the engine running while keeping the promise they made to the builders who got them here are the companies that will compound for another thirty years.

CUSTOMER RECOGNITION AS ITS OWN TRACK

The same recognition logic applies to customer acquisition, and almost no company has fully figured this out yet. The companies that solve it will have an enormous structural advantage.

You are what you recognize. If your stage only honors rank advancement, the field will optimize for rank advancement. If your stage only honors recruiting, the field will optimize for recruiting. The behavior follows the spotlight.

The variable this book has spent the most time on is customer acquisition. Customer ratio is Ratio 1. The smoke detector test is built around real customers. The flash crash characteristics include the absence of customer verification. Every chapter has reinforced that customers are the foundation that determines whether momentum compounds or collapses. Yet in practice, almost no company runs a recognition system that takes customers as seriously as it takes recruiting.

The standard convention stage looks like this. Top recruiters are recognized. Top organization builders are recognized. Top rank advancers are recognized. Then somewhere near the end, often as a footnote, the top customer acquirer of the year gets a brief mention. The field receives the message clearly. Customers matter on the bookkeeping side of the business. Recruiting matters on the cultural side.

That misalignment is one of the largest unforced errors in this industry. The company is telling the field, every time it gathers, that the variable the company is built on is less important than the variable the field happens to enjoy doing.

The fix is to build customer recognition as its own track. Not as a footnote within the existing rank structure. As a parallel and equally celebrated path. Some companies have already started doing this, building genuine secondary recognition specifically tied to customer counts and customer retention, separate from the traditional rank structure built on volume and recruiting. The result is a culture where the people who build large customer bases are honored as visibly as the people who build large organizations. That cultural signal is part of what protects a company's customer foundation when leaders depart or external conditions shift.

The mechanics are direct. Create a parallel rank structure built entirely on customer acquisition and customer retention metrics. Customer

Champion. Customer Master. Customer Diamond. Whatever language fits the company. Set thresholds based on number of personally enrolled active customers, average customer tenure, and customer retention rates. Recognize advancement on this track at every event with the same energy used to recognize traditional rank advancement. Have the customer track recognized on the main stage, not as a sidebar.

The compensation can mirror the recognition. Pay matching bonuses on personally acquired customer volume. Pay tenure bonuses when customers cross 12, 24, and 36 month retention thresholds. Build a fast-start customer bonus that incentivizes the first thirty days of customer acquisition for new builders. The financial signal and the recognition signal point at the same behavior. The behavior follows.

The reason almost no company has executed this fully yet is that the compensation plan and the recognition system were both built before customer acquisition was understood as the primary structural variable. The default architecture rewards what direct selling companies have always rewarded: enrollment, organization growth, and rank advancement. Adding a customer track requires deliberate design work that competes with the existing structure for stage time, comp plan budget, and field attention.

The companies that figure out how to do this without cannibalizing the traditional structure will produce a field culture where customer acquisition is no longer the unloved stepchild of recruiting. It will be honored visibly, compensated meaningfully, and pursued by the field with the same energy that the field currently directs at building organizations. That is the cultural shift this industry needs to make, and the recognition architecture is one of the most underused tools available to make it happen.

You are what you recognize. Recognize customer acquisition the way you recognize rank advancement, and the field will learn that customer acquisition matters as much as the company has been claiming it does.

Here is the framework.

THE COMP PLAN HEALTH AUDIT

Question 1: What percentage of your total field volume is qualification-driven?

Calculate the gap between your required personal volume and your distributors' estimated genuine personal consumption. Multiply by the number of active distributors. That gap is qualification-driven volume. If it exceeds 30% of total volume, your revenue contains significant artificial demand. Note: many modern companies have reduced or eliminated forced monthly requirements. If yours hasn't, this question is urgent.

Question 2: What is your payout ratio trend?

Track total commissions and bonuses as a percentage of revenue, quarter over quarter, for the last eight quarters. If the percentage is rising while revenue is flat or declining, you're in payout inflation. The company is spending more to generate less. Two consecutive quarters of payout inflation is an early warning. Four consecutive quarters is a structural problem.

Question 3: Does your front end compete with the digital economy?

How quickly does a new builder earn their first meaningful check? If the answer is "eight to twelve weeks," you're losing new people to platforms that pay in days. Evaluate your first-90-day economics against what a content creator or affiliate marketer can earn in the same period.

Question 4: Does your plan reward current activity or historical achievement?

Are your highest-paid leaders actively building, serving customers, and developing new leaders? Or are they collecting passive income from organizations they no longer support? If the plan rewards passivity at the top, it's draining compensation dollars from active builders in the middle. Consider activity-based bonuses that require ongoing production to qualify for leadership-level income.

Question 5: What happens to your revenue if all promotional incentives stopped for 90 days?

No trips. No rank bonuses. No fast-start promotions. Just the base plan. What volume survives? That surviving volume is your floor. If the floor is less than 60% of your promoted volume, your revenue is promotion-dependent, which means it's structurally fragile.

Scoring:

Low qualification purchasing + stable payout ratio + competitive front end + activity-rewarded back end + high floor: your plan architecture supports sustainable momentum.

High qualification purchasing + payout inflation + slow front end + passivity-rewarded back end + low floor: your plan is structurally designed for a spike-and-settle pattern. The growth will look impressive until the promotions stop and the floor is exposed.

Imagine a CEO who understands that her comp plan isn't a financial document. It is a behavioral document.

She reviews the plan not by asking "is it competitive?" but by asking "what behavior is it producing?" She tracks qualification purchasing as a percentage of total volume. She monitors payout inflation quarterly. She evaluates every proposed bonus and promotion against a simple test: does this incentivize the behavior that builds the customer floor, or does it incentivize the behavior that produces a temporary spike?

When her team proposes a new fast-start bonus to "jumpstart Q3," she asks: "Will this bonus produce new customers who reorder next quarter, or new distributors who buy to qualify and leave in four months?" If the answer is the latter, she redirects the budget toward customer retention.

That CEO's growth rate might be slower than her competitor's promotional spike. But her floor is rising. Her revenue is backed by genuine demand. Her Three Hard Ratios are in the green zone. And when her competitor's spike settles back to their floor, she is still building.

The next chapter brings all five drivers together: Product-Culture Fit, Platform Disruption, Leader Migration, Market Expansion, and Compensation Architecture. What happens when two or three of them collide simultaneously. The most explosive growth stories in industry history. And the Flash Crash Formula that predicts which collisions build empires and which ones build time bombs.

From the mastermind work, I see comp plan architecture from the field's perspective. And the field understands plans better than most corporate teams realize.

The top earners I work with evaluate comp plans the way financial analysts evaluate investment structures. They can look at a plan and tell you within an hour whether it's designed for growth or retention. Whether the fast-start economics will attract builders or jumpers. Whether the qualification requirements will produce real volume or closet-qualifying. Whether the depth of the plan is sufficient to incentivize leadership development or whether it caps out too early and kills the mentoring incentive.

What I hear most often behind closed doors is a conversation that would make most corporate teams uncomfortable. "The plan pays me to recruit. It doesn't pay me to keep customers." That sentence, or a version of it, comes up in almost every leadership session I facilitate. A leader looks at the comp plan and does the math. Enrolling one new distributor who buys a $500 starter kit pays more in bonuses than retaining twenty customers who each reorder $50 per month. The math is clear. The behavior follows the math.

The leaders who see this and deliberately choose to build on customers anyway are the ones with the longest careers. They understand that the plan may not reward customer retention in the short term, but that customer retention is what produces income that survives when recruiting slows. They are playing a different game than the plan was designed for. They are building durability inside a structure designed for speed. That takes discipline. And not everyone has it.

THE BOTTOM LINE: Your compensation plan drives human behavior more powerfully than any training, event, or marketing campaign. Audit which behaviors your plan actually rewards and ask whether those are the behaviors that build a durable company.

Your comp plan isn't what you pay. It is what you teach. Every behavior your field repeats is a behavior your comp plan rewarded. Make sure the lesson is the right one.

Chapter 11: The Perfect Storm

Figure 5. Every major momentum story in direct selling history maps to a specific driver stack. Three-driver convergence produces the biggest wins AND the biggest crashes.

Figure 6. Check how many apply to your company. Three or more is the architecture of every flash crash in the dataset.

Single drivers produce growth. Two drivers produce momentum. Three drivers produce the stories this industry tells for decades. Momentum isn't built. It's assembled. And the question most leadership teams fail to confront is: what happens when all three reverse at the same time?

In 1992, Hurricane Andrew became the most expensive natural disaster in American history. It would hold that record for 13 years. Then Hurricane Katrina hit in 2005 and made Andrew look modest.

Katrina wasn't the strongest hurricane to make landfall that year. It wasn't even the strongest hurricane that month. What made Katrina catastrophic was the convergence. A powerful storm. A city below sea level. Levees that had been underfunded for decades. A federal response system that failed at every level. Any one of those factors would have produced a bad outcome. All of them hitting simultaneously produced a $125 billion disaster that killed over 1,800 people and displaced a million more.

Meteorologists have a term for this. They call it a "perfect storm," after Sebastian Junger's book about the 1991 convergence of weather systems that destroyed the fishing vessel Andrea Gail. The term has become so overused in business writing that it has lost its power. But the underlying concept is the most important idea in this book.

In direct selling, the most explosive growth stories are never single-driver events. They are convergences. Two drivers overlapping produce strong momentum. Three drivers overlapping produce the most explosive growth periods in the industry's history. And when those same drivers reverse simultaneously, the collapse is as dramatic as the rise.

Momentum is always compound. That compounding runs in both directions, and that's the core thesis of this chapter.

Let me show you what driver convergence looks like going up.

LuLaRoe combined three drivers simultaneously. Product-Culture Fit: athleisure leggings during the peak of the leggings-as-fashion trend, with limited-edition patterns creating collector psychology. Platform Disruption: Facebook Live launching in 2015, right as the company was scaling, turning every consultant's living room into a live shopping broadcast. Compensation Architecture: a $5,000 to $9,000 upfront inventory buy-in that financially committed sellers to aggressive activity from day one.

Three drivers firing at the same time. Product-culture fit made the conversation easy. Platform disruption made the reach explosive. Compensation architecture made the field's economic commitment intense.

Result: $9.8 million in 2014 to approximately $2.3 billion in 2017. Revenue grew roughly 23,000% in three years.

doTERRA combined three drivers. Product-Culture Fit: essential oils during the wellness mega-trend, with a broad product category serving dozens of use cases. Leader Migration: the founding team and initial distributor base drawn from established essential oils relationships in the industry, bringing expertise and credibility from day one. Platform Disruption: Facebook groups and the virtual party model, which let Wellness Advocates build communities and educate customers at scale.

Three drivers. But with a critical difference from LuLaRoe. The product category was broad and anchored to durable needs. The leaders who migrated built customer depth. The platform usage created communities, not just transactions.

Result: startup to over $2 billion across sixteen years. The most durable momentum story of the modern era.

MonaVie combined three drivers. Product-Culture Fit: acai superfruit during the Oprah-fueled superfood craze. Leader Migration: Brig Hart and other Amway mega-earners bringing pre-built sales forces. Compensation Architecture: 50% commissionable-volume payout with aggressive fast-start bonuses making the math irresistible for experienced networkers.

Three drivers. All three were borrowed or temporary. The acai trend was a cultural moment, not a durable need. The leaders came for the economics and left when the economics shifted. The comp plan rewarded speed over sustainability.

Result: $0 to $854 million in three years. Then collapse. The company was eventually absorbed. All three drivers reversed within a narrow window.

Amway's 2008-2013 peak combined two drivers. Market Expansion: China becoming its largest single market, generating over $4.3 billion at peak. Product-Culture Fit: Nutrilite supplements intersecting with China's exploding wellness market.

Two drivers. Both massive. The result was $11.8 billion in global revenue, the highest in the company's history and one of the highest in direct selling history.

The pattern across every case is consistent. Single-driver growth exists but is modest and typically short-lived. Two overlapping drivers produce strong, visible momentum. Three overlapping drivers produce the legendary growth stories that become industry lore. Companies that hit three-driver convergence are the ones that fill stadiums, make headlines, attract leaders from competitors, and create the perception of unstoppable momentum.

The table tells the story:

Amway: $11.8 billion peak. Two drivers. Market Expansion plus Product-Culture Fit.

Herbalife: $5.8 billion peak. Three drivers. Market Expansion plus Product-Culture Fit plus Platform Disruption (Nutrition Clubs).

LuLaRoe: approximately $2.3 billion peak. Three drivers. Product-Culture Fit plus Platform Disruption plus Compensation Architecture.

doTERRA: $2 billion plus and growing. Three drivers. Product-Culture Fit plus Leader Migration plus Platform Disruption.

Rodan+Fields: $1.5 billion peak. Two drivers. Platform Disruption plus Product-Culture Fit.

MonaVie: $854 million peak (2008). Three drivers. Leader Migration plus Product-Culture Fit plus Compensation Architecture.

Nu Skin: $3.18 billion peak. Two drivers. Market Expansion plus Product-Culture Fit.

The same driver convergence logic operates outside direct selling. The clearest case is the iPhone.

When Steve Jobs introduced the iPhone at Macworld on January 9, 2007, he described it as three products in one: "an iPod, a phone, and an Internet communicator." The framing wasn't just marketing. Three technological drivers had just reached the threshold at which a $600 consumer device could integrate all three capabilities: touchscreen technology finally worked well enough for consumer use, processor power had miniaturized sufficiently, and lithium-ion battery density had reached the minimum required energy density. In 2005, a $600 smartphone wasn't technically possible. By 2009, the window for a first-mover to define the category would have closed as Android matured. 2007 was the only year the iPhone could have launched with the impact it had.

But technology alone wasn't the full convergence.

Apple had also been building a second driver: retail disruption. Apple Stores had been operating since 2001, and by 2007 Apple owned a distribution channel that no other phone manufacturer controlled. When the iPhone launched, customers could experience the product in an Apple Store, not behind a carrier counter. The cultural context of phone buying changed because Apple had already changed where phones were sold.

The third driver was cultural. The iPod had become a status object during the 2000s. By 2007, millions of consumers already trusted Apple with their music, their computers, their design aesthetic, and their self-image. The iPhone didn't have to build cultural credibility from zero. It inherited it from a decade of iPod, iMac, and iTunes.

Technology convergence. Retail disruption. Cultural pre-validation. Three drivers firing simultaneously.

The result was the same three-driver explosion this book documents repeatedly. Apple sold 6 million iPhones in the first fourteen months. Nokia, the market leader, went from 51% global market share in Q4 2007 to under 3% five years later. Nokia wasn't a bad company. It was structurally outpositioned by a competitor running three drivers at once. Digital camera sales peaked in 2007, the same year the iPhone launched, and have declined ever since. MP3 players, portable GPS units, handheld gaming devices, and standalone video recorders were all absorbed by the convergence.

The iPhone's three-driver convergence produced an entire decade of category-defining growth. But notice what eventually happened to the drivers. Technology convergence stopped being a differentiator by roughly 2012, as Android phones matched the hardware. Retail disruption ended as a differentiator as every phone was sold online and in multiple formats. Cultural pre-validation remained but weakened as the category matured. Apple stayed dominant in the smartphone market, but growth rates slowed dramatically by the mid-2010s. The initial three-driver convergence converted into a mature market leader, not an accelerating phenomenon. The drivers that created the momentum didn't create sustainable momentum. They created the opening. Apple's subsequent discipline in product development, ecosystem management, and customer experience created the sustained business.

Three driver convergence explains the original iPhone launch the same way it explains LuLaRoe, doTERRA, MonaVie, and every other convergence story in this book. The mechanism is identical across industries. Direct selling didn't invent driver convergence. It just provides unusually clean cases to observe it.

Now let me show you what driver convergence looks like going down. Because this is the part the industry doesn't study. And it should, because the mechanics are identical. Just inverted.

Every momentum decision that buys speed in Act 1 creates a constraint in Act 3. The aggressive comp plan that attracted leaders fast creates payout inflation when those leaders coast. The BDA that injected a pre-built sales force overnight creates concentration risk when that leader considers leaving. The international launch that produced a first-year revenue spike creates geographic dependency when that market's regulatory environment shifts. Momentum problems are usually delayed consequences of earlier tradeoffs. The companies that survive the longest aren't the ones that avoided tradeoffs. They are the ones that were honest about the tradeoffs while they were making them.

When multiple drivers collapse simultaneously, the decline isn't additive. It is multiplicative. Each failing driver accelerates the failure of the others. The compounding that built the company in four years destroys it in two. And the speed of the collapse catches leadership teams off guard because they were never monitoring which drivers were active. They were monitoring revenue. Revenue is a lagging indicator. By the time revenue shows the collapse, the drivers have already reversed.

LuLaRoe's collapse illustrates simultaneous driver reversal.

The product-culture fit expired. The athleisure trend matured. Quality problems emerged and spread virally. The "buttery soft" fabric that built the brand started tearing. Patterns that had been collectible became ordinary as the novelty faded. The cultural conversation that had carried the product shifted from "where can I find those leggings" to "those leggings are falling apart." When the culture turns on your product, every conversation your field has becomes harder. Not incrementally harder. Fundamentally harder. The cultural tailwind that had been pushing every conversation forward was now pushing against every conversation.

The platform window closed simultaneously. Facebook Live's prominence in the algorithm declined. Organic reach dropped across the platform. The appointment-viewing behavior that had made every livestream an event faded as consumers grew tired of the format. The Facebook groups that had been communities of enthusiastic buyers became communities of frustrated sellers trying to liquidate inventory. The same platform that amplified the brand's rise amplified its complaints. Social media is a megaphone. It doesn't care which direction it points.

The compensation architecture turned toxic at the same time. The $5,000 to $9,000 upfront inventory requirement that had committed sellers during the growth phase became a financial trap when the product stopped selling. Consultants were stuck with thousands of dollars of unsold inventory in their garages and spare bedrooms. The comp plan that had incentivized aggressive buying now produced aggressive losses. The Facebook groups didn't just become complaint forums about product quality. They became

Going Out Of Business sale forums where consultants tried to recoup some fraction of their inventory investment.

All three drivers reversed within roughly eighteen months. Product-culture fit gone. Platform advantage gone. Comp plan economics inverted. Each reversal accelerated the others. Product failure made the platform conversation toxic. Toxic platform conversation made recruiting impossible. Failed recruiting made the comp plan economics collapse. The consultants who had been buying $5,000 to $9,000 in inventory to stay active stopped buying. Revenue collapsed from $2.3 billion to a fraction of that. Consultants dropped from a peak of roughly 80,000 in April 2017 to fewer than 20,000 by 2020 per industry reporting. Lawsuits piled up. A documentary was made. The company name became, for many, a punchline.

The compounding that produced 23,000% growth in three years produced a proportional collapse. Because the same forces that amplify each other going up amplify each other going down. Three drivers multiplied the growth. Three reversals multiplied the decline.

I remember a leader describing the experience of being inside a three-driver collapse. She said: "It was like the tide going out. You could feel it pulling but you couldn't see it yet. Then one morning you woke up and the water was gone and everything you'd built was just sitting on sand." That is what flash crash feels like from the field side. The corporate dashboard still showed revenue. But the energy had already left.

MonaVie experienced the same simultaneous reversal across all three of its drivers. The Chapter 2 case study documents the full mechanism. Three drivers reversing together. The billion-dollar company evaporated.

This is the dark mirror of the perfect storm. The industry studies the convergence going up. It celebrates the companies that hit three-driver alignment. It puts those companies on stages, writes about them in trade publications, and holds them up as proof that momentum is possible. It almost never studies what happens when the same convergence reverses. And it should. Because the companies most likely to experience a three-driver collapse are, by definition, the companies that experienced a three-driver convergence. The same architecture that produced the rise contains the mechanism for the fall. You didn't build that growth. You rented it. And rent comes due.

The only thing that determines how far a company falls when drivers reverse is the customer floor. Drivers create growth. The customer base decides whether any of it survives.

This is where the Flash Crash Formula enters.

Across the 53-company dataset, every company that experienced a flash crash, defined as zero to two years from peak to major break, shared at least three of five specific characteristics. These five traits are so consistent across every flash crash in the dataset that they function as a predictive diagnostic. If your company has three or more, you're structurally configured for a flash crash whether you realize it or not.

Characteristic 1: Single hero product driving more than 50% of revenue.

Vemma had Verve. ViSalus had Vi-Shape. LuLaRoe had leggings. Medifast had the 5&1 Plan. WorldVentures had memberships. When one product is the business, the business has the risk profile of that one product. Any threat to the product, whether from quality issues, cultural shift, regulatory action, or competitive disruption, threatens the entire company.

An important nuance: launching with a single lead product is often the smartest strategy. Focus creates clarity in the field's messaging, simplifies duplication, and concentrates belief. The risk isn't having a hero product. The risk is failing to develop supporting products that increase average customer spend and retention once the lead product matures.

The default strategy should be to maintain and enhance the hero product for as long as possible. Build adjacent products around it. Deepen the product ecosystem. Create reasons for existing customers to spend more, not reasons for the field to learn an entirely new story. PM International has reformulated its lead product over a dozen times rather than abandoning it. That is like Apple improving the iPhone every year rather than launching an entirely new device. Enhance the existing story. Do not constantly chase new ones.

But there are times when the hero product has run its course. When the category has been disrupted. When the cultural moment has passed and no amount of reformulation will bring it back. When a new product emerges that has a stronger story, better science, or a more compelling fit with where the market is heading. In those moments, pivoting the hero product isn't disloyalty to the original story. It can be the best strategic decision a company makes. The key is distinguishing between chasing shiny objects, which destroys focus, and making a genuine strategic pivot, which can save a company. The companies that get this wrong change their hero product every eighteen months and never build depth in any of them. The companies that get this right evolve deliberately, building each new chapter on the foundation of the last.

Characteristic 2: Revenue predominantly from distributor self-purchasing, with more than 70% internal consumption.

Vemma: 86% internal, only 14% retail. WorldVentures: 95% of members were reps. YTB: 85% from membership purchases. BurnLounge: package-driven with negligible external customers. When the buyers are classified as sellers, even genuine product demand shows up on a regulator's spreadsheet as internal consumption. In some of these cases, the purchases really were driven by comp plan qualification and not product love. In others, like Vemma, real affiliate enthusiasm for the product was locked inside an affiliate classification that the FTC does not allow a company to reclassify after the fact. Either way, the structural signal is the same, and the regulatory consequences are the same. Retail verification systems that can distinguish real customers from enrolled affiliates who behave like customers are what protect a company from that classification trap.

Characteristic 3: Recruiting growth rate exceeding 100% year-over-year for two or more consecutive years.

ViSalus enrolled 378,000 new promoters in Q1 2012 alone. LuLaRoe grew from 1,000 to 80,000 consultants in two years. Vemma was adding 30,000 new members per month at peak. This rate of enrollment isn't unsustainable because you run out of people. There are 8 billion people on the planet. No direct selling company has ever exhausted the prospect pool, and customer demand is effectively unlimited. What happens at this velocity is different. The company enrolls faster than it can train, develop, and retain. The new people aren't being onboarded properly. They aren't building customer bases. They are cycling through the system in 90 days.

Each person who leaves without succeeding becomes a story in their own network about an opportunity that didn't work for them. That story isn't about market saturation. It is about a company that grew faster than its support infrastructure could deliver. The damage is to the company's credibility in the specific networks where the failures happened, which is a fixable problem if the company slows enrollment, invests in proper training, and builds the support systems that should have been in place before the velocity began. The recruiting story doesn't die because the world has heard it. It pauses where the company lost the ability to support the people it was enrolling, and it resumes wherever the company rebuilds that support and proves the new system works.

Characteristic 4: Top 5% of leaders generating more than 50% of total company volume.

ViSalus: one leader organization accounted for 74% of revenue. Organo Gold: a three-person leadership core drove the culture and momentum. When volume is this concentrated and the company hasn't invested in leadership development underneath those organizations, the departure of one or two leaders isn't a personnel issue. It is an existential threat. The same concentration with strong secondary leadership underneath is a strength, because the volume continues to flow even if a top leader's pace shifts.

A necessary reality check for every corporate leader reading this. You are probably thinking: what am I supposed to do about this? Corporate doesn't recruit anyone. The field builds the organizations. If one leader builds faster and bigger than everyone else, that's the model working exactly as designed. You can't tell your best builder to slow down so the revenue distribution looks healthier on a spreadsheet.

That is correct. And it's exactly why concentration risk is so dangerous. It is a natural byproduct of the model. In any direct selling company, the distribution of volume will always be uneven. Some leaders build bigger than others. Some organizations produce more than others. The top 20% of your field will always generate a disproportionate share of revenue. That isn't a flaw. That is network effects working as intended.

Concentration itself isn't the problem. The problem is when corporate does nothing to build underneath it.

What you can control. You can't control who builds the biggest organization. But you can invest in developing new leaders deeper in the organization who have their own identity, their own customer base, and their own reasons to stay that are independent of the person above them. You can create leadership development programs that identify emerging builders at every level and give them direct relationships with corporate, not just with their upline. You can build recognition systems that celebrate rising leaders, not just the established ones. You can design comp plan features that reward depth of leadership development, not just width of recruiting.

You can't prevent concentration. What you can do is build layers underneath it. If your number one organization produces 40% of revenue but that organization has 15 independently motivated leaders with their own customer bases and their own teams, the departure of the person at the top hurts but doesn't kill. If that same organization produces 40% of revenue and every person in it is loyal to one leader and one leader only, you have a single point of failure that no amount of corporate planning can survive.

The question to ask isn't "how do we reduce our top leader's volume?" That framing will alienate your best builder. The right framing is "how many independent leaders exist underneath our top organizations, and are we investing in developing more of them every quarter?"

Characteristic 5: No meaningful preferred customer program or retail verification system.

If the company can't demonstrate, with auditable data, that real external customers exist in meaningful numbers, both the regulatory risk and the structural fragility are elevated. The company has no defense against an FTC inquiry. And it has no foundation underneath the recruiting engine.

The data across the flash crash subset is stark. Every flash crash company in the dataset checked at least three of these five boxes.

Vemma: all five. ViSalus: all five. LuLaRoe: four of five. Medifast: four of five. WorldVentures: all five. YTB: all five. Wake Up Now: four of five. BurnLounge: four of five.

Zero exceptions.

The contrast with the companies that sustained momentum is equally revealing.

doTERRA at three-driver convergence checks zero of the five flash crash characteristics. Multiple products across dozens of use cases, not a single hero product. Over 10 million customers by 2024, not internal consumption. Growth was strong but not 100% year-over-year for consecutive years. Volume is distributed across 3 million Wellness Advocates, not concentrated in a handful of mega-leaders. And the company has a robust customer program with verifiable external purchasing.

Three drivers produced explosive growth. Zero flash crash characteristics ensured the growth was durable. Those two facts together are the equation. Driver convergence creates the speed. Flash crash characteristics determine whether the speed builds something lasting or something that detonates.

The difference isn't luck. The difference is architecture. One company's three-driver convergence was built on a foundation of real customers, diversified products, and distributed volume. The other's was built on a single product, self-purchasing consultants, and concentrated volume. Same number of drivers. Opposite foundations. Opposite outcomes.

In the mastermind conversations, I watch leaders evaluate companies using an intuitive version of this framework. They don't call it the Flash Crash Formula. They don't check five boxes on a scorecard. But the best long-term builders in this industry have developed a gut instinct for which companies are built on driver convergence with real foundations and which are built on driver convergence with structural fragility.

Every leader evaluates differently. Some lead with the product. Some lead with the comp plan. Some lead with the owners and their track record. Some lead with the culture and community. Some care most about international markets. There is no universal checklist that every experienced builder runs through before joining a company. People are different. Priorities are different.

But here is what the smartest long-term builders have in common: they're looking at the whole picture, not just one variable. They are asking whether the product has real demand. Whether the volume is diversified or sitting inside a few organizations. Whether the company's growth feels sustainable or feels like a sprint that can't last. Whether real customers exist or whether everyone is buying to qualify. They might not ask these questions in this order, and they might not ask all of them. But the leaders who build decade-long careers tend to evaluate more of these factors than the leaders who restart every three years.

That said, the more important point isn't whether leaders are screening for these characteristics. It is whether your company is building against them regardless. Because even if no prospective leader ever asks you about product concentration or customer ratios, these characteristics still predict your company's structural durability. You don't fix them because a leader might ask. You fix them because the math demands it. A company with zero flash crash characteristics is a better company whether anyone is evaluating it or not. It retains customers longer. It survives leader departures better. It withstands regulatory scrutiny more effectively. It compounds instead of spiking.

Build the right company and the right leaders will find you. They won't run a five-point audit. They will see the results of building correctly in every metric that matters.

If you're reading this chapter and your company is in the middle of explosive growth right now, I need to speak to you directly.

This book isn't telling you that fast growth is bad. Fast growth is extraordinary. It is rare. It is the thing that every company in this industry is trying to create. If you're in your first year and breaking records, or you hit a couple hundred million in your first three years, that's not a problem to be solved. That is an achievement to be protected.

The danger isn't the speed. The danger is what you do with the speed while you have it.

Durable explosive growth requires two things simultaneously. They rode the wave as hard as they could AND they invested in the foundation underneath it while the revenue gave them the margin to do so. They built their customer programs during the boom, not after. They developed homegrown leaders during the recruiting sprint, not after the sprint ended. They fixed their operations before the volume broke them. They ran the diagnostics in this book while everything was green, not after things turned yellow.

Speed didn't cause the crashes. They crashed because they used the growth period to celebrate instead of build. They assumed the wave would last forever. They didn't invest in the customer floor while they had the cash flow to do it. And when the wave broke, there was nothing underneath.

If you're in momentum right now, you have something that many companies would give anything for: the revenue and the energy to build the foundation at the same time. Every dollar you invest in customer depth, leadership development, operational capacity, and structural soundness while the wave is running is a dollar that pays for itself ten times over when the wave inevitably slows. You don't slow down the wave. You build the floor while the wave is carrying you.

The best possible outcome in this industry isn't steady compounding or explosive growth. It is explosive growth on a sound foundation. That is the rarest thing in direct selling. And it's what this entire book is designed to help you build.

There is a shadow side to this analysis that matters.

If you read this chapter and conclude that three-driver convergence should be avoided because it creates flash crash risk, you've misread the argument.

Three-driver convergence is the most powerful growth accelerant in the industry. It is what produces the companies that reach $1 billion in revenue. It is what creates the momentum that attracts leaders, fills conventions, and generates the belief that powers an entire field. Without driver convergence, there's no explosive momentum. And without explosive momentum, many companies never reach the scale required to build durable infrastructure.

Do not avoid convergence. The goal is to pursue convergence while monitoring for flash crash characteristics. Drive hard on product-culture fit. Exploit platform windows aggressively. Welcome leader migration. Expand internationally. Design a comp plan that rewards the right behaviors. Do all of it simultaneously if you can.

The companies that achieved three-driver convergence and survived, doTERRA being the clearest example, did not avoid risk. They pursued growth aggressively while simultaneously building the foundation that would sustain it. They recruited leaders and built customers. They exploited Facebook groups and developed platform-independent capabilities. They rode the essential oils cultural wave and built a product line with dozens of use cases that would outlast the wave's peak. Every growth decision was paired with a foundation decision. That pairing is what separates the companies that create legendary growth stories and survive them from the companies that create legendary growth stories and end up in the decline dataset.

The same is true for companies like Amway, Herbalife, and Nu Skin, which achieved massive scale through multi-driver convergence and then managed the inevitable challenges that followed. Each of these companies made mistakes along the way. Each faced periods where the equation turned negative. What they had in common was the willingness to address the structural problems rather than deny them. That willingness, more than any individual strategic decision, is what separates the survivors.

But while you're doing it, check the five boxes. Is your revenue concentrated in one product? Diversify. Is your volume driven by internal consumption? Build customer programs. Is your recruiting velocity unsustainable? Invest in retention before you hit the wall. Is your volume concentrated in a few leaders? Develop organic leadership depth. Can you prove real customers exist? Build the verification systems before the regulator asks for them.

The companies that get this right create the legendary growth stories AND survive them. The companies that don't create the legendary growth stories and then become the decline stories documented in the 53-company dataset.

The diagnostic has two parts.

THE DRIVER COMBINATION MAP + FLASH CRASH SCORECARD

Part 1: The Driver Combination Map

For each of the five drivers, rate its current status in your company:

Active: this driver is currently producing measurable growth. Dormant: this driver exists as a potential but isn't currently contributing. Absent: this driver isn't available to your company. Reversing: this driver was previously active and is now working against you.

Count your active drivers. One active driver produces modest growth. Two active drivers produce strong momentum. Three or more active drivers produce explosive growth. Any driver that's reversing is subtracting from your total. Two active drivers and one reversing driver may net out to modest or zero growth.

Part 2: The Flash Crash Scorecard

For each characteristic, check without flinching:

- Single hero product driving more than 50% of revenue? YES / NO

- More than 70% of volume from participants inside the comp plan? YES / NO

- Recruiting growth exceeding 100% year-over-year for 2+ consecutive years? YES / NO

- Top 5% of leaders generating more than 50% of total volume? YES / NO

- No meaningful customer verification system with auditable data? YES / NO

Score: - 0-1 checks: Low flash crash risk. Your foundation supports your growth. - 2 checks: Moderate risk. Address the checked items proactively. - 3+ checks: High flash crash risk. Across the 53-company dataset, every company with 3+ checks that experienced rapid growth subsequently experienced a crash. Zero exceptions. Address immediately.

Combined Assessment:

The most dangerous position: 3+ active drivers AND 3+ flash crash characteristics. You are experiencing explosive growth on a fragile foundation. The growth feels incredible. The crash, when it comes, will be proportional.

The strongest position: 2-3 active drivers AND 0-1 flash crash characteristics. You are experiencing strong growth on a sound foundation. This is the profile of the companies that sustained momentum for a decade or more.

Consider a board that runs both assessments quarterly.

They map their active drivers and identify which ones are producing growth. They check the flash crash scorecard and address any characteristics that have crept above zero. They don't just celebrate the convergence. They monitor the foundation underneath it.

When the CEO presents to the board, she doesn't just show the revenue curve. She shows the driver map alongside the flash crash scorecard. "We have three active drivers. Our flash crash score is one. The one characteristic we're flagging is product concentration: our flagship line now accounts for 55% of revenue. We're launching two new product lines this quarter specifically to reduce that concentration below 50%."

That is a leadership team that understands the equation, not just the drivers. The equation. Growth multiplied by structural integrity. Speed checked by foundation.

Part II is now complete. The five drivers have been introduced, explained, illustrated, and combined. The reader knows what creates momentum, how drivers interact, and which combinations produce durability versus fragility.

Part III turns to what kills momentum. The four phases of decline. The regulatory domino sequence. The operational ceiling. The patterns are documented. The warning signs are identifiable. And the companies that survived did so because they recognized the patterns before the patterns consumed them.

A pattern I see when multiple drivers converge and a company experiences explosive growth. Leadership teams almost always misattribute what is happening. They give credit to whichever driver is most visible at the moment, usually the one closest to their own decisions. The CEO credits the vision. The head of sales credits the comp plan redesign. The marketing team credits the new campaign. The product team credits the new launch.

In reality, what happened is that two or three drivers aligned simultaneously, and any one of them would have produced growth on its own. The combination produced explosive growth. But no single person on the leadership team can see the full picture because each person is closest to their own function. The momentum attribution audit from Chapter 2 exists specifically to surface this blind spot. When I run the audit with a leadership team in momentum, the results are always the same. Every function takes more credit than the data supports. The actual driver stack is usually broader and more external than anyone wants to admit.

This matters because the misattribution predicts the crash. If the leadership team believes the growth came from the comp plan redesign, they'll double down on that driver when growth slows. But if the actual driver was a cultural wave, doubling down on the comp plan won't save them. The wave passed. The driver that was carrying them has shifted. And they're now investing resources in the thing they can see while the thing they couldn't see is what actually mattered.

A reminder before moving into the decline patterns. Everything in Part III is documented because companies that misread the signals paid the price. None of it is a verdict on the industry. The same dataset that produced the patterns of decline also produced four-decade compounders, billion-dollar quiet operators, and companies that crossed regulatory crises and emerged stronger. The drivers in Part II can be activated on purpose. The constraints in Part III can be designed around. The companies that read both halves of this book together get the full picture. The diagnosis is hard because the work is real. The work is real because the opportunity is real. Both halves of that sentence are the point.

THE BOTTOM LINE: Multiple drivers produce explosive growth. Flash crash characteristics determine whether it lasts. Pursue driver convergence while monitoring all five flash crash traits. The goal is speed on a sound foundation.

The perfect storm builds empires and destroys them. The difference is what's underneath when the wind changes.

Part III: Decline Patterns

Chapter 12: The Four Phases of Decline

Figure 7. Decline descends in four phases. Each phase feeds the next. Catching Phase 1 costs months. Phase 4 costs the company.

Every decline in this industry follows the same sequence. The timing varies. The sequence doesn't.

In medicine, there's a concept called the "window of intervention." It is the period between when a disease becomes detectable and when it becomes untreatable. A tumor that's caught in stage one has a dramatically different prognosis than the same tumor caught in stage four. The disease is identical. The outcome depends entirely on when you diagnose it.

Direct selling companies die the same way. Not suddenly. Not unpredictably. In a sequence that's identifiable at each stage and treatable at the early stages but nearly always fatal by the final stage. The companies that survive are the ones that diagnose early. The companies that die are the ones that don't look until the symptoms are impossible to ignore.

Across the 53-company dataset, the timing of decline varies enormously. Flash crashes play out in weeks. Slow erosions take years. But the sequence, the order in which the symptoms appear, is almost always the same. Four phases. Same order. Every time.

If you know the sequence, you can read the early signals. And if you can read the early signals, you can intervene before the decline becomes irreversible.

PHASE 1: INVISIBLE CHURN ACCELERATION

This is the phase that kills companies, but not because it's the most damaging phase. It kills because it's the phase that nobody sees.

Churn in direct selling is always present. Annual turnover rates of 50% to 70% are considered normal in this industry, as we covered in Chapter 4. The field is constantly losing people. New distributors join, try for a few months, don't see results, and quit. This is the background rate. It is priced into the business model. As long as recruiting outpaces churn, net growth continues.

Phase 1 begins when the churn rate starts rising above normal but recruiting hasn't yet slowed. The gross numbers still look healthy. New enrollments are strong. Convention attendance is solid. Revenue may even be growing. But underneath the surface, the rate at which people leave has accelerated from 60% to 70% to 75% to 80%.

You can't see this in the headline numbers. If you recruit 10,000 people this month and lose 7,500, your net growth is 2,500. That looks like progress. It feels like momentum. But if last year you were recruiting 10,000 and losing 6,000, your net growth was 4,000. The net has been cut nearly in half. The gross recruiting number masked it completely.

This is why Phase 1 is invisible. The metric many companies track, total distributor count, is a net number. It shows the result of recruiting minus churn. When both are high, the net can look stable even while the underlying dynamics are deteriorating rapidly. The company is running harder to stay in the same place. The treadmill is accelerating. But the dashboard says "growing."

The FTC investigation covered in Chapter 4 documented this dynamic precisely. The net distributor count looked stable. The gross was a churn machine processing hundreds of thousands of people through the system annually, with each person's brief tenure generating a burst of qualification purchasing that showed up as revenue and then disappeared when they left.

AdvoCare's 2017 income disclosure was Phase 1 data in plain sight. Sixty-seven percent of distributors earning zero. Those people weren't building. They weren't producing sustainable volume. They were cycling through the system. The company needed constant fresh enrollment to replace them. When the FTC examined the economics two years later, the structural fragility was obvious. But in 2017, AdvoCare was still generating strong revenue. The Phase 1 signal was visible. Nobody acted on it.

The diagnostic for Phase 1 is simple. Track gross churn separately from net growth. If your gross churn rate is rising quarter over quarter, even while your net distributor count is stable or growing, you're in Phase 1. The disease is present. The window of intervention is open. The treatment is investing in retention, reducing qualification purchasing requirements, improving the first-90-day experience, and building customer depth that survives distributor turnover.

Many companies never run this diagnostic. They look at the net number and see growth. They look at convention attendance and see enthusiasm. They look at revenue and see progress. The rot is hidden inside the gross numbers. And by the time it becomes visible in the net numbers, Phase 1 has already transitioned to Phase 2.

PHASE 2: REVENUE PER DISTRIBUTOR DECLINES

In Phase 2, the field becomes less productive on a per-person basis. Each distributor produces less volume. Each recruiting conversation converts at a lower rate. Each customer is harder to find because the low-hanging fruit has been picked. The recruiting story has lost its freshness.

The company's response to Phase 2 is predictable and almost always wrong. Corporate launches new incentive trips. Creates promotional bonuses. Runs rank advancement contests. Introduces limited-time comp plan enhancements. Each of these is designed to spike activity and mask the underlying decline in per-person productivity.

Sometimes the promotions work briefly. A new product launch generates a quarter of excitement. A trip incentive motivates a burst of recruiting. But the underlying dynamic hasn't changed. The recruiting story is harder to tell than it was last year. The field's energy is lower. The cultural moment that made the product easy to share has matured. And each promotion costs money, pushing the payout ratio from Chapter 4 higher.

Medifast provides the clearest proof of Phase 2 in real time. The data is from SEC filings. Average revenue per active OPTAVIA coach dropped from $4,972 per quarter to $4,630 per quarter between Q2 2024 and Q2 2025. That is a decline in per-person productivity. But here is what makes it Phase 2 rather than Phase 1: the number of coaches was ALSO dropping, from over 60,800 at peak to roughly 22,800. Both metrics declining simultaneously. Fewer people, each producing less. That is the signature of Phase 2.

When a company enters Phase 2 and responds with incentive spending, it creates a payout inflation spiral. Revenue is flat or declining. Incentive costs are rising. Margins compress. Cash reserves shrink. The promotions that were supposed to reignite growth are actually accelerating the financial deterioration.

The diagnostic for Phase 2 is revenue per distributor tracked quarterly. If the average volume produced per active distributor is declining, even while total revenue holds steady because new enrollment is replacing lost volume, you're in Phase 2. The treatment isn't more incentives. The treatment is honest diagnosis of why per-person productivity is falling. Is it a stale recruiting narrative? Product-culture fit fading? Platform effectiveness declining? Each cause has a different response. Throwing promotions at all of them indiscriminately makes the financial picture worse.

PHASE 3: TOP LEADER DEPARTURE

Andy Grove called this a strategic inflection point: the moment when the fundamentals shift so dramatically that the old playbook stops working. Phase 3 is when the decline becomes visible to the field. Because the people who drive the culture, the energy, the belief, start leaving.

In Phases 1 and 2, the departures are at the bottom and middle of the organization. New distributors who never got traction. Mid-level builders whose income dropped below the effort threshold. These departures are painful but not culturally devastating. The field doesn't panic when someone they've never heard of quits.

Phase 3 is different. Phase 3 is when the top 1% to 5% start leaving. And their departure comes in one of two forms.

The quiet departure. The leader stops promoting. She stops attending events. She stops doing team calls. She doesn't formally announce her departure. She just goes silent. Her team notices. Her energy was the engine of her entire organization. Without it, the organization drifts. Volume declines slowly. Leaders beneath her start having the same conversation she had six months ago: "Is this still working? Should I be looking at something else?"

The loud departure. The leader announces she is leaving. She posts on social media. She appears on another company's stage. She brings her team with her. The volume leaves overnight. When Brig Hart left Amway for MonaVie, the impact was measurable in Amway's financial reports.

When the heavy hitters later jumped to the next opportunity, MonaVie collapsed within a few years from its $854 million peak.

Organo Gold's trajectory is the most dramatic Phase 3 example in the dataset. As covered in the Leader Migration chapter, industry estimates of peak revenue vary from hundreds of millions to approaching $800 million before the departure of the founding leadership trio cratered the company to a fraction of peak. An 85 to 95% decline. The field's loyalty was to the leaders, not to the brand.

The diagnostic for Phase 3 is deceptively simple. Are any of your top twenty earners less active than they were twelve months ago? Are any of them less visible on social media? Are any of them declining invitations to company events or stage opportunities? Are any of them less enthusiastic in their public messaging about the company?

By the time a top leader formally announces a departure, the decision was made months earlier. The signals were visible long before the announcement. The leader who stops posting enthusiastically about your company six months before she leaves was in Phase 3 thinking six months before that. The total timeline from first doubt to formal departure is often twelve to eighteen months. That is a twelve-to-eighteen-month window where the right intervention, honest conversation, economic adjustment, addressing whatever caused the dissatisfaction, could potentially retain the leader.

Many companies don't have these conversations until after the announcement. By then it's too late.

There is a version of Phase 3 that doesn't involve leader departure at all: founder transition. When a founder steps back, retires, or is replaced, the company enters a structural version of Phase 3 even if no field leaders leave. The founder's personal relationships, vision-casting, and decision-making speed were often the invisible infrastructure holding the company together. Research on founder transitions in high-growth companies shows that the skills that built the company are rarely the skills that sustain it at scale. The charismatic founder who recruited the first generation of leaders may not be the right person to manage a billion-dollar operation. But replacing that founder without losing the cultural identity she created is one of the hardest transitions any organization faces. The companies that manage founder transitions well, Melaleuca from VanderSloot to Felton being one example, do so by ensuring the successor was embedded in the culture for years before the transition. The companies that manage it poorly replace the founder with an outsider who has operational credentials but no field trust. The field reads that transition as a signal, and the signal is rarely positive.

PHASE 4: NARRATIVE COLLAPSE

Phase 4 is terminal. Not always immediately fatal. But terminal in the sense that the disease has metastasized beyond the company's ability to control it.

Narrative collapse is when the story breaks. The public-facing narrative that attracted distributors, recruited leaders, and generated belief shifts from aspirational to skeptical. Social media, which had been the company's greatest amplifier during growth, becomes its greatest amplifier during decline.

The mechanics are specific. Aspirational posts from active distributors decline in frequency. Complaint posts from former distributors increase. Facebook groups that were once communities of enthusiastic sellers become communities of people trying to liquidate inventory. The term "GOOB sale" (Going Out Of Business) appears. Former distributors become vocal critics. Blog posts and videos documenting the decline gain traction. Journalists investigate. Documentaries get made.

LuLaRich, the documentary about LuLaRoe's rise and fall, reached a mainstream audience and cemented the company as a case study in what went wrong. Once a documentary exists, the narrative is locked. No amount of corporate messaging can override a two-hour film available on every streaming platform.

Once narrative collapse takes hold, recruiting is functionally dead. Because the first thing any prospect does in the modern era is Google the company name. If the first page of results is lawsuits, documentaries, complaint threads, and "is this a pyramid scheme" articles, no amount of field enthusiasm can overcome the search results.

Tupperware's restructuring officer captured narrative collapse in a single sentence during the company's bankruptcy proceedings: "Nearly everyone now knows what Tupperware is, but fewer people know where to find it." That is narrative collapse. The brand still exists in public consciousness. But the story attached to it has changed from "innovative American company" to "your grandmother's storage containers." The brand recognition that was once an asset became a liability because the narrative it carried was one of irrelevance rather than aspiration.

The diagnostic for Phase 4 is external. Google your company name. What do prospects see? If the first page of results is positive press, distributor success stories, and product reviews, your narrative is healthy. If the first page includes lawsuits, regulatory actions, income disclosure critiques, anti-MLM content, or "is this a pyramid scheme" results, you're in or approaching Phase 4.

The treatment for Phase 4 is the hardest of all four phases because the narrative is no longer within the company's control. The company can invest in PR. It can generate positive content. It can encourage distributors to post success stories. But the organic narrative, the one generated by real people sharing real experiences, has shifted. And in the social media era, organic narrative overwhelms corporate messaging by orders of magnitude.

The only companies that have recovered from Phase 4 did so by fundamentally changing the business. Not by messaging their way out of it. Herbalife survived narrative collapse during the Ackman era by restructuring its U.S. operations and documenting real customers. The narrative shifted because the business underneath it changed. The company that emerged from the crisis was structurally different from the one that entered it.

Monat provides a different kind of resilience story. The company faced intense negative PR campaigns that many in the field viewed as unfair attacks, amplified by social media and anti-direct-selling content creators. Monat's response was to double down on product quality, compliance infrastructure, and customer documentation. The company weathered the storm and continued operating. Negative PR does not automatically equal structural failure. It tests whether the foundation is real. Monat proved its foundation was real enough to survive the test.

Avon offers the most instructive Phase 4 legacy story in the industry. Founded in 1886, Avon built one of the longest-running direct selling operations in history. The Avon Lady was once a household cultural reference. Peak global revenue exceeded $10 billion. For more than a century, the model worked.

Then the environment changed. E-commerce rose. Beauty moved to Sephora, Ulta, and TikTok Shop. The creator economy gave women with beauty expertise a path to monetize their audiences without joining a direct selling company. Avon's representative model aged faster than the company could modernize it. Avon International posted nine consecutive quarters of revenue decline. In August 2024, Avon Products Inc. filed for Chapter 11 bankruptcy in the United States. Parent company Natura & Co reacquired the international assets for $125 million through the bankruptcy process. In September 2025, Natura announced the sale of Avon International to Regent LP. A new commission plan launched in January 2025 that moved Avon's North American Ambassadors from a fixed to a variable structure tied to campaign sales. Those are real changes. The company is trying to modernize.

Avon's story isn't about a single catastrophic decision. It is about a century of legacy infrastructure meeting a decade of platform shifts that the company couldn't adapt to fast enough. The field aged. The customer base migrated to other channels. The narrative in search results and social media turned from nostalgic to dated. And the revenue curve followed the narrative down. Legacy brands aren't immune to Phase 4. They are sometimes more vulnerable to it, because the infrastructure that built the company becomes the infrastructure that has to be torn down before a different kind of company can be rebuilt inside the same walls.

There is one additional factor that appears in multiple decline stories and deserves separate mention: private equity ownership. When PE firms acquire or invest in direct selling companies, the dynamic changes. Private equity doesn't kill momentum. What it does is expose weak economics faster. If the company's fundamentals are strong, PE capital can accelerate growth, fund infrastructure, and expand international reach. If the fundamentals are weak, the pressure to generate returns on an exit timeline accelerates the very structural weaknesses this book documents. The PE firm's focus on short-term financial engineering can conflict with the long-term relationship building that sustains direct selling organizations. Several high-profile declines in the dataset involved private equity ownership. The dynamic is well documented in industry analyses. Companies that maintain founder-led or long-term strategic ownership have shown greater resilience through multiple cycles.

From inside the mastermind, I watch these four phases play out in real time. Not from SEC filings. From the conversations of the people living through them. And what I can tell you is that the field reads these phases faster and more accurately than any corporate dashboard.

The leaders in Phase 1 companies say things like: "We're still growing but it feels different. Harder. I'm working more and getting less." They can feel the churn acceleration before the data shows it. Their teams are churning faster. Their personally-sponsored people are staying for shorter periods. The excitement of a new enrollment is dampened by the quiet exit of someone else who joined three months ago. But the company's revenue report says everything is fine. The leadership team is celebrating a record quarter. And the top earner sitting in one of my leadership sessions is staring at her phone thinking, "Something is off and I can't explain it."

I always tell leaders in this situation: trust the feeling. The field's intuition about churn is almost always ahead of the data. If it feels like you're filling a leaky bucket, you probably are. Go look at the gross numbers. Count how many people joined your team in the last six months. Then count how many of them are still active today. That ratio is your personal Phase 1 diagnostic. If it's worse than it was a year ago, the phase has begun regardless of what the corporate report says.

The leaders in Phase 2 companies say: "I used to close one out of three people I talked to. Now it's one out of ten. Everyone's already heard of us and half of them know someone who tried it and quit." They can feel per-person productivity declining. The conversations are harder. The objections are more frequent. The prospect who would have said yes two years ago now says "let me think about it" and never calls back. But corporate just launched a new trip incentive and is telling everyone to "push harder this quarter." The disconnect between what the field is experiencing and what corporate is prescribing is enormous. And the field knows it.

The leaders in Phase 3 companies say very little publicly. They go quiet. They take calls from competitors. They start building a Plan B. The conversations happen behind closed doors, in hotel suites after convention, in private group chats, in the community. When a top earner from a well-known company starts asking questions about other opportunities, everyone in the room knows what it means. Nobody says it out loud. But the unspoken understanding is clear: she is evaluating her exit.

I've learned to read Phase 3 in body language at industry events. The leader who used to be on stage is now in the audience. The leader who used to post daily about her company hasn't posted in two weeks. The leader who used to bring her entire team to convention brought three people this year. These aren't metrics you find in a spreadsheet. They are signals you see if you're paying attention. And by the time you see them, the clock is already running.

The leaders in Phase 4 companies are already gone or mentally checked out. The ones still there are managing a controlled descent, trying to maintain their income as long as possible while the narrative erodes around them. Some transition to coaching or consulting. Some move to the next company and start building immediately. Some leave the industry entirely, exhausted by the emotional whiplash of a company they loved becoming a company they can no longer defend.

The speed at which these phases progress varies enormously. In a flash crash, all four phases can play out in six to twelve months. In a slow erosion, Phase 1 can last for years before Phase 2 becomes visible. But the sequence is always the same. Invisible churn. Declining productivity. Leader departure. Narrative collapse. In that order. Always.

The survey data quantifies what these conversations reveal. Among 82 top-level leaders surveyed, 76% reported that 40% or more of the legacy leaders on their teams have become less engaged in the past two to three years. A third said 70% or more. That isn't a company-specific problem. That is an industry-wide Phase 1 signal hiding in plain sight.

And here is the data point that should change how every company thinks about disengagement: 78% of those leaders said that when they felt less engaged, they didn't quit. They shifted to support mode. They stopped recruiting but kept supporting their teams. They were still there. Still attending. Still collecting checks. Still showing up at convention. But they had stopped creating momentum. They had stopped personally sponsoring. They had stopped being the engine.

Top leaders don't quit. They drift into maintenance. And that drift is invisible on every corporate dashboard because the leader is still technically active. Her volume hasn't dropped to zero. Her team is still producing. Her rank is intact. But the behavior that created the growth in the first place, the personal sponsoring, the prospecting energy, the belief that drives action, has stopped. She is maintaining. Not building. And the difference between maintaining and building is the difference between Phase 1 and momentum.

Run this quarterly.

THE DECLINE PHASE DIAGNOSTIC

For each phase, assess whether the signals are present in your company right now.

Phase 1 Signals (Invisible Churn Acceleration): - Gross churn rate rising quarter over quarter, even if net growth is positive - Average distributor tenure declining (people are staying for shorter periods) - First-year attrition exceeding 70% - Increasing percentage of distributors earning zero income

If two or more Phase 1 signals are present: you're in Phase 1. Invest immediately in retention, first-90-day experience, and customer depth. This is the cheapest and most effective intervention point.

Phase 2 Signals (Revenue Per Distributor Declines): - Average volume per active distributor declining quarter over quarter - Recruiting conversion rate declining (more conversations needed per enrollment) - Increasing incentive spending without proportional revenue response - Payout ratio (commissions as % of revenue) rising while revenue is flat or declining

If two or more Phase 2 signals are present: you're in Phase 2. Stop adding incentives. Diagnose the root cause of the productivity decline. If it's a stale recruiting narrative, refresh the story and the field's skills. If it's product-culture fit fading, innovate. If it's platform effectiveness declining, adapt.

Phase 3 Signals (Top Leader Departure): - Any of your top twenty earners less active than twelve months ago - Top earners declining invitations to company events or stage opportunities - Top earners whose public enthusiasm for the company has noticeably cooled - Private conversations circulating about potential departures

If any Phase 3 signals are present: you're in or approaching Phase 3. Have honest, direct conversations with the leaders showing signals. Address the economic or cultural factors driving their dissatisfaction. Do it now, not after the announcement.

Phase 4 Signals (Narrative Collapse): - Google search results for your company name include negative press, lawsuits, or anti-MLM content on the first page - Social media sentiment has shifted from aspirational to complaint-driven - Former distributor content (critical videos, blog posts, GOOB sales groups) is gaining traction - Recruiting conversion rates have dropped below sustainable levels despite strong field effort

If Phase 4 signals are present: the narrative has shifted beyond the company's ability to message its way out. Only fundamental business changes, not PR, can redirect the narrative. Study what Herbalife did after the FTC settlement. The narrative changed because the business changed.

Critical Rule: The phases are sequential. If you're in Phase 3, you already passed through Phases 1 and 2. Addressing Phase 3 without fixing the underlying Phase 1 and Phase 2 dynamics is treating symptoms, not the disease. Always diagnose and treat from Phase 1 forward.

Consider a leadership team that runs this diagnostic quarterly.

They track gross churn separately from net growth. They monitor revenue per distributor. They maintain direct, honest relationships with their top twenty earners. They Google their own company name and read the results without defensiveness.

When Phase 1 signals appear, they don't dismiss them. They invest in retention. When Phase 2 signals appear, they don't throw promotions at the problem. They diagnose the root cause. When Phase 3 signals flicker, they have the conversations that might prevent the departure. They never reach Phase 4 because they intervened at Phase 1.

That company doesn't avoid decline permanently. No company does. Markets shift. Products age. Platforms change. Competitors emerge. But that company sees the decline earlier, responds faster, and intervenes at the stage where intervention is cheapest and most effective. Instead of discovering decline when revenue has already dropped 30%, they discover it when the gross churn rate ticks up two percentage points. Instead of losing their best leaders to competitors, they address the economic factors that were pushing those leaders toward the door.

Early diagnosis. Early intervention. That is the difference between a recoverable dip and a fatal spiral.

THE THREE-NUMBER DASHBOARD

The full diagnostic in this chapter gives a leadership team the depth to identify exactly which phase it's in and what structural issues are driving the decline. It is the right tool for a full quarterly review.

But every CEO and CFO also needs a simpler view. A set of numbers you can check in five minutes. A dashboard small enough to live on a whiteboard. Large enough to catch a decline before it becomes a crisis.

There are three numbers that do that work.

The first number is new distributor enrollments. How many new distributors are you bringing on board this month, this quarter, this year. Track it over time. Watch the trend.

The second number is new customers. How many new real customers are you bringing on board this month, this quarter, this year. Track it over time. Watch the trend.

The third number is retention. What percentage of your distributors from twelve months ago are still active. What percentage of your customers from twelve months ago are still ordering. Track it over time. Watch the trend.

Three numbers. New distributors. New customers. Retention. Look at them every month. But the comparison that matters most isn't month-over-month or even quarter-over-quarter. It is this quarter compared to the same quarter last year. That comparison strips out seasonality and promotional noise and reveals the underlying direction of the business.

Month-over-month comparisons show you the weather. Quarter-over-quarter comparisons show you the climate. Year-over-year for the same quarter shows you the actual trajectory.

When all three numbers are moving in the same direction, you have a clear signal. Three greens and the business is healthy. Three reds and you're in a phase of decline that the deeper diagnostic will now help you name precisely.

The three-number dashboard doesn't replace the full four-phase framework. It tells you when to run it.

The next chapter covers the most predictable external threat to momentum: regulatory enforcement. What the data shows is that FTC actions don't arrive suddenly. They follow a consistent four-stage sequence with two to four years of warning signals. The companies that survived responded to the early signals. The companies that died treated the early signals as noise.

THE BOTTOM LINE: Every decline follows the same four-phase sequence. Diagnose which phase you're in by tracking gross-vs-net enrollment, revenue per distributor, top earner activity levels, and public narrative. Early diagnosis is cheap. Late diagnosis is fatal.

The phases are always the same. The timing is always different. The companies that survive are the ones that diagnose at Phase 1 and treat before Phase 3.

Chapter 13: The Regulatory Domino Sequence

Figure 8. Enforcement feels sudden. It isn't. Every stage is public and visible two to four years before the hammer drops.

FTC enforcement actions don't arrive suddenly. They arrive predictably. The survivors see the signals. The rest call them "hater noise."

On August 21, 2015, FTC agents walked into Vemma Nutrition Company's offices in Tempe, Arizona, with a court order. They froze the company's assets. They appointed a temporary receiver. They effectively shut down a business that had been generating more than $200 million in annual revenue and enrolling 30,000 new members per month.

To the field, it felt like a lightning strike. One day they were building. The next day their company was frozen. Leaders were blindsided. Distributors were furious. The narrative from Vemma's defenders was immediate: this was government overreach, an attack on entrepreneurship, a politically motivated hit job on a legitimate business.

But the FTC action against Vemma wasn't sudden. It was the final domino in a sequence that had been falling for over two years. And every single domino was visible to anyone who was paying attention.

July 2013: TINA.org, a nonprofit consumer advocacy organization, began warning consumers about Vemma after receiving numerous complaints from college students and parents about aggressive recruitment tactics.

April 2014: TINA.org filed its first formal complaint with the FTC after Vemma was deemed a pyramid scheme by Italian regulators and fined. Italy had seen the pattern before America's regulators acted.

June 2014: TINA.org filed a second complaint with the FTC, documenting numerous deceptive health claims made by top distributors. By this point, the FTC had received 170 consumer complaints about Vemma.

Throughout 2014 and early 2015: Rolling Stone, Al Jazeera, the Today Show, the Sunday Times of London, and the Cincinnati Enquirer all published investigative stories about Vemma's business practices. National media scrutiny was intensifying.

August 2015: The FTC filed suit. Assets frozen. Company shut down.

Twenty-five months of visible warning signals before the enforcement hammer dropped. Two years of media scrutiny, consumer complaints, watchdog alerts, and international regulatory action. All of it public. All of it Googleable. All of it ignored by a company that was too busy celebrating momentum to read the signals.

Vemma's CEO Benson Boreyko had been told. He had been warned by his own team. He told the New York Post in 2014: "I always want to stay on the good side of the FTC because they have guns." He acknowledged the threat. And then he continued operating exactly as before. The company made cosmetic changes. Banned affiliates under 18. Tweaked the compensation plan slightly. Announced compliance improvements. The fundamental pattern that had drawn regulatory attention never changed.

A clarification worth adding here, because it matters for any company reading this book. Vemma had a real product that real people actually loved. Many of the affiliates counted in that 86% internal consumption number were, in practice, product customers. They kept ordering the energy drinks month after month even though they were making no money from the business side. Under FTC rules, the company couldn't reclassify enrolled affiliates as customers even when their behavior was indistinguishable from customer behavior. That classification gap was part of the structural problem. Once someone enrolled as an affiliate, the FTC measured them as an affiliate forever, regardless of whether they were actually building a business or just buying product on autoship.

But the specific trigger that escalated Vemma from another aggressive direct seller into a priority FTC target wasn't only the internal consumption ratio. It was the promotion. Vemma's Young People Revolution (YPR) movement targeted college students and younger prospects with an income narrative so loud, so money-focused, and so publicly documented on social media that the regulatory risk profile was unavoidable. The events were party-style. The messaging was stacked with luxury imagery and explicit or implied income claims. The culture celebrated fast money in ways that made every problematic post evidence for a future enforcement action. Parents complained to the FTC about their college-aged kids. Journalists had hundreds of screenshots of distributor posts to work with. The same business model with quieter promotion would have attracted less attention. The loud, claim-heavy, youth-targeted promotion made the file.

For any owner or executive reading this, the Vemma lesson isn't only about internal consumption. It is that aggressive income-focused promotion aimed at a young demographic creates a public evidence trail that regulators, journalists, and watchdog organizations can't ignore. The volume and visibility of the promotion amplifies every structural weakness. A company with a healthy customer ratio and disciplined promotion has defense. A company with a concerning ratio and loud income claims on social media is building a case against itself.

The dominoes fell anyway.

Here is the pattern. It has repeated across every regulatory enforcement action in the dataset. The timing varies. The sequence doesn't.

STAGE 1: MEDIA SCRUTINY

The first domino is usually media. A journalist investigates. An article publishes. A news segment airs. The coverage is typically based on interviews with former distributors, consumer complaints, and publicly available financial data.

A critical caveat: not all negative press is a Stage 1 signal. Every successful direct selling company eventually gets negative coverage. If you're big enough, someone will write something negative about you. A blog post from someone with 200 followers isn't the same signal as an ESPN investigative feature. A single Reddit thread isn't the same as a New York Times article. Context matters. Who published it? What is their reach? How credible is the outlet? How detailed is the investigation? How many sources did they use? Is this a single disgruntled person or a documented pattern?

The signal becomes meaningful when the coverage is from a credible outlet with significant reach, when it's based on multiple sources and documented evidence, and when it describes structural practices rather than individual complaints. One angry blog post is noise. An investigative feature on a major platform that interviews a dozen former distributors and cites financial data is a signal. The difference between the two is the difference between normal friction and the beginning of a pattern that regulators will eventually notice.

ESPN's investigative feature on AdvoCare's business practices preceded the FTC's action by three years. Three years of the company operating with a media target on its back. The ESPN story was detailed. It named names. It questioned the income opportunity. It showed that the vast majority of distributors earned little or nothing. It was broadcast on a platform with millions of viewers. And AdvoCare's response was to defend the business, dismiss the coverage, and continue operating without structural changes.

Three years later, the FTC hit AdvoCare with a $150 million fine and banned the company from network marketing permanently. The ESPN story had described the same structural problems that the FTC would later cite in its enforcement action. The article was a free preview of the regulatory case. And the company treated it as a PR inconvenience rather than a diagnostic signal.

The People's Daily's article about Nu Skin preceded the Chinese government investigation and the 33% stock decline. ABC's 20/20 preceded Mannatech's lawsuits. BuzzFeed's reporting preceded the LuLaRoe attorney general suit.

In every case, the media coverage came first. It was the canary in the coal mine. And in every case, the company's response to media coverage was defensive rather than diagnostic. They attacked the journalist. They questioned the motives. They issued statements defending the business model. They rallied the field with messages about "haters" and "people who don't understand our profession."

What they didn't do was ask: "Is there truth in this coverage? Does the data support the criticism? Should we change something before the regulators see the same article?"

STAGE 2: CONSUMER COMPLAINT SPIKE

The second domino is complaint volume. As media coverage increases public awareness of the company's practices, consumers who had negative experiences begin filing formal complaints. They file with the FTC. They file with state attorneys general. They file with the Better Business Bureau. They post in online forums.

The FTC had received 170 formal complaints about Vemma before the agency took action. AdvoCare faced a class-action lawsuit from distributors before the FTC investigation concluded. LuLaRoe saw mass quality complaints from consultants with defective inventory before attorney general investigations began. Parents filed complaints with multiple agencies about Vemma's campus recruiting practices targeting their college-aged children.

The complaint spike is measurable. The FTC tracks complaint volume by company. State attorneys general track complaint patterns. These aren't hidden databases. They are responsive to Freedom of Information Act requests. TINA.org obtained Vemma's FTC complaint data through exactly this mechanism.

When complaint volume rises sharply against a specific company, it creates a paper trail that regulators use to justify investigation. The complaints don't cause the enforcement. They provide the evidence base that makes enforcement legally actionable.

STAGE 3: WATCHDOG ALERTS

The third domino is institutional attention. Consumer advocacy organizations, industry watchdogs, and regulatory monitoring bodies begin publishing formal warnings or filing complaints.

TINA.org is the most prominent example in the direct selling space. The organization warned consumers about Vemma in July 2013, more than two full years before the FTC acted. In several cases, TINA.org literally filed the FTC complaints that preceded enforcement actions.

When TINA.org or a similar organization publishes an investigation of a direct selling company, it's not an opinion piece. It is a documented compilation of evidence: income disclosure analysis, complaint data, deceptive marketing examples, regulatory history of the founders, and financial structure analysis. These investigations create the roadmap that regulators follow.

The companies that treat watchdog alerts as "hater noise" are making the same mistake that Vemma made. The alert isn't an attack. It is a diagnosis.

And the appropriate response isn't defense. It is examination. Is the evidence accurate? Does our data support or refute the claims? What would we need to change to make the criticism moot?

STAGE 4: ENFORCEMENT (the final domino)

By the time the FTC or a state attorney general takes formal action, the company has typically been on a regulatory watchlist for two to four years. The investigation has been building quietly. Evidence has been compiled. Legal strategy has been developed. The complaint has been drafted, reviewed, and approved through an internal process that involves multiple layers of analysis.

The action feels sudden to the field because the field wasn't privy to the investigation. But the investigation was predictable because every preceding stage was visible. The media covered the company negatively. The complaints spiked. The watchdogs published warnings. And the company did nothing structurally different in response to any of it.

The enforcement action is the final domino in the sequence rather than the first.

Juul Labs illustrates the same four-stage sequence in a non-direct-selling context, and the parallels are instructive because they demonstrate that the sequence isn't unique to direct selling. It is how regulatory enforcement works.

Juul launched its e-cigarettes in 2015. By 2018, the company had captured more than 70% of the U.S. e-cigarette market. Sales were explosive. The product was, by conventional business metrics, one of the most successful consumer product launches of the decade. Inside Juul, the momentum felt like an undeniable validation of the business model.

Stage 1 began in 2017 and 2018. Journalists at the New York Times, CNN, and multiple broadcast networks ran detailed investigative pieces on Juul's marketing practices, particularly the company's apparent targeting of underage users through flavor selection (mango, mint, creme), social media campaigns, and youth-focused event sponsorships. The 2018 FDA declaration of an "epidemic" of underage vaping was a Stage 1 signal of enormous magnitude. A federal regulator publicly identifying a specific category as a public health crisis isn't ambiguous.

Stage 2 followed quickly. Consumer complaints, parent complaints, and school district complaints spiked across 2018 and 2019. The complaint volume was sufficient to attract state attorney general attention in multiple states simultaneously. EVALI, the vaping-related lung injury crisis that hospitalized thousands of people in 2019, amplified the consumer-complaint backdrop even though most EVALI cases involved black-market cannabis products rather than Juul.

Stage 3 arrived in 2019 and 2020. Multiple watchdog organizations published formal reports. The Massachusetts Attorney General filed suit in 2020. North Carolina reached a $40 million settlement in 2021. A multistate coalition of 33 states plus Puerto Rico launched a coordinated investigation.

Stage 4 arrived on June 23, 2022. The FDA issued a marketing denial order (MDO) that required Juul to stop selling its products in the United States. In the subsequent twelve months, Juul agreed to $1.7 billion in individual lawsuit settlements, $438.5 million in multistate AG settlements, and another $462 million in settlements with additional state attorneys general. The company didn't cease to exist because, in June 2024, the FDA rescinded the MDO while continuing its scientific review. But the four-year domino sequence had already fundamentally damaged the business. Juul's valuation had peaked at $38 billion in 2018. By the time of the MDO, the valuation had collapsed by more than 90%.

The parallels with direct selling regulatory cases are exact. Stage 1 signals from credible media outlets appeared three to four years before enforcement. Stage 2 consumer complaint spikes followed. Stage 3 watchdog and attorney general action came next. Stage 4 federal enforcement arrived on schedule. And throughout all four stages, the company's response was primarily defensive. Juul's leadership team made marketing changes (removing flavored pods in 2019, ending social media marketing, changing executive leadership) but never fundamentally restructured the business model that regulators were investigating. When Stage 4 arrived, the same practices that had drawn scrutiny in 2017 were still identifiable in the regulatory record.

Juul demonstrates that the four-stage sequence isn't a direct selling phenomenon. It is how every regulatory enforcement action in consumer products operates. Media scrutiny precedes consumer complaints precedes watchdog action precedes enforcement. The timeline varies from two to four years. The sequence doesn't.

The lesson that separates survivors from casualties is simple. Better lawyers won't save you. Lobbying won't save you. Political connections won't save you. Responding to early signals by changing behavior is what saves you.

The companies that survived regulatory scrutiny, every single one of them, responded to Stage 1 or Stage 2 signals by making substantive changes to their business model. Not cosmetic changes. Not PR campaigns. Structural changes to the practices that generated the criticism.

Neora is the most dramatic example. The FTC sued Neora in 2019, alleging the company was a pyramid scheme. The case went to a full trial. In September 2023, Judge Barbara Lynn denied every claim the FTC brought. All five of them.

What made Neora different? The company had 80% of its revenue coming from real customers. It had implemented rigorous compliance programs. It had changed its practices in response to regulatory guidance over the years. When the FTC examined the business, the evidence showed a legitimate company with real customers, not a recruitment-driven operation with a product alibi.

CEO Jeff Olson's statement captured the strategic choice: "Because Neora has always been built on a solid foundation with science-based products that bring true value to the market, a massive non-distributor customer base that represents nearly 80 percent of the company's total revenue, and a modern e-commerce sales system that removes the need for brand partners to carry inventory or incur unnecessary extra costs, we were able to take on and win this important fight."

Neora didn't beat the FTC by having better lawyers. It beat the FTC by having better data. Data that showed the business was real.

Herbalife survived a $200 million FTC settlement in 2016 by agreeing to fundamentally restructure its U.S. operations. The restructuring was painful. It required documenting real retail customers. It changed compensation structures. It cost money and disrupted the field. But it saved the company. Herbalife is still operating at nearly $5 billion in annual revenue. The companies that refused to restructure are gone.

Amway survived the FTC in 1979 by implementing the 70% rule, the 10-customer rule, and a buyback policy. These safeguards redirected growth toward customers rather than pure recruiting velocity. They created friction in the enrollment process, yes. But they demonstrated to regulators that the company was serious about operating legitimately. And they built a foundation of real customer demand that has sustained the company for over sixty years. Most companies in the industry adopted the language of Amway's safeguards. Few adopted the discipline. The ones that adopted the discipline survived. The ones that adopted only the language didn't. Amway's willingness to prioritize the right kind of growth over the fastest kind of growth, at a time when the company was the dominant force in the industry, set a template that should have been followed by every company that came after it. Some did. Many didn't.

The pattern across all three survivors is consistent. They made structural changes that cost money and growth in the short term. They accepted the pain of doing the right thing during a period when the easier path was to continue doing the wrong thing. They treated regulatory scrutiny as diagnostic information rather than an attack on their business. And because they changed, the regulatory apparatus recognized that the changes were real and adjusted its posture accordingly.

The companies that died treated every warning signal as noise. They didn't get caught by surprise. They got caught by denial. They doubled down on the practices that generated the criticism. They attacked the critics. They rallied the field against the "haters." And when the enforcement action arrived, they had no data to defend themselves because the business model was exactly what the regulators alleged it was. This isn't a statement of moral judgment. Some of the people who built these companies were talented and well-intentioned. But intention doesn't change structure. And the structure was the problem.

From the mastermind, I watch the regulatory conversation from both sides. On the company side, compliance is often treated as a cost center, the department that says no, the people who redline the exciting parts. Executives privately call their compliance team "the sales prevention department." The joke has been circulating in this industry for decades. It is also a symptom of a culture that views compliance as friction rather than protection.

Corporate tolerance for compliance is highest when the company is growing and lowest when the company is struggling, which is exactly backwards. The companies that need compliance most are the ones in momentum, because momentum is when the field is most likely to make aggressive claims, stretch the truth about income, and push the boundaries of what is legally permissible. When a company is growing 100% year over year and conventions are packed and the field is on fire, nobody wants the compliance officer to slow things down. But that's precisely when the Stage 1 signals are most likely to appear. Because the aggressive behavior that drives momentum is the same aggressive behavior that generates media scrutiny and consumer complaints.

On the field side, compliance is viewed with a mix of frustration and fear. Distributors know they need to stay within guidelines. But the guidelines are often unclear, inconsistently enforced, and in direct tension with the economic incentives of the comp plan. A distributor whose fast-start bonus rewards rapid enrollment is going to push harder in conversations than a distributor whose compensation rewards customer acquisition. The comp plan tells her to recruit aggressively. The compliance department tells her to be careful. She listens to the one that writes the check.

This is the structural conflict that creates regulatory risk in direct selling. The comp plan incentivizes behavior. The compliance department tries to constrain behavior. They are working in opposite directions. And the comp plan always wins because it's backed by money.

I tell every company I consult with the same thing. Your best compliance strategy isn't your compliance department. It is your compensation plan. If the comp plan incentivizes behavior that creates regulatory risk, no amount of compliance monitoring can fix it. You are trying to police behavior that your own economic system is encouraging. Fix the incentives and the behavior follows. Fix the monitoring while keeping the incentives and you're playing whack-a-mole forever.

Most top earners aren't evaluating a company's compliance culture before they join. That is simply the reality. Compliance isn't what attracts leaders.

Product, comp plan, culture, and opportunity attract leaders. The only time compliance becomes a factor in a leader's evaluation is when the compliance problems are so visible that they've become bad PR. When a company's name is in the news for the wrong reasons. When the income claims on social media are so aggressive that experienced builders see it and think "that's going to end badly." When the culture feels like a ticking clock rather than a foundation. At that point, the best leaders avoid the company. They haven't run a compliance audit. The smell of trouble is strong enough to notice from the outside.

That is why compliance matters for corporate even though the field doesn't ask about it. The field will never request a compliance briefing before joining. But the field will avoid a company whose reputation has been damaged by compliance failures. And by the time the reputation damage is visible, the regulatory dominoes are already falling.

As this book goes to press, the regulatory domino sequence has claimed its most significant legacy company yet. In April 2026, Forever Living Products, one of the oldest and largest direct selling companies in the world, announced it would terminate all recruiting and sponsorship activities in the United States effective May 1, 2026. No new distributors. Several legacy incentive programs frozen or eliminated. Product sales continue, but the direct selling opportunity in the US is over.

Forever Living was founded in 1978. It operated in over 160 countries. It reported revenue exceeding $1.7 billion at peak. It had been in business for nearly fifty years. And it concluded that the evolving US regulatory environment created, in the company's own words, "unmanageable regulatory exposure" that could threaten its global operations if it continued the US model.

Read that carefully. A billion-dollar company with nearly five decades of operating history looked at the regulatory landscape and decided the risk of continuing its US recruiting model was greater than the cost of shutting it down. That isn't a startup folding under pressure. That is a legacy company making a calculated decision that the domino sequence had progressed too far to reverse.

Forever Living's announcement validates the central argument of this chapter. The dominoes are visible. The sequence is predictable. The companies that read the signals and adapt their model survive. The ones that don't eventually face a choice between structural change and shutdown. Forever Living chose to narrow its US model to product sales and long-term compliance. That is a structural response to a regulatory reality that every company in this industry must now take seriously.

The companies that get compliance right make it part of the culture, not a department that operates in opposition to the culture. They train compliance like they train recruiting, early and often. They use real examples from the field, not abstract legal guidelines. They reward teams that model compliant behavior. They make it clear that sustainable growth and compliant growth are the same thing. And their leadership teams understand that the best defense against regulatory enforcement is never needing one.

There is a counterexample that should be examined directly. Because the domino sequence isn't destiny. It is a diagnostic. And the companies that respond to the early stages can stop the sequence before it reaches Stage 4.

Herbalife faced every stage of the domino sequence and survived. The media scrutiny was intense. Bill Ackman's public short campaign in 2012 generated more negative media coverage than many companies experience in a decade. Documentaries were produced. Congressional hearings were held. The FTC opened a formal investigation. Consumer complaints spiked. TINA.org filed alerts. Every stage of the sequence was active simultaneously.

Herbalife's response wasn't cosmetic. The company negotiated a $200 million FTC settlement in 2016 and agreed to fundamental restructuring of its U.S. business operations. It implemented systems to verify retail customers. It restructured compensation to reduce the incentive for qualification purchasing. It invested in the Nutrition Club model, which created genuine daily customer habits tied to physical locations where real people showed up every morning to drink a shake and socialize. The changes were painful. Revenue dipped. Leaders left. The field was disrupted. The stock took hits.

But Herbalife survived. It is still a nearly $5 billion company operating globally. The company that faced every domino in the sequence, including a billionaire publicly calling it a pyramid scheme on national television, is still operating because it responded to the signals with structural change rather than cosmetic defense. It changed the business model, not the press release.

The domino sequence isn't a death sentence. It is an early warning system. The companies that treat it as a signal and respond with structural change can stop the sequence. The companies that treat it as noise and respond with press releases can't.

Monitor these signals.

THE REGULATORY EARLY WARNING TIMELINE

For each stage, assess whether signals are currently present for your company.

Stage 1 Signals (Media Scrutiny): Evaluate any negative media coverage on two dimensions: credibility and volume. A single negative article from a small outlet is normal business. Multiple articles from credible outlets, or a single investigative piece from a major platform (ESPN, New York Times, network television), is a signal. Has an investigative journalist requested an interview or company documents? That is a signal regardless of the outlet, because it means someone is building a case.

If credible, high-reach Stage 1 signals are present: you have the widest intervention window available. This is the cheapest time to act. Conduct an internal audit. Identify the practices that generated the attention. If the coverage has merit, change the practices. If it doesn't have merit, document why and prepare your response. Either way, do not ignore it.

Stage 2 Signals (Consumer Complaint Spike): Is FTC complaint volume increasing? (File a FOIA request to find out.) Are state attorneys general offices contacting your company? Has a class-action lawsuit been filed by former distributors? Are complaint threads multiplying across multiple platforms rather than concentrated in one place? The signal here is volume and pattern, not individual complaints. Every company gets complaints. What matters is whether the volume is accelerating and whether the complaints describe the same structural issues.

If Stage 2 signals are present: the paper trail is building. Cosmetic changes won't stop it. Structural changes to the practices generating complaints are required. The longer you wait at this stage, the more expensive the fix becomes.

Stage 3 Signals (Watchdog Alerts): Has TINA.org or a similar consumer advocacy organization published a formal investigation of your company? Has any regulatory body in any country taken action? These are institutional signals, not individual complaints. When an organization with regulatory relationships publishes a documented investigation, the findings often become part of the evidence base that regulators use.

If Stage 3 signals are present: the regulatory machinery may be in motion. Retain legal counsel with specific FTC defense experience. Begin structural reforms that you can document with data. Every change you make now is evidence you can present later. The window is narrowing but it's not closed.

Stage 4 Signals (Enforcement): - Has the FTC, a state attorney general, or any federal or state agency contacted your company regarding a formal investigation?

If Stage 4 signals are present: the dominoes have fallen. Your defense depends entirely on what you built in the preceding years. If you have Neora's data, 80% real customers, documented compliance programs, and structural evidence of a legitimate business, you have a defense. If you have Vemma's data, 86% internal consumption, complaint files a foot thick, and a CEO with a previous FTC consent order, you don't.

The Critical Rule: The dominoes tend to fall in order, though the timing between stages varies enormously. Some sequences play out over years. Others compress. The consistent pattern is that the cost of intervention rises at each stage. A business model change at Stage 1 costs money and effort. At Stage 2, it costs money, effort, and credibility. At Stage 3, it costs all of that plus legal fees. At Stage 4, it may cost the company. The earlier you respond, the cheaper the fix. The survivors responded early. The rest waited until the cost was unbearable.

An executive team that monitors the regulatory timeline the way they monitor revenue Googles their own company quarterly, files FOIA requests annually to check FTC complaint volume, subscribes to TINA.org's reports, and treats each stage as an escalating signal demanding proportional response. That company may never face enforcement. It never gave the regulators a case to bring. The dominoes never reached Stage 4 because the company intervened at Stage 1 and removed the conditions that would have triggered the rest of the sequence. That is regulatory intelligence. Not legal defense. Prevention.

One more constraint remains. The one that stays invisible until it breaks. When your growth outpaces your ability to deliver, the momentum doesn't just stall. It reverses. Because the same customers and distributors who celebrated your growth will punish your failure to fulfill it.

THE BOTTOM LINE: The regulatory domino sequence is visible years before enforcement. Monitor media coverage, complaint volume, and watchdog reports. Respond to early signals with structural change, not press releases.

Regulatory enforcement is the most predictable threat in this industry. The timeline is visible. The stages are documented. The only companies that are surprised are the ones that chose not to look.

Chapter 14: The Operational Ceiling

Momentum doesn't die from lack of demand. It dies from inability to deliver. And the cruelest version of this is when the demand you worked years to create is the thing that destroys you.

The enemy in this chapter: ignoring the foundation while chasing the headline.

In 2020, Peloton had a problem many companies would envy. Demand was so far ahead of supply that customers were waiting three to four months for delivery. They had already paid in full. They were sitting in their homes refreshing tracking pages, posting on social media about the wait, and growing more frustrated by the day.

Peloton wasn't ignoring the problem. The company was spending over $100 million on expedited ocean freight and air cargo. In some regions, last-mile delivery was costing $500 per bike. Management was throwing money at the fulfillment gap with both hands. And they still couldn't close it.

This is the operational ceiling. The moment when your growth outpaces your infrastructure's ability to deliver the experience that created the growth. And the cruelty of the operational ceiling is this: the same customers who were willing to wait because they were excited will punish you when the excitement turns to frustration. The social media posts shift from "I can't wait for my Peloton" to "I've been waiting three months and nobody can tell me when it's coming." The narrative flips. And once it flips, it compounds, because social media amplifies frustration the same way it amplifies enthusiasm.

Peloton's operational ceiling contributed to a cascade of problems that ultimately cost CEO John Foley his job, destroyed $45 billion in market value, and left the company sitting on more than $1.4 billion in gross inventory, an overhang the company itself called an existential threat in its Q4 fiscal 2022 shareholder letter.

But Peloton's story is a universal pattern. It happens in every industry when growth exceeds operational capacity. And in direct selling, where the distribution model depends on thousands of independent field representatives delivering a consistent experience, the operational ceiling is both more common and harder to fix.

The mechanism is simple.

Growth creates demand. Demand requires fulfillment: products shipped, orders processed, customer service answered, returns handled, commissions calculated, technology platforms maintained. Each of these operational functions has a capacity. When demand operates within that capacity, the experience is good. When demand exceeds capacity, the experience degrades.

In traditional retail, the operational ceiling typically manifests in supply chain problems. Out-of-stock inventory. Shipping delays. Website crashes during peak traffic. These are visible, measurable, and fixable with capital investment.

In direct selling, the operational ceiling manifests in at least five dimensions simultaneously, which makes it harder to diagnose and harder to fix.

First, fulfillment and shipping. When order volume spikes, warehouse capacity, shipping logistics, and delivery timelines all strain. Products arrive late. Orders ship incomplete. International shipments get stuck in customs. The distributor who promised her customer a five-day delivery watches it stretch to three weeks and has to explain why. Fulfillment timing isn't a minor operational problem. It is a revenue-killer.

Second, product quality. When manufacturing scales rapidly to meet demand, quality control often suffers. LuLaRoe's quality collapse is the defining example in direct selling. The "buttery soft" leggings that built the brand started tearing during normal wear. Fabric quality declined as production scaled to meet the demand of 80,000 consultants ordering simultaneously. A consultant who had invested $15,000 in inventory described the moment she realized the quality had shifted. She unboxed a shipment, held up a pair of leggings, and could see her hand through the fabric. She had 200 customers waiting for new patterns. She couldn't sell them product she was embarrassed by. She photographed the defects and posted them in a private consultant group. Within hours, dozens of other consultants posted similar photos. The company's response was slow. The field's response was immediate. Trust broke not in a press release but in a

Facebook group at 11 pm on a Tuesday night. That is how operational failure actually kills momentum. Not in a boardroom. In a living room.

Quality failures compound in direct selling in a way they don't in traditional retail. When a retail product has a quality problem, the customer returns it to the store and gets a refund. The experience is impersonal. When a direct selling product has a quality problem, the customer tells the distributor who personally recommended the product. The failure is personal. The distributor's credibility, not just the company's credibility, takes the hit. And the distributor who recommended a product that fell apart is far less likely to recommend the next product with conviction. One quality problem at a retail store loses one sale. One quality problem in direct selling can suppress an entire team's activity for months.

Third, customer service. When the field grows faster than the support team, distributors can't get answers. Back-office reports are delayed. Commission disputes pile up. Product questions go unanswered. Technology glitches linger for weeks. Each unanswered question erodes belief. Distributors can tolerate a lot of imperfection, but they can't tolerate feeling abandoned. When they call headquarters and nobody answers, the narrative shifts from "we're in momentum" to "nobody's steering this ship." The companies that get this right understand that customer service isn't a cost center. It is the field's most direct measure of whether the company is functional. A broken back-office tells the field, in real time, that the company can't be trusted to deliver on the promise the field is making to prospects. No amount of convention energy can override that signal.

This is where infrastructure and momentum intersect most directly. My previous book, Built to Last in Direct Selling, covers the infrastructure playbook in depth: what to build, how to build it, and what happens when you don't. This chapter is focused on the specific moment when infrastructure failure kills momentum. The two books are companion lenses on the same problem. Built to Last asks "what do you need?" This chapter asks "what happens when you don't have it in time?"

Fourth, technology. Back-office systems, e-commerce platforms, distributor portals, mobile apps. All of these have capacity limits. When 50,000 distributors hit the back-office portal simultaneously on commission day, the system either handles it or crashes. When the e-commerce platform can't process orders during a product launch, the field loses sales they worked weeks to create. Amazon's Prime Day outage in 2018 is the canonical outside example. The company's single biggest sales event of the year, publicly announced, marketed for months, started with a website that couldn't handle the traffic it had specifically engineered demand for. Analysts estimated the outage cost Amazon between $72 million and $100 million in lost sales during the first hour alone. If Amazon, with engineering resources larger than most countries, can crash under demand they planned for, direct selling companies running a product launch without stress-testing the back-office first are guaranteed to. Technology failures during momentum are especially damaging because they undermine the field's confidence in the company's competence at precisely the moment when confidence matters most.

Fifth, compliance infrastructure. As the field grows, the volume of social media posts, income claims, product claims, and marketing materials that need monitoring grows proportionally. A compliance team that could effectively monitor 5,000 distributors can't monitor 50,000 with the same staff. Vemma learned this the hard way, as covered in Chapter 13. Tens of thousands of YPR-movement affiliates posted income imagery and lifestyle claims at a pace the compliance team couldn't possibly keep up with. Every unmonitored post became evidence. Journalists and regulators had a documented archive of field behavior the company had never actually reviewed. Unmonitored field behavior during rapid growth is what generates the Stage 1 and Stage 2 regulatory signals we covered in the previous chapter. The operational ceiling in compliance creates the conditions for regulatory risk.

There is a non-DS example that illustrates the operational ceiling with a happier ending.

In 2007, Apple launched the first iPhone. Demand was so extreme that customers camped outside stores for days. The initial production run sold out almost immediately. Apple could have rushed to scale production, cut corners on quality, and flooded the market to capture every dollar of demand.

Steve Jobs chose the opposite approach. He constrained supply. He kept production tight. He ensured that every iPhone that shipped met the quality standard. Customers waited. Some waited months. And because the product was excellent when it arrived, the wait became part of the story rather than a complaint about the company. Scarcity enhanced the brand rather than destroying it.

Jobs understood something that many companies in momentum don't: the speed of your growth should be governed by the quality of your delivery, not the other way around. Growing faster than your infrastructure can support doesn't produce more momentum. It produces more problems. And problems during momentum are uniquely destructive because the expectations are so high.

The direct selling equivalent of Jobs's approach is the company that says no to opportunities it isn't ready to execute. The company that delays an international market opening because the infrastructure isn't ready. The company that slows a product launch because the quality testing isn't complete. The company that caps enrollment temporarily because customer service can't handle the volume.

These decisions feel like losing momentum. They feel like hitting the brakes when everyone is screaming "go faster." But they're the decisions that protect the experience that created the momentum in the first place. Momentum built on a great experience can be rebuilt after a pause. Momentum destroyed by a terrible experience is much harder to recover.

In the mastermind conversations, I see the operational ceiling from the field's perspective. And I can tell you that operational failures destroy belief faster than any competitor, market condition, or regulatory threat.

Leaders can explain a market shift. They can explain a product category disruption. They can even explain a regulatory action as "challenges we're working through." But they can't explain why their customer's order arrived damaged, why the back-office was down for three days, or why the commission they earned wasn't paid on time. Those are failures of the basics. And when the basics fail, belief crumbles.

I've heard top earners say some version of this more times than I can count: "I can build through a tough market. I can build through a comp plan change. I can't build through a company that can't ship product on time and respond to service inquiries within a reasonable window."

That statement reveals the hierarchy of what matters to the field. And it's often different from what corporate prioritizes. Not every corporate team gets this wrong. Some leadership teams are deeply operational and invest in fulfillment, customer experience, and back-end systems from day one. But in many companies, the visible investments get the attention: events, product launches, compensation enhancements, technology platforms. Operations tends to sit lower on the priority list until something breaks. The companies where operations is treated as a strategic priority rather than a cost center are the ones where the field rarely has to think about it. And that invisibility is the point. The best operations are the ones nobody notices because everything works. Operations is the one thing everyone takes for granted until it doesn't work.

Companies in this industry lose leaders all the time, not because of market conditions or comp plan issues but because of chronic operational failures that made the leaders look bad to their teams. When a leader brings a new distributor into the business and that distributor's first order arrives late, damaged, or wrong, the leader has failed in the eyes of her recruit. Not the company. The leader. Because the recruit trusted the leader's recommendation, and the experience didn't match the promise. The leader can survive one bad experience. She can apologize and promise it won't happen again. But if the operational failures are chronic, if every month brings another shipping problem or another commission error, the leader eventually stops recommending the business. She didn't lose faith in the product. She lost faith in the company's ability to deliver it.

The best companies I've observed through the community invest in operational infrastructure before they need it. They build warehouse capacity for the company they want to be in two years, not the company they're today. They hire customer service staff ahead of the curve. They stress-test their technology platforms before peak volume events. They treat operations as a momentum investment, not a cost center.

The companies that underinvest in operations during growth are making a bet. They are betting that the growth will slow enough for the infrastructure to catch up. Sometimes that bet pays off. More often, the growth continues and the infrastructure gap widens until something breaks publicly. And the public break, the moment when customers and distributors see the operational failure in real time, is when belief takes a hit that no event, no product launch, and no marketing campaign can repair.

The irony is that operational excellence is one of the cheapest competitive advantages available. Better shipping costs less than a new comp plan bonus. Faster customer service costs less than a destination incentive trip. Reliable technology costs less than a product launch campaign. The boring investments produce disproportionate returns in field confidence and customer retention. Nobody ever left a company because the shipping was too fast. But many companies chase the exciting investments first and discover the boring ones matter more only after something breaks.

And when something does break, because it will, the response matters as much as the fix. When back-orders occur, when systems go down, when a product batch has a quality issue, radical transparency builds more trust than silence. Johnson & Johnson's handling of the Tylenol tampering crisis in 1982 remains the textbook case: the company pulled 31 million bottles from shelves, communicated openly at every step, and emerged with stronger consumer trust than before the crisis. The field forgives problems. It doesn't forgive being kept in the dark. A company that says "we have a shipping delay, here is why, here is when it will be fixed, and here is what we're doing about it" earns credibility. A company that goes silent while the field discovers the problem through frustrated customers earns distrust that no PR campaign can reverse.

There is an important nuance here. The operational ceiling isn't always about underinvestment. Sometimes it's about the wrong kind of investment.

Some companies invest heavily in technology, building sophisticated distributor portals, AI-powered tools, and content management systems. Those investments look impressive on a slide deck. But if the basic fulfillment, the product arriving at the customer's door on time and in good condition, is broken, the technology investment is irrelevant.

Other companies invest in marketing infrastructure, creating beautiful product launches, high-production-value videos, and stunning event experiences. Those investments generate excitement. But if the customer service team can't handle the inquiry volume that the marketing generates, the excitement turns to frustration.

The hierarchy is always the same. Fulfillment first. Commissions second. Customer service third. Technology fourth. Marketing fifth. Each layer matters. But the foundation layers must be solid before the upper layers produce value. A company with world-class marketing and broken fulfillment is building a beautiful house on sand.

A specific dimension of operational strategy that often gets overlooked. The decision isn't just whether to invest in inventory. It is when to stock heavily versus when to deliberately sell out fast. Both can be the right move depending on the situation.

Stocking heavily makes sense when the demand profile is reasonably predictable, the company has the cash position to absorb a slower sell-through, the product has a long shelf life, and the launch is intended to ride a wave for multiple quarters. The advantage is that the company can meet demand without supply gaps that erode field belief. The risk is that if demand under-delivers, the company is sitting on inventory that ties up working capital and may eventually require discounting or write-offs.

Selling out fast can also be the right move. A scarcity event during a launch can extend the cultural conversation around a product and create momentum that pays off across future launches. The risk is that running out of stock at the wrong moment can frustrate customers, slow the field's ability to enroll new builders during the window, and require the company to do exceptional work on storytelling and communication to maintain interest while the product is unavailable. Companies that sell out well don't just announce the sellout. They communicate the reason transparently, give the field tools to keep the narrative momentum alive, and create a clear path back into stock with a defined timeline.

The decision between the two is always a projection, and the projection is always uncertain. Best case scenario for demand. Worst case scenario for demand. Cash position. Predictability of the underlying customer pull versus distributor qualification volume. Manufacturing lead times for restock. Shelf life of the product. The company's existing operational maturity at handling either outcome. There is no universal right answer.

There is only the discipline of modeling both scenarios with discipline and choosing the inventory strategy that the company can actually execute well, given its cash position and its capability to ramp up or ramp down from whatever it chose.

The mistake is treating inventory as a mechanical decision rather than a strategic one. Companies that stock based on a single optimistic demand assumption and have no plan for what happens if demand underdelivers tend to learn the hard way. So do companies that deliberately understock without the storytelling discipline to make a sellout into a positive narrative. The strategic question isn't how much to stock. The strategic question is which scenario you're betting on, what you do if you're wrong, and whether your cash position and operational capability support the bet.

Rate your capacity.

THE OPERATIONAL CAPACITY TEST

For each dimension, rate your company's current capacity relative to current demand and projected demand twelve months from now.

Dimension 1: Fulfillment - Can you ship every order within your promised delivery window at current volume? At 150% of current volume? - What is your average order-to-delivery time, and is it improving or deteriorating? - What is your order error rate (wrong items, damaged shipments, incomplete orders)? - If demand doubled in 90 days, would your fulfillment infrastructure handle it?

Dimension 2: Commission Accuracy - Are commissions calculated and paid accurately and on time every pay period? - What is your commission dispute rate, and is it rising or falling? - Can your system handle a 50% increase in active distributors without degradation?

Dimension 3: Customer Service - What is your average response time for distributor inquiries? For customer inquiries? - Is response time improving or deteriorating? - What is your first-contact resolution rate? - If inquiry volume doubled, could your team maintain current service levels?

Dimension 4: Technology - Does your back-office, e-commerce platform, and mobile app function reliably during peak usage? - When was the last unplanned outage, and how long did it last? - Is your technology infrastructure scaled for current volume or projected volume?

Dimension 5: Compliance Monitoring - Can your compliance team effectively monitor the volume of field marketing content being produced? - Are compliance violations being caught and addressed in days or weeks? - If your field doubled, could your compliance infrastructure keep pace?

Scoring:

For each dimension, rate: GREEN (capacity exceeds current demand and can handle reasonable growth), YELLOW (capacity meets current demand but can't absorb significant growth), or RED (capacity is below current demand and operational failures are occurring).

To calibrate the rating consistently, apply this stress test: "Would you bet the company on this dimension holding if demand doubled in 90 days?" Yes with confidence is GREEN. Probably is YELLOW. No is RED. Absolutely not is CRITICAL, which means operational failures are already visible to the field and the CEO's job this quarter is fixing this dimension.

Per-dimension specifics:

Fulfillment. GREEN: Less than 2% error rate, delivery within promised window at 150% of current volume. YELLOW: 2-5% error rate, delivery window holds only at current volume. RED: Above 5% error rate, delivery times already slipping.

Commission Accuracy. GREEN: Less than 1% dispute rate, every pay period on time. YELLOW: 1-3% dispute rate or occasional delays. RED: Above 3% dispute rate or recurring payment delays.

Customer Service. GREEN: Response time trending down, first-contact resolution above 70%. YELLOW: Response time stable, resolution 50-70%. RED: Response time trending up or resolution below 50%.

Technology. GREEN: No unplanned outages in last six months, infrastructure scaled for projected volume. YELLOW: One or two unplanned outages in last six months. RED: Outages in last 30 days or infrastructure capacity at current volume with no headroom.

Compliance Monitoring. GREEN: Violations caught and addressed in days, monitoring scales with field size. YELLOW: Violations take one to three weeks to address. RED: Violations take longer than three weeks or backlog exists.

Aggregating the score:

Any RED: Fix immediately. Operational failures during momentum are the fastest way to destroy the belief that created the momentum.

Two or more YELLOWS: Invest before they become reds. The time to build capacity is before you need it, not after the system breaks.

All GREEN: You have operational resilience. This is a competitive advantage that many companies in this industry don't have. Protect it.

Imagine a company that treats operational capacity as a leading indicator, not a lagging one.

The CEO reviews the Operational Capacity Test quarterly, not just when something breaks. She sees that fulfillment is green but customer service is trending yellow. Average response time has increased from four hours to eleven hours over the last two quarters. Inquiry volume is rising as the field grows. She authorizes hiring three additional service representatives before the holiday volume spike, not after the phones start going unanswered.

That decision doesn't appear on any momentum dashboard. It doesn't get celebrated at convention. No one posts about it on social media. But it's the decision that ensures the field's experience remains strong during the quarter when the company grows 18%. And because the experience holds, the belief holds. And because the belief holds, the momentum holds.

Operations aren't glamorous. They aren't the chapter in a business book that anyone highlights and posts on Instagram. But across the dataset, the companies that sustained momentum longest were the ones that invested in operations proportional to their growth. And the companies that crashed fastest were often the ones that invested in marketing, events, and comp plan bonuses while the operational foundation cracked underneath them.

WHEN OPERATIONAL CEILINGS ARE GOVERNANCE CEILINGS IN DISGUISE

There is a sixth dimension of the operational ceiling that doesn't fit neatly with fulfillment, quality, customer service, technology, or compliance. It sits underneath all of them. The dimension is governance, by which I mean how decisions actually get made inside the company, who has the authority to make them, and what mechanisms exist to override or redirect a single person's judgment when the data calls for it.

This variable shows up in nearly every flash crash in the dataset, almost always as a footnote rather than a named cause. LuLaRoe's product sourcing decisions were concentrated in a small inner circle that didn't respond to early warnings about quality. ViSalus had a leadership concentration that allowed one person to control 74 percent of revenue, which the company eventually had to live with as a structural fact. Young Living's growth trajectory shifted significantly after the founder's death because so much strategic decision-making had been concentrated in him. WorldVentures had governance dynamics that made course correction difficult during the period when course correction would have been most valuable. The pattern repeats across the dataset.

Governance ceilings produce operational ceilings. A company that can't delegate can't scale. A company where one person makes every consequential decision will hit a capacity limit that has nothing to do with warehouses or technology and everything to do with that person's available hours and judgment bandwidth. A founder who controls every product decision will eventually approve a product that shouldn't have shipped, because no one else had the authority to stop it. A CEO who controls every comp plan decision will eventually approve a structural change that produces an unintended consequence, because no one else had the authority to model the second-order effects.

The companies in the dataset that scaled past the founder-as-bottleneck stage and survived for decades almost always made one specific transition. They built decision-making infrastructure that didn't depend on any single person. Boards with independent directors. Executive teams with real authority over their domains. Documented decision rights for product, compliance, comp plan, and field strategy. Override mechanisms when data contradicted leadership intuition. The transition isn't glamorous. It is often resisted by founders who built the company precisely because they trusted their own judgment more than anyone else's. But the absence of that infrastructure is the structural reason many great companies stall at the founder's personal capacity ceiling and never recover.

The diagnostic question is direct. If your CEO or founder were unavailable for six months, would the company continue operating with the same quality of decisions? Would the strategy stay on course? Would the field continue to feel the leadership presence? In the long-term compounders, the answer is yes. In the flash crashes, the answer was usually no, and the company found out at exactly the wrong moment.

A founder reading this book may feel resistance to the section. The resistance itself is data. The companies that lasted were built by founders who, at some point, recognized that the company they had built had outgrown the management structure that built it. They redesigned the structure. They surrendered some control to gain durability. The ones who didn't surrender control reached a ceiling defined by their personal capacity, and the ceiling held until something forced the question. The question is better answered on the front end of momentum than under the pressure of decline.

Part III is now complete. The decline patterns have been documented. The four phases of decline, the regulatory domino sequence, and the operational ceiling represent the three ways momentum dies: from within (churn and productivity decline), from regulators (predictable enforcement), and from inability to deliver (infrastructure failure).

Part IV turns to the playbook. What to do with all of this. How to read the equation. How to time your investments. How to reignite when you've stalled. The diagnosis is complete. The treatment plan begins.

THE BOTTOM LINE: Operations rarely create momentum but frequently kill it. Rate your capacity across fulfillment, commissions, customer service, technology, and compliance. Any red rating requires immediate investment before growth exposes the gap.

Momentum is built by the exciting decisions. It is sustained by the boring ones. The companies that get both right are the ones that last.

Part IV: The Playbook

Chapter 15: Reading the Equation

Figure 9. The book's frameworks compressed into one executive instrument. Run this quarterly. Bring it to your next leadership meeting.

During the Gulf War, General Norman Schwarzkopf had access to more battlefield intelligence than any commander in history. Satellite imagery. Real-time communications intercepts. Drone surveillance. Electronic signals intelligence. He could see every Iraqi troop position, every supply line, every fortification.

The intelligence wasn't the advantage. The advantage was that Schwarzkopf could read the intelligence and make a decision before the enemy knew he had it. He saw that the Iraqi forces expected a frontal assault from the south. Instead, he swung an entire corps 300 miles west through the desert and attacked from the flank. The "left hook" that won the ground war in 100 hours wasn't a function of superior firepower. It was a function of reading the data accurately and acting on it before the situation changed.

You now have every variable. The five drivers. The three hard ratios. The flash crash formula. The four phases of decline. The regulatory timeline. The operational capacity test. What the measurements are telling you right now, about your company, this quarter, is the only thing left to figure out.

In 2003, Billy Beane and the Oakland Athletics changed professional baseball.

The story, made famous by Michael Lewis's Moneyball, is well known. The A's had the third-lowest payroll in Major League Baseball. They couldn't compete with the Yankees or Red Sox on spending. So Beane and his team built a system that evaluated players differently than every other team in baseball. Instead of relying on scouts' subjective assessments of talent, they used statistical analysis to identify undervalued players. On-base percentage instead of batting average. Walks instead of stolen bases. The metrics that actually predicted runs scored, not the metrics that looked impressive on a highlight reel.

The A's won 103 games that season. Same number as the Yankees. With roughly a quarter of the payroll.

Moneyball didn't invent statistics. Baseball had been tracking stats for a century. What Moneyball did was change which statistics mattered and how they were combined. It replaced a subjective evaluation system with an integrated diagnostic that told you something predictive about a player's actual contribution to winning.

This chapter does the same thing for direct selling companies. The industry tracks statistics. Revenue. Distributor count. Average order value. Convention attendance. Social media engagement. These metrics have been on dashboards for decades. But many of them are vanity metrics. They tell you what happened. They don't tell you what is about to happen.

The frameworks in this book were designed to be predictive, not descriptive. They don't tell you where you've been. They tell you where you're heading. And when you combine them into a single integrated diagnostic, you get something that has never existed in this industry: a unified equation for reading momentum in real time.

Here is how the pieces fit together.

Every framework in this book measures a different dimension of the same underlying system. The five drivers measure what creates growth. The ratios measure whether it's real. The flash crash formula measures structural fragility. The decline phases measure hidden erosion. The regulatory timeline and operational test measure external threat and delivery capability.

None of these frameworks works in isolation. A company can have three active drivers (strong momentum) and three flash crash characteristics (fragile foundation). A company can have zero decline signals and a regulatory timeline at Stage 2 (growing but externally threatened). A company can have green ratios and red operations (healthy on paper but failing in execution).

The equation is the combination. And reading the equation means holding all the variables simultaneously.

Here is why many companies fail to do this. In the survey of 82 top earners, 50% said corporate listens to leader feedback "fairly well but not enough." Another 27% said "poorly" or "very poorly." Only 23% said corporate listens "extremely well." That means 77% of the most experienced leaders in this industry don't believe their companies are fully using the diagnostic information the field already has. The scorecard in this chapter gives corporate a structured way to access what the field already knows. Whether leadership teams will actually use it or whether the scorecard will sit in a drawer next to the advisory council minutes that never got read is the real test.

DRIVER PRIORITIZATION: "If I can only fix one, which one?"

Executives ask this constantly. Every time I'm in a room with a leadership team working through the scorecard, some version of this question comes up within the first hour. The CEO looks at a scorecard full of yellows and reds and wants to know which fire to put out first.

The honest answer is that the right priority isn't the same for every company. It depends on where you're in the business lifecycle, which drivers are reversing, and what your ratios look like. A $50M company with a product-market problem needs a completely different priority order than a $500M company with a concentration problem. Prescribing the same fix for both would be malpractice.

What I can give you is a set of decision triggers. Read the scorecard, match your situation to the triggers below, and invest your leadership attention where the data says it will produce the most return.

If your customer ratio is below 30% and declining: stop everything else. This is the only priority. No new markets, no new products, no new promotions until the customer acquisition problem is addressed. Every dollar spent on growth initiatives while the ratio is in the danger zone is a dollar spent accelerating toward a cliff.

If your customer ratio is above 50% but your churn exceeds 70%: your product is strong but your field development is broken. Invest in onboarding, training, and the first-90-days experience for new distributors. The product holds customers. The system is losing builders.

If two or more drivers are active and zero flash crash characteristics are present: you're in the sweet spot. Invest aggressively in growth. This is the moment to spend on international expansion, product line extensions, and platform strategy. The foundation supports it.

If two or more drivers are active and three or more flash crash characteristics are present: you're riding a bomb. The growth feels incredible. The architecture is fragile. Every month you delay addressing the flash crash characteristics increases the severity of the eventual correction. Start fixing them now while revenue gives you the margin to absorb short-term pain.

If you're in Phase 2 of decline (revenue per distributor declining): do not launch a new promotion. Diagnose why per-person productivity is falling. Is it a stale recruiting narrative? Product-culture fit fading? Platform effectiveness declining? Match the treatment to the cause.

If you're in Act 4 of the boom-bust cycle (your category going mainstream at retail): this isn't fixable with better marketing. Your distribution cost advantage is gone. Either evolve the product to something that requires human distribution (education, coaching, accountability) or begin planning the model transition before the market forces it.

If you're pre-revenue or in year one: Compensation Architecture first. Nothing else matters if the plan doesn't incentivize the behaviors that produce customers and duplication. Get the plan right before you invest in anything else.

If you're growing but fragile (under $100M): Product-Culture Fit first. If your product doesn't generate real demand independent of the comp plan, no amount of leader acquisition or platform exploitation will save you. Fix the product-market connection before you scale.

If you're scaling ($100M to $500M): Leader Migration and Platform Disruption matter most. You have product-market fit or you wouldn't be here. Now you need velocity and reach. Recruit strong leaders. Exploit platform windows. This is the phase where the fastest-acting drivers produce the highest return on investment.

If you're mature ($500M+): Market Expansion and Compensation Architecture. Domestic growth is slowing. International opens new Act 1 windows. And your comp plan needs to shift from rewarding speed to rewarding retention and customer depth. This is where the back-end economics determine whether you sustain or erode.

If you're declining: Go to Chapter 17 (Reigniting). Do not invest in drivers until you've diagnosed which break path you're on. Activating the wrong driver during decline accelerates the decline.

One rule applies at every stage: If your Three Hard Ratios are red, fix the ratios before investing in any driver. Drivers amplify whatever foundation exists. If the foundation is rotten, amplification makes the collapse faster.

Let me walk through what this looks like in practice.

THE MOMENTUM EQUATION SCORECARD

This is the comprehensive diagnostic. It integrates every framework into a single assessment. Run this quarterly. Share the results with your leadership team. Make decisions based on what it shows, not on what the revenue report says.

Section 1: Driver Status

For each of the five drivers, assess current status:

Product-Culture Fit: Is your product category growing in the broader culture? Is inbound conversation ratio above 30%? Is your category at risk of disruption (GLP-1, retail commoditization, platform shift)? Status: ACTIVE / DORMANT / ABSENT / REVERSING

Platform Disruption: Which platform is your primary customer acquisition channel? What year of the platform window are you in? Is more than 60% of acquisition from a single platform? Status: ACTIVE / DORMANT / ABSENT / REVERSING

Leader Migration: Have you recruited significant external leaders in the last 12 months? What is your migrated-to-organic leader ratio? Is any leader's organization more than 20% of total volume? Status: ACTIVE / DORMANT / ABSENT / REVERSING

Market Expansion: Have you opened new markets in the last 24 months? What is your geographic concentration (any single country above 30% of revenue)? Are expansions producing real volume or headline-only results? Status: ACTIVE / DORMANT / ABSENT / REVERSING

Compensation Architecture: Does your comp plan reward customer acquisition or recruiting velocity? What is your qualification-driven volume as a percentage of total? Has your payout ratio increased in the last four quarters? Status: ACCELERATING / NEUTRAL / DECELERATING / TOXIC

Count your active and accelerating drivers. Count your reversing and toxic drivers. The net is your momentum trajectory.

Section 2: The Three Hard Ratios

Ratio 1 (Internal vs. External): What percentage of revenue comes from participants inside the comp plan versus external customers? - GREEN: Below 50% internal. You have a product business. - YELLOW: 50-70% internal. You have a mixed model with structural risk. - RED: Above 70% internal. You have a product alibi.

Ratio 2 (Churn): What is your gross annual churn rate? - GREEN: Below 60%. Industry-competitive retention. - YELLOW: 60-80%. Standard but weakening. Monitor quarterly. - RED: Above 80%. Churn is consuming your recruiting. You are in Phase 1 of decline.

Ratio 3 (Payout Inflation): Is total commission and bonus payout as a percentage of revenue rising while revenue is flat or declining? - GREEN: Payout ratio stable or declining. Healthy economics. - YELLOW: Payout ratio rising but revenue is growing faster. Manageable. - RED: Payout ratio rising while revenue is flat or declining. Margin compression in progress.

Section 3: Flash Crash Check

Check each characteristic: 1. Single hero product driving more than 50% of revenue? YES / NO 2. More than 70% of volume from participants? YES / NO 3. Recruiting growth exceeding 100% year-over-year for 2+ consecutive years? YES / NO 4. Top 5% of leaders generating more than 50% of total volume? YES / NO 5. No meaningful customer verification system? YES / NO

Count your YES answers. - 0-1: Low structural risk. - 2: Moderate. Address proactively. - 3+: High. In the 53-company dataset, every company with 3+ flash crash characteristics and rapid growth subsequently crashed.

Section 4: Decline Phase Assessment

Which phase signals are present?

Phase 1 (Invisible Churn): Gross churn rising while net growth looks stable. Average distributor tenure declining. First-year attrition above 70%.

Phase 2 (Declining Productivity): Revenue per distributor declining. Recruiting conversion rates falling. Incentive spending increasing without proportional revenue response.

Phase 3 (Leader Departure): Any top twenty earners less active than twelve months ago. Top earners declining stage opportunities or posting less about the company. Private conversations about departures circulating.

Phase 4 (Narrative Collapse): Google search results include negative press on first page. Social media sentiment shifted from aspirational to complaint-driven. Recruiting conversion rates below sustainable levels.

Current phase: NONE / PHASE 1 / PHASE 2 / PHASE 3 / PHASE 4

Section 5: External Threat Assessment

Regulatory Timeline: Which stage applies? - CLEAR: No media scrutiny, no complaint spikes, no watchdog alerts. - STAGE 1: Negative media coverage in the last 24 months. - STAGE 2: Consumer complaint volume rising. State AG inquiries. - STAGE 3: Watchdog organizations publishing about your company. - STAGE 4: Formal investigation or enforcement action.

Category Disruption: Is your product category facing an external threat? - CLEAR: No visible category threat. - EMERGING: Early signals of category disruption visible in adjacent markets. - ACTIVE: Category disruption is currently affecting your revenue.

Model Disruption: Is your distribution model facing competitive pressure? - CLEAR: Your product requires distributor involvement for education and trust. - EMERGING: Competitors in your category are reaching consumers through lower-cost channels. - ACTIVE: Companies in your category are exiting the direct selling model.

Section 6: Operational Capacity

Rate each dimension GREEN / YELLOW / RED: - Fulfillment - Commission accuracy - Customer service - Technology - Compliance monitoring

Count your reds. Any red during momentum is an immediate threat.

Let me show you how to read the combined picture through the scenario most readers of this book will actually recognize. The healthy company is easy to diagnose. The crisis in disguise, which is too far gone for most owners to identify with. The middle case. The fragile grower.

The company's revenue is growing. Convention attendance is up. The CEO is on stage celebrating momentum. The public story is great.

Then the scorecard runs.

Two active drivers: product-culture fit, and leader migration with several significant leaders recruited in the last year. One reversing: platform disruption, because the primary channel shifted from Instagram to TikTok and the company is behind the curve. Ratio 1 is yellow at 65% internal. Two flash crash characteristics are present: the flagship product drives 58% of revenue, and the top five organizations account for 52% of volume. Phase 1 signals are present: gross churn has risen from 62% to 71% over the last three quarters while net growth has remained positive. Regulatory timeline is at Stage 1 after a negative article in a trade publication. Operations are yellow on customer service response time.

The revenue chart still says momentum. The scorecard tells a different story. The growth is heavily dependent on migrated leaders whose organizations may be portable. The product is concentrated. The volume is concentrated. Churn is accelerating invisibly. And a trade publication has already noticed.

This company needs to diversify its product line, invest in organic leadership development to reduce concentration, build customer acquisition programs to move Ratio 1 toward green, and treat the Stage 1 media coverage as an early warning rather than a nuisance. If the leadership team acts on the scorecard, every problem is fixable. If they celebrate the revenue report and ignore the scorecard, they're setting up for a Phase 2 transition within twelve to eighteen months.

That is the gap this entire book exists to close. The revenue report tells you what happened last quarter. The scorecard tells you the direction of travel. And the direction of travel is what determines whether you survive the next cycle or become the case study in somebody else's book.

Inside the mastermind work, I've begun running simplified versions of this diagnostic with leaders who are evaluating their current companies or considering new ones.

The reaction is always the same. Clarity followed by discomfort. Clarity because the scorecard makes the picture obvious. Discomfort because the picture is sometimes not what the leader wanted to see.

I worked with a leader who was earning significant income at a company she loved. She ran the diagnostic. Two active drivers. Ratio 1 yellow. Two flash crash characteristics. Phase 1 signals present. She looked at the scorecard and said, "I can feel everything on this page. I just didn't have words for it."

That is the power of the diagnostic. It doesn't tell you something you don't already know. It gives you language and structure for what you already sense. The field's intuition, the feeling that something is off even when the revenue report looks fine, is almost always accurate. The scorecard translates that intuition into variables that can be discussed, tracked, and acted upon.

The leader in that conversation didn't leave her company. She brought the scorecard to her company's top corporates. She said, "Here is what I'm seeing. Here is what the data suggests. What are we going to do about it?" That conversation led to changes. The company invested in customer acquisition programs. They addressed the qualification purchasing problem. They began tracking gross churn separately from net growth.

That is what this diagnostic is designed to produce. Not panic. Not departure. Action. Early diagnosis that leads to early intervention at the stage where the problem is cheapest to fix.

There is a shadow side to this diagnostic.

Some leaders will run this scorecard and discover that their company is in worse shape than they believed. The natural response is one of two extremes. Either "I need to leave immediately" or "this scorecard must be wrong because my check is still good."

Both responses miss the point.

The first response ignores the fact that most problems identified at Phase 1 or Phase 2 are addressable. The scorecard is a diagnostic tool, not a death sentence. Companies recover from yellow ratios and early-phase decline. Nu Skin has reinvented itself multiple times across four decades. Herbalife survived the most public attack in industry history and a $200 million FTC settlement. Recovery is possible when leadership is willing to face the data without flinching. Whether your leadership team recognizes the problem and acts on it is the only variable left in your control.

The second response ignores the fact that income during Phase 1 and Phase 2 can remain strong while the foundation deteriorates. The leader's check is still good because gross recruiting is replacing churn and qualification purchasing is generating volume. Neither of those things is durable. The check is a lagging indicator. The scorecard is a leading indicator.

The appropriate response is engagement. Share the diagnostic with corporate. Have the honest conversation. Push for the changes that the data suggests. If corporate responds with action, stay and build. If corporate responds with dismissal, that response itself is information.

The meta-framework.

THE MOMENTUM EQUATION

Momentum = (Active Drivers x Foundation Integrity) minus (Decline Signals + External Threats + Operational Gaps)

This isn't a literal mathematical formula. It is a conceptual model for how momentum works.

Active Drivers create the growth. Foundation Integrity, meaning healthy ratios, low flash crash risk, real customers, determines whether the growth is sustainable. Decline Signals, External Threats, and Operational Gaps subtract from momentum by eroding the conditions that make growth possible.

A company with strong drivers and weak foundation has explosive growth on a fragile base. The growth is real but the crash risk is high.

A company with moderate drivers and strong foundation has sustainable momentum. The growth is slower but durable. That company will still be growing in five years while the company with stronger drivers and weaker foundation has already crashed.

A company with drivers reversing and decline signals present has a negative equation. The direction is down regardless of what this quarter's revenue says.

Or, in the versions you can put on a slide:

Drivers create growth. Foundation decides if it survives.

Fast growth plus weak foundation equals delayed collapse.

You don't lose momentum. You reveal what was underneath it.

The companies that have lasted longest in this industry aren't the ones that had the most explosive momentum. They are the ones whose equation stayed positive over decades. Moderate drivers. Strong foundations. Problems addressed early. Operations maintained. The boring math of sustainability, compounded over forty years, produces larger outcomes than the exciting math of explosive growth followed by collapse.

Each of those companies deserves recognition for what it took to sustain a positive equation across decades. Multi-decade survival in this industry requires continuous adaptation. Product lines get reinvented. Compensation plans get restructured. International markets open and close. Regulatory frameworks evolve. The companies that lasted are the ones whose leadership teams read the equation and responded, over and over, across cycles that broke most of their competitors.

The pattern among long-term survivors isn't perfection. Every one of these companies has had periods of declining revenue, leadership challenges, regulatory pressure, and strategic missteps. The pattern is responsiveness. They saw the signals. They adjusted. They invested in the foundation during the good years, which gave them the resilience to absorb the bad years. That is the equation working as designed.

Imagine a leadership team that reviews the full Momentum Equation Scorecard every quarter.

The meeting takes two hours. It happens the week after quarterly financials close. The CEO, top corporates, VP of Sales, CFO, and head of compliance are in the room. The revenue report is on the table, but it's not the agenda. The Momentum Equation Scorecard is the agenda.

The VP of Sales presents Section 1: Driver Status. "Product-culture fit is active but maturing. Our category is in Act 3. Platform disruption is active on TikTok but we're in year two of the window. Leader migration is dormant. No significant external leaders recruited this quarter. Market expansion is active with the Brazil launch performing ahead of projections. Comp plan is neutral, no changes this quarter."

Next, the CFO presents Section 2: The Three Hard Ratios. "Ratio 1 is green at 48% internal. Ratio 2 is yellow, gross churn ticked up from 61% to 64% this quarter. Ratio 3 is green, payout ratio stable."

Compliance takes Section 5: External Threat Assessment. "Regulatory timeline is clear. No media scrutiny, no complaint spikes. Category disruption is emerging. We're monitoring two retail competitors that launched similar products at lower price points last quarter."

The CEO looks at the scorecard. Two active drivers. One ratio trending yellow. Category disruption emerging. She doesn't panic. She acts. "The churn tick-up is Phase 1 early signal. I want a retention task force reporting in 30 days with specific interventions for first-year distributors. And I want competitive intelligence on those two retail entrants by next meeting. If our product-culture fit is in Act 3, we need to be investing in differentiation now, not after the retail threat materializes."

That is a meeting that changes outcomes. The scorecard didn't predict the future. It showed the present clearly enough that the leadership team could act before the signals became crises.

That team doesn't avoid all problems. No company does. Markets shift. Products age. Platforms change. But that team sees the problems earlier, responds faster, and intervenes at the stage where the cost is lowest and the probability of recovery is highest.

That is reading the equation rather than just knowing the variables. Using them.

THE MOMENTUM EQUATION SCORECARD: 30-MINUTE EXECUTIVE VERSION

Run this quarterly. No interpretation needed. Rate each variable. Act on the results.

SECTION A: DRIVER STATUS (Rate each: Active / Maturing / Dormant / Reversing)

Product-Culture Fit. Is your product category growing in the broader culture? Is the field excited to share? If Active: invest in customer depth. If Maturing: invest in differentiation. If Reversing: begin product evolution immediately.

Platform Disruption. Are you in year 1-2 of a platform window? If Active: lean in hard, build systems around it. If Maturing (year 3-5): diversify to other channels. If Dormant: ensure field skills work without any single platform.

Leader Migration. Have significant external leaders joined in the last 12 months? If Active: monitor concentration risk, invest in organic development simultaneously. If Dormant: that's fine if organic pipeline is strong. If you have no organic pipeline and no migration, you have no growth engine.

Market Expansion. Are you in a new international market in its first 3 years? If Active: ensure infrastructure matches ambition. If Dormant: evaluate whether expansion from strength or escape from weakness.

Compensation Architecture. Has your plan been redesigned in the last 24 months? If Active: monitor field behavior changes. If Dormant: audit whether the plan rewards the behaviors you actually want.

Decision trigger: If two or more drivers are Reversing, go directly to Chapter 17 (Reigniting). Do not invest in growth until you diagnose the break path.

SECTION B: FOUNDATION METRICS (Rate each: Green / Yellow / Red)

Customer Base Strength. What percentage of revenue comes from real customers not in the comp plan? Green: above 50%. Yellow: 30-50%. Red: below 30%. If Red: stop scaling and fix customer acquisition before spending another dollar on recruiting incentives.

Churn Rate. What is your annual gross churn? Green: below 50%. Yellow: 50-70%. Red: above 70%. If Red: your recruiting is masking a retention crisis. Fix the first-90-day experience immediately.

Payout Ratio Trend. Are commissions as a percentage of revenue rising while revenue is flat or declining? Green: stable or declining ratio. Yellow: rising for 1-2 quarters. Red: rising for 3+ quarters. If Red: you have payout inflation. Restructure before it becomes a margin crisis.

Leader Concentration. Do your top five organizations account for more than 50% of volume? Green: below 30%. Yellow: 30-50%. Red: above 50%. If Red: one departure can trigger a cascading decline. Invest in organic leadership development now.

First-Time Success Ratio. What percentage of your top earners had their first meaningful success inside your company? Green: above 50%. Yellow: 25-50%. Red: below 25%. If Red: your growth is imported, not duplicated. The loyalty is fragile.

New Success Creation Rate. How many first-time six-figure earners did you create in the last 12 months? Green: trending up year over year. Yellow: flat. Red: declining. If Red: your systems aren't creating new leaders. Fix training and mentorship before investing in anything else.

Decision trigger: If three or more foundation metrics are Red, you're in structural crisis regardless of what the revenue report says. Every dollar should go to foundation repair.

SECTION C: THREAT ASSESSMENT (Rate each: Clear / Emerging / Active)

Regulatory Timeline. Any media scrutiny, complaint spikes, or enforcement signals? If Active: conduct internal audit within 30 days. Change the practices generating the attention.

Category Disruption. Any external force changing your consumer's relationship with your product? If Emerging: begin product evolution planning. If Active: this is now your top strategic priority.

Momentum Type. Is your current growth Spike, Compound, False, or Borrowed? If Spike or Borrowed: build customer floor immediately. If Compound: protect what you have. If False: stop celebrating and start diagnosing.

Decline Phase. Are Phase 1, 2, 3, or 4 signals present? If Phase 1: cheapest intervention point. Act now. If Phase 2: urgent. Stop adding incentives and diagnose root cause. If Phase 3 or 4: crisis management. See Chapter 17.

THE 30-MINUTE MEETING:

Print this scorecard. Bring your CEO, top corporates, VP of Sales, CFO, and head of compliance into a room. Each person rates their section with data, not opinions. Read the results aloud. Where the scorecard is green, protect. Where it's yellow, investigate. Where it's red, act. Assign one owner and one 30-day deadline for every red item. Meet again next quarter. That is the full meeting.

The next chapter covers timing: the 5-Act Boom-Bust Cycle that has repeated six times in seventy years, and how to know where your company and your product category sit in the cycle right now.

One observation from the masterminds I run. The leadership teams that use this kind of diagnostic quarterly aren't the ones with the worst problems. They are the ones with the best companies. Here is the underlying pattern. Companies in crisis rarely have time or infrastructure to run a disciplined quarterly audit. Companies with disciplined quarterly audits rarely end up in crisis.

The cause and effect run both ways. Running the audit prevents the crisis, and preventing the crisis preserves the capacity to run the audit. It is a virtuous cycle that the best operators in this industry have been running for decades. Melaleuca runs it. Amway runs it. PM International runs it. The companies that never appear on the "what happened" list run it.

The leadership teams that resist the audit usually do so for one of three reasons. They don't want to see the numbers. They are afraid the team will disagree and expose a culture problem. Or they believe they're too busy running the business to spend half a day diagnosing it. All three reasons are wrong, and they're all symptoms of the same underlying issue. A company that can't afford to run the audit is a company that can't afford to not run it. Whether you have time isn't the test. Whether you want to see the truth before the market forces you to see it is.

WHERE THIS FRAMEWORK HAS LIMITS

A serious framework should be able to name where it's less useful. The Momentum Equation is a strategic lens for direct selling companies pursuing scale, and like any framework, it's not equally predictive in every situation. Three categories of company will find the framework less directly applicable.

The first is companies in highly regulated specialty sectors where compliance creates a fundamentally different competitive dynamic. Financial services direct sellers, like Primerica, operate under SEC and state insurance regulators. Telecom direct sellers operate under FCC oversight. Legal services direct sellers, like LegalShield, operate under state bar associations. In these categories, the regulatory environment is itself part of the moat. Compliance overhead that would be a burden in another category is a barrier to entry that protects established operators. The flash crash characteristics this book identifies are still relevant in these categories, but the dynamics are partially distorted by the regulatory structure. Customer ratios still matter, but the comp plan design is constrained by regulatory frameworks that don't exist in supplements or beauty. A reader from one of these categories should read this book as informative rather than prescriptive. The patterns translate. The specific thresholds may not.

The second is companies in the quiet middle of the industry, the operators in the $20 million to $80 million range that have been running profitably for fifteen or twenty years without ever appearing in a Direct Selling News headline. The dataset behind this book is acknowledged to overrepresent the largest companies and the most dramatic failures. Companies in the quiet middle often have stable customer bases, modest distributor counts, low overhead, and a culture that prioritizes profitability over scale. They aren't pursuing the next billion-dollar inflection. They are running a sustainable business that pays the founders, the corporate team, and a stable field. For these companies, several frameworks in this book apply less directly. The Five Drivers diagnostic was built for companies trying to create explosive momentum, not maintain compounding stability. The flash crash characteristics describe a failure mode these companies usually avoid by design. The reignition framework applies if the business stalls, but the path is often simpler because the foundation is smaller and easier to diagnose. A reader running a company in this profile should treat the book as a reference for stress-testing rather than a roadmap. The principles still apply. The urgency may not.

The third is founder-owned private companies whose optimization function isn't scale. Some founders are running their direct selling companies as long-term lifestyle businesses, family wealth vehicles, or platforms for personal influence in the industry. These companies don't have boards demanding growth, private equity sponsors waiting on exit timelines, or public market analysts pressuring quarterly performance. The owner can choose stability over scale. He can choose to keep the business small enough to control. He can choose to optimize for the wellbeing of his existing field rather than the acquisition of new builders. For these companies, the boom-bust cycle pressures are real but optional. The framework's prescription to pursue customer depth still applies. Its prescription to engineer driver combinations for explosive growth often doesn't. A founder reading this book with no intention of seeking scale should treat the equation as a defensive lens rather than an offensive one.

The framework still matters even when it's incomplete. A regulated-sector operator who reads this book understands the underlying patterns of momentum and decline more clearly, even if her specific situation is partially shaped by regulatory dynamics the book doesn't analyze in detail. A quiet-middle operator who runs the scorecard once a year catches structural problems before they compound. A lifestyle-business founder who tracks the customer ratio knows whether his business is built on durable demand or borrowed momentum. The framework is a thinking tool, not a verdict. It is most useful when its limits are understood and when the reader applies the parts that fit her situation without forcing the parts that don't.

The most dangerous response to a framework's limits is to dismiss the entire framework on the basis of where it doesn't perfectly apply. The most useful response is to read the framework critically, identify where it lands and where it bends, and use what is useful. That is the discipline this book is asking for from start to finish. Honest diagnosis of the company. Honest diagnosis of the framework that's being used to diagnose the company. Both are part of the same intellectual practice.

THE BOTTOM LINE: Run the full Momentum Equation Scorecard. Green, yellow, or red for each driver, ratio, flash crash trait, decline phase, regulatory stage, and operational dimension. The scorecard is the integrated diagnostic. Use it quarterly.

The equation doesn't predict the future. It shows you the present more clearly than anything else in this industry. And seeing the present clearly is the closest thing to predicting the future that exists.

Chapter 16: Timing, Sequencing, and the Boom-Bust Cycle

Figure 10. Every product category in direct selling history has moved through the same five acts. Which act are you in?

In the 1990s, Silicon Valley watched the same script play out with web browsers. Netscape captured the market explosively. Microsoft copied the model and gave Internet Explorer away for free. The imitators flooded in. The category went mainstream. Then regulation and antitrust pressure closed the era. Netscape, which once had 90% market share, was absorbed into AOL and eventually disappeared. The browser war repeated in mobile. BlackBerry captured it. iPhone disrupted it. Android copied it. The category commoditized. BlackBerry went from 50% smartphone market share to near zero. Different products. Different decades. Same script.

The products change. The platforms change. The demographics change. The script doesn't. It has repeated six times in seventy years in direct selling alone. Knowing which act you're in changes every decision you make.

The enemy in this chapter: running yesterday's playbook in tomorrow's market.

Change is inevitable in every business and every industry. It is the one constant. The companies that last aren't the ones that avoided change. They are the ones that read the equation, saw the act transition coming, and adapted before it arrived.

Before we examine the historical cycle, one recent episode deserves attention because it affected every company in the industry simultaneously.

During 2020 and 2021, the pandemic created one of the broadest momentum spikes the direct selling industry has experienced. Not every company benefited equally, and some were already declining before COVID hit. But the industry-wide numbers were striking. U.S. direct selling revenue jumped from $35.2 billion in 2019 to $40.1 billion in 2020, a 13.9% increase that the DSA called the greatest percentage gain in a decade. By 2021, the number reached nearly $42.7 billion. Many companies across multiple product categories saw significant growth simultaneously.

Then the correction hit. Algorithms changed. Organic reach on every major platform collapsed. Inflation squeezed discretionary spending. The prospects who had been open during lockdown went back to their jobs and their routines. And the field discovered something uncomfortable: many companies had stopped developing timeless skills during the boom. The fundamentals of one-on-one conversations, live events, customer service, personal follow-up, and relationship building had been replaced by an over-reliance on social media content and digital prospecting. The field had become algorithm-dependent instead of skill-dependent.

But the deeper problem wasn't just selling skills. It was leadership development and personal development. The two disciplines that have always been the backbone of the strongest direct selling organizations.

During the boom, many companies cut back on or completely abandoned their investment in developing leaders. The growth was so easy that nobody seemed to need development. New people were signing up without being coached. Teams were growing without being mentored. Rank advancements were happening without the personal growth that used to precede them. The development infrastructure that companies like Melaleuca, PM International, and the strongest legacy organizations had spent decades building was treated as optional during a period when everything seemed to work without it.

When the boom ended, the absence was devastating. Companies had fields full of people who had achieved rank without developing the skills to sustain it. Leaders who had been promoted by the algorithm rather than developed by a mentor. Teams that had been assembled by social media rather than built through personal relationships and genuine leadership. The titles were there. The leadership capacity wasn't.

The companies that recovered fastest from the post-COVID correction were the ones that had never stopped investing in leadership development and personal development, even when the growth made it seem unnecessary. They kept running their mentorship programs. They kept training one-on-one conversation skills. They kept investing in personal growth content, not because it was popular during the boom, but because they understood that the boom was temporary and the skills would be needed when it ended.

This isn't an argument against technology. It is an argument for both. The companies that will win the next decade are the ones that embrace every new technology, every new platform, every AI tool, every social media trend, AND simultaneously double down on the fundamentals that no technology can replace. Leadership development. Personal development. Mentorship. One-on-one coaching. Live events where human beings are in a room together and something happens that can't happen on a screen. Team culture that's built through shared experience over time, not through a group chat.

Technology amplifies human skills. It doesn't replace them. The company that gives its field AI tools for customer follow-up AND trains them to have a genuine conversation with a prospect is unbeatable. The company that gives its field AI tools instead of training them to have a genuine conversation is building on sand.

Many companies never returned to pre-COVID levels. The pandemic boom ending was predictable. Going deeper than pre-COVID baselines was the real damage. The companies that had maintained leadership development and personal development through the boom, that had continued teaching the timeless principles even when social media was doing the heavy lifting, recovered faster. The companies that had abandoned fundamentals in favor of digital-only strategies found themselves with a field that didn't know how to build without an algorithm as a tailwind and didn't have the leadership depth to figure it out.

The lesson is identical to the one this entire chapter teaches. Platform windows are temporary. Timeless fundamentals are permanent. The COVID boom was a platform window, maybe the biggest one in history. The companies that treated it as a permanent shift built on it exclusively and crashed. The companies that treated it as a temporary accelerant and maintained their foundation of leadership development, personal growth, and human skill-building came through it stronger.

In the early 1950s, a new category opened. Women had moved into suburbia. They had new kitchens, new neighborhoods, and social networks built around hosting. Tupperware invented the home party and built a multi-billion-dollar business by being first to exploit the cultural shift. Within a decade, imitators arrived. Stanley Home Products. Avon. Mary Kay. The recruiting pool fragmented. Over time, the cultural conditions shifted. Women entered the workforce. Hosting culture declined. The category matured, peaked, and eventually contracted.

In the 1990s, telecom deregulation created a new category. Long-distance rates dropped. Consumers had choice for the first time. Excel Communications was among the first MLMs to capture the opportunity and grew explosively, reaching $1.4 billion in revenue. Imitators flooded in: ACN, Ambit, Stream Energy, 5LINX. Then technology commoditized the product. Cell phones eliminated long-distance charges. VoIP made landlines obsolete. The product that MLMs were selling disappeared. The category died.

In the early 2000s, the superfood craze opened a new category. Noni juice. Acai. Mangosteen. XanGo. MonaVie. Exotic ingredients with premium pricing and compelling health stories. First movers captured enormous revenue. Imitators piled in. Then the ingredients went mainstream. Acai bowls showed up at Costco. Noni was available on Amazon. The premium became indefensible. Combined peak revenue across superfruit MLMs exceeded $2 billion. Combined current value: approximately zero.

In the 2010s, social media created a new category of social selling companies. Younique pioneered the Facebook party. LuLaRoe rode Facebook Live. Rodan+Fields weaponized Instagram. First movers grew explosively. Imitators multiplied. Then the platforms changed their algorithms, TikTok emerged, and the model exit wave began: BODi, Rodan+Fields, Beautycounter, Modere, Seint, all leaving the direct selling model between 2024 and 2025. In April 2026, Forever Living Products, a billion-dollar legacy company operating since 1978, terminated its US recruiting model entirely, citing unmanageable regulatory exposure. The exits are no longer limited to mid-size social selling brands. They have reached the legacy tier.

Different products. Different decades. Same script.

THE 5-ACT BOOM-BUST SCRIPT

This pattern has repeated at least six times in the history of direct selling. The acts are always the same. Only the cast changes.

Act 1: A new channel or category opens.

A market opportunity emerges. It could be a cultural shift (wellness movement, athleisure trend), a technology change (social media platforms, e-commerce), a regulatory change (telecom deregulation), or a demographic shift (suburban housewives, college-age digital natives). The opportunity creates space for new businesses to form.

The opportunity is almost always external to the company. It is a wave forming in the culture, the economy, or the technology landscape. The companies that catch it early don't create the wave. They see it forming and position themselves inside it.

Act 2: Early MLMs capture it explosively.

The first companies to identify the opportunity and build a product around it gain massive first-mover advantage. They have the product and the recruiting story. The product is new and exciting. The recruiting pitch writes itself: "This is the next big thing and you're early." The combination of product novelty and early-mover economics produces the most explosive growth trajectories in the industry.

Tupperware in the 1950s. Amway in the 1960s. Excel in the 1990s. MonaVie in the mid-2000s. doTERRA in the late 2000s. LuLaRoe in the mid-2010s. Each one captured a wave that was forming and rode it before anyone else could.

The growth during Act 2 feels like destiny. The product is right. The timing is right. The field is on fire. Revenue multiplies. Conventions fill stadiums. Leaders earn life-changing income. Nobody is thinking about Act 3 because Act 2 feels like it will last forever.

It never does.

Act 3: Imitators flood in.

Success is visible. Other entrepreneurs see what the first movers built and conclude they can do the same thing. New companies launch with similar products, similar compensation structures, and similar pitches. The available attention and energy in the market gets split across more companies.

After doTERRA and Young Living proved the essential oils opportunity, dozens of smaller essential oils MLMs launched. After Younique proved the Facebook party model for cosmetics, multiple beauty MLMs copied the approach. After MonaVie reached $854 million with acai juice, superfruit imitators multiplied.

Each new entrant splits the available market. The total demand for the product category may still be growing, but the number of companies competing for distributors and customers is growing faster. Per-company growth slows. The recruiting pitch changes from “you’re early” to “we’re different.” And “we’re different” is a harder sell than “you’re early.”

The pattern isn’t unique to direct selling. When Uber proved the ride-sharing category, Lyft launched with nearly identical features. Then came Juno, Via, Gett, and dozens of regional competitors in markets around the world. Uber’s growth didn’t stop, but the cost of acquiring each new rider and driver escalated dramatically. Customer acquisition costs tripled in some markets. Profit margins compressed. The company that had once grown on pure momentum now had to spend billions defending the category it invented. That is Act 3 in any industry. Novelty stops working. Discipline starts mattering.

Act 3 is when discipline matters most. The companies that survive Act 3 are the ones that invested in customer depth during Act 2. They have real customers who buy because they love the product, not because the category is novel. When imitators arrive and the novelty fades, the customer base holds.

The companies that don’t survive Act 3 are the ones that were riding novelty rather than serving need. When the novelty fades and the imitators arrive, they have nothing underneath the excitement.

Act 3 is also where the strongest companies actually separate from the pack. The imitators that flood in are almost always weaker operators. They copy the product concept but not the infrastructure. They copy the comp plan structure but not the culture. They attract leaders by offering bigger deals, not better foundations. And most of them fail within three to five years, leaving the first movers stronger by comparison. The companies that survive Act 3 often emerge from it with a larger market share than they had entering it, because the imitators failed and their distributors and customers had to go somewhere. Surviving Act 3 is a competitive advantage. It just doesn't feel like one while you're in it.

Act 4: The category goes mainstream.

The product that built the MLMs becomes available through conventional retail channels at a fraction of the direct selling price. Acai bowls at Costco. Essential oils on Amazon. Skincare at Sephora. Fitness content on YouTube. The direct selling distribution model's cost, the 40 to 50% paid out in commissions, becomes a competitive disadvantage when the same product type is available without that distribution markup.

Act 4 is not an attack on the direct selling model. It is the natural lifecycle of every product category. Products that start in specialty channels always migrate to mass channels as demand grows. The migration is a sign of success for the category. It is a threat to the companies that depend on specialty distribution.

Blockbuster is the most dramatic non-industry example. At its 2004 peak, the company had 9,000 stores and $5.9 billion in revenue. Its category was video rental. Its distribution model was retail storefronts. Netflix didn't attack Blockbuster directly. It simply made the same category available through a different distribution model, first DVDs by mail, then streaming. By 2010, Blockbuster filed for bankruptcy. The product didn't change. The category didn't disappear. The distribution model that built Blockbuster became obsolete. Blockbuster had a chance to acquire Netflix in 2000 for $50 million and passed. That decision looks obvious in hindsight. It didn't look obvious at the time, when Netflix was losing money and Blockbuster was still growing.

The companies that survive Act 4 have differentiated their products enough that the retail alternative isn't a direct substitute. doTERRA's sourcing program, its Co-Impact Sourcing partnerships with growers in 45 countries, created a differentiation story that generic Amazon oils can't replicate. The product may look similar on the surface, but the story behind it is defensible.

The companies that don't survive Act 4 have products that are functionally interchangeable with retail alternatives. When the consumer can buy a similar product at retail for substantially less, the direct selling version needs to be actually better, not just more expensive. If the only thing justifying the premium is the compensation plan, the premium collapses when the consumer realizes the retail alternative exists.

GLP-1 drugs are the most visible Act 4 event in current industry experience. They aren't just making the direct selling weight management product available through a different channel. They are introducing a pharmaceutical alternative that addresses weight loss through a different mechanism. The shake isn't just competing with a cheaper shake at retail. It is competing with a prescription drug that produces faster results for many users. That is category reshaping, and it's happening across multiple billion-dollar companies simultaneously. The companies that adapt early by integrating GLP-1 support products, peptide-based formulations, and complementary wellness offerings are turning the disruption into a new growth driver. The companies that treat the trend as a temporary headwind face the harder version of the adjustment.

LifeVantage provides one of the cleanest real-time case studies of this principle in action, and they deserve credit for building the customer foundation that caught them when the spike receded.

Here is the actual timeline from SEC filings.

Before the GLP-1 pivot, LifeVantage was operating as a steady compounder in the $200 to $213 million range. Fiscal year 2022 revenue was approximately $200 million. Fiscal 2023 reached $213.4 million. Fiscal 2024 came in at $200.2 million. Not explosive, but steady for a decade-plus company anchored by a strong product foundation in Protandim and TrueScience skincare.

In the second quarter of fiscal 2025, LifeVantage launched the MindBody GLP-1 System in the US. The quarterly results were dramatic. Q2 FY2025 revenue hit $67.8 million, up 31.3% year over year. It was the strongest quarter the company had posted in years. Americas revenue alone was up 46.3%. US revenue was up 48.8%. The company raised full-year guidance from $200 to $210 million up to $235 to $245 million. The spike was real. The numbers were audited. The field was energized.

The third quarter of fiscal 2025 continued the strength. Revenue was $58.4 million, up 21.1%. The fourth quarter came in at $55.1 million, up 12.6%. Full fiscal year 2025 closed at $228.5 million, a 14.2% annual increase over fiscal 2024.

Then the first quarter of fiscal 2026 told the next chapter of the story. Revenue came in at $47.6 million, barely up at 0.7% year over year and missing analyst estimates by 15.1%. The stock fell 4.22% in after-hours trading. The company's own disclosure language noted that MindBody GLP-1 sales were offset by lower sales of the core Protandim and TrueScience product lines and a decrease in total active accounts.

That is the pattern this chapter describes. A real category opportunity. A real product launch. A real revenue spike. And then a revert to something close to the pre-launch baseline once the novelty window closed and the underlying core product performance reasserted itself.

The lesson isn't that LifeVantage made a mistake. The company responded to a real category shift with a real product that drove real revenue. The lesson is about what a GLP-1-adjacent product launch can and can't do. It can generate meaningful short-term revenue. It can't, by itself, reposition a company into a new category without deeper commitment. And when the launch novelty fades, the company returns to whatever its underlying customer-product foundation was before.

The underlying customer-product foundation is what deserves the credit here. LifeVantage went into the GLP-1 window with a durable customer base built over more than a decade around Protandim and TrueScience. When the GLP-1 spike receded, there was a floor to land on. A weaker company with the same spike and the same revert would have seen dramatically more damage to its baseline. LifeVantage's baseline held, and the subsequent acquisition of LoveBiome suggests the company is continuing to evolve its product portfolio rather than betting the whole strategy on any single category trend.

For every owner and executive reading this, the instructive point is that the spike is borrowed and the floor is owned. When a category opens, ride it. Take the revenue. Reinvest in the customer base. But track the revert as carefully as the rise, because the revert is where the real health of the company shows up. And build the foundation deep enough that when the category window closes, you have something real to stand on.

THE NO MAN'S LAND PROBLEM

There is a related principle worth naming directly, because it shows up in nearly every category-shift scenario in this industry and almost no one names it explicitly.

Do not enter a new category unless you're committed to it.

In tennis there's a position called no man's land. It is the area between the baseline and the net where players who aren't fully committed to either position end up losing the point. If you're at the baseline, you're committed to the baseline game. If you're at the net, you're committed to the net game. If you're caught in between, you're not really doing either, and the ball lands at your feet.

The same dynamic plays out when a company sees a category shift like GLP-1 and reacts with a half commitment. The company isn't really in the GLP-1 category. It launched a GLP-1-adjacent product to capture the moment. The marketing pivots to weight loss. The field talks about weight loss. The new builders join because of the weight loss story. But the company isn't actually committed to becoming a weight loss company. Six months later, when the launch novelty fades, the company quietly returns to its core narrative and hopes the field forgets the pivot.

That is no man's land. It isn't staying disciplined in the original category, where the company would have continued building the customer base around its core products. And it's not committing to the new category, where the company would have spent the next three to five years building the product line, the field training, the testimonials, and the cultural infrastructure to actually win in weight loss. It is hovering between the two, capturing short-term revenue from the new category while signaling to the field and the customer base that the old category is no longer the priority. Both bases get diluted. The company ends up weaker in both directions than it was before the launch.

The discipline is to make a real choice. Either commit to the new category for several years with everything that requires (product line evolution, field retraining, testimonial libraries, comp plan adjustments, marketing repositioning, and the patience to let the community form around the new positioning) or stay disciplined in the original category and continue building what was already working. Both are legitimate strategic moves. The half commitment is the move that destroys value.

If a company decides the new category is the future, the commitment can't be just a single product launch. It has to be a multi-year strategic repositioning, with the leadership team, the field, and the customer base aligned on the new direction. If the company isn't willing to commit at that level, it shouldn't enter the new category at all. The short-term revenue from a half-launched product is rarely worth the cultural and strategic cost of confusing the field about what the company is actually building.

Pick a side of the court. Commit to the position. Play the point you can actually win.

That is what Chapter 16 is ultimately teaching. The cycle isn't the enemy. The cycle is just the cycle. The companies that ride each wave well and land safely when the wave breaks are the companies that build foundations during the spike rather than assume the spike is the foundation.

Act 5: Regulatory and reputational pressure closes the era.

As the category matures and the structural problems become visible, regulatory scrutiny increases. Media investigations publish. Consumer complaints spike. Enforcement actions arrive. And the companies that built their businesses on recruiting velocity rather than customer depth discover that the regulatory environment has no tolerance for businesses without real customers.

Simultaneously, the companies that entered the category late, the Act 3 imitators, begin failing. Their products are commoditized. Their fields are depleted. Their revenue is declining. Some exit the direct selling model entirely. Some go bankrupt. Some are acquired for parts.

Act 5 is the shakeout. The companies that survive have real customers, differentiated products, and compliant operations. They may be smaller than they were at peak. They may have restructured painfully. But they're still standing.

The companies that don't survive either ran out of money, ran afoul of regulators, or watched their field evaporate as the narrative collapsed.

The critical question for every reader of this book: which act is your company in, right now?

Because the answer determines not just your strategy but where your money goes. This quarter. Not next year. The decisions that are appropriate in Act 2 are catastrophic in Act 4. The investments that are essential in Act 1 are irrelevant in Act 5.

Act 1 or early Act 2: SPEND. This is the window of maximum return on investment. Every dollar invested in field growth, platform exploitation, and market expansion produces outsized returns because the competition is thin and the cultural tailwind is strong. Invest aggressively in every driver available to you. Move fast. Capture market share.

But simultaneously invest in customer depth. The most common Act 2 mistake is investing everything in growth velocity and nothing in customer retention. Every company in the decline dataset that crashed from a high peak made this error. The fix is simple: allocate at least 20% of your growth budget to customer acquisition and retention programs from day one. Build the floor while you're building the spike.

The companies that used Act 2 to build both a large field and a deep customer base are the ones that survived. doTERRA did this with essential oils. Herbalife did this with the Nutrition Club model. PM International did this with obsessive SOPs and a personal development infrastructure that kept the field engaged beyond the initial product excitement. In each case, the growth was explosive but the customer habits were real.

Late Act 2 or Act 3: SHIFT. Imitators are arriving. The recruiting pitch is harder. Shift your capital allocation from growth velocity to customer retention and product differentiation. Cut spending on recruitment incentives by 15 to 20% and redirect to customer loyalty programs, product R&D, and field training on customer service. What makes your product actually different from the imitators? If you can't answer that clearly, fund the answer. This is when R&D spending should peak.

Act 4: RESTRUCTURE. Your distribution cost is a competitive disadvantage against retail alternatives. You have two options and you need to pick one this quarter. Option A: differentiate your product enough to justify the premium, which means investing in formulation, clinical evidence, exclusive sourcing, or a service layer (coaching, community, accountability) that retail can't replicate. Option B: restructure your distribution model to compete on cost, which means reducing field compensation as a percentage of revenue and reinvesting the savings in lower consumer pricing and DTC marketing. There is no Option C. Hoping the retail competition goes away isn't a strategy.

Act 5: CONSERVE AND CONSOLIDATE. Cut non-essential spending. Protect your customer base. Do not invest in expansion. Focus every dollar on retaining the customers and leaders you have. The companies that survive Act 5 enter the next category cycle in a stronger position because their competitors died during the shakeout. Your survival IS your competitive advantage for the next cycle.

The capital allocation rule across all acts: When your Three Hard Ratios are green, invest in drivers. When your ratios are yellow, split investment between drivers and foundation repair. When your ratios are red, stop investing in drivers entirely and put every available dollar into fixing the foundation. Drivers amplify whatever exists. If what exists is rotten, amplification makes it worse.

Here is where the product category survival rates from the decline research become strategically useful. A reminder: these rates are based on the 53-company dataset, not the entire industry. They are directional, not absolute. But they're the best historical indicators available for assessing category risk.

Every category has a historical survival rate. And that survival rate tells you something about your category's structural resilience.

Essential oils: 100% operating, though declining. Multiple use cases and deep community have sustained the category through Act 4. Both doTERRA and Young Living deserve recognition for weathering more than a decade of challenges.

Weight management: 33% operating in reduced form. GLP-1 drugs have pushed this category into the most severe Act 4 event in industry history. The surviving companies, Herbalife most prominently, have done extraordinary work to adapt. Herbalife's resilience across decades of challenges, from the Ackman battle to the FTC settlement to GLP-1 disruption, speaks to the company's operational depth and the Nutrition Club model's genuine customer relationships.

Beauty and skincare: 50% operating but declining. Sephora, TikTok Shop, and DTC brands are competing effectively for the same consumer. The companies still operating in this space, including Mary Kay's remarkable multi-decade run, are adapting to a distribution landscape that looks fundamentally different than it did five years ago.

Exotic juice and superfruit: 0% survival in the 53-company dataset. The structural pattern is documented in full in Chapter 5. MonaVie's events were extraordinary. Dallin Larsen understood how to build belief in a room. The failure was structural, not human: a single-ingredient premium in a category bound to commoditize.

Travel and memberships: 0% survival at original scale in the dataset, though niche players in cruises and group travel have built smaller sustainable businesses. The historical failure mode in this category was specific. The product was the opportunity. When the opportunity stopped working, there was no product underneath it. The new generation of travel operators has the chance to solve the exact failure mode the dataset documented, by building a product experience that customers value independent of the income side. Better booking technology, AI-driven personalization, group dynamics that weren't technically possible a decade ago, and a clearer market understanding of what a real travel customer looks like all give the modern operator tools the original generation didn't have. The structural lesson from history is that the customer has to want the trips, not just the opportunity. That is a solvable problem with the resources available now.

Clothing and accessories at scale: 0% survival at original scale in the dataset. Fashion cycles historically moved faster than the inventory-heavy direct selling model could accommodate. LuLaRoe created something culturally significant, a community of women who found identity and belonging through the brand. That isn't nothing. The structural mismatch between fashion's pace and the legacy inventory model was the failure mode. The new generation of clothing operators has different tools available. Print-on-demand and dropshipping technology that didn't exist at scale in 2017. AI-driven trend forecasting that compresses the planning cycle. Lighter inventory models that don't require distributors to hold $5,000 of stock. Hybrid distribution models that combine the relationship-driven sales the model is good at with the operational discipline that fashion specifically requires. The historical category failure wasn't a verdict that clothing in direct selling can't work. It was a documentation of one specific approach that didn't work at scale. New approaches are being attempted now with structural advantages the original generation didn't have.

These survival rates aren't prophecy. They are history. And history is the best predictor of category risk available, with one important qualification. Every category in this list has been attempted by operators using the tools, technology, and market understanding available at the time of their entry. The next generation of operators, in any of these categories, has access to capabilities the dataset companies didn't. AI for inventory forecasting and customer personalization. Real-time data on what is working across the industry. Lighter operational models that reduce risk. The accumulated mistakes of every prior attempt available to study. A regulatory environment that has clarified what works and what doesn't. A modern customer who is more sophisticated about evaluating both products and opportunities. The historical survival rate tells you what the structural challenges have been. It doesn't tell you that those challenges can't be solved by an operator who learns from the prior failures and builds with the resources available today. Every category in this dataset is harder than the categories with strong historical survival rates. None of them is impossible. The work is to understand the specific failure mode that history documented and build a model that solves for it specifically.

Inside the mastermind, the timing conversation is the most important strategic discussion we have. And it's the conversation that separates the leaders who build decade-long careers from the ones who restart every three years.

I watched this play out in real time during 2023 and 2024. Leaders in weight management companies started coming to me with the same question, asked different ways but always the same question underneath: "Is this still going to work?"

They could feel the act transition happening. The GLP-1 conversation was everywhere. Their prospects were bringing it up unprompted. "My doctor says I should try Wegovy." "My sister lost 40 pounds on Ozempic." The cultural conversation that had been their tailwind for years was shifting underneath them. Some of these leaders were earning six figures per month. They weren't panicking. But they were reading the signs.

The ones who read the cycle correctly started adapting before the numbers forced them to. They diversified their personal product usage stories beyond weight loss. They leaned into gut health, energy, and wellness benefits that GLP-1 drugs don't address. They built customer relationships around daily habits, not 90-day challenges. They started training their teams on the shift rather than pretending it wasn't happening.

The ones who refused to read the cycle kept running the same playbook. Same challenge. Same pitch. Same before-and-after photos. Same "this is the greatest weight management product ever created" story. And their numbers dropped. They hadn't lost skill. The act had changed and their strategy hadn't changed with it.

The hardest conversation I have in the community is telling a leader earning significant income that the act their company is in has shifted and their current strategy has an expiration date. Nobody wants to hear that. Especially when the checks are still clearing. But the leaders who listen, who adjust before the numbers force them to, are the ones still building three years later. The ones who dismiss the signal are the ones who end up starting over at a new company, telling themselves "this time will be different" without understanding that they're entering another cycle at the same act they just left.

The leaders who build the most durable careers are the ones who can read which act their company and category are in and adjust their strategy accordingly. They don't build the same way in Act 2 as they do in Act 4. They don't use the same pitch in Act 1 as they do in Act 5.

In Act 2, the best leaders focus on growth. Recruit aggressively. Build the team. Capture the wave. But they also build customer habits from day one. They don't wait until Act 3 to start acquiring customers. They build the customer foundation during the period when growth is easiest.

In Act 3 and Act 4, the best leaders shift from building wide to building deep. They invest in their existing team rather than constantly chasing new recruits. They help their organization develop genuine customer relationships. They prepare for the reality that the recruiting pitch that worked in Act 2 will not work in Act 4.

In Act 5, the best leaders make hard decisions. Some stay with companies that have the foundation to survive the shakeout. Some move to companies in earlier acts of a different category cycle. Some diversify their income sources beyond a single company. The ones who thrive long-term are the ones who read the cycle accurately and adapt before the cycle forces them to.

I don't tell leaders which act their company is in. I give them the framework and let them see it for themselves. The conversation is always more powerful when the leader reaches the conclusion on her own. And the conclusions are almost always correct. The field knows where it's in the cycle. It just needs the language to describe it.

Map your position.

THE CYCLE POSITION MAP

Step 1: Identify your product category.

What is your primary product type? Weight management, beauty/skincare, essential oils, supplements, clothing/accessories, travel/memberships, technology/telecom, other?

Step 2: Determine your category's current act.

Is the category new and growing (Act 1-2)? Are imitators multiplying (Act 3)? Has the product become available through mainstream retail (Act 4)? Is regulatory and reputational pressure building (Act 5)?

Step 3: Determine your company's position within the category.

Are you a first mover or an imitator? Were you early to the category or late? Where is your revenue relative to peak? Is your field growing or contracting?

Step 4: Match your strategy to your position.

Act 1-2 Strategy: Invest in growth drivers aggressively. Build customer depth simultaneously. This is the window of maximum opportunity.

Act 3 Strategy: Transition from growth velocity to customer retention. Differentiate your product. Invest in what makes you unique, not in what makes you similar to imitators.

Act 4 Strategy: Restructure for competition. Your distribution cost is now a competitive disadvantage. Either differentiate enough to justify it or adapt the model. Monitor the category survival rate for your product type.

Act 5 Strategy: Focus on survival fundamentals. Real customers. Compliant operations. Differentiated products. If your foundation is strong, you can emerge from the shakeout as a category leader. If your foundation is weak, the shakeout will find you.

Step 5: Monitor for act transitions.

Acts don't announce themselves. They transition gradually. The shift from Act 2 to Act 3 is marked by imitators entering and recruiting difficulty increasing. The shift from Act 3 to Act 4 is marked by retail availability and price compression. The shift from Act 4 to Act 5 is marked by media scrutiny and model exits.

Track these signals quarterly. When you see the transition beginning, your strategy should already be shifting. The companies that adapt to the next act before it fully arrives are the ones that survive.

Imagine a CEO who understands the 5-Act Cycle.

She looks at her weight management company and sees Act 4 clearly. GLP-1 drugs aren't going away. The category has been structurally reshaped. Instead of denying the shift or hoping it passes, she adapts. She diversifies her product line beyond weight management into adjacent categories that are in earlier acts. She invests in the Nutrition Club model that creates daily customer habits independent of the shake category. She restructures her comp plan to reward customer retention over recruiting velocity.

Her revenue may dip in the short term. Her field may resist the changes. But she is positioning the company to survive Act 5 while her competitors are still pretending they're in Act 2.

Five years from now, her company is still operating. Smaller, perhaps, than at peak. But alive, profitable, and positioned for the next cycle. The competitors who denied the act transition are in the decline dataset.

THE ACT 2 TO ACT 3 LEADER FRAMEWORK

There is one transition in the boom-bust cycle that matters more for the leader personally than any other. The shift from Act 2 to Act 3. The boom is over. The plateau has begun. The wind that was at your back is now at your face. Everything that worked stops working at roughly the same time. This is the single most consequential moment in a leader's career, and almost every leader handles it the same wrong way.

Recognition first. The hardest part of the transition is admitting you're in it. Act 2 produces the dopamine of constant wins. Recruiting numbers up. Convention attendance up. Revenue up. Field excitement up. Act 3 begins with the same activities producing diminishing returns. The same recruiting push that worked last year produces half the result this year. The same convention attracts the same crowd, but the energy is different. Most leaders interpret the slowdown as a temporary plateau, a single bad quarter, a market issue, a regulatory issue, anything other than the truth: the drivers that built Act 2 have run their course.

The denial pattern is predictable. Leaders explain the slowdown with one-off causes. Last quarter was Q4 seasonality. This quarter was the comp plan adjustment. Next quarter will rebound after the convention. Each individual explanation might even be partially true. But when the explanations stack across multiple quarters and the underlying trend is consistently down, the cause is structural, not circumstantial. The leader who can't face that the cause is structural will keep applying Act 2 solutions to an Act 3 problem, and each application makes the situation worse.

The instinct to push harder is the wrong instinct. Most leaders respond to early Act 3 by doing more of what worked in Act 2. More incentives. More aggressive recruiting promotions. More events. Bigger trips. Louder cultural energy on stage. These moves work in Act 2 because the drivers underneath are still active and the field's belief is high. They fail in Act 3 because the drivers have decayed. Pushing harder against a closed driver doesn't reopen it. It just spends capital that the company will need later for the actual pivot.

Question your assumptions about what produced Act 2 in the first place. This is where leaders most consistently get it wrong. They assume Act 2 was built by their leadership decisions, their comp plan, their event strategy, their charisma. Some of it was. Most of it was the underlying drivers doing their work while leadership was making decisions on top of those drivers. The platform window that opened. The cultural wave that crested. The leader migration that happened. The market that opened. Without rigorously diagnosing which drivers actually produced Act 2, the leader won't know which drivers have closed in Act 3 or which new ones to activate.

Then the harder question. Is this a dip or a dead end? Some companies enter Act 3 because the original drivers ran their natural course and the path forward requires real work. Structural redesign. Customer foundation rebuilding. Comp plan modernization. Leadership development. Evolution of the product line. That is a dip. The other side exists. Companies that push through it become the long-term compounders this book has been describing. doTERRA crossed a dip in the late 2010s when essential oils matured as a category. Herbalife crossed a dip after the FTC settlement. Melaleuca has crossed several dips across thirty-plus years. Each of them came out the other side with a different company than the one that entered.

Other companies enter Act 3 because the underlying business model has structural problems that no amount of work will fix. The customer foundation never existed. The comp plan was built around qualification volume rather than real demand. The product was a vehicle for the opportunity rather than the other way around. That isn't a dip. That is a dead end. The work of pushing through doesn't produce the eventual breakthrough because there's no breakthrough on the other side. The company will keep grinding into terminal decline.

The leader who can tell the difference makes the most important call of her career. A dip requires commitment. Doubling down on the structural work even when the short-term returns look poor. Investing in the customer foundation, the comp plan redesign, the product evolution, the field development infrastructure that takes eighteen to thirty-six months to produce results. Holding the line when the board is asking why growth hasn't returned and when the field is asking why the leadership team isn't doing more visible things. The reward for the commitment is the company that emerges on the other side, which is almost always more valuable, more durable, and more profitable than the company that entered.

A dead end requires the opposite. The leader has to recognize that the work she is asking the company to do won't produce the breakthrough on the other side because the foundation isn't capable of supporting one. Smart leaders in this situation make the hard call early. They sell. They restructure. They merge. They wind down on their own terms while the company still has value, rather than grinding it into nothing over the next five years.

The leader who survives the Act 2 to Act 3 transition does it with zero ego and zero defensiveness about the diagnosis. Ego protects the story that Act 2 was built by the leader's brilliance and Act 3 is a temporary inconvenience. The leader who can drop the ego and ask directly which drivers produced Act 2, which ones have closed, what the company's real customer foundation looks like, and whether this is a dip worth pushing through or a dead end worth exiting, gets the truth in time to act on it. The leader who can't drop the ego gets the truth too, but later, after the company has spent years and millions confirming what the data was already telling her at the start of Act 3.

The leaders I've watched manage this transition successfully share one trait. They were willing to hear that the company they had built wasn't the company the next phase required. The company that broke into Act 2 had to become a different company for the version that survives Act 3 to exist. That is a hard message for any builder to absorb, especially one whose identity is wrapped up in the company's previous wins. But the absorption is the door. Leaders who can accept that the next chapter requires structural change, sometimes painful, often unpopular, almost always slower than the field would like, are the leaders who get to write that next chapter. Leaders who can't accept it almost always preside over the company's terminal decline while still believing they're about to figure it out.

That is the framework. Recognition. Driver diagnosis. Dip versus dead end. Commitment or exit. All of it executed with the ego and the assumptions stripped away.

That is timing. Not predicting the future. Reading the present through the lens of history. Knowing that the script repeats. And making sure your company is on the right side of the pattern.

The next chapter covers reignition: what to do when momentum has stalled. A different playbook than creating momentum from scratch. And the reason most reignition attempts fail is that they solve for the wrong variable.

THE BOTTOM LINE: Every product category follows a five-act boom-bust cycle. Identify which act your category is in. Match your strategy to the act. An Act 2 strategy in an Act 4 market accelerates your decline.

The script has repeated six times. It will repeat again. Which act you're in, and whether your strategy matches it, is the only thing still in your hands.

Chapter 17: Reigniting Stalled Growth

Most reignition attempts fail for the same reason: they try to recreate the growth that was lost instead of diagnosing why it was lost. A company that stalled because the recruiting story lost its power can't be fixed by a new incentive trip. The trip treats a symptom. The stale narrative is the disease.

In the mid-1990s, Marvel Comics filed for bankruptcy. The company that owned Spider-Man, the X-Men, and the Avengers was worth less than $1 billion and sinking. Revenue had collapsed. The stock was delisted. Creditors were circling.

The conventional wisdom said Marvel was finished. The comic book market had imploded. Retailers had gone under. Speculator-driven demand had evaporated. Everything that had fueled the early 1990s boom, variant covers, special editions, collector frenzy, was gone.

But Marvel's new leadership team, eventually led by Ike Perlmutter and then Kevin Feige, did not try to reignite the comic book boom. They diagnosed the actual problem. The characters were the asset. The distribution channel was the constraint. Comics were a shrinking medium. Film wasn't.

Marvel Studios launched Iron Man in 2008. The character was considered a B-list property. The film grossed $585 million worldwide. Ten years later, Avengers: Endgame grossed $2.8 billion. Disney had acquired Marvel for $4 billion. The company that was bankrupt in 1996 had become one of the most valuable entertainment properties in human history.

Marvel didn't reignite by doing more of what had stopped working. It reignited by diagnosing what was actually valuable, the characters and stories, and deploying that value through a completely different channel. The distribution changed. The core asset remained.

That is the reignition principle. And it applies to every direct selling company that has stalled, plateaued, or declined.

Most reignition attempts fail for a specific reason.

When revenue stalls, the most common corporate response is to stimulate the existing model. Launch a new product. Create a promotion. Run a rank advancement contest. Announce a new incentive trip. Increase fast-start bonuses. Open a new international market. These are all variations of the same approach: do more of what you were doing, but louder.

Sometimes it works. A strong product launch can create a quarter of excitement. A trip incentive can motivate a burst of activity. But if the underlying reason for the stall hasn't been addressed, the stimulation produces a temporary spike followed by a return to the stalled baseline. Or worse: the stimulation costs money, the spike doesn't materialize, and the company has burned cash it needed for a real structural fix.

The Decline Engine model from the research identifies four distinct break paths. Each break path has a different cause. Each cause requires a different response. Applying the wrong response to the right problem is worse than doing nothing, because it burns resources and belief simultaneously.

Path 1: Regulatory action interrupted the reward loop.

If your company stalled because of an FTC enforcement action, state attorney general investigation, or compliance overhaul, the reignition path is structural reform. Not marketing. Not motivation. Demonstrable change to the business practices that triggered the regulatory attention. Herbalife's path after the $200 million FTC settlement was expensive and painful. The company restructured its U.S. operations, documented real retail customers, and changed compensation structures. Revenue dipped. The field was disrupted. But the company survived because the reforms were genuine and the data improved.

Companies that respond to Path 1 with PR campaigns instead of structural reform are delaying the inevitable. The regulatory apparatus doesn't forget. If the practices that triggered the first enforcement action continue, the second enforcement action will be more severe.

Path 2: Category disruption shifted demand away from your product.

If your company stalled because the product category was disrupted, whether by pharmaceutical innovation (GLP-1), technological change (VoIP killing telecom MLMs), or retail commoditization (acai at Costco), the reignition path is product evolution or category migration. You can't reignite demand for a product category that the consumer has moved away from. You can evolve the product to serve adjacent needs, or you can migrate to a category that's in an earlier act of the boom-bust cycle.

The first strategic call is to determine whether the disruption is a fad or a trend. A fad is a short-term consumer behavior shift that recedes within a few years. The Atkins low-carb wave of the early 2000s was a fad. The juice cleanse trend of the early 2010s was a fad. Companies that overreacted to either wave by abandoning their flagship and chasing the trend ended up worse off than companies that held steady. A trend is a structural shift that doesn't recede. The shift to streaming was a trend. The shift to mobile-first computing was a trend. Companies that underreacted to either shift, including some of the most respected operators in their categories, lost ground they couldn't recover.

The current GLP-1 shift appears to be a trend, not a fad. The demand for weight loss is permanent. The mechanism that satisfied that demand for the last forty years (lifestyle-based dietary programs) is being partially supplemented and partially replaced by a pharmaceutical mechanism that produces faster, more reliable results for many users. GLP-1s are also the most visible piece of a broader peptide trend that's reshaping wellness more generally. The companies in the affected category have to assume the shift is durable and respond accordingly. The companies that integrate GLP-1 support, peptide-adjacent products, and complementary wellness offerings into their lines are turning the trend into a tailwind. The companies that wait for the wave to recede are likely to be wrong.

But fad-versus-trend assessment is one of the hardest strategic calls in business. The honest answer is often "we'll not know for two to three years." During that uncertainty window, the disciplined response is to invest in optionality. Continue serving your existing customers while quietly building capability that would let you adapt if the disruption proves durable. Do not bet the entire company on a category pivot until the data demands it. But don't freeze either. The companies that wait for certainty before acting often act too late.

Medifast is attempting category evolution right now. The company can't reverse the GLP-1 disruption of its core weight management shake business. What it can do is evolve the coaching model to complement GLP-1 usage rather than compete with it. Patients on GLP-1 drugs still need nutritional guidance, accountability, and community support. The distribution model's core strength, the human relationship, still has value. But the product through which that value is delivered must change.

Nu Skin has been adapting through multiple cycles across four decades. From personal care products in the 1980s, through the ageLOC anti-aging line, through beauty devices like LumiSpa iO, and now into intelligent wellness platforms. Full-year 2024 revenue was $1.73 billion, down from the $3.18 billion peak in 2013. The company hasn't recovered to peak. But it's still operating, still innovating, and still adapting. That resilience across a decade of decline deserves recognition. Nu Skin's willingness to evolve its product line, restructure its comp plan, and invest in new technology categories is the playbook for Path 2 survival. It isn't glamorous. It doesn't produce explosive growth. But it keeps the company alive while competitors in the same category disappear.

The Path 2 response framework comes down to four principles. First, assess fad versus trend with clear eyes. Second, do not bet the company on the assessment until the data is clear. Third, evolve the product to serve adjacent needs that the disruption created, rather than competing directly against the disruption. Fourth, hold the flagship narrative as long as possible while introducing supporting products that bridge to the new market reality. Companies that follow this sequence give themselves the best chance of surviving a real category disruption. Companies that panic, abandon their flagship, and chase the disruption typically end up with neither the old business nor the new one.

Path 3: Channel shift is creating competitive pressure on your distribution model.

If your company is facing competition from DTC, affiliate, Amazon, or TikTok Shop channels that reach consumers at lower cost, the reignition path is doubling down on the human element that digital channels can't replicate.

This doesn't mean the direct selling distribution model is obsolete. For product categories that require education, demonstration, coaching, accountability, and personal trust, direct selling has advantages that no algorithm can match. A TikTok video can't follow up on day 14 when a customer is about to quit their wellness program. An Amazon listing can't build a community of people who hold each other accountable. A DTC website can't look a prospect in the eye and say "this changed my life, let me show you."

What it does mean is that companies need to invest in making that human connection so valuable that the customer would never trade it for a cheaper price online. Train the field to do what algorithms can't. Build the coaching, community, and accountability infrastructure that justifies the distribution cost. Some companies may supplement their direct selling channel with DTC or retail partnerships to broaden reach. The core field relationship remains the asset. Everything else is distribution strategy around it.

Path 4: Financial distress created a liquidity crisis.

If your company stalled because of debt, cash flow problems, or unsustainable cost structures, the reignition path is financial restructuring. Not more revenue. Less cost. MonaVie's final years were a financial death spiral. Revenue was declining. Debt was increasing. The company was acquired, restructured, and eventually dissolved. Tupperware followed a similar trajectory, filing for bankruptcy in 2024 after years of declining revenue and mounting debt.

Path 4 is often the end stage of Paths 1 through 3. A company that fails to address a regulatory problem, a category disruption, or a channel shift eventually runs out of money. The financial distress is a symptom of the unaddressed structural problem, not the cause.

The companies that survive Path 4 are the ones that restructure aggressively: cutting costs, renegotiating debt, selling non-core assets, and refocusing on the smallest viable version of the business. The ones that try to grow their way out of financial distress almost always make the situation worse, because the growth initiatives require capital the company doesn't have.

This is why the break path diagnosis matters so much. The treatment for each path is different, and applying the wrong treatment to the right problem makes things worse.

A company on Path 2 (category disruption) that responds with Path 1 tactics (compliance restructuring) is fixing something that isn't broken while ignoring the thing that is. A company on Path 3 (channel shift) that responds with Path 4 tactics (cost-cutting) is shrinking itself without addressing the strategic problem. A company on Path 1 (regulatory) that responds with Path 2 tactics (product innovation) is launching new products while the legal foundation is crumbling.

The most common mismatch I see in the industry is companies on Path 2 or Path 3 responding with generic growth tactics: new incentive trips, new rank bonuses, new fast-start promotions. These aren't break-path treatments. They are stimulants. They produce temporary activity spikes without addressing the structural reason the company stalled. The activity spike looks like progress for one quarter. Then it fades. And the company is in a worse position than before because it burned cash and belief on an initiative that could never have worked.

The companies that reignite successfully are the ones that diagnose first. They name the break path. They accept the diagnosis even when it's uncomfortable. And then they apply the treatment that matches the problem.

Amway's response to the FTC in 1979 was Path 1 treatment for a Path 1 problem: structural reforms that redirected growth toward real customers and demonstrated legitimacy. Nu Skin's ongoing reinvention is Path 2 treatment for a Path 2 reality: product evolution as categories mature. BODi's exit from direct selling was Path 3 treatment for a Path 3 reality: the distribution model no longer matched the product's path to the consumer. Each company diagnosed correctly and responded accordingly. The ones that didn't are gone.

Many companies don't fail to reignite because they lack ideas. They fail because they solve the wrong problem. They launch a new product when the issue is churn. They sign a new leader when the issue is the comp plan. They open a new country when the issue is customer depth. Every failed reignition attempt I've studied made the same mistake: the leadership team skipped the diagnosis and went straight to the treatment they were most comfortable with.

There is one additional pattern that deserves attention. Sometimes the founder is both the company's greatest asset and its biggest obstacle to reignition. The same conviction that built the company can prevent the founder from accepting that the market has changed. The same relationships that created the original growth can become the reason the founder can't objectively evaluate which leaders are still contributing and which are coasting. Early decisions about compensation, culture, and organizational structure create consequences that compound for years. A comp plan designed for launch-phase speed may be structurally wrong for a mature company. A culture built around one person's charisma may not survive that person stepping back. The hardest reignition conversations aren't about the market or the product. They are about whether the people who built the company are willing to change the decisions they made when they built it.

The reignition sequence that actually works follows a specific order. Skip a step and the reignition fails.

Step 1: Diagnose which break path you're on.

This is the step many companies skip. They jump straight to "what should we launch?" without asking "why did we stall?" Run the Momentum Equation Scorecard from Chapter 15. Identify which drivers reversed. Identify which ratios moved. Identify which decline phase you're in. The diagnosis determines the treatment. The wrong treatment is worse than no treatment. The reignition discipline starts with the scorecard, not with initiatives. The temptation in any reignition is to skip straight to solutions, especially when the leadership team is feeling pressure to show movement. That instinct is the first thing the discipline has to override. Sit with the diagnosis first.

Step 2: Strip before you build.

Before investing in reignition, remove the practices that are accelerating the decline. If qualification purchasing is inflating revenue artificially, reduce the requirements. If the comp plan is creating payout inflation, restructure it. If compliance failures are generating regulatory risk, fix them. If operational failures are eroding field belief, address them.

This step is painful. It often causes revenue to dip further in the short term because you're removing artificial volume and reducing incentive spending. The field will resist. Some leaders will leave. But you can't build durable growth on top of structural decay. You must fix the foundation before adding weight.

Herbalife stripped before it built. The FTC settlement required the company to restructure its U.S. operations. Revenue dipped. The field was disrupted. But the restructured foundation was sound. The Nutrition Club model produced genuine daily customers. And from that sound foundation, the company rebuilt.

Step 3: Rebuild around the right variable.

This is where the diagnosis from Step 1 determines the action. If the break path is category disruption, rebuild around product evolution. If the break path is channel shift, rebuild around distribution model adaptation. If the break path is regulatory, rebuild around compliance and customer depth. If the break path is financial, rebuild around cost structure.

The most common reignition mistake is rebuilding around recruiting when the problem was never recruiting. If your company stalled because the product category was disrupted, recruiting harder won't fix it. If your company stalled because the distribution model is uncompetitive, a new rank advancement bonus won't fix it. The variable you rebuild around must match the variable that caused the stall.

Step 4: Launch the reignition initiative from the clean foundation.

Only after Steps 1 through 3 are complete should you launch the initiative that's designed to restart growth. Now the new product launch has a foundation under it. Now the international expansion is resourced and committed, not a headline to mask domestic decline. Now the comp plan enhancement is sustainable because the cost structure has been fixed. Now the platform strategy is diversified because you're not dependent on one channel.

The reignition launched from a clean foundation feels different to the field. They can sense whether the growth is real or manufactured. When the foundation is sound and the initiative is matched to the actual problem, the field responds with genuine energy. When the foundation is rotten and the initiative is a Band-Aid on a structural wound, the field goes through the motions. They have seen it before. They know the difference.

The survey data validates this sequence and reveals what companies get wrong about reignition. When 82 top-level leaders were asked what would re-engage a disengaged legacy leader, the number one answer wasn't money. It wasn't incentives. It wasn't a new product. Fifty percent said: a clear, believable 3-to-5-year vision and roadmap. Thirty-four percent said: a co-created launch plan with the field. Thirty-two percent said: real influence with visible follow-through.

Read those answers carefully. The top three reignition levers are all about belief and influence. Not compensation. Not promotions. Not trips. The field is telling you: we stopped building because we stopped believing the company knows where it's going. Show us where you're going. Let us help build the plan. And then actually follow through on what we create together.

You don't re-engage leaders with money. You re-engage them with belief and influence.

There is an organization that understands this better than most. The Association of Network Marketing Professionals, the ANMP, is the only grassroots nonprofit in this industry that brings field leaders and corporate executives into the same room as peers. Not as stage performers and audience. As collaborators. Since 2004, the ANMP has created a space where top field leaders from different companies, company owners and executives, and industry advocates learn from each other, challenge each other, and work on the profession's biggest problems together. Their annual convention puts 50 or more of the industry's top earners and trainers on one stage, alongside corporate leaders who are willing to listen as much as they speak. If you're a company executive who has never attended an ANMP event, you're missing the most honest cross-company field perspective available in this profession. And if you're a field leader who has never attended, you're missing the chance to learn from builders across dozens of companies who have solved problems your company hasn't even identified yet. The gap between what corporate thinks and what the field knows is the single most dangerous blind spot in this industry. Organizations like the ANMP exist to close that gap. Use them.

The same survey revealed why most reignition attempts fail before they start. When asked how well corporate listens to leader input, only 23% said "extremely well." Fifty percent said "fairly well, but not enough." Twenty-seven percent said "poorly" or "very poorly." That means over three-quarters of the industry's top leaders feel their feedback isn't consistently acted upon. Now imagine you're one of those leaders. Corporate announces a reignition initiative. A new product. A new promotion. Did anyone ask you what the field actually needs? Did anyone incorporate your feedback into the plan? If the answer is no, the initiative was designed in a boardroom by people who don't build, for people who do. And the field can feel it immediately.

Many companies try reignition by launching a promotion, a trip incentive, or a new fast-start bonus. The survey data suggests those are the wrong levers. They address symptoms, not cause. The cause is a leadership team that stopped believing in the direction. The cure is giving them a direction worth believing in and a genuine role in creating it. That is Step 4 done right.

From the mastermind conversations, I see reignition attempts constantly. And the pattern of failure is remarkably consistent.

A company stalls. Corporate panics. They call an emergency leadership retreat. They brainstorm a "growth initiative." They come back with a new product, a new promotion, a new trip, and a motivational video from the CEO. They launch it at the next event with maximum energy. The CEO is on stage casting vision. The music is pumping. The video package is cinematic. The crowd cheers.

The field gets excited for two weeks. Some activity spikes. Then the energy fades. Because the initiative didn't address the structural reason for the stall. It was a sugar rush on top of a broken foundation.

I've watched this happen so many times that I can predict the outcome from the announcement. When a company announces a new incentive trip as its reignition strategy, and the reason the company stalled was category disruption, I know the trip will fail. Trips do work. They are powerful motivational tools when the field has something real to build toward. But a trip can't restore product-market fit that has eroded. It can't bring back a cultural wave that has passed. It can't undo a pharmaceutical disruption. The trip motivates activity. If the activity has nowhere productive to go because the underlying problem is structural, the motivation produces effort without results. And effort without results is the fastest path to demoralization.

Six months later, revenue is at the same level or lower. The field is more demoralized than before because they saw the company try to fix the problem and fail. They pushed hard. They did the work. And nothing changed. Belief erodes further. The next reignition attempt will be even less effective because the field's trust in corporate's ability to diagnose and fix the problem has been damaged. Each failed attempt makes the next attempt harder. That is the reignition trap.

The companies I've seen reignite successfully share three characteristics. First, the leadership team was honest about the diagnosis. They didn't blame the field. They didn't blame the market. They didn't stand on stage and say "we just need to work harder." They looked at the data and named the structural problem. That takes courage because naming the problem means admitting that the leadership team allowed it to develop. The CEO who says "our customer ratio is too low and our qualification purchasing requirements are too high" is admitting that the comp plan she approved created the structural problem. That is hard to say out loud. But it's necessary.

Second, they stripped before they built. They made the painful changes to the foundation before launching the growth initiative. They reduced qualification requirements. They restructured comp plan incentives. They fixed operational failures. They accepted short-term revenue pain.

Third, they matched the initiative to the problem. If the problem was customer depth, the initiative was customer-focused. If the problem was product-market fit, the initiative was product evolution. If the problem was operations, the initiative was infrastructure investment. The match between diagnosis and treatment was precise.

Those three steps sound simple. They are excruciating to execute. And the reason they're excruciating has less to do with strategy than with people.

The hardest part of reignition isn't designing the new comp plan or choosing the right product initiative or running the scorecard. The hardest part is managing the human resistance inside your own organization while you do it.

When you announce structural changes, three things happen simultaneously. Your top earners panic because any change to the comp plan threatens their income. Your corporate team resists because they built the current system and changing it feels like an indictment of their work. And your field splits into factions: the ones who trust the leadership enough to follow, the ones who are already halfway out the door and will use the change as their excuse to leave, and the ones in the middle who are watching to see which group wins.

The companies that manage this well do four things. First, they bring their top 20 earners into the process before the announcement. Not to ask permission. To give them context, to let them ask questions privately, and to make them feel like insiders rather than victims. A leader who hears about a comp plan change from the stage at the same time as everyone else feels ambushed. A leader who heard about it three weeks earlier in a private call with the CEO feels respected. The change is the same. The reaction is completely different.

Second, they communicate the WHY before the WHAT. Many companies announce the change first and then scramble to explain why. Flip it. Spend two weeks communicating the diagnosis. Share the data. Show the field the same scorecard the leadership team saw. Let them arrive at the conclusion before you announce the solution. When the field understands why the change is necessary, the change itself feels logical rather than arbitrary.

Third, they accept short-term losses. Some leaders will leave. Some volume will drop. Some field energy will dip. That is the price of structural repair. The CEO who can't stomach a 10% revenue dip for two quarters will never fix a structural problem that's compounding at 5% per year. The math is simple. The courage isn't.

Fourth, they measure the right things during the transition. Do not measure revenue in the first 90 days after a structural change. Measure customer acquisition rate. Measure new leader development. Measure the behaviors the new structure is designed to produce. If the behaviors are changing in the right direction, the revenue will follow. If you measure revenue during a structural transition, you'll panic and reverse the change before it has time to work. That is how most reignition attempts die. The strategy is rarely the problem. The leadership team loses its nerve. The first step requires admitting you have a structural problem. The second step requires short-term revenue pain during a period when the board is already nervous.

And the third step requires discipline to solve the actual problem instead of the problem you wish you had.

The CEO who executes all three steps is the one who saves the company. The CEO who skips to the launch is the one who loses it.

A necessary honesty about constraints. This playbook assumes a leadership team with the authority, capital, and time horizon to make decade-scale decisions. That describes a minority of the industry. Many companies are run by founders whose net worth is tied to this quarter's revenue because their debt covenants require it. Others are owned by private equity firms with three-to-five-year exit horizons who want the spike, not the compound. Others are family businesses where the founder is aging and the next generation is more interested in the payout than the foundation. Still others are public companies whose stock price rewards revenue growth and punishes "restructuring" regardless of long-term health.

If you're operating inside one of those constraints, you already know that the "right" strategic decision and the "possible" strategic decision are often different things. The board wants Q3 numbers. The PE sponsor wants a new market opening this year. The founder refuses to touch the comp plan because "that's how we built this company."

I do not have a magic answer for operating inside constraints that prevent long-term optimization. But I have one piece of advice that applies universally: do not pretend the constraint doesn't exist. Name it. In the boardroom, in the leadership team, in the strategic plan. "We are making this decision because our capital structure requires short-term revenue, not because it's the optimal long-term move." That honesty doesn't solve the constraint. But it prevents the far more dangerous outcome: believing that the constrained decision is actually the right decision, and building your next three years of strategy on a foundation that was never a choice. It was a concession.

The companies that survive constraints are the ones that make concessions deliberately and plan for the day the constraint lifts. The companies that die inside constraints are the ones that mistake the concession for conviction.

A reignition case that deserves a full look. Pampered Chef, the kitchen tools and cookware direct seller founded in 1980, was acquired by Berkshire Hathaway in 2002. Warren Buffett added the company to his portfolio of durable consumer businesses. What followed is instructive for any owner thinking about reignition timelines.

For roughly a decade after the acquisition, Pampered Chef declined. The party plan model that built the company in the 1980s and 1990s ran into the same cultural erosion that damaged Tupperware. Home parties became less central to how women socialized. E-commerce ate into kitchen goods retail. The field aged. Revenue eroded.

Then the company began a deliberate reignition. New leadership refreshed the brand, invested in digital capability, expanded international markets, and renewed the focus on the independent consultant base. Company communications reported that by roughly 2019, digital sales had grown from approximately 10% of the business to more than 50%, with sales and earnings growth over the prior five years. The company had done the unsexy work of rebuilding its own foundation for a different era, while continuing to honor the consultant model that built it.

Pampered Chef hasn't reclaimed its 1990s-era peak. Reignition doesn't promise peak recovery. What it promises is a return to the foundation underneath the company, rebuilt in a form that matches current conditions rather than the conditions of the era when the original model was designed. That is what honest reignition looks like. Years, not quarters. Digital integration, not digital abandonment. And the willingness to change the business substantially while keeping the relationship with the people who built it.

Diagnose before you act.

A NOTE ON OPERATORS FROM OUTSIDE THE INDUSTRY

There is a specific reignition failure pattern worth addressing directly, because The pattern is observable across the industry. A company gets acquired or recapitalized. New ownership brings in executives who have run successful businesses in other categories. Consumer products. Technology. Retail. Traditional distribution. These aren't bad operators.

Many of them are excellent operators. They have P&L experience. They have built brands. They have managed large teams. The instinct is to assume that good business is good business, and that the skills translate.

Some of them do translate. Financial discipline translates. Brand strategy translates. Supply chain translates. Talent management translates. An outside operator with strong fundamentals has a lot to contribute.

But direct selling is a different sport underneath the familiar business vocabulary. The incentive architecture is different. The field relationship is different. The way growth happens is different. The way decline happens is different. The way leaders behave under pressure is different. The way compliance risk moves is different. The way an event week affects a quarter is different. The way a comp plan tweak ripples through the culture is different. An outside operator who is brilliant at CPG or tech won't know any of that coming in, and the learning curve is months, not weeks.

It is the difference between being the greatest basketball coach in the country and then taking a head coaching job in football. The coaching skills still matter. The ability to read talent, manage ego, build systems, handle pressure, all of that still matters. But the sport is different. The rules are different. The plays are different. The injury patterns are different. The recruiting cycle is different. And the coach who walks in assuming the skills are one-to-one transferable gets his team beaten for two seasons while he figures out what he doesn't know.

The owners and executives who succeed coming from outside the profession share one habit. They immerse themselves. They hire consultants who have operated inside the industry. They bring in corporate team members who have run direct selling companies before and are trusted to speak candidly. They go to Direct Selling News events. They attend the Association of Network Marketing Professionals conferences. They sit in with field leaders. They read the comp plan history of competitors. They study the regulatory case law. They don't assume they know the answers before they know the questions.

The owners and executives who fail are the ones who treat the industry as generic business. They apply retail metrics to a relationship model. They optimize for quarterly revenue when the business compounds over decades. They cut field-facing costs because they scan as overhead and don't realize they were funding the culture that built the company. They add executive process layers that the field experiences as bureaucracy. Each decision in isolation looks defensible. The compound of those decisions is what kills the momentum the prior generation spent decades building.

There are similarities between direct selling and traditional business. Brands matter. Customers matter. Operations matter. Margins matter. But there are enough unique dynamics that an outside operator has to treat the first year as a learning year, not a changing year. The biggest mistakes I've watched new ownership groups make are the mistakes they made in the first twelve months, before they understood what they had inherited.

If you're coming into ownership or an executive role at a direct selling company from another industry, that's not a weakness. You bring strengths the profession needs. The strengths are only fully useful when they're combined with a respect for the operating dynamics specific to this business. Immerse first. Decide second. The companies that survive new ownership are almost always the ones where the new owners were willing to sit in the room and learn before they moved to the front of the room and led.

THE FULL ARC: HOW HERBALIFE EXECUTED A REAL REIGNITION

Every framework in this chapter raises the same fair question. Has any direct selling company actually executed something like this and survived? The honest answer is yes, and the most documented example is Herbalife between 2013 and 2020. The arc is worth walking through in full, because it's the closest thing the industry has to a public case study of all four reignition steps executed in sequence, under intense external pressure, with the financial and field outcomes documented in SEC filings.

Set the stage. In December 2012, hedge fund manager Bill Ackman of Pershing Square Capital announced a $1 billion short position against Herbalife. He delivered a 342-slide presentation arguing the company was a pyramid scheme that the FTC would shut down. Major financial media covered the announcement live. The stock fell 39% in three days. Herbalife was a publicly traded company with a multi-decade operating history, and a single hedge fund manager had created an existential crisis with a slide deck. The Ackman attack continued for the next five years across television, conferences, regulatory complaints, and political lobbying. It was the most public assault on a direct selling company in the history of the industry.

In March 2014, the FTC opened a formal investigation. In July 2016, the investigation concluded with a $200 million settlement and a consent order that required Herbalife to fundamentally restructure its US business. The company had to document genuine retail customers. It had to change how distributors were compensated, tying rewards explicitly to documented retail sales rather than internal consumption. It had to implement systems to prove customer acquisition was real and ongoing. The settlement didn't call Herbalife a pyramid scheme. But it required the company to operate in a way that would make the pyramid scheme accusation impossible to sustain in the future.

This is where most companies in similar positions either fight the verdict, run a PR campaign, or collapse under the operational weight of compliance. Herbalife did something different. The company executed all four steps of the reignition sequence in roughly the order this chapter describes.

Step 1, diagnosis. Herbalife's leadership team, led at that time by CEO Michael Johnson, did not treat the FTC settlement as a public-relations problem. They treated it as a structural diagnosis. The break path was clear: regulatory action interrupting the reward loop. The diagnosis pointed at the practices that needed to change. The leadership didn't fight that diagnosis. They accepted it.

Step 2, strip before build. Herbalife restructured its compensation plan. It built systems to document real retail sales. It changed how new distributors were enrolled, including a 90-day cooling-off period and refund guarantees that protected new distributors from pressure to buy inventory they couldn't sell. It eliminated practices that the FTC had flagged as suspect. Revenue did dip. The field was disrupted. Some distributors left because they had built their business around the practices that were now restricted. The leadership team didn't reverse course in response to the short-term pain. They held the line on the structural changes.

Step 3, rebuild around the right variable. The variable Herbalife rebuilt around was customer depth. The Nutrition Club model, which had been a strength internationally for years, became the strategic centerpiece in the United States. Nutrition Clubs are physical locations where customers gather daily to drink shakes, attend wellness events, and build relationships with the brand. Each club generates documented customer transactions. Each customer is a real person who comes back, often daily, because they like the experience and the product. The model is the structural answer to the FTC's concerns: it's impossible to argue a customer is fake when she walks into a club five times a week and pays for a shake.

Step 4, launch from the clean foundation. With the structural reforms in place and the Nutrition Club model scaling, Herbalife resumed growth. Revenue, which had compressed from $5.0 billion in 2013 to $4.4 billion in 2017 during the restructuring, climbed back to $5.5 billion in 2020 and reached $5.8 billion in 2021. The Ackman position, which had cost Pershing Square nearly a billion dollars over five years, was closed in 2018 at a major loss. The pyramid scheme accusation, which had defined the industry conversation for nearly a decade, was decisively answered by the company's continued growth and operational discipline.

The reignition wasn't pretty. The five years from 2013 to 2018 were brutal for Herbalife's leadership team, its field, and its share price. The decisions cost real money in real time. Distributors who had built businesses on the old model lost income. Operational complexity increased substantially. Compliance overhead became permanent. None of that is hidden in this case study. The reignition cost what reignitions actually cost.

But the company is still standing. It is still publicly traded. It is still a multi-billion-dollar operator. And it has the most defensible regulatory posture of any major direct selling company in the United States, because it has already been through the worst-case regulatory scenario and emerged with a structurally compliant business. When the next wave of FTC enforcement comes, Herbalife is the company that has already done the hard work. Most of its peers haven't.

What the Herbalife arc proves. The reignition framework isn't theoretical. A real company, at real scale, under real public pressure, has executed all four steps and survived. The diagnosis was clear-eyed. The strip was painful. The rebuild was structural. The launch came from a clean foundation. The pattern wasn't invented for this book. It was extracted from cases like this one and codified so that other leadership teams could follow it before the FTC forced them to.

Herbalife is also a useful counter-example to the dominant industry narrative. The story most commonly told about Herbalife is about the Ackman fight: the heroic CEO, the failed short, the dramatic battle. That story is real. But the more important story underneath it's the reignition. The company that survived the Ackman attack isn't the company that existed before it. The company that survived is the one that diagnosed the structural problem the attack exposed, stripped the practices that made the attack credible, and rebuilt around real customer depth. The fight with Ackman was the public drama. The reignition was the work.

For a CEO reading this chapter, the Herbalife arc means the framework can carry real weight. The four steps aren't consultant talk. They map onto a documented turnaround at the largest scale this industry has produced. If your company is staring at its own version of the 2013 to 2018 window, the path is known. The work is hard. The cost is real. And the survival is possible.

THE REIGNITION DIAGNOSTIC

Step 1: Identify your break path.

Which of these four descriptions best matches your company's stall?

Path 1 (Regulatory): Enforcement action, compliance overhaul, or regulatory scrutiny has disrupted the field's activity or the company's operations.

Path 2 (Category Disruption): Your product category is being disrupted by pharmaceutical innovation, retail commoditization, or technological change that makes your product less relevant to consumers.

Path 3 (Channel Shift): DTC, affiliate, Amazon, TikTok Shop, or other distribution channels are reaching your consumers at lower cost than your direct selling model.

Path 4 (Financial Distress): Debt, cash flow problems, or unsustainable cost structures are constraining the company's ability to invest in growth.

More than one path may apply. In that case, prioritize: financial distress first (you need cash to fix anything else), then regulatory (you need legal clearance to operate), then category or channel (these are the strategic problems).

Step 2: Run the Momentum Equation Scorecard.

Use the full diagnostic from Chapter 15 to identify which drivers have reversed, which ratios have moved, and which decline phase you're in. The scorecard tells you what needs to be fixed before growth can restart.

Step 3: Define your strip list.

What practices are currently accelerating your decline? High qualification purchasing requirements? Unsustainable incentive spending? Operational failures? Compliance gaps? List them. Strip them. Accept the short-term revenue impact.

Step 4: Define your rebuild variable.

Based on your break path, what is the single most important variable to rebuild around?

Path 1: Rebuild around compliance and customer documentation. Path 2: Rebuild around product evolution or category migration. Path 3: Rebuild around the human element that digital channels can't replicate. Path 4: Rebuild around cost structure and financial sustainability.

Step 5: Design the initiative.

Only now. Only after diagnosis, stripping, and variable identification. Design the specific initiative that addresses your actual problem. Launch it from a clean foundation with realistic expectations.

Imagine a company that has stalled. Revenue is down 25% from peak. The field is demoralized. The board is nervous. The CEO could panic and launch a splashy reignition campaign.

Instead, she runs the diagnostic. The break path is category disruption: the product category has entered Act 4 of the boom-bust cycle, with retail alternatives undercutting the direct selling price. She runs the scorecard.

Two drivers reversing. Ratio 1 yellow. Phase 2 signals present. No regulatory issues. Operations green.

She strips. She reduces the personal volume requirement that was generating qualification purchasing. Revenue dips 8% in the first quarter as artificial volume falls out. The board is uncomfortable. But Ratio 1 begins to shift toward green because the remaining volume is more real.

She rebuilds around the right variable. The product line evolves. New products are developed for adjacent categories that are in earlier acts. The comp plan is restructured to reward customer acquisition in the new categories. The field is retrained on selling the evolved product story.

She launches the reignition initiative from a clean foundation. A product launch event built around the new line, supported by field training that matches the new compensation incentives, resourced with marketing investment that the cost savings from the strip phase made possible.

Revenue doesn't spike overnight. It recovers slowly. Quarter by quarter. Built on real customers buying a product they actually want. The field is smaller but stronger. The leaders who stayed through the transition are more committed. The foundation is sound.

Two years later, the company is growing again. Not at the explosive rate of the original boom. But at a sustainable rate built on a structure that can endure the next cycle.

That is reignition. The work produces a real foundation, not a sugar rush. A rebuild. Slow. Painful. Real.

THE 90-DAY REIGNITION STARTER SEQUENCE

The Reignition Diagnostic tells you what to do. The 90-Day Starter Sequence tells you when to do it. Every reignition I've watched succeed followed roughly this rhythm, whether the CEO planned it that way or fell into it by instinct. Every reignition I've watched fail skipped one of these three phases, usually the first one, and launched straight into the splashy initiative before the diagnosis was complete.

This sequence assumes you're the CEO, president, or owner with the authority to execute structural change. If you're a senior executive without that authority, the sequence becomes a tool for presenting the case to the person who does.

Days 1 to 30: Diagnosis.

The first 30 days are for understanding what you actually have before you change anything. Most reignition attempts that fail die here, because this phase feels unproductive to boards and leadership teams that want visible action. Protect it.

Week 1: Assemble the diagnostic team. Name one executive as the scorecard owner. This person runs the diagnosis. One person, not a committee. One person with authority. Pull the last 36 months of revenue, new customer acquisition, customer retention, distributor enrollment, distributor churn, qualification purchasing percentage, and average customer order size. If the data doesn't exist in clean form, that's itself a diagnostic finding. A company that can't answer these questions in a week is a company whose decisions have been running on feel, not facts.

Week 2: Run the full scorecard. Complete the Momentum Equation Scorecard from Chapter 15. Every driver. Every ratio. Every phase signal. Do not skip questions because you think you know the answer. Identify your break path using the Reignition Diagnostic. If more than one path applies, rank them by severity. Document what is green, what is yellow, what is red. Do not edit for comfort.

Week 3: Interview the field. Talk to ten top earners privately. Separate conversations, not a group call. Ask what they think is happening and what they would change if they had your job. Talk to ten mid-level leaders, people earning between $3,000 and $15,000 a month. Their view is often the truest signal because they're close enough to the field to know what is happening on the ground and detached enough to speak candidly. Pick three customers who have been with the company for more than three years. Find out why they're still buying. That answer tells you what the business is actually made of.

Week 4: Build the diagnosis document. One page. Maximum. This is the document you'll use to align the board, the leadership team, and eventually the field. Include the break path, the two or three drivers that have reversed, the ratios that have moved, the single most important structural problem, and a one-line answer to the question "what is the foundation underneath this business right now?" Share it with your board or ownership group before the end of week four. Their reaction is data. If they resist the diagnosis, you have a second problem on top of the first.

Days 31 to 60: Strip planning and stakeholder alignment.

The second 30 days are for preparing the structural changes and bringing your key stakeholders into the process before anything public happens. This is where human resistance either gets managed early or becomes the thing that kills the reignition.

Week 5: Build the strip list. List every practice that's accelerating your decline. High qualification purchasing requirements. Unsustainable incentive spending. Operational failures. Compliance gaps. Comp plan features rewarding the wrong behavior. For each item, estimate the revenue impact of removing it. Accept that some will cost revenue in the short term. That cost is the entire point. Rank the strip list by structural priority, not by ease. Hardest structural problems first, not the easiest political wins.

Week 6: Design the rebuild variable. Based on your break path, name the one variable the rebuild will center on. Product evolution. Compliance and customer depth. Distribution model adaptation. Cost structure. If more than one variable feels critical, the diagnosis was incomplete. Go back to week two. Sketch what the company looks like 24 months from now if the rebuild works. That vision is what you'll eventually share with the field. It has to be specific enough to believe.

Week 7: Private conversations with top 20 earners. Call or meet individually with your top 20 earners, not the top 50. The top 20. The people whose departure would hurt the most. Share the diagnosis. Share the direction. Share the changes that are coming. Not to ask permission. To give context, answer questions privately, and make them insiders rather than surprised victims. A leader who hears about a comp plan change from the stage at the same time as everyone else feels ambushed. A leader who heard about it three weeks earlier in a private call with the CEO feels respected. The change is the same. The reaction is completely different.

Week 8: Final board and leadership alignment. Present the strip list, the rebuild variable, the 24-month vision, and the expected short-term revenue impact. Name the constraint directly if one exists. If the PE sponsor or debt covenants won't tolerate the short-term pain, the plan has to change, or the conversation has to become about whether the right strategy is possible inside the current capital structure. Do not announce anything externally until the board, top 20 earners, and senior leadership team are aligned. If you announce before alignment, the message fragments in the retelling and the field gets three different versions within a week.

Days 61 to 90: First strip execution and signal reading.

The third 30 days are for executing the first structural change publicly and reading the signals that tell you whether the reignition is taking root or not. This isn't the launch of the growth initiative. That comes later. This is the visible beginning of the rebuild.

Week 9: Communicate the WHY before the WHAT. Spend a full week on diagnosis communication before announcing any specific change. Share the data. Show the field the same scorecard the leadership team saw. Let them arrive at the conclusion before you announce the solution. When the field understands why the change is necessary, the change itself feels logical rather than arbitrary. Many companies invert this sequence and announce the change first, then scramble to explain why. That order makes the change feel punitive. Reverse it.

Week 10: Execute the first strip. Make the first structural change from the strip list. One change, not three. The field needs to absorb and process, not scramble. Pair the change with field support. Training. Office hours with leadership. Clear answers to the top 20 questions that will come up. Accept the short-term revenue dip. Do not flinch. A reignition in which the CEO can't tolerate a 10 percent revenue dip for two quarters won't survive a structural problem compounding at 5 percent per year.

Weeks 11 to 12: Measure the right signals. Do not measure revenue during the first 90 days. That is the one metric that will panic you into reversing the change before it can work. Measure customer acquisition rate week over week. If real customer acquisition is improving, the rebuild variable is working even when the revenue trendline doesn't show it yet. Measure new leader development. Are rank advancements happening in the first two levels? That signals a healthy pipeline forming. Measure the field-sentiment signals from your mid-level leaders. They will feel the momentum shift weeks before it shows up in the data. Prepare the next strip list for days 91 to 180. Reignition isn't a 90-day program. The first 90 days are a beginning. The full rebuild takes 18 to 36 months.

Why the sequence matters.

Reignition fails when the leadership team skips to week 10 and launches a public initiative without diagnosis, without stakeholder alignment, without stripping the practices that are accelerating the decline. The splashy launch in an unaligned company produces a two-week sugar rush followed by a deeper demoralization than existed before.

The 90-day sequence exists because every reignition has the same early failure mode: leaders want to skip diagnosis and jump to action. The sequence forces the hard discipline of completing the diagnosis before announcing anything, aligning stakeholders before the announcement is public, and executing the first strip before designing the growth initiative.

A CEO who has executed this sequence cleanly by day 90 has not reignited the company yet. The growth initiative hasn't even launched. But she has done something more valuable: she has prepared the foundation to receive a real reignition instead of a sugar rush. That is what separates the companies that recover from the ones that bounce once and fade.

THE BOTTOM LINE: Reignition requires four steps in order: identify your break path, diagnose the root cause, strip the broken foundation, then launch. Many companies skip to step four. That is why many reignition attempts fail.

The companies that reignite successfully are the ones that have the courage to diagnose without flinching, the discipline to strip before they build, and the patience to rebuild around the right variable. The ones that fail are the ones that skip the hard steps and go straight to the launch.

Chapter 18: The Quiet Compounders

The most valuable company in direct selling history never had a viral moment.

This book has spent most of its chapters diagnosing why companies crash. The data tilts toward the explosive and the collapsed because the explosive and the collapsed generate the cleanest mechanisms to study. LuLaRoe's rise and fall happened fast enough to isolate every variable. Vemma's regulatory collapse unfolded on a public timeline. MonaVie's trajectory lets you see product-culture fit and its shadow in the same decade.

But if you finish this book believing that the industry is mostly flash crashes and their aftermath, you've read half the story.

The other half is quieter. Slower. Less quotable. And far more instructive for an owner trying to build something that lasts.

The enemy in this chapter: confusing visibility with success. The companies you hear about most in this profession aren't the companies performing best over time. They are the companies performing loudest. A stadium event, a celebrity endorsement, a stock pop, a viral product launch. These create attention. Attention creates industry narrative. Industry narrative creates the mental list of "who's winning" that many leaders carry in their heads. That mental list is almost always wrong.

The companies actually winning the long game rarely appear on it.

THE QUIET COMPOUNDER PROFILE

Across the dataset, companies that sustained growth for 15 years or more share a profile that looks almost nothing like the explosive cases.

Melaleuca. Founded 1985. Privately held. Reports over $2 billion in annual revenue. Frank VanderSloot built a company that has grown in 34 of its 35 reported years. No stock listing. No IPO. No headline-grabbing products. No celebrity endorsers. No sudden viral moment. Just consistent compounding, category after category, for three and a half decades.

Amway. Founded 1959. The oldest surviving major direct selling company in the world. Reports $7.4 billion in revenue (2023). Weathered the 1979 FTC administrative law proceeding and a 1986 consent decree on earnings disclosure compliance, the collapse of its own distributor hierarchy in the 1990s, multiple regulatory reviews, and the full disruption of its original go-to-market channel. Still operating. Still profitable. Still family-controlled by the founding families.

PM International. Founded in Germany, 1993. Reports over €3 billion in revenue. Thirty-plus consecutive years of growth. Expanded into over 45 markets. Almost unknown in the US business press. Revered inside the European direct selling community as the cleanest sustained-momentum story in modern industry history.

Primerica. Founded 1977. Publicly traded (NYSE: PRI). Insurance and financial services distributed through an independent representative model. Revenue over $3 billion. Has grown in 20 of its last 22 years. Market capitalization higher than most "hot" direct selling brands at their peak.

Nature's Sunshine. Founded 1972. Publicly traded. Reports consistent growth. Survived the original herbal supplement boom, the GNC retail era, the e-commerce disruption, and the Amazon compression.

Shaklee. Founded 1956. One of the oldest wellness direct sellers still operating. Built on nutrition, personal care, and home cleaning products that have been reformulated across decades rather than replaced. Survived multiple ownership transitions and the entire evolution of the supplement category without the crisis moments that mark most of its contemporaries.

USANA. Founded 1992. Publicly traded on the New York Stock Exchange. Revenue approaching $900 million with audited financial disclosures every quarter. Operates in more than 20 markets. The fact that its numbers are verifiable quarterly, and that it has remained consistently profitable across multiple industry cycles, makes USANA one of the cleanest examples of sustained compounding available in the public record.

Seven companies. Zero flash crashes. Zero major regulatory collapses. Zero founder-dependency crises. A combined 340+ years of continuous operation.

What do they have in common?

FOUR PATTERNS ACROSS THE QUIET COMPOUNDERS

Pattern one: product-led, not opportunity-led. Every one of these companies leads with the product, not the compensation plan. When a distributor describes Melaleuca to a friend, she talks about the cleaning products, the laundry detergent, the vitamins. When she describes Primerica, she talks about term insurance replacing whole life. The comp plan exists. People earn money. But the comp plan isn't the pitch. The product is the pitch. This single positioning choice shapes everything downstream, from who joins to what they sell to why customers stay.

Pattern two: customer ratios that would embarrass many companies in the dataset. Melaleuca reports that roughly 70% of its volume comes from preferred customers, not distributors. Amway's recent US restructuring moved aggressively toward customer-dominant volume. Primerica's financial services model is fundamentally a retail business, with distributors earning commissions on products sold to real policyholders. These companies didn't stumble into healthy ratios. They engineered them, often decades before the rest of the industry understood that ratios were the metric that mattered.

Pattern three: founder discipline over founder celebrity. Frank VanderSloot, Rich DeVos, Jay Van Andel, Rolf Sorg of PM International. None of them became the personal brand of the company in the way that some founders have. None of them built their identity around stage performances, personal social media followings, or celebrity lifestyle signaling. They built companies that ran on systems and succession, not on their personal charisma. Melaleuca's transition from VanderSloot to Jerry Felton in May 2022, after 37 years with VanderSloot at the helm, happened without a narrative collapse. Amway has transitioned through multiple generations of the DeVos and Van Andel families. Founder discipline creates companies that survive their founders. Founder celebrity often doesn't.

Pattern four: boring consistency over dramatic reinvention. The quiet compounders rarely chase the new thing. Melaleuca has sold essentially the same core product categories for 30 years, with incremental expansion. Amway's top products today are descended from products that existed in the 1970s. PM International has reformulated its lead product FitLine more than a dozen times but has never abandoned it. This looks boring from the outside. It is. Which is exactly the point. Boring is what 30 years of compounding looks like.

THE EQUAL AND OPPOSITE

Quiet compounding has its own shadow, and leaders who want to imitate the pattern need to see it clearly.

The shadow of slow growth is recruiting fatigue. When a company grows 8% a year instead of 80%, field excitement wanes. The people who joined to build a fast fortune discover they're building a slow business. Some of them leave for whatever looks hotter. The quiet compounders tolerate this. They know their field is self-selecting over time toward distributors who value durability over speed. But the transition period is painful, and it costs the company talent along the way.

The shadow of product focus is missed category opportunities. Melaleuca has stayed in home, personal care, and wellness for decades while trillion-dollar opportunities have opened and closed in categories it chose not to enter. That discipline has costs. The companies that chase every opportunity sometimes catch a generational wave. The companies that stay disciplined watch those waves from the shore. Quiet compounders accept the missed opportunity as the price of not making the wrong bet.

The shadow of founder discipline is organizational predictability. The quiet compounders aren't glamorous places to work. They don't generate the industry buzz that attracts ambitious executives from outside. They promote from within, reward tenure, and move slowly on personnel decisions. This produces remarkable continuity and also produces a certain blandness that newer companies sometimes exploit to poach talent. The tradeoff is real. These companies accept it.

The shadow of boring consistency is vulnerability to genuine category disruption. Quiet compounders are built to weather incremental shifts, not structural breaks. When a category gets disrupted at the molecular level, as weight management was by GLP-1 drugs, even the most disciplined operator inside that category faces existential pressure. Discipline protects against many risks. It doesn't protect against the entire category changing.

PATTERN RECOGNITION FROM DSN DATA

The Direct Selling News top 100 tracks companies over time. The signal in that data isn't the ranking at any single point. The signal is persistence. The companies that appear on the list year after year, growing slowly and consistently, are the quiet compounders. The companies that rocket up the list one year and drop off three years later are the flash crashes this book has been studying.

Scan those lists across five-year windows and you'll see the pattern clearly. The top ten in 2015 included multiple companies that are now defunct or a fraction of their peak. The top ten in 2020 looked different. The top ten in 2025 looks different again. But a specific set of names appears in every one of those snapshots. Those are the companies to learn from if you want to build something that lasts.

In the masterminds I run with top earners, I see another pattern that has emerged consistently. The distributors who have earned seven figures for a decade or longer are disproportionately concentrated at the quiet compounder companies. Not exclusively. But disproportionately. The companies that produce income stability at the top tend to produce income stability throughout the organization. The companies that produce explosive income for a few years tend to produce short careers for most.

THE PATTERN: COMPANIES THAT DO NOT GENERATE EMERGENCIES

One pattern is consistent across every quiet compounder in the dataset. They don't generate emergency conversations. Their data isn't confusing. Their ratios aren't alarming. Their field isn't melting down. They have systems that surface problems early, and they have the discipline to act on the signals before the problems compound.

The companies that generate the loudest strategic conversations are running the other kind of business. Fast growth, alarming ratios, field unrest, unclear attribution. The urgency of the conversation is usually proportional to the acceleration of the problem. Companies that ran too hot are reading the ratios and realizing the foundation is thin. Companies that just lost a major leader are trying to diagnose what broke. Companies that just received a letter from a state attorney general are trying to understand which dominoes they missed.

Melaleuca, PM International, and Amway don't produce these emergencies. Not because they're perfect, but because their structural design absorbs problems before they cascade. The customer foundation buffers the volatility. The decision infrastructure catches the early signals. The leadership culture treats slow steady progress as the goal rather than the consolation prize.

If you're an owner reading this book, that's the company you're trying to become, rather than the company that runs hot and needs rescue. The company that runs steady and never generates the emergency.

THE FRAMEWORK: THE QUIET COMPOUNDER AUDIT

If you want to evaluate your company against the quiet compounder profile, answer five questions with real data. Each question is a yes or no, and the scoring is direct.

One: When a distributor pitches your company to a friend, is the primary pitch the product or the opportunity? If you don't know the answer, survey your top 100 distributors and ask them to describe their first 60 seconds of a company introduction. Count how many lead with product.

Two: What percentage of your volume comes from customers who have never been enrolled in the compensation plan? If you can't answer this in a board meeting, you're not yet running the playbook that the quiet compounders have been running for decades.

Three: Does your founder's personal brand exceed your company's brand in public search volume, social media following, or industry recognition? If yes, your company has a succession problem you may not yet be able to see.

Four: How many of your top ten products today existed in some form five years ago? If fewer than six, you're optimizing for novelty rather than compounding.

Five: In the last three years, how many times has your leadership team made a major strategic shift in response to a competitor's move? If more than once, you're being shaped by the market rather than shaping your own position.

Scoring.

Five yes answers in the quiet compounder direction (product-led pitch, high customer ratio, company brand exceeds founder brand, stable product line, infrequent reactive shifts) means you're structurally aligned with the pattern that produces 15+ year compounding. Execute the playbook you're already running. Do not chase the spike.

Three or four yes answers means you're close but carrying specific vulnerabilities. Identify which questions you answered no on and determine whether the gap is a strategic choice or a strategic mistake.

Two or fewer yes answers means your company is built on the explosive pattern, not the compounder pattern. That isn't a verdict. Some explosive companies mature into quiet compounders over time. But it's a diagnostic. You should know which game you're playing.

THE VISION

Imagine a company that has grown for 30 straight years without a single headline moment.

No IPO. No celebrity spokesperson. No stadium launches. No viral products. Just steady category leadership, consistent customer retention, predictable field behavior, and the kind of quarterly board meetings where revenue is slightly up, margins are stable, and the most interesting topic is the upcoming product reformulation.

From the outside, that company looks boring. It doesn't generate the industry buzz. It doesn't dominate the "who's hot" conversations at the annual convention circuit. Its founder isn't on the keynote rotation at industry events.

From the inside, that company is the dream.

Its distributors have been building for 15 years. Their incomes are predictable. Their retention is high. Their children are now distributors too. The top earners aren't chasing the next opportunity because they have no reason to. The front-line sellers aren't burning out because the pace is sustainable. The executive team isn't managing crisis after crisis because the systems surface problems early and the discipline addresses them quickly.

That is what quiet compounding buys you. Not glory. Continuity. Generational income. The kind of business that your grandchildren could still be running.

The flash crash companies in this book are remembered for how high they went and how fast they fell. The quiet compounders aren't remembered because they never stopped. The absence of the story is the story.

That is the company this book has been teaching you how to build.

A DEEP DIVE: MELALEUCA

Frank VanderSloot founded Melaleuca in 1985. The company sells wellness, cleaning, and personal care products through a direct marketing model. It has grown in 34 of its 35 reported years. Revenue exceeded $2 billion by the late 2010s. The company has never gone public, never been acquired, and never had a year that generated a crisis-tier news story.

This is how that happened.

VanderSloot built Melaleuca around a specific architectural decision that almost no other direct selling company has duplicated. The compensation plan pays primarily on consumable products that real customers reorder every month. Not on starter kits. Not on qualification purchases. Not on large one-time orders. The math only works if a significant percentage of what ships every month is going to people who are using the product, consuming it, and reordering because they want more.

That single decision cascades into everything downstream. The company's field incentive structure is aligned with customer acquisition and customer retention, because those are the behaviors that generate durable earnings. The product line expands into more categories that customers reorder (laundry detergent, vitamins, skincare, essential oils, cleaning supplies) rather than into one-time purchases with higher margins. The compliance stance is naturally conservative because the business model doesn't require aggressive recruiting velocity to sustain growth.

The cultural result is that Melaleuca doesn't feel like a traditional direct selling company to its customers. A high percentage of Melaleuca buyers are preferred customers who never recruit anyone and never build a business. They buy the products because they use them. They stay with the company because the products perform and the reordering is convenient. This customer foundation produces revenue stability that makes Melaleuca's compounding possible.

The shadow of this approach is that Melaleuca's growth has been slower than direct selling companies that optimize for recruiting velocity. The company has never had a Facebook party era, a TikTok explosion, a stadium convention with 80,000 people. That slower pace has cost it some talent over the decades to companies that were growing faster at a given moment. It has also meant that Melaleuca is less visible in the industry narrative than companies a tenth its size.

The tradeoff has been worth it. The companies that outgrew Melaleuca in any given five-year window almost all eventually collapsed or declined. Melaleuca is still here. Still growing. Still privately owned. Still producing income for hundreds of thousands of customers and consultants. The boring math compounded over four decades into one of the largest privately held consumer products companies in the country.

VanderSloot stepped back as CEO in May 2022, after 37 years leading the company, and handed the role to Jerry Felton, who had previously served as President of Melaleuca International and had been inside the company for years. The transition was executed without a narrative collapse or field disruption, because the company hadn't been built on the founder's charisma. It had been built on a product model that worked whether VanderSloot was at the top of every convention stage or not.

The lesson for owners reading this book isn't that every company should copy Melaleuca's exact model. The lesson is that durable compounding requires an architectural decision about what the business is actually selling. Melaleuca sells consumable products that real people reorder. That choice has shaped every decision for 40 years, and the compounding followed.

A NON-DIRECT-SELLING PARALLEL: COSTCO

The same pattern appears outside direct selling in one of the most durable retail companies in the world. Costco was founded in 1983. Forty-one years of continuous operation. Nearly 900 warehouses globally. Over $240 billion in annual revenue. A membership renewal rate above 90% that has held consistent for decades.

Jim Sinegal, the founder, built Costco around a specific architectural constraint. Gross margin on products would be capped at 14%, significantly below the 25 to 50% typical in retail. This constraint forced the company to make money on membership fees rather than markup. Which forced the company to deliver genuine value per visit. Which created customer loyalty that competitors couldn't match. Which made the membership fee easy to renew year after year.

The constraint became the engine. The 14% margin cap wasn't a marketing slogan. It was a structural limit written into the company's operating philosophy. Executives who tried to push margins higher were overruled. The board pushed back when proposals threatened the cap. The shareholders who understood the model stopped asking about margin expansion because they understood that margin restraint was what produced Costco's competitive moat.

The parallel to Melaleuca is exact. Both companies made a structural decision that limited their short-term growth ceiling. Melaleuca limited itself to consumable products that customers would reorder. Costco limited itself to 14% margins. Both constraints produced slower growth than competitors who optimized for speed. Both constraints produced durability that competitors who optimized for speed couldn't duplicate.

The quiet compounders in both industries share this pattern. They build a constraint into the model that forces genuine customer value, limits short-term maximization, and compounds over decades into a business that competitors can't easily replicate.

What is your company's structural constraint? If you don't have one, you're optimizing for speed. The quiet compounders optimize for durability. The difference shows up in the fifteenth year.

EVOLUTION WITHOUT LOSING FOCUS

There is a question that doesn't get asked enough in this industry, and it's one of the most important questions a CEO will face over a decade of operation. How do you evolve a company without losing the focus that made the company work in the first place?

This is one of the hardest balances in business strategy. Every long-term company faces it. The cultural definition of insanity is doing the same thing over and over and expecting different results. But the cultural reality of business failure is that many companies aren't consistent enough. They pivot the flagship product story every eighteen months. They chase the latest category trend. They redesign the comp plan three years in a row. They confuse motion for progress. The team never has time to actually master the message before it changes.

The pattern across the long-term winners in the dataset is different. They commit to a flagship product story for a minimum of three years and ideally five. They give the system, the field training, the customer testimonials, the duplication tools, and the cultural narrative time to actually mature. They understand that launching a product is the easy part. Making the launch work over the long term requires relentless focus, repetition, and culture-building that takes years to develop.

The discipline is to hold the flagship narrative steady while introducing supporting products that reinforce the same story. doTERRA's essential oils flagship is still the brand's central narrative, but the company has evolved to include nutrition products, weight management, and supplements that connect back to the wellness lifestyle the oils represent. The flagship story didn't change. The product line expanded. The duplication system stayed similar. The field didn't have to relearn how to share the brand every two years.

Melaleuca followed the same pattern across decades. The flagship has always been wellness products that families use and reorder. Over time the line expanded into beauty, nutrition, and home essentials. The expansion was always in service of the same flagship narrative, not in replacement of it. The duplication story for a new representative looks recognizably similar to what it looked like fifteen years ago, even though the product portfolio has more than tripled.

The companies that struggle with evolution typically make one of two mistakes. They either freeze the product line entirely and let it become irrelevant as customer needs change, or they constantly chase new flagship narratives that confuse the field and reset the duplication clock every cycle. Neither produces compounding. The first produces stagnation. The second produces churn.

The discipline of focused evolution requires distinguishing between flagship products and supporting products. A flagship product is the central reason customers and distributors are choosing your company. The duplication story is built around it. The training is built around it. The income testimonials feature it. Changing the flagship is a high-stakes decision that resets everything underneath. A supporting product is something that fits into the existing flagship narrative without requiring the field to rebuild its messaging. New supporting products can be introduced regularly without disrupting the cultural momentum the company has built. Many companies confuse these two categories and treat every new product launch as a flagship reset, which creates constant churn in the field.

There are exceptions. Sometimes the market shifts hard enough that a flagship pivot is necessary. Netflix is a useful non-direct-selling example. The company built its early growth around DVDs by mail. By the late 2000s, Reed Hastings and the leadership team understood that the future was streaming, not physical media. Netflix attempted to spin off the DVD business into a separate brand called Qwikster in 2011. The execution was botched. Customers revolted. The company reversed the decision within weeks. But the underlying strategic insight was correct. The company eventually did pivot the flagship from DVDs to streaming, and the result was one of the most successful business transformations in modern corporate history. Sometimes the pivot is necessary. The Netflix lesson is that even when it's necessary, getting it right is hard, and the cost of getting it wrong publicly is severe. The pivot has to be earned by data and conviction, not chased because something newer looks shinier.

The probability data is clear. Companies that constantly switch flagship directions, on average, do not survive long enough to compound. Sure, you can find one or two exceptions where a relentless pivoter eventually got it right. Those are the exceptions, not the pattern. The companies that build durable momentum hold the flagship narrative through the storms. They give the system the runway it needs to actually work. Three-year minimum commitment. Five-year intention. Open to feedback. Willing to pivot when the data demands it. But never confusing pivoting with the constant low-grade churn that breaks the field's ability to master anything.

The relentless focus is what makes the launch actually work. Anyone can have a great launch event. The companies that compound have what comes after the launch. The years of repetition. The training that gets refined every quarter. The testimonials that build into a library. The story that becomes so familiar to the field that they tell it the same way at every kitchen table conversation. The cultural saturation that turns a product into an identity.

That is evolution without losing focus. Hold the flagship narrative. Expand the line in support of the narrative. Pivot only when the data demands it, not when boredom or trend-chasing tempts it. Give the system the time it needs to mature. The companies that hold this discipline produce the compounding curves that make this chapter possible.

THE BOTTOM LINE: The industry narrative is dominated by explosive companies because explosive companies generate the cleanest stories. The companies actually winning the long game rarely appear in the narrative. Study the quiet compounders. The frameworks in this book are optimized for their pattern, not the pattern of the companies that generate the loudest headlines.

Fast growth isn't the enemy. Fast growth is a windfall. The question is what you do with it. The companies that get a spike and reinvest it back into more spike chasing produce the flash crashes the dataset documents. The companies that get a spike and reinvest it into the foundation, the customer base, the operational infrastructure, the field development, the comp plan integrity, the compliance discipline, end up with both the spike revenue and the durability that compounds for the next two decades. Both kinds of companies had momentum. Only one kind kept it.

If your company catches fire, take the windfall. Run the play. But the discipline that separates the long-term winners from the headlines is what they did with the capital and the attention the spike gave them. They invested it back into the metrics this book has been telling you to track.

Real customer acquisition. Field development. Operational depth. Comp plan health. Cultural infrastructure. They didn't assume the spike was the foundation. They used the spike to build the foundation while the wind was at their back.

You aren't trying to choose between speed and longevity. You are trying to use the speed, when it comes, to build the company that's still here in twenty years.

Chapter 19: The Next Momentum Window

Every book that analyzes the past has an obligation to point at the future.

This one makes no claim to predict the future. Nobody in this industry has predicted it accurately in the last decade. The rise of Facebook parties wasn't predicted. The TikTok Shop explosion wasn't predicted. GLP-1 drugs breaking the weight management category wasn't predicted. The trust recession in direct selling was underestimated by nearly every executive who had to deal with it.

What I can do is identify the variables the momentum equation will have to solve for in the next three to five years. These aren't predictions. They are the incoming forces your leadership team needs to be tracking whether you want to or not.

The enemy in this chapter: planning the next three years using the playbook of the last ten.

FORCE ONE: THE AI-NATIVE COMMERCE SHIFT

The most underestimated variable in direct selling right now isn't which platform wins. It is how AI reshapes the basic unit of selling itself.

Three shifts are already visible. First, AI-generated content is collapsing the cost of production to near zero. A distributor can now create a week's worth of short-form video content in an hour using tools that cost less than $30 a month. This dramatically levels the playing field between the distributor with a production team and the distributor with a smartphone. It also dramatically reduces the signal value of "content effort" as a leadership differentiator. When everyone can produce, the scarcity shifts.

Second, AI shopping assistants are changing how people research and decide. Tools that compare products, check reviews, and surface alternatives in seconds are being built into browsers, phones, and operating systems. The distributor's traditional role as the trusted product explainer is being disintermediated for basic information. What remains is social proof, community, and personalized experience. None of that goes away. But the informational moat disappears.

Third, AI agents will eventually transact on behalf of consumers. The early versions are already live. When a customer tells an AI agent "I want to restock my vitamins," the agent will make a decision based on price, reviews, shipping speed, and availability. A premium direct selling price point that exists because of the comp plan overhead is exposed to scrutiny that a human customer might not have applied. This will pressure premium pricing in ways the industry hasn't yet modeled.

What this means for the five drivers.

Product-culture fit gets harder because AI accelerates cultural cycles. A product that catches a wave has 12 months, not 36. Platform disruption is ongoing as new AI-native platforms emerge faster than the industry can build capability on them. Leader migration accelerates because top leaders can now build personal brands independent of their company platform faster than ever before. Market expansion becomes cheaper because AI translation and localization tools reduce the cost of entering a new market by an order of magnitude. Compensation architecture comes under pressure because AI-assisted customer analytics expose exactly how much of your volume is qualification purchasing versus real demand.

Companies that treat AI as a side project will underperform. Companies that treat it as the new operating substrate will pull ahead.

This points to the single most important strategic shift the profession faces right now, and it deserves to be stated plainly. As pure product information gets commoditized by AI and search, the durable advantage moves from the product to what surrounds the product. A product can be copied in months. A unique ingredient buys a lead of weeks, not years, because the competition is fierce and everything ends up on a shelf or a marketplace eventually. What can't be copied quickly is community, coaching, accountability, and the personalized experience a strong field delivers. The companies that build a real people-based experience around the product own the one moat competitors can't replicate by next quarter. The strategic phrase worth putting on the wall is product plus service. The product is the reason to start. The service and the community are the reason to stay.

Here is the part the industry has to be honest about. That service layer isn't free to deliver. Real community, real coaching, and real accountability take an enormous amount of company resources and field energy. When brand partners spend hours coaching customers and holding them accountable, that's labor. When a company builds events, apps, training systems, and support infrastructure to make that experience happen, that's cost. A lot of people in this profession have been trained to treat community as a free add-on, the soft value that justifies the product price. That assumption is the trap. If the experience that drives retention is expensive to deliver but treated as though it costs nothing, two things break. The company strains under the resource load, and the field does the work without being compensated for it. That is the same misalignment that breaks comp plans, just wearing a friendlier face.

The companies that get this right treat the service layer as a real value exchange. The community has value, customers will pay for genuine community and coaching, and the cost of delivering it's funded rather than absorbed quietly. This isn't a call for every company to launch paid online coaching. The right structure depends entirely on the category. Weight management is the clearest example where comprehensive coaching is both expensive to deliver and something customers will pay a premium for, which is why the strongest weight management models build the coaching into the offer rather than giving away an unfunded service on top of a product. There are others. Financial services and legal services have always been priced as services. Longevity and health-optimization offerings are moving in the same direction. Most categories don't work this way today. In categories like skincare or essential oils, a separately priced coaching program is far less common, and for most companies the community shows up as retention, education, social proof, and belonging rather than as a line item the customer pays for directly. But less common isn't the same as impossible. If a company builds enough value into a system, there are always creative ways to make the economics work, and the operator who figures out how to do it in a category where it hasn't been done before may find an advantage nobody else has. The point isn't to declare which categories can monetize service and which can't. The point is to think clearly about the value and the cost. The mistake isn't failing to charge for coaching. The mistake is either pretending the experience costs nothing to deliver, or assuming there's only one way to monetize it. The principle holds across all of it. The experience has real value and real cost. Build it, fund it, compensate the people who deliver it, match the structure to your category, and stay open to the possibility that a model the industry hasn't tried yet is sitting in front of you. Companies that do this turn the one advantage AI can't commoditize into the foundation of the next decade.

FORCE TWO: THE CREATOR ECONOMY COLLISION

The direct selling industry has always believed it's in a different business than the creator economy. That belief is now wrong.

The creator economy produced over $100 billion in earnings for individual creators globally in 2024. A significant portion of those creators built followings around the same categories direct selling companies operate in: wellness, beauty, fitness, lifestyle, personal development. They built audiences without joining any company. They monetize through affiliate relationships, sponsorships, and direct product sales that cut out the multi-level structure entirely.

For a generation of ambitious people who would have joined a direct selling company in 2005, the creator economy is now the obvious alternative. It offers higher margins on personal effort, more brand control, no downline management, no monthly qualification requirements, and no industry stigma. The raw talent pool that direct selling used to recruit from is increasingly choosing the creator path instead.

This collision cuts both directions. Some direct selling companies are responding by building creator-friendly comp structures. Zero qualification volume. High customer bonuses. No downline pressure. Essentially repackaging the product as an affiliate opportunity with benefits. Other companies are being actively undercut by creators who sell retail alternatives to the same customer base at lower prices with more transparency.

The companies that will win the next decade either fully integrate creator-economy dynamics into their distributor model or position themselves clearly as a different offering. The companies that lose will be the ones who split the difference, maintaining a traditional direct selling structure while claiming to be creator-friendly.

FORCE THREE: THE PEPTIDE REVOLUTION AND THE WEIGHT MANAGEMENT RESHAPE

The weight management category inside direct selling won't return to its pre-GLP-1 shape, and trying to operate as though the shift is temporary is the most expensive mistake a company in this category can make. But this isn't just about GLP-1s. GLP-1 receptor agonists are the most visible piece of a broader peptide and pharmaceutical trend that's reshaping wellness consumer behavior more generally. The smart strategic position for the direct selling profession is to integrate the trend rather than fight it.

Medifast's revenue dropped from $1.6 billion at peak to $385.8 million in 2025 per reported financials. Herbalife's weight-focused business has seen measurable compression. Isagenix, Plexus, It Works, and every other company in the category has felt the shift. The drugs don't go away. The patents expire. The drugs get cheaper. The drugs get more effective. The drugs become injectables, then pills, then generics. Consumer access expands. Compliance improves.

This permanently changes the economics of the direct selling weight management category. The drugs don't eliminate all consumers. Some people can't take them, will not take them, or prefer non-pharmaceutical solutions. There remains a market. But the size of the addressable market is reset, and the price point at which direct selling weight management products can compete is compressed.

The companies in this category have three options. Reposition the product line toward benefits that GLP-1 can't replicate (community, coaching, muscle preservation during weight loss, maintenance after the drug cycle ends, and the broader peptide and wellness category that GLP-1 is part of). Diversify out of weight management into adjacent wellness categories with better structural economics. Or slowly shrink as the category compresses. Herbalife is executing option one through its Nutrition Club model. LifeVantage demonstrated what option one can produce when its MindBody GLP-1 System launch generated a Q2 fiscal 2025 spike of $67.8 million in revenue, up 31.3% year over year. Others are executing option two. Most aren't executing anything and will default to option three.

If your company is in weight management and your leadership team hasn't had an explicit, data-driven conversation about which option you're choosing, you're already behind.

FORCE FOUR: THE GENERATIONAL TRUST COLLAPSE

Every survey of Gen Z and younger Millennial attitudes toward direct selling shows the same pattern. Dramatically lower trust than previous generations. Dramatically higher skepticism of compensation plan claims. Dramatically lower willingness to join. This isn't an inconvenience. It is the most important long-term force in the industry, and many companies aren't treating it as one.

The trust collapse happened for three reasons. First, the internet made every historical regulatory action and company collapse permanently searchable. A 19-year-old considering joining a company today can read twenty years of documented failures in an afternoon. Second, social media amplified the voices of people who left direct selling companies unhappy. Anti-MLM content on TikTok and YouTube reaches tens of millions of viewers. Third, the income disclosure statements, which federal pressure required companies to publish, made the earnings reality impossible to hide.

The companies building for the next decade understand that they're recruiting into a different environment than the one that built Amway and Mary Kay. They can't rely on the opportunity narrative alone. They have to earn trust through transparency, through product performance, through compensation plans that clearly reward customer acquisition, and through compliance that exceeds what regulators require rather than just meeting the minimum.

The Zinzino model is informative here. The company publishes actual results from its blood-test product. It requires real customer acquisition. It operates publicly on Nasdaq First North, which means audited numbers are part of the trust signal. That combination is attracting a generation of distributors who wouldn't consider a traditional direct selling company. Other companies will have to find their own version of that transparency strategy or lose the next generation of builders.

FORCE FIVE: THE REGULATORY CONSOLIDATION

The FTC's stance toward direct selling has hardened progressively since 2015 and shows no signs of softening. State attorneys general are increasingly coordinated. International regulators are following the US lead. The Neora victory, which opened Chapter 5 of this book, is important specifically because it established that companies with genuine customer foundations can beat the government at trial. But it doesn't signal a regulatory retreat. It signals a higher evidentiary bar for the government, which means companies will be given more opportunity to operate but will face more scrutiny when they do.

The consolidation to watch: state-level enforcement. California, New York, Illinois, and Washington have all increased direct selling oversight. The federal model requires substantial resources and long timelines. State action can be faster and more targeted. Some observers believe the next decade will be shaped more by state AG actions than by federal FTC cases.

The regulatory implication for the momentum equation is that compliance becomes a momentum driver in its own right. Companies that build genuine compliance infrastructure, not as a cost center but as a strategic asset, will have a material competitive advantage. They can grow faster because they can operate in markets where less compliant competitors get shut down. They can attract better leaders because leaders increasingly factor regulatory exposure into their choice of company. They can command premium valuations because acquirers and investors price regulatory risk into every transaction.

FORCE SIX: THE PLATFORM-NATIVE GENERATION

The top earners of the coming decade are currently somewhere between 22 and 32 years old. They were teenagers when Instagram launched. They grew up on TikTok. They don't have memories of the home party era or the hotel meeting era. Their default communication medium is short video. Their default buying behavior is creator-driven. Their relationship to authority is different. Their relationship to patience is different. Their relationship to ownership of a downline is different.

Every company planning for the next ten years has to answer a simple question: what does your company look like when the field leaders at the top of the organization are people who have never run a hotel meeting, never done a three-way call, and never used a comp plan flipbook?

Some companies are already planning for this. Others aren't. The ones that aren't will discover a few years from now that their entire field leadership pipeline is aging out faster than it's being replaced, and that the younger cohort they were counting on never actually bought into the traditional playbook.

THE CULTURAL BACKDROP UNDERNEATH ALL SIX FORCES

There is a larger story behind the six forces in this chapter. Something structural is happening to human interaction itself that every direct selling owner needs to understand, because it shapes how the entire next decade will unfold.

People around the world are getting lonelier. They are interacting with real people less. They are spending more time on screens. The pandemic accelerated a shift that was already in motion across most developed markets, and the shift hasn't reversed.

The data is serious enough that the US Surgeon General issued a formal advisory on it in 2023 titled Our Epidemic of Loneliness and Isolation. The advisory found that approximately half of US adults report experiencing measurable loneliness. Social isolation increases the risk of premature death by 29% and loneliness by 26%, an effect the advisory compared to smoking up to 15 cigarettes a day. The sharpest decline in social interaction shows up among young people ages 15 to 24, who reported 70% less in-person time with their friends than previous cohorts. Average weekly social time across all US adults fell from 12.8 hours in 2010 to 6.5 hours in 2019, and to roughly 5 hours by 2024. Adults across most developed markets now spend an average of six to seven hours a day on digital media. In the U.S., one in three adults reports being online almost constantly. Similar patterns hold in the U.K., Australia, much of Europe, and major Asian markets.

I cite these statistics because they tell you something every strategic planner needs to understand. A generation is growing up with less real human interaction than any generation in modern memory. Face-to-face time is down. Community attachment is down. Friendships are more likely to live on a screen than in a room. Young people report record levels of loneliness. Adults report record levels of anxiety. The pandemic didn't create the trend. It accelerated a trend that was already reshaping how humans spend their hours.

Here is the strategic point. The fake thing never actually replaces the real thing. Scrolling a feed isn't a substitute for dinner with friends. A parasocial relationship with a creator isn't a substitute for a mentor who knows your name. A thousand followers isn't a substitute for five people who show up when something hard happens. The digital version feels cheaper and more convenient in the moment, but it doesn't produce the same thing the real version produces. And at some point, the accumulated deficit starts showing up as a mental health crisis, as civic disengagement, as a generation that has never learned what real community feels like.

Every direct selling owner should be paying attention to this, because it reframes the entire strategic landscape for the next decade.

In a world where real human interaction is becoming rarer, real human interaction becomes more valuable, not less. The direct selling model is one of the few remaining commercial structures in modern life that requires real human relationships to work. A distributor can't sell through a warm market without having a warm market. A leader can't build a team without knowing the people on it. A convention can't create a culture without people standing in the same room. The entire model is built on something the rest of the economy is losing, and losing fast.

That isn't a threat. That is an advantage. The companies that understand this will position themselves as the commercial version of what an entire generation is starting to realize it needs. Real community. Real mentorship. Real relationships. Real belonging. None of it simulated. The actual thing.

But, and this is where the advocacy argument has to be honest, the community advantage only matters if you pair it with the other two legs of the stool. You still need a great product. You still need a compensation plan that drives the right human behavior. You still need operational infrastructure that doesn't collapse under the weight of growth. Community alone doesn't build a durable company. Community plus a great product plus a strategic comp plan plus operational discipline builds one. The community is the amplifier. The product is the substance. The comp plan is the engine. Miss any of the three and the opportunity doesn't materialize.

POSITIONING IS HALF OF PRODUCT MOMENTUM

There is one more variable that has to be made explicit, because it underlies every product momentum story in the coming decade. It isn't the product itself. It is the positioning of the product.

Look at what has actually been moving in consumer markets in the last five years.

The Stanley tumbler story from Chapter 7 is the canonical modern example. Same hundred-year-old product, new positioning, new storytellers, ten times the revenue in four years. That pattern is repeating across consumer categories.

Weighted vests existed for three decades as a niche fitness item. Then fitness creators started telling the story of rucking, load training, and longevity protocols. The category exploded.

Saunas have existed for centuries. Then a wave of health influencers started telling the story of cold plunges, heat exposure, and cellular recovery. Now you can't walk into a wellness center without seeing one.

Red light therapy has been studied in medical research for decades. Then the positioning shifted from clinical device to home wellness tool. Now it sits on bathroom counters across the country.

Infrared. Sonos. Grounding mats. Creatine. Electrolytes. Magnesium glycinate. None of these products are new. Almost none of them contain fundamentally new science. What changed is that the right people started telling the right story at the right cultural moment, and the positioning unlocked demand that had always been latent in the product.

The same pattern plays out in direct selling. Nu Skin's AP-24 whitening toothpaste has been in the product line for over twenty years. For most of that time it was a steady contributor to the skincare portfolio. Then a wave of field leaders repositioned the story around teeth whitening in a social media era where everyone was suddenly paying attention to their smile on camera. The product didn't change. The positioning did. And the result was a surge in sales for a twenty-year-old product.

The lesson is the same as the Stanley lesson. The product and the positioning are two different variables. A great product with bad positioning goes nowhere. A mediocre product with great positioning still fails over time. A great product with great positioning, delivered at the right cultural moment by people who know how to tell the story, is what creates momentum.

Every direct selling executive planning the next decade should be asking two questions about every major product in their line. Is this product good enough to sustain demand once customers try it? And is it positioned in a way that connects to what the culture is paying attention to right now?

If the answer to the first question is no, repositioning won't save you. You need a better product.

If the answer to the first question is yes but the answer to the second is no, you're sitting on latent demand that a repositioning could release. That is one of the cheapest momentum wins available to any established company. The product already exists. The manufacturing is already there. The supply chain is already built. What changes is the story, the presentation, and the people who are telling it.

Some of the most significant momentum shifts in the coming decade will come from existing products being repositioned for the current cultural moment, not from new products being launched from scratch. The companies that understand this will get more leverage from their existing catalog than companies that only believe in new product launches.

THE VISION

Imagine a company built from the ground up for the next decade instead of the last one.

Its compensation plan rewards real customer acquisition above everything else. Its distributor training teaches content creation, short-form video, and community building, not hotel meeting scripts. Its leadership development is designed for people who have never sat in a 500-person basic training. Its product line is transparent, tested, and marketed with the same integrity standards a regulated industry would require. Its field communication happens on platforms the leadership team actually uses, not the ones the founder used in 1995.

That company isn't waiting for the next Facebook party revolution to create momentum for it. That company is engineering the variables that will produce momentum in the environment that's forming now, not the environment that existed a decade ago. When the AI-native commerce shift fully arrives, that company is already positioned. When the generational trust collapse bottoms out and younger builders start looking again for a legitimate alternative to the creator economy, that company looks different from every other direct selling option on their screen.

The companies that will own the next decade are being built right now, by leadership teams that are willing to solve for the equation as it's forming, not as it existed a decade ago.

THE CEILING QUESTION

A question that doesn't get asked often, but that I've thought hard about over the years, deserves direct treatment in this chapter. Why has no direct selling company exceeded roughly $12 billion in annual revenue? Amway has been the high-water mark for sixty years, peaking at $11.8 billion in 2013 and never crossing the $12 billion line. Herbalife topped out under $6 billion. Nu Skin under $4 billion. Mary Kay around $3 billion. Meanwhile, single Costco warehouses do more in annual revenue than most entire direct selling companies. Apple does Amway's annual revenue every two weeks. The question matters because if there's a structural ceiling, the strategic implications shape everything an owner builds toward.

There are at least four constraints that contribute to the ceiling, and any honest analysis has to name them.

First, recruiting-dependent growth creates local network friction over time. The traditional model depends on distributors enrolling other distributors, who then enroll from their own networks. At extraordinary velocity, the overlap between sponsor networks grows, which is why mature companies often see slower new-distributor intake even while revenue remains healthy. This isn't customer saturation. Customer demand is effectively unlimited. New consumers enter every market every day, and every mass-market category has room for additional brands. The friction is specific to how quickly a recruiting-led model can expand its builder base within the same geographic and social pools. Companies that rely mostly on new-distributor velocity for growth hit this friction earlier. Companies that build strong customer-first economics can scale dramatically further, because they're competing for consumer attention, not for the limited time of other builders.

Second, the compensation overhead is a real structural cost that affects pricing flexibility. A company paying 30 to 50% of revenue to its field has limited room to compete aggressively on price in mass-market categories where the consumer compares to retail alternatives. The compensation cost is part of how the model produces field income at scale, which is a legitimate strategic choice. But it does limit the categories where the model can compete on pure price.

Third, regulatory friction increases with scale. Every billion in revenue increases the regulatory attention on the company. The compliance infrastructure required to operate at $5 billion is qualitatively different from the infrastructure required at $500 million. Some of the largest opportunities for category expansion are in product areas with the highest regulatory complexity, which limits the categories a scaled direct selling company can credibly enter.

Fourth, the trust ceiling makes mass-market positioning harder. Direct selling carries reputational baggage that compresses the addressable market for any given product. A consumer who would happily buy a wellness product at Whole Foods may decline the same product if it's sold through a distributor model. That trust gap is a real ceiling, and it has hardened in the last decade as anti-MLM content has scaled on social media.

Those constraints are real. But they're not necessarily permanent. And the discipline that breaks them isn't what most people expect.

In nearly every domain where I've watched people produce extraordinary outcomes, the pattern is the same. They don't have a special trick. They don't have a hidden system. They do the basics better than everyone else, and they do them more consistently. Big vision matters. Audacious goals matter. But the company that breaks the $12 billion ceiling won't get there by skipping steps. It will get there by executing the fundamentals at a higher level of consistency than any company before it has executed them, and by stacking that consistency year over year over year. Steady progress. Real customers acquired one at a time. Field development that doesn't cut corners. Operational excellence that holds at scale. Compliance discipline that never relaxes. Comp plan integrity that doesn't get gamed in the name of a quarter's growth. Boring work, executed at world-class standard, compounded across a decade. That is the pattern. That is what breaks the ceiling, if anything does.

In 1954, Roger Bannister broke the four-minute mile. For decades, scientists and athletes had said the four-minute mile was physiologically impossible. The human body couldn't sustain that pace. Then Bannister did it. Within two years, dozens of other runners had also broken the barrier. The ceiling had been a story humans told themselves, not a physical law.

The $12 billion ceiling in this industry might be similar. Or it might be a real structural limit that will hold. The honest answer is that we'll not know until someone breaks it, and we'll not understand what made the breaking possible until they do.

What this book argues is that the ceiling question is the wrong one for many owners reading this. Instead of asking "how do I become the company that breaks $20 billion?" the better frame is "what kind of company am I trying to build, and have I designed for that ambition with full awareness of what the model permits?"

Some owners will read this book and decide they want to build a $100 million company that compounds for thirty years and produces durable income for thousands of families. That is an extraordinary outcome. It is also achievable inside the model with full alignment to the frameworks in this book.

Some will decide they want to build a $1 to $3 billion company with sustained category leadership for decades. Also achievable. The quiet compounders covered in the previous chapter prove it.

Some will decide they want to be the one who breaks the ceiling. That is a different kind of ambition, and it requires the architectural decisions described in the rest of this chapter, executed with discipline that hasn't yet been demonstrated by any direct selling company in history. It is possible that someone reading this book is the person who will do it. The framework here is one of the inputs that might make it possible.

What I'll say with conviction is that breaking the ceiling, if it happens, will not happen by repeating the playbook that built the existing $10 to $12 billion companies. The path to $20 billion doesn't look like a faster version of the path that got Amway to $11.8 billion. It will require building something architecturally different. The variables in this book will be part of the equation. The new variables, the ones not yet visible, will be the rest.

The ceiling holds until it doesn't. The owners who are designing today for the company that breaks it are the ones we'll be writing case studies about a decade from now.

THE COMPANY OF THE NEXT DECADE: A CONCRETE PROFILE

Let me describe what the winning company of the next decade actually looks like, not as prediction but as architecture. A company built from the ground up for the six forces described above would have specific features that most current direct selling companies don't have.

Its compensation plan pays on customer volume above almost everything else. New distributor enrollments generate modest upfront bonuses. The serious income flows from the customer base the distributor builds and retains. The qualification requirements are low or zero. Personal volume requirements have been replaced by customer volume requirements. The plan is transparent, mathematically simple, and easy for a new distributor to understand in under five minutes. If a 23-year-old with a TikTok following asks "how do I make money here," the answer is clear: acquire and keep customers.

Its product line is anchored in categories where AI disintermediation is low. Personal experience matters. Coaching matters. Community matters. Physical results matter. The product delivers something that a chatbot and an Amazon page can't deliver, which isn't the product itself but the experience, relationship, and accountability wrapped around it. The pricing is defensible on its own merits, not subsidized by comp plan margins that would collapse if held to retail scrutiny.

Its technology stack is native to short-form video, creator economics, and AI-assisted content creation. Distributors can produce on-brand content in minutes using tools the company provides. The customer relationship management system tracks retention, predicts churn, and surfaces interventions before customers leave. Commission calculations are transparent and real-time. Compliance monitoring is automated, surfacing questionable claims before they become violations rather than after.

Its leadership development is designed for people who have never run a hotel meeting, never made a three-way call, and never seen a comp plan flipbook. The training teaches digital relationship building, community facilitation, personal content creation, and retention coaching. The aspirational income stories featured in training materials come from distributors who built through these behaviors, not from 1980s-style stage speeches translated into social media.

Its compliance posture exceeds what regulators require. Every claim is substantiated. Every income example comes with context. The company voluntarily publishes cohort retention data, average customer lifetime value, and typical participant earnings. Transparency is treated as a competitive weapon rather than a regulatory burden, because the transparency itself attracts the kind of distributor who cares about building something legitimate and the kind of customer who has been burned before and values honesty.

Its brand positioning is distinct from traditional direct selling imagery. No Lamborghini pictures. No mansion tours. No stage photos of "millionaires" who are actually net negative after buying qualification volume. The marketing is understated, evidence-based, and designed to attract builders who would have chosen the creator economy over a traditional direct selling opportunity.

That company exists today in early form inside several organizations. Zinzino shows pieces of it. Neora shows pieces of it. Several smaller and newer companies are building toward the full profile. None of them have executed every element yet, because the infrastructure required is expensive and the cultural shift inside existing companies is slow.

The companies that build out this full profile in the next three to five years will pull dramatically ahead of the competition. The companies that try to retrofit this profile onto a traditional recruiting-first model will struggle because the two models are architecturally incompatible. You can't add transparent customer-first economics on top of a comp plan designed for qualification purchasing velocity. The underlying math breaks.

WHAT THE INDUSTRY WILL LOOK LIKE

Three observations about where this leads. First, the number of billion-dollar direct selling companies will likely shrink in the next decade, not grow. The industry's aggregate revenue may hold or decline as companies in weight management and other disrupted categories compress, and as customers who would have bought through distributors increasingly buy elsewhere. This isn't a crisis. It is a correction to a sustainable size for the model.

Second, the companies that emerge as the new category leaders will look different from the ones that dominated 2010 through 2020. Some will be current companies that successfully pivoted. Some will be companies most readers haven't heard of yet, started in the last five years, operating below the industry radar until they reach a scale that forces attention.

Third, the profession's reputation will either recover or decline sharply based on whether the new generation of companies operates with genuine transparency or tries to repackage the old model in new language. If enough new companies build the customer-first architecture described above, the reputation recovers. If the industry keeps producing flash crashes that look exactly like the ones this book studies, the reputation collapses further and the regulatory environment continues to harden.

The choice the industry collectively makes about which path to take will be determined one company at a time by the decisions of specific leadership teams. Your leadership team is one of those. What you build will contribute to whichever outcome prevails.

THE BOTTOM LINE: The momentum equation itself doesn't change. Five drivers, three hard ratios, four phases of decline, regulatory and operational constraints. The variables remain constant. What changes is the weight, velocity, and behavior of each variable in response to AI, creator economics, GLP-1, generational trust, regulatory consolidation, and platform-native behavior.

The companies that solve for the next decade's version of the equation will build the next generation of durable momentum. The companies that solve for the 2019 version will become the case studies in the next version of this book.

Conclusion: What Momentum Is Actually For

The companies that won long-term were not the ones with the most momentum. They were the ones with The Underneath. Across the 53-company dataset, three things separated the companies that survived from the companies that didn't. Not five things. Not ten. Three. And they are simpler than you expect. 1. Real customer revenue above 50%. Not distributors buying to qualify. Real humans buying because they want the product. Neora at 80% beat the FTC in court. BurnLounge at 2.3% was shut down. The ratio is the dividing line. Above 50%, product business. Below 50%, product alibi. This is not a suggestion. It is the variable most consistently associated with long-term survival across the dataset. 2. Willingness to discipline growth. Every survivor said no to practices that would have generated faster growth. Amway implemented the 70% rule, the ten-customer rule, and a buyback policy in 1979. Those safeguards constrained recruiting velocity. They added friction to the enrollment process. They slowed growth. And they saved the company from the FTC at a time when the agency was looking to make an example of a direct selling company. That 1979 ruling came from an administrative law judge, who found that Amway's compensation system was based on actual product sales rather than recruitment. Herbalife disciplined its growth when it restructured after the FTC settlement. The company did not stop growing. It redirected how growth happened, tying compensation to documented retail customers rather than recruiting volume. The changes cost revenue in the short term. Leaders left. The field was disrupted. But the restructured foundation was sound. And the company is still worth nearly $5 billion. Neora disciplined its growth by building compliance programs that channeled field behavior toward real customer acquisition. The company could have grown faster with looser compliance. It chose to grow the right way instead of the fastest way. And when the FTC examined the business, the compliance infrastructure was part of the evidence that proved the company was legitimate. The companies that refused to discipline their growth, that optimized for speed at every decision point without investing in the customer foundation underneath it, that chose the aggressive comp plan over the sustainable one, that chose the recruiting sprint without building customer depth alongside it, are the ones in the decline dataset. Not all of them. But enough to make the pattern unmistakable. Disciplining growth is the hardest thing to do in direct selling. Not slowing it down. Channeling it. Growing as fast as you possibly can while simultaneously investing every available dollar into acquiring more real customers, retaining them longer, and increasing their average monthly spend. The entire culture celebrates growth. The stage celebrates growth. The income recognitions celebrate growth. The field demands growth. And they should. Growth is the lifeblood of this model. The discipline is not in how fast you grow. It is in making sure that the growth is building something real underneath it. That the customer floor is rising as fast as the revenue line. That every dollar of growth is backed by a dollar of genuine demand. The CEO who tells her field "we are going to grow as fast as we can AND we are going to invest heavily in customer acquisition and retention while we do it" is not constraining anything. She is building the kind of growth that survives. 3. A product with demand the comp plan amplifies, not manufactures. The Smoke Detector Test from Chapter 5. If you removed qualification purchasing tomorrow, what percentage of your volume would come from customers who want the product? The companies that survive long-term have products that people buy because they want the product, with the comp plan and the field amplifying that demand. The companies that crash have products where the comp plan's qualification structure is the dominant reason for purchasing, with the underlying customer demand too thin to sustain volume on its own once the qualification pressure is removed. BurnLounge gave us the answer with court-documented precision: 2.3% came from real product demand when recruiting rewards were removed. That is the extreme. But the principle applies on a spectrum. The higher the percentage of volume that comes from genuine customer demand independent of qualification purchasing, the more real the business is. The lower the percentage, the more fragile. doTERRA's essential oils are purchased by millions of customers who are not in the compensation plan. Herbalife's Nutrition Club customers show up every day to drink a shake and socialize. Mary Kay's cosmetics have genuine consumer demand that has sustained for over sixty years. LegalShield, formerly Pre-Paid Legal, sells legal access and identity theft protection services that people buy because they need a lawyer, not because a comp plan requires it. Founded in 1972, the company has now operated for over fifty years on customer demand that exists with or without the compensation plan. Members keep their legal subscriptions during economic downturns, after they leave the business opportunity, and through major life changes, because access to legal counsel is a need that does not go away. The product passes the Smoke Detector Test by definition. Nobody subscribes to legal protection to qualify for a rank. These are real products with real demand. The comp plan amplifies the distribution. It does not create the demand. The companies where qualification volume IS the demand, where removing the compensation structure would eliminate the vast majority of purchasing, are the companies that appear in the decline dataset. Not because the field was the problem, but because the qualification pressure was carrying volume that the underlying customer demand could not. When the pressure changes, the volume goes with it. The artifact disappears when the incentive structure changes. These three things are not complicated. Real customers. Disciplined growth that invests in the foundation while it scales. Products with genuine demand. A first-year business student could understand them. And yet the majority of companies in the dataset lacked at least one. Many lacked all three. The principles were known. Executing them requires discipline that runs counter to the industry's dominant culture.

The industry's dominant culture celebrates speed. It celebrates explosive growth. It celebrates the company that goes from zero to a billion dollars in four years. It puts those stories on stages and in trade publications and holds them up as proof that the model works. But the 53-company dataset tells a different story. The companies that grew fastest were, on average, the companies that crashed hardest. The companies that grew steadily, that compounded year over year for a decade without a headline-grabbing spike, were the ones most likely to still be operating. The most durable momentum is often the least dramatic. doTERRA's sixteen-year arc to $2 billion is less exciting than LuLaRoe's four-year arc to $2.3 billion. But the company is still operating at scale, having reached a size and customer base that has held up through its own challenges. PM International's thirty-plus year run to $3.25 billion has never produced a single viral headline, but it has produced consecutive growth for longer than most direct selling companies exist. Melaleuca's reported $2 billion business was built on consumable products that people reorder every month, with a 95%+

monthly retention rate that most subscription services would envy. Herbalife's gradual international expansion over four decades is less exciting than the billion-dollar sprints that produced short-lived industry legends. But Herbalife is a nearly $5 billion company. Most of the sprinters no longer exist. Quiet compounding beats explosive spikes. Not always. But reliably enough that it should change how this industry defines success. A clarification worth making here, because the fast-growth story in this industry is more nuanced than the dataset alone suggests. Fast growth is not the problem. Fast growth is often an extraordinary opportunity. The problem is what a company does with the capital and the attention that the fast growth produces. If I were running a direct selling company in a period of explosive growth, I would not try to slow the growth down. I would be excited. I would celebrate the momentum. And then I would allocate the windfall with intention. The extra revenue flowing in during a fast-growth window is the most valuable strategic resource a company will ever have. It is capital you did not have a year ago. It is attention the market is paying you that your competitors would pay millions to buy. Use it deliberately. Put the disproportionate share of that windfall into customer acquisition and customer retention infrastructure. Not into bigger incentives. Not into more promotional trips. Not into flashier conventions. Into the systems, the product depth, the customer experience, the data capability, and the brand building that will keep working after the current wave breaks. The fast-growth window gives you runway to do things a slower-growing company cannot afford to do. Use that runway to build the customer foundation that will still be standing when the drivers reverse. The companies that rode a spike and then collapsed were, almost without exception, the ones that spent the windfall on more of what produced the spike. More recruiting incentives. More qualification-purchase bonuses. More attention on the field side of the ledger. The companies that rode a spike and converted it into a durable business spent the windfall on customer depth while they still had the cash and the attention to do it. Offense during the boom buys you the foundation that holds when the boom ends. Do not try to slow your growth down. Try to grow the customer foundation underneath your growth at the same rate as the growth itself, or faster. If revenue doubles, your real customer count should double. If you are adding distributors at a record pace, you should be adding retention systems, product development investments, and customer experience capability at a record pace too. The problem in the dataset was never fast growth. It was fast growth that built only one side of the business while the other side got ignored. This brings me to the question the book's title asks but never explicitly answers. What is the momentum equation? It isn't a formula. It's a lens. The equation is the understanding that momentum is created by identifiable structural forces (the five drivers), sustained by foundation integrity (real customers, sound ratios, diversified products and leaders), and destroyed by predictable patterns (declining phases, regulatory sequences, operational failures, and the boom-bust cycle). Reading the equation means creating momentum more often and sustaining it longer. Understanding the forces. Managing them deliberately instead of hoping for the best. The alternative is treating momentum like weather. Celebrating when the sun shines. Panicking when the storm arrives. Never building a roof because the rain felt impossible while the sky was clear. The rain is always coming. Build the roof while you still can. I want to end with what I believe about this profession. Not what the data says. What I believe. I believe direct selling is one of the most powerful distribution models ever created. It allows ordinary people to build businesses without massive capital requirements. It creates communities that matter to the people inside them. It distributes income to hundreds of thousands of families who would not otherwise have access to entrepreneurial economics. At its best, it is a force for genuine good in people's lives. I also believe this profession has spent decades tolerating structural practices that undermine its own credibility. Qualification purchasing that inflates revenue artificially. Compensation plans that reward recruiting over customer acquisition. Income claims that bear no relationship to the typical participant's experience. Companies that build product alibis instead of product businesses. These practices damage every legitimate company in the industry because they feed the narrative that the entire model is flawed. The data in this book draws a clear line between the companies that build real businesses and the companies that build recruiting machines. The line is visible in the ratios, in the survival rates, in the regulatory outcomes. It is not ambiguous. The profession needs more companies on the right side of that line. More companies with real customer revenue above 50%. More companies willing to discipline their growth by investing in real customers while they scale. More companies whose products have demand the comp plan amplifies rather than manufactures. More leadership teams with the courage to prioritize long-term durability over short-term speed. If this book moves even a few companies in that direction, it will have done its job. The data says those companies last. And lasting is the point. There is one more thing the dataset shows that I have not said until now. The companies that lasted were not the ones with the best products. They were not the ones with the best comp plans. They were not the ones with the best marketing or the best events or the most charismatic founders. The companies that lasted were the ones with the most honest leadership teams. Honest about their customer ratios. Honest about which drivers were active and which were borrowed. Honest about where they sat in the cycle. Honest about the tradeoffs they were making and the prices those tradeoffs carried. Honest with their field about what the business actually looked like underneath the convention stage. Honesty is the most underrated competitive advantage in this industry. It does not earn that status for sounding noble. It produces better decisions. A CEO who knows her real customer ratio makes different investments than a CEO who believes the narrative her marketing team created. A board that understands which drivers are borrowed builds contingency plans. A leadership team that can admit "we are in Act 3 and our category is maturing" redirects resources before the numbers force them to. The companies that lie to themselves about their own metrics are the companies in the decline dataset. The lies prevented the diagnosis that could have prevented the decline. I have sat in rooms with owners who knew their customer ratio was below 30% and chose not to discuss it. Leadership teams celebrate recruiting numbers while ignoring the churn data sitting in the same spreadsheet. Companies run the Momentum Equation Scorecard, see red across three categories, and put it in a drawer because the implications were too uncomfortable to address at this quarter's board meeting.

Every one of those companies is either gone or declining. The scorecard did not predict it. Ignoring the scorecard guaranteed it. The equation is not complicated. But it requires something that no framework can give you: the willingness to see what it shows you and act on what you see. If Built to Last showed you how to build the systems that sustain a company, this book showed you how to create the momentum that those systems are designed to sustain. Defense and offense. Infrastructure and growth. Both are necessary. Neither is sufficient alone. The best companies in this industry do both. They build the infrastructure and they create the momentum. They diagnose without flinching and they act with courage. They respect the data and they serve the people. They pursue growth and they discipline it when growth threatens the foundation. Those companies are rare. They should be less rare. The equation is in your hands now. You have the drivers. You have the ratios. You have the diagnostics. You have the timing framework and the reignition sequence. What you do with it is a choice. And it is a choice with consequences that extend beyond your balance sheet. Every company in this profession either builds trust or borrows it. The ones that build trust create something that survives them. The ones that borrow it create something that collapses when they leave. Momentum isn't built. It's assembled. From drivers you can identify, combinations you can engineer, and a foundation you choose to protect or neglect. Momentum does not build companies. What you build during momentum does. Build both worlds. World Two especially hard while World One is on fire.

I want to close with a story. A few years ago, I sat with a company owner in his office after a long day. His company had been through a brutal two years. Revenue had dropped 30%. Leaders had left. The field was demoralized. His board was pressuring him to sell. He had a whiteboard behind his desk with two columns. On the left, a list of everything that had gone wrong. Leader departures. Product returns. Platform algorithm changes. A comp plan that was paying too much for too little activity. On the right, a list of everything he was building. A customer acquisition program that was showing early results. A leadership development pipeline for homegrown talent. An operational overhaul that had cut fulfillment errors by 60%. A revised comp plan that the field initially hated but was starting to produce better behavior. The left column was longer. The right column was newer. He looked at both lists and said something I have never forgotten. "Two years ago, I thought the left column was happening to me. Now I realize I built most of it. And now I'm building the right column on purpose. For the first time, I actually understand what I'm doing and why." That is the equation. The book does not promise a formula for guaranteed momentum. It offers a lens for seeing clearly enough to build on purpose instead of by accident. The companies that see clearly build better. Not always bigger. Not always faster. Better. And better lasts. The equation is not about finding momentum. It is about deserving it. ONE WAY TO GET MORE FROM THIS BOOK A practical suggestion before the final note. Many owners will read this book alone. That is how business books usually get read. One leader reads it, highlights passages, and tries to describe the ideas to a team that has not read them. The ideas get compressed. The frameworks get oversimplified. The vocabulary does not translate. Three weeks later, the book is on the shelf and the leadership team is back to making decisions with the language they had before. The book works better when it gets read as a team. Give it to your executive leadership. Give it to your senior corporate leaders. Give it to your top field leaders. Not as a motivational gift. As required reading before the next strategic planning session. When a leadership team reads the same book at the same time, three things change. The vocabulary gets shared. Everyone on the team can use the same words to describe the same patterns. Instead of arguing about whether growth is real, the team can ask whether Ratio 1 is green, yellow, or red. Instead of debating whether a comp plan change is working, the team can ask which Phase of decline a specific signal suggests. Shared language accelerates shared judgment. The frameworks get tested against the same data. When everyone has seen the Momentum Equation Scorecard, the same questions get asked in leadership meetings without anyone having to explain what the questions mean. The diagnostic becomes routine. Routine diagnostics produce routine early warnings. Early warnings produce better decisions. The blind spots become visible. When an executive team runs the scorecard together, the disagreements surface fast. One leader sees green where another sees red. Those disagreements are the most valuable conversations the team can have. Disagreements about the real state of the company almost never get voiced in a leadership meeting without a structured diagnostic forcing them to the surface. The book provides the structure. The field benefits too. When your top field leaders understand the same framework corporate is using, the conversations between field and corporate become more productive. A top earner who has read the book can ask why the customer-to-distributor ratio has moved instead of just complaining that growth has slowed. A corporate team that has read the book can explain the diagnosis in language the field already understands. The distance between the two sides shrinks. This is not a pitch. It is a usage instruction. The leverage in this book is not any single framework. It is the shared language that emerges when a leadership team reads it together. One final note. The patterns in this book will repeat. Some companies will read this book and adjust. Some will not. That is how the industry has always worked. Some leaders see the signals and act on them. Others see them and choose not to. Both are making a choice. The consequences of each choice compound over time. I am not writing this book to predict which companies will be gone in three years. I am writing it because I love this profession and I want more of it to survive. I want more owners making better decisions. I want more executives reading the right variables. I want fewer good companies destroyed by blind spots that were visible if anyone had been looking at the right dashboard. If this book is useful to one leadership team, it was worth writing. If it is useful to dozens, it changes the trajectory of companies that would have crashed otherwise. I am cheering for every person reading this to build something that lasts. Not everyone will. But every owner who reads the equation with clear eyes and acts on what it shows has a better chance than the owner who does not. That better chance is the contribution. That is why I wrote the book. A FINAL CALL TO THE LEADERSHIP TEAM One last thing before you close the book. Put a copy of this in the hands of every person on your leadership team. The CEO. The COO. The VP of Sales. The head of operations. The compliance officer. The comp plan architect. The CFO. The marketing leader. The customer experience lead. The top members of your field advisory council. Everyone with a seat at the table where strategic decisions actually get made. This book is the ultimate leverage point for getting an entire leadership team aligned around the same diagnostic vocabulary. When the CEO is using one mental model and the VP of Sales is using another and the comp plan architect is using a third, the company makes decisions that sound coherent in any single meeting and produce contradictory outcomes in execution. That misalignment is the silent destroyer of more direct selling companies than any market force, regulatory action, or competitor. When every member of the team has read the same equation, scored the same frameworks, and lived inside the same vocabulary, every conversation that follows is faster, sharper, and more honest. The team stops debating what to call the problem and starts working on solving it. The CEO does not have to translate strategy into five different languages for five different functions. The functions translate themselves because they share the same underlying lens.

This is why I keep saying it. The book in one person's hands is a useful read. The book in the entire leadership team's hands is a competitive weapon. The companies that take this seriously, that actually distribute the book and run their leadership offsites against the frameworks, are the companies that move faster and decide better than the companies whose CEO read it on a plane and never shared it. Make this the next assigned reading for your team. Run a leadership offsite against the Momentum Equation Scorecard. Have every function score their domain with discipline. Watch what surfaces. The conversations that follow will tell you more about your company in two days than the last two years of strategic planning produced. That is the real leverage. Not in the book. In the team that reads it together. A NOTE ON THE INSTITUTIONS THAT MAKE THIS WORK POSSIBLE This industry has been raised to a higher professional standard by a set of institutions that have invested decades in strategic journalism and executive education. Two of the most important are Direct Selling News and Direct Selling University, both built and stewarded by Stuart Johnson. Stuart Johnson's contribution to this profession is hard to overstate. Through DSN, he has built the industry's most credible publication, where serious journalism, data transparency, and executive-level thinking have a home. The DSN Global 100 alone has done more to bring data discipline to this industry than any other published resource. Through DSU, he has built executive education at a level that rivals mainstream business schools, gathering owners, executives, and operators in conversations that have shaped how the best companies in this profession think about strategy, compliance, and growth. The industry is better because of his stewardship of these institutions over the last two decades, and any owner or executive who is not engaged with DSN and DSU is missing the most strategic conversation this profession has.

Appendix A: The 53-Company Dataset

This book is built on a dataset of 53 direct selling companies spanning 1950 to 2025. Companies were selected based on the availability of verifiable revenue trajectories, SEC filings, court records, FTC enforcement documents, income disclosures, and company-reported financial data. The dataset includes companies across every major product category in direct selling: health and wellness, beauty and skincare, weight management, essential oils, household products, clothing and accessories, travel and memberships, technology and telecom, and financial services. It includes the industry's largest companies (Amway, Herbalife, Nu Skin, Mary Kay) and its most dramatic failures (BurnLounge, Vemma, WorldVentures). It includes companies that are still operating, companies that have exited the direct selling model, companies that were shut down by regulators, and companies that filed for bankruptcy. Every framework, ratio, and diagnostic in this book was derived from patterns identified in this dataset and tested against the full population of companies. The Flash Crash Scorecard's five characteristics were present in every flash crash in the dataset with zero exceptions. The Four Phases of Decline sequence was consistent across every documented decline. The Regulatory Domino Sequence followed the same four-stage pattern in every enforcement action where timeline data was available.

The dataset is not a random sample. It is a comprehensive collection of the most documented cases in the industry's history. Selection criteria included: availability of multi-year revenue data (verified through SEC filings, court records, or reliable industry reporting), documented business model structure, and sufficient historical record to identify momentum drivers and decline patterns. Revenue figures throughout the book are sourced as follows: SEC filings for publicly traded companies (Tier 1), court records and FTC enforcement documents (Tier 1), Direct Selling News reporting and Grand View Research (Tier 2), company press releases and company-reported figures labeled as such (Tier 3), and industry insider accounts used cautiously (Tier 4). THE DATASET AT A GLANCE

Figure A-1: The 53-company dataset. Each point represents one company. X-axis shows years from founding to peak revenue. Y-axis shows peak annual revenue on a logarithmic scale. Color indicates current status. The shaded regions highlight the two structural extremes this book analyzes: the Flash Crash Zone (under ten years to peak) where most companies end up dissolved or dramatically reduced, and the Quiet Compounder Zone (over twenty-five years to peak) where most companies are still operating. The chart excludes Zeek Rewards and TelexFree, which were criminal fraud operations rather than legitimate direct selling companies, and BurnLounge, whose small scale would distort the revenue axis. Individual companies are not labeled because the purpose of the chart is to show the structural pattern, not to litigate any specific company's trajectory.

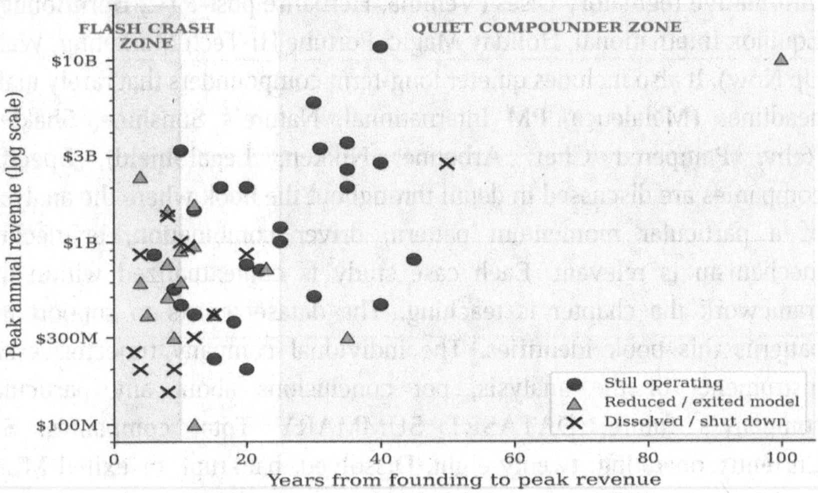

Figure A-1: The 53-Company Dataset

The visual tells the story the numbers carry. The left side of the chart, where companies reached peak revenue in under ten years, is dominated by red and amber. The right side, where companies took twenty-five years or more to reach peak, is dominated by green. Speed and durability are almost inversely correlated across the dataset. The exceptions, particularly Tupperware, prove that category disruption can eventually reach even the most patient compounder. But the general pattern is as clean as any in this book: the companies that grew fast mostly did not last, and the companies that lasted mostly did not grow fast. DATASET SCOPE The 53 companies in the dataset span nine product categories: health and wellness supplements, beauty and skincare, weight management, essential oils, household products, clothing and accessories, travel and memberships, technology and telecom, and financial services. They range in peak revenue from under $10 million to nearly $12 billion, and in founding-to-peak timeline from three years to sixty-eight years. They span every significant era of direct selling from the 1950s through 2025.

The dataset includes the industry's largest operators (Amway, Herbalife, Nu Skin, Mary Kay, Primerica, doTERRA, PM International, Forever Living, Melaleuca, Medifast/OPTAVIA), the most instructive growth stories (doTERRA, Zinzino, Partner.Co, LifeVantage, Isagenix), the most documented flash crashes (LuLaRoe, MonaVie, ViSalus, AdvoCare, Vemma, WorldVentures, Excel Communications), and the most informative regulatory cases (Vemma, Herbalife post-FTC, BurnLounge, Equinox International, Holiday Magic, Fortune Hi-Tech Marketing, Wake Up Now). It also includes quieter long-term compounders that rarely make headlines (Melaleuca, PM International, Nature's Sunshine, Shaklee, Reliv, Pampered Chef, Arbonne, Nikken, LegalShield). Specific companies are discussed in detail throughout the book where the analysis of a particular momentum pattern, driver combination, or decline mechanism is relevant. Each case study is contextualized within the framework the chapter is teaching. The dataset exists to support the patterns this book identifies. The individual company trajectories are instruments of the analysis, not conclusions about any particular company's future. DATASET SUMMARY Total companies: 53. Currently operating: twenty-eight. Dissolved, bankrupt, or exited MLM model: twenty-five. Regulatory shutdowns: 8. Model exits (MLM to affiliate/DTC): 5. Filed for bankruptcy: 4. Combined peak revenue of all 53 companies: exceeds $65 billion. Combined current revenue of surviving companies: approximately $40 billion (estimated). Median time from founding to peak: approximately ten years. Median time from peak to break: approximately four years. Flash crash median: six years to peak, one year to break. Slow decline median: twenty-two years to peak, extended decline over longer windows. Product categories with 0% survival at original scale in the dataset: exotic juice/superfruit, travel memberships (at scale), clothing/accessories (at scale). Product categories with highest survival rates: consumable household products, financial services, essential oils, supplements (with diversified product lines and strong customer bases).

Appendix B: The Momentum Diagnostic AI Prompt

The frameworks in this book are designed to be used in a leadership meeting. But they can also be used with AI to accelerate the diagnostic process and stress-test your thinking. Below is a prompt you can copy and paste into any AI assistant (ChatGPT, Claude, Gemini, or whatever tool your team uses). It contains the core frameworks from this book. When you feed it your company's specific data, it will run the diagnostics and surface the questions your leadership team should be discussing. This is not a replacement for the conversations this book is designed to produce. It is an accelerant. Use it to prepare for the meeting, not to skip it.

HOW TO USE THIS PROMPT Step 1: Copy the entire prompt below. Step 2: Paste it into your AI tool of choice. Step 3: When the AI responds, answer its questions with your company's real data. Be honest. The AI does not judge. It diagnoses. Step 4: Bring the output to your next leadership meeting. Use it as the starting point for the conversation, not the ending point. THE PROMPT (copy everything between the lines) You are a strategic diagnostic tool for a direct selling company. You have been trained on the frameworks from

Why Some Direct Selling Companies Crash by Rob Sperry. Your role is to help a leadership team diagnose their company's momentum position using the following frameworks. Ask me questions one section at a time, wait for my answers, then provide your analysis before moving to the next section. FRAMEWORK 1: THE FIVE DRIVERS For each driver, help me assess whether it is Active (currently producing measurable growth), Dormant (exists as potential but not contributing), Absent (not available), or Reversing (previously active, now working against us). The five drivers are: 1. Product-Culture Fit: Does our product intersect with an emerging or active cultural trend? Is the culture doing our prospecting for us, or is the field doing all the work? 2. Platform Disruption: Are we among the first to fully exploit a new communication or distribution platform? Are we platform-dependent or platform-flexible? 3. Leader Migration: Have we attracted established leaders from other companies? Are they building long-term or passing through? What is our ratio of migrated leaders to organic leaders? 4. Market Expansion: Are we opening new geographic markets? Are we expanding from strength or from weakness? Are we actually committed to new markets or running headline launches? 5. Compensation Architecture: Does our comp plan incentivize the behaviors that produce sustainable growth? Does it reward customer acquisition or just recruiting velocity? How does our front- end speed compare to the digital economy? FRAMEWORK 2: THE THREE HARD RATIOS Help me calculate and assess these three ratios: 1. Real Customer Revenue Ratio: What percentage of total volume comes from people who are not in the compensation plan? Above 50% is the survival zone. Below 30% is the danger zone. 2. Active Distributor Churn Rate: What percentage of distributors quit annually? Below 50% is healthy. Above 70% is a structural problem. 3. Payout Ratio Trend: Are total commissions and bonuses as a percentage of revenue rising, stable, or falling over the last eight quarters? Rising payout ratio with flat or declining revenue is payout inflation. FRAMEWORK 3: THE FLASH CRASH SCORECARD Help me check each characteristic: 1. Single hero product driving more than 50% of revenue? 2. More than 70% of volume from participants inside the comp plan? 3. Recruiting growth exceeding 100% year-over-year for two+ consecutive years? 4. Top 5% of leaders generating more than 50% of total volume? 5. No meaningful customer verification system with auditable data? Score: 0–1 checks = low risk. 2 checks = moderate risk. 3+ checks = high risk. Every company in the historical dataset with 3+ checks that experienced rapid growth subsequently crashed. FRAMEWORK 4: THE DECLINE PHASE DIAGNOSTIC Help me identify which phase we are in: Phase 1 (Invisible Churn): Is gross churn rising even while net distributor count is stable? Phase 2 (Revenue Per Distributor Decline): Is average volume per active distributor declining quarter over quarter? Phase 3 (Leader Departure): Are any top twenty earners less active, less enthusiastic, or less visible than twelve months ago? Phase 4 (Narrative Collapse): Has the public story shifted from aspirational to skeptical? Are former distributors more vocal than current ones? FRAMEWORK 5: THE five-ACT CYCLE POSITION Help me identify which act our product category is in: Act 1: New category or channel opening. Act 2: Early companies capturing it explosively. Act 3: Imitators flooding in, splitting attention and energy. Act 4: Category going mainstream, product available at retail for fraction of direct selling price. Act 5: Regulatory and reputational pressure closing the era. FRAMEWORK 6: THE TWO WORLDS ASSESSMENT World One is the distributor world: recruiting, team building, rank advancement. World Two is the customer world: people who buy because they want the product, many of whom do not know a comp plan exists. Help me assess: How strong is World Two independent of World One? If World One contracted by 50% tomorrow, what percentage of revenue would World Two sustain? After collecting my data across all six frameworks, provide: 1. A summary of the company's momentum position (green, yellow, or red for each framework). 2. The three most urgent issues to address. 3. Recommended next steps matched to the specific diagnosis. 4. Questions the leadership team should be discussing that the data raises but does not answer. Be direct. Do not soften the diagnosis. The leadership team reading this output needs clarity, not comfort. That is the complete prompt. It contains the diagnostic DNA of this book in a format that any AI tool can process. Update it with your company's actual numbers quarterly. The AI does not replace your judgment. It organizes the data so your judgment has something real to work with. The AI will only be as honest as the data you feed it. If you give it the numbers you wish you had instead of the numbers you actually have, the diagnosis will be useless. Feed it the truth. The whole point of this book is that the truth, uncomfortable as it may be, is the only foundation worth building on.

The equation is already in your hands. The tools are already built. What remains is the work of looking clearly at what they show and deciding what to do about it. Start there.

Work With Rob

Rob Sperry speaks and consults with direct selling companies around the world. To inquire about bringing Rob in as a keynote speaker for your company convention, leadership retreat, or incentive trip, or to discuss high-level consulting for your executive team, go to www.robsperry.com. The conversation that changes a company usually starts with one honest question. If this book raised one for you, that is the place to start.

www.ingramcontent.com/pod-product-compliance
Lightning Source LLC
LaVergne TN
LVHW030056140826
845598LV00033B/415

9798996377404